Born in 1920, educated at O'Neill College Elsternwick, Loreto Convent Toorak and the University of Melbourne, Moira graduated with a Bachelor of Science in 1941 and joined the Women's Auxiliary Australian Air Force. She was involved in the hazardous work of the Chemical Research Unit and the mustard gas trials in World War II.

After the war, she worked as a research scientist for CSL and CSIRO and enjoyed a busy social life, which was frequently reported in the social pages along with details of her stylish clothes and exquisite hats. In 1950, Moira married Melbourne lawyer, John F Dynon and they enjoyed a glorious six-month honeymoon abroad before settling down in Malvern and raising five children.

For most women of her generation, indeed any generation, this would have been enough.

But Moira had only just started.

MOIRA DYNON:
An Inspiring Life

JOHN F DYNON

Edited and compiled by Michele Trowbridge
and Jacinta Efthim with material on the
author and his family history

Moira Dynon: An Inspiring Life

John F Dynon

Edited and compiled by Michele Trowbridge and Jacinta Efthim with material on the author and his family history

Copyright text © Michele Trowbridge and Jacinta Efthim
Copyright imagery © Michele Trowbridge and Jacinta Efthim

We respect the rights of copyright holders. In this book we have quoted text from letters, telegrams, reports and other documents. Before publishing, we obtained legal advice as to the copyright status of this material. We have endeavoured to contact all copyright holders and we express our appreciation to the many persons who gave us permission to publish copyright material, including The Herald and Weekly Times. We invite and request any person who claims a copyright interest in any material published in this book, which interest has not been acknowledged, to contact the editors by email (copyright@moiradynon.com.au).

Published by Jacinta Efthim
PO Box 68 Black Rock Victoria 3193 Australia
(info@moiradynon.com.au)

 A catalogue record for this book is available from the National Library of Australia.

First edition 2020

ISBN: 978-0-6487747-1-6 (paperback)

All rights reserved. No part of this publication may be reproduced in whole or in part, stored in a retrievable system, or transmitted in any form or by any means, electronic, mechanical, photocopying, recording or otherwise, without written permission of the copyright holder or publisher.

Front cover image: Moira c. 1948

Back cover image: John F Dynon holding pages of signatures for the petition to Her Majesty, seeking disallowance of section 28 (m) of the *Matrimonial Causes Act 1959*. October 1960

Cover design and typesetting – Michelle Pirovich
Printed by Ingram Spark

Dedication

May those who glance through these pages recognise the girl they knew, the sister, the wife, the mother, the courageous loving and compassionate woman and citizen of 'the world' as she understood it.

John F Dynon

Contents

Preface	11
Moira, my wife	15
1 'Those whom the gods love, die young.'	17
Early years and war service	21
2 Moira Lenore Shelton—the early years	23
3 Moira's war service and the mustard gas trials	30
4 Moira's brother, RAAF Flying Officer Alan Shelton	37
Social life and marriage	55
5 Moira's post-war social activities and her newsworthy hats	57
6 Wedding and honeymoon	62
Community activism	91
7 The Spirit of Loreto Federation	93
8 Australian Association for the United Nations Malvern Branch	103
9 President and Secretary of Stonnington Branch of the Liberal Party	109
10 Section 28 (m)	125
11 The petition to Her Majesty	145

12	Australian-Japanese children in Kure	151
13	Italian welfare	168
14	Catholic Women's League	176

Aid for India 183

15	Milk for India	185
16	Feeling sorry won't help—milk will	201
17	Reconsidering the policy of Prime Minister Menzies	205
18	A Pleasant Sunday Afternoon	218
19	Politicians, politics and resilience	226
20	Offer from Shipping Corporation of India	251
21	Eight weeks in India	256
22	The ABC 'Noises Off' Affair	266
23	Making a difference	275
24	The Prosecution	282
25	India revisited—Letters between Moira and John	295
26	Surplus Australian wheat for India	317
27	Twenty-five million pints of milk	321
28	Disasters in East Pakistan	327

Winding down 341

29	Winding down the Campaign	343
30	Into Eternity	350

CONTENTS

Appendix A.
Reports, documents and letters — 363

Appendix B.
About the author John F Dynon—aspects of his life and family history by Michele Trowbridge and Jacinta Efthim — 419

Appendix C.
Three autobiographical chapters by John F Dynon — 469

Appendix D.
Just Mum and Dad—the 'Dynon children' share some reflections and memories of their parents and life at home by Michele Trowbridge, Jacinta Efthim, James Dynon and David Dynon — 486

Acknowledgements — 499

Index of names — 502

References — 511

All around you are possibilities of doing good and of making the world a better place for you having lived in it.

Mother Gonzaga Barry IBVM[1]

Preface

Moira and John were our parents. They were involved in public life. Whenever they saw an injustice or someone in need, they had to *do something*. We saw the Milk for India years close-up, but there was so much more.

After Moira died in 1976, John began writing her biography. This was The Manuscript. He stored records in cardboard milk boxes. It started with three or four boxes against the wall in the dining room at The Righi. Each time we visited, there were more. When John died in 1984, there were about 50 boxes. Together with our brothers James and David, we opened some.

As expected, there was a huge amount of material about Milk for India. We all knew what a big part of her life Moira gave to this. There were records on the Stonnington Branch of the Liberal Party when our parents were President and Secretary and, in particular, records leading to the first national divorce legislation and the contentious section 28 (m) of the *Matrimonial Causes Act 1959*. We found Moira's war service account of her work as a scientist during World War II and the mustard gas trials; also, records of her efforts for the Australian-Japanese children and the Loreto Federation. There were letters and telegrams to and from world leaders: Lal Bahadur Shastri, Indira Gandhi, Robert Kennedy, Mother Teresa and Australian prime ministers. There were also medals, including the well-deserved honours they both received from the Italian Government for helping Italian immigrants and reuniting families. We also found some family treasures—there was John's diary of his 1929 family trip to Europe with the autographed photo he received from Mussolini, and, still mostly intact, was the magnificent diary of James Dynon, John's father, about his journey to England and the Continent in 1881.

We didn't really know what to do with all this material. At the time we were busy with young families. When Michele went overseas, the boxes moved to the attic of Jacinta's home in Black Rock. When Michele returned to The Righi, so did the boxes. It was John's wish that Michele have the papers so, when Michele moved to Drouin, the boxes followed her. Finally in 2011, we started to work through the material.

The Manuscript was a detailed account of events. John had done careful and thorough research. But it was still a draft. We sifted through the mountain of documents in the boxes and found more letters to add. Moira's life story could fill a dozen volumes. Many documents have been edited. However, some letters, telegrams and reports are reproduced in full, so that the relevant message is set out in its proper context. These are historical records.

The various causes and campaigns that our parents promoted from the early 1950s until the early 1970s are related in some detail. Moira's work for the needy in India certainly stands out and her achievements are all the more remarkable considering the resistance that she encountered from some Australian

Government quarters. Her resilience and perseverance to continue doing what needed to be done are part of Moira's story.

Moira was regularly called upon to speak to various groups. She journeyed throughout Australia addressing conferences, seminars, schools and community organisations. She also spoke on several occasions in India, including at the Guild of Service/UNESCO Human Rights Seminar in Madras in 1969. Moira was well read and thoughtful. She was a courageous advocate for peace, justice and human rights. She welcomed practical solutions and common sense.

We have included material about our father. John was a huge part of Moira's inspiration and support. From an early age, John had been concerned for the good of his fellow man. He believed in social and economic justice and he promoted the message of *Rerum Novarum*, the encyclical letter of Pope Leo XIII on the rights and duties of Capital and Labour.

In 1951, when John asked for Moira's help to establish a Malvern Branch of the Australian Association for the United Nations, this was the beginning of their public work together. Over the next 20 years, Moira's good works elevated her to another level—her care for the needy and the vulnerable; her driving force to organise, to inspire others and to get things done; and her ability to make a difference. As the problems of the Indian sub-continent increased through the 1960s and early 1970s, so did Moira's involvement. John knew the importance and value of Moira's work and he supported her every step of the way. John was a lawyer with a conscience; a champion for justice and fairness. He had been captain of Xavier College; captain of the football, cricket and athletics teams and president of various groups and causes—he was a natural leader but he readily adapted to a supporting role. He was always there for Moira as he was for us. Moira's biography would be incomplete without due recognition of John's contribution.

John wrote three chapters for an autobiography and these are included. His family history is fascinating. With the benefit of the internet and digitally recorded Australian newspapers, it has been exciting to jump back into history and discover more about the lives of our paternal grandparents and great-grandparents in Melbourne in the late 1800s and early 1900s.

There is so much evidence of good work by two Christian people and of two lives well lived. Our parents were exceptional and they made a difference to the lives of many. But, to us, they were still Mum and Dad and we, together with our brothers, have added some thoughts and recollections of life at home. Mum always said to us that each good deed was just a drop in the ocean, but that the ocean was made up of drops.

Towards the end, as illness forced her to slow down and she had time to reflect, she said—typically understated—'I've done my bit'.

Michele and Jacinta

MOIRA, MY WIFE

1

'Those whom the gods love, die young.'

The venetian blind was down, shutting out the eclipse—in that world which then seemed so remote. It was 23 October 1976 at Cabrini Hospital in Malvern. My brother sat beside the bed, quietly reading his breviary. I was standing on the left side with Michele next to me. I was holding Moira's hand in mine.

I recall so well our last words together. I said simply, 'I love you always'. She had heard, smiled and, with her eyes still closed, replied clearly and softly, 'That's beautiful'.

She was calm. The minutes ticked by. The room seemed so quiet. All at once I became aware that Moira was very pale and motionless. There was no sign of a pulse. I motioned to my brother. He checked her breathing and called the sister in charge. Moira was dead and at peace. That instant was a time for tears in my heart. So much flooded through my mind on this encounter with death—the death of a dear, gentle, intelligent and loving girl with whom I had shared my life and who was so loving to me and to our five children.

As I later looked back on Moira's life, I recalled what Professor FM Powicke had said:

> No man can live for long without becoming aware of the fact that he and his neighbours are directly involved in the struggle for freedom and justice; What in the New Testament is called love or charity springs from a source that lies very deep in man, so deep that faith and experience cannot be separated from each other. It is there that awareness of God gives meaning to human life.[2]

Moira certainly was aware of this struggle, and I believe that it was her very awareness of God that led her to devote herself to the service of others.

Prior to that dreadful day, if I had ever been asked what had affected me most in all my life, I think I would probably have replied that it was the death of my mother. She had been a superbly wonderful mother to me. It was she who handed on to me the true value of family. My mother had brought me up to do what I believed was right, no matter what others thought, did or threatened. My mother's qualities I found in Moira, and many more besides.

It was on 14 June 1977, the anniversary of the birthday of Moira's mother, Lily, that I made up my mind to set down on paper a few things about Moira's life. What I have written is not a complete picture of the depth, volume and value of her work, struggles and initiatives. I have endeavoured to record a number of things she did for others. She did not do things for herself, but for others. The facts and the achievements speak for themselves and the love, compassion and dedication shine out like a beacon.

During those last weeks, I especially remember celebrating Moira's birthday on 4 September in her hospital room. She had insisted that any presents given were to be for use in the home—a vertical griller and frying pan. A cake was made by the kitchen staff at Cabrini Hospital and sent to Moira for the occasion. She considered this a lovely gesture. Two weeks before Moira died, she came home as she wished to be there with the family. She spent most of her last days at home in what was her 'study' or 'den'. It was there that together we watched two splendid operas on Sunday nights on television. This gave her great joy.

Finally, Moira returned to her room at the hospital. On that day, I telephoned Sister Ruth Winship IBVM[3] and told her that Moira had returned to hospital. I was then unable to speak another word to her on the telephone. The family kept vigil in Moira's room. My brother flew over from Perth, arriving in Melbourne in the very early hours of Saturday morning.

I was to realise later how I was saved from sheer annihilation by my brother and every member of our family, and the support of Moira's mother and of all the Sheltons.

This is my testimony to the memory of Moira's courage and love. Even if I were granted ample time, I doubt if I could adequately relate the full story of Moira's intense toil, fertile thought and devotion. We went through it all together—in our love, our faith in God and belief in the importance of family life. We shared our thoughts and life in various fields—politics, family reunion, religion, immigrants, conscription of youth, underprivileged children, the needy, education, and against violence, intimidation and gross persuasion. We shared too in the hope of improving a world for our children and for other children.

Moira chose in her own way to express her practical concern for those who obviously needed special care. Moira set things going and she supported her causes with all she had to give. She made no financial gain from her works. She and all her co-workers gave their time and energies in fully honorary capacities. True, Moira did not enter into all fields of need. Who could? She, however, made her own choice and her own contribution in her own way to the life of the land and people she loved and she was prepared to look beyond our shores and demonstrate an understanding and compassion for others outside. This shows not only a Christ-like love but helps to build a bridge of peace in a militant world. Jesus was the Prince of Peace, and it was he who in his Sermon on the Mount called on those who believed in him to follow him.

EARLY YEARS AND WAR SERVICE

2

Moira Lenore Shelton —the early years

Moira was born on 4 September 1920 at Londa private hospital in Elsternwick. She was the eldest child of Lily and Percy Shelton. Shortly after her birth, Moira needed a small chest operation to draw away some fluid and, although it wasn't serious, she was baptised at the hospital and given the name 'Moira'. Lily told me that when the birth was registered, she added 'Lenore', after her brother Len.

Moira's grandparents on her father's side were Susan Ryan from Killaloe, County Clare, Ireland and Henry Shelton, a Latin scholar and schoolteacher. Their son, Percy, was the second-youngest of six children: Elsie (Murphy), Grantley, Harry, Eileen (Newman), Percy and Jim. All four boys won scholarships to the University of Melbourne. Harry became a lawyer and the other three brothers became doctors. Percy was 21 when he graduated. He was a hard-working GP who ran his medical practice from the family home at 230 Glenhuntly Road, Elsternwick.

On her mother's side, we go back to Moira's great-grandfather George Keane Johnston who was born in Drumshanbo,

County Leitrim, Ireland in 1817. He married Charlotte Howard Burd in 1840 and they emigrated to Melbourne in 1853. Sometime later, Charlotte died and in 1865 George married thrice-widowed Eliza Brophy, who was the fourth daughter of Tabetha and Benjamin Wickham of Adelaide. George and Eliza had a son, William Bowen Johnston, who married Margaret Ellen McCarthy in 1895. Their daughter Lily, Moira's mother, was born on 14 June 1898. She was baptised Lilian Eliza but to her family she was always Lily. Lily had three brothers: Len, Alan and Maurice. Len was an ear, nose and throat surgeon. He married Mary Peppard and they had five children. Alan enlisted with the army and was killed at Sandakan in 1944. Maurice died young, leaving a wife Nancy (Rutherford-Smith) and six children.

On 16 October 1919, Lily Johnston married Dr Percy Shelton at St Patrick's Cathedral, Melbourne. The wedding was reported in some detail in *Table Talk*.[4] Lily and Percy had five children—Moira, Valda, Alan, June and David. They grew up in a warm and loving family. Percy called on Mother Bernard at O'Neill College, Elsternwick and arrangements were made for Moira to commence her schooldays there and the other children followed.

Moira always expressed warm affection for her primary school. After our wedding in 1950, Moira and I visited Mother Bernard and the other Presentation Convent sisters, including Sister Katherine Curtain and Sister Lazerian. After Moira's death, Sister Katherine spoke with me of her memories of Moira:

> Moira was always carefully dressed, sweet and cheerful. I used to teach the girls to be courteous. I gave an example of ringing the doorbell when calling at a

> home; that one should wait a substantial time before ringing the bell again if the first ring brought no response. Perchance I had to call one day at the Shelton home and rang the bell once. I could not hear the ring and fearing that I had not rung properly, I rang a second time. Moira had a great joke with me about the incident afterwards.
>
> I set the class an essay on the hero they liked best in reality or fiction. Moira wrote pages on 'Daddy'—'he cures the sick; he is not always paid and is kind.' It was considered to be most original. She was a warm-hearted person and popular. She remained at O'Neill College up to Grade 7. After she had started at Loreto she came back to see me. My lasting impressions of Moira were her simplicity, her lack of any affectation, her warmth, her generous nature and her loyalty. I have only a beautiful memory of her school days spent here. Afterwards we were so proud of all the good and generous work that Moira performed.[5]

Sister Lazerian recalled teaching Moira in the Junior Certificate class.

> Moira was beautifully refined and courteous and also had a sense of fun. I recall a fete that Moira attended; she came with 5 shillings and had to take home 6 pence. I remember the family coming to see Mother Bernard at Christmas. Percy so much admired Mother Bernard and vice versa. They were a lovely family. Moira had a real Madonna face.[6]

Moira's sister, Valda, was born on 4 March 1922. The sisters were close. Valda was Moira's matron of honour at her wedding. Valda married William Martin, who was later appointed a County Court Judge and they had five children—Bill, David, Paul, Geoff and Margie. Alan was born on 18 April 1923. Following his father's footsteps, Alan commenced a medical degree but before completing it, he joined the RAAF as a pilot. A few weeks before the end of the war in Europe, on 4 March 1945, he died when his plane was shot down during air operations over England. June was born on 24 June 1924 and was school captain of Loreto, Toorak. June married Dr Charles McCann and they had six daughters—Liz, twins Margie and Judy, Joan, Trish and Genevieve. David was the youngest, born on 3 December 1926, and he attended Christian Brothers' College, St Kilda and St Kevin's College. He was a businessman and ran Downards transport company. He married Valery Mornement, a dental nurse and they had four children—Jill, Mark, Carol and Katrina.

For over 30 years, a married couple, Tot and Les, lived in the room at the back of the Shelton home in Elsternwick. June recalled:

> Tot would do the cleaning and the cooking. Friday was their only day off, so Lily would cook fish (the only thing that June knew how to cook when she was married!).

> Les would do the garden. He planted a huge potato crop in the back yard, which later produced the biggest potatoes in the area. He also looked after the tennis court and the two cars. The cars were always cleaned and polished, and Percy's 1928 Dodge coupe was always waiting at the door ready for his morning calls.[7]

As a schoolgirl, Moira seldom missed an 'at home' football match at South Melbourne. She had great admiration for Laurie Nash and Bob Pratt. Every Saturday, the family car was decorated with the 'South' colours. It was a big event in the family. Percy was very attached to South. His father, Henry, had played for South in its amateur days. Percy 'treated the South Melbourne football players for more than 20 years and did all their x-rays, rarely receiving payment'.[8]

From 1933 to 1937, Moira attended Loreto Convent, Toorak and in March 1938 Moira matriculated at the University of Melbourne. Her subjects were mainly in the arts. She returned to Loreto for five weeks before deciding to study science at university. She enrolled at Taylors College in chemistry, physics and biology, which were not then offered at Loreto.

Moira began her science degree at the University of Melbourne in 1939, aged 18. During a 'swot vac', Moira took part in influenza virus tests, conducted in a confidential 10-day camp by Dr F Burnet.[9] *The Herald* reported:

> How a group of Melbourne University medical students recently volunteered to be inoculated with 'flu virus as part of an experiment in immunisation against influenza was revealed today by Dr. F. Burnet, assistant director of the Walter and Eliza Hall Institute, who made the tests.
>
> While other University students were on "swot" vacation, 12 senior medical students—six men and six women—accompanied by Dr. and Mrs Burnet, a nurse and a cook, left Melbourne on a "hush hush" mission in the cause of science.
>
> The tests to which they submitted lasted 10 days. Dr. Burnet based experiments on methods which had proved effective in ferrets and mice. The aim, he said, was to discover whether the infusion of a weak virus would, as in the case of these animals, produce an

immunity against a virulent type of virus. Inoculations of successively more virulent types of virus were given to the students by throat and nose sprays. The strain used in the last inoculation was isolated from the mild influenza epidemic in Melbourne last winter.

If the volunteers had behaved exactly like ferrets, none of them should have suffered from influenza after the last inoculation, said Dr. Burnet. In fact, three out of the 12 did contract influenza within a day or two. The tests were therefore not wholly successful; but the extent of the success could not be gauged until blood tests of the subjects were taken.

Dr Burnet claimed no startling results, but regarded the attempt as an essential first step in the transition from laboratory immunisation tests to human application. He said that human volunteers had been used before for research on infectious disease in Australia. In 1917 Professor Cleland had carried out important researches on dengue or "breakbone" fever by these methods. Early this year, before immunisation against tetanus was made compulsory in the army, a group of volunteers in Melbourne was inoculated to prove that the procedure was harmless.

Should Dr. Burnet attempt any further tests, he will need more volunteers. Braving 'flu germs may yet become a matter of course for medical students.[10]

Moira graduated with a Bachelor of Science degree from the University of Melbourne on 20 December 1941. Her subjects included bacteriology, biochemistry, chemistry, physiology, botany, natural philosophy, nutrition and food economics, zoology and German.

Douglas Kay shared some of his memories about Moira's life as a teenager:

> My contact with her was during our teen years when the family lived in Glenhuntly Road, Elsternwick, during which time I played tennis there regularly and sometimes croquet and attended social functions with her group…Mrs. Shelton would preside at afternoon tea on tennis afternoons which turned into rather formidable affairs for the lesser fry. Dr. Percy Shelton was seldom in evidence.
>
> I should imagine, knowing a little of her personality, that Moira may have kept a diary and, if so, I could well be mentioned in it in the mid to late 1930's. I remember once her saying to our group, who were then her close friends, "To think we shall be friends all our lives". It was not to be so but it is something I remember through nearly fifty years because it gave me then considerable pleasure to be held, among others, in such affection.
>
> I remember various occasions at Glenhuntly Road; one in particular was when a band was employed for a private ball. It played in the fire alcove in the reception room which was divided by glass doors from the dining room. It was a large party which seemed to go off very well.
>
> Perhaps my most useful recollection is of the great joy we all found at that time in each others company. We were profoundly innocent; naive even for the 1930's. The war was years away when we met and there were many simple things to do and enjoy.[11]

3

Moira's war service and the mustard gas trials

Following her graduation, Moira lost no time becoming involved in the war effort. Between January and July 1942, she carried out food analysis at a WAAAF (Women's Auxiliary Australian Air Force) training station under the direction of Surgeon Rear Admiral Carr, Director of Naval Medical Services.

The record shows that, on 17 August 1942, Moira Lenore Shelton (number 104057) was 'attested'[12] into the Royal Australian Air Force as aircraftwoman. After attending the School of Administration at the University of Melbourne, Moira was granted a Commission on 10 October, appointed Assistant Section Officer and posted to 1 WAAAF Training Depot (Staff) Preston.[13] *The Age* reported:

> Accounting and cyphering duties now performed by men at R.A.A.F. stations will be taken over by members of the W.A.A.A.F., who yesterday completed a two months' course of training at the School of Administration...

> Not all of the newly fledged officers will undertake accountancy or cyphering. A.S.O. Shelton, who holds the degree of Bachelor of Science, and has specialised in domestic science, will be in charge of messing arrangements at a large W.A.A.A.F. training station. Her work will be of great importance in planning suitable meals for women performing varying types of work, and living under varying climatic conditions.[14]

It was not long before Moira was called to work in the gas and chemical field as a technical adviser in the RAAF Directorate of Armament—a far cry from planning suitable meals for members of the WAAAF.

Among Moira's personal papers was a detailed account of her war service that she wrote after the war.[15] *The Argus* published an article describing Moira's hazardous work in the chemical research unit:

> Probably one of the most hazardous war jobs done by any member of the women's services in the war was that undertaken by Flight-Officer Moira Shelton, WAAAF, with a chemical warfare experimental unit.
>
> She worked in tropical jungles, unloaded chemical munitions from the hold of a ship, and served as volunteer observer on an experimental flight in a Beaufort bomber contaminated with mustard gas.
>
> Flight-Officer Shelton joined the WAAAF in 1942 to do food analysis, but when a chemical research unit was set up in Australia she was appointed as an assistant to Wing-Commander R.J.W. Le Févre because of her qualifications as a science graduate in bio-chemistry and bacteriology.

About the time of her appointment British and Australian scientists and Army, Navy and Air Force officers had concluded from experimental work under tropical conditions that a considerable amount of investigation of the effects of gas in tropical climates was necessary. Accordingly an Army unit, to which were attached inter-Allied and civilian scientists, was set up at Innisfail, and later an inter-service establishment operated from Proserpine. Flight-Officer Shelton was attached to this unit, where volunteers were sometimes used to test out the effect of gas.

Long before she was sent to this unit as Air Force HQ Directorate of Armament Liaison Officer in April, 1944, Flight-Officer Shelton had received rather rugged training in her new work. She did courses in chemical warfare at Hamilton, Shepparton, and Nhill. During this time she took part in manoeuvres, throwing smoke-bombs, and learning how to deal with leaking and dangerous gas bombs. In February, 1943, she was present in Sydney at the unloading of a ship of gas munitions. Once again she was the only woman on this job, which entailed working in the hold of the ship.

The most hazardous part of her work began when she was sent to Innisfail, and there most of her time was spent working in the dense jungles in that area and on tropic islands off the North Queensland coast. Her work here was connected principally with trials using the aircraft attached to the unit. These aircraft, principally Beaufort bombers, would drop chemical bombs, and Flight-Officer Shelton and other scientists would analyse the effects on volunteers, who went into the bombed areas wearing special clothing giving varying degrees of protection.

During one trial a party which included Flight-Officer Shelton went by barge to an island which had been attacked with mustard bombs and when they attempted to rejoin the main party they discovered that the tide had gone out and their barge was stuck fast on a coral reef. So they had to spend all night on this reef awaiting the tide in company with hordes of mosquitoes with the overpowering smell of the coral, and with no food.

Another spectacular exploit of Flight-Officer Shelton's occurred when she was a volunteer observer on a two hours' experimental flight in a Beaufort bomber that had been specially sprayed with mustard gas. On another occasion she accompanied a convoy of live bombs from Innisfail to Cairns.[16]

After the war, RJW Le Févre, then a Professor at the University of Sydney, wrote a letter of reference for Moira:

I am very glad to have this opportunity of supporting Miss M. Shelton's application and paying a tribute to her war service. This I can do so from close personal knowledge gained during my 19 months war-time attachment to HQ. RAAF., Melbourne, as a "chemical adviser". Early in this period it was necessary to start an organisation by selecting two Australian officers, at first to assist me, and later to carry on after my return to U.K. At that stage it was clear that duties would involve not only the routine normal to HQ. Staff Officers, but would require in addition the understanding of much chemical and toxicological research proceeding in this and other countries, frequent personal contact with those persons and units in the Air Force who were practically concerned with the handling, maintenance and storage of various types of special weapons and equipment, the training and instructing of many groups of R.A.A.F. and W.A.A.A.F. in modern methods of gas identification and defense, and the establishment of inter-service and inter-departmental liaisons on technical planes.

Miss Shelton, then an Assistant Section Officer, W.A.A.A.F. was selected from the science graduate members of the Royal Australian Air Force. The choice was fully justified by her performance. She rapidly acquainted herself with the literature (largely "secret") of her new background and then applied herself with energy and success to all the tasks before the three of us. She took the rough with the smooth, both in the field and the office. In the nature, as well as the quantity and quality, of her work she proved more than equal to a man. To her was naturally allotted the responsibility for commencing the training of the W.A.A.A.F. in various anti-gas matters and she made many tours to units in the NE coast region, at the time when an invasion or air-raids were still a possibility, to lecture and demonstrate on these subjects.

Subsequently she took a prominent part in the Air Force share of an inter-service tropical research station, set up at Proserpine towards the end of 1943. This was an unforeseen development when she joined me. Here her work lay in the laboratory as well as the experimental ranges. She was a member of the team who staged the historic "Brook island" trial—an event notable for its unprecedented scale and for the orientation its results gave to the allied understanding of the potentialities of chemical warfare materials and weapons under hot and humid conditions.

During all this period she participated in the regular inspection of storage dumps and when the occasion demanded performed the difficult (and sometimes dangerous) task of withdrawing samples for analysis from suspicious bombs or other containers.

Her success in these arduous activities drew commendations from all sides. She was recognised as a hard and willing worker with a good scientific knowledge allied to sound common sense. She was undoubtedly helped by her natural politeness and cheerful personality which often enabled necessary contacts to be made smoothly with many persons who sometimes themselves lacked these qualities.

Although I am ignorant of her work on anti-biotics since her demobilisation, I can submit my opinion that she is just the type of Australian who could give and receive benefit by a research tour in the U.K. I have seen and worked with many over there to whom I could not apply the previous paragraph. She entered the "closed" chemical warfare field with vigor and distinction but without previous knowledge. If she is now seeking to widen her knowledge in a field in which she already has experience and qualifications, I am confident as to the result.

On the above grounds, therefore, I recommend her as strongly as I am able.

R.J.W. Le Févre
Professor of Chemistry[17]

The leader of the interservice chemical research unit, 'The Australian Field Experimental Station', was British scientist Lieutenant Colonel FS (Freddie) Gorrill, RAMC. Lily Shelton remembered that Lieutenant Colonel Gorrill attended a party given by Moira at their home in Elsternwick at the end of the war. I met Lieutenant Colonel Gorrill and his wife in December 1964 when they visited us at our home in Malvern during their trip to Australia. I attempted to contact Lieutenant Colonel Gorrill in 1982, but Mrs Gorrill advised me that her husband had died seven years earlier. She said that 'Freddie' took the greatest pride in the brilliance and dedication of the people in his unit to the end of his life.

I was often to wonder why an instruction was given to the RAAF to make the mustard gas experimental tests with aircraft impregnated thoroughly with mustard gas, in flight. When I read the story in *The National Times*[18] titled 'Churchill Wanted to Gas the Germans', the penny dropped. In June 1944, Winston Churchill had told his Chiefs of Staff that he wanted an urgent practical assessment on the use of poison gas, mainly mustard, on a vast scale over Germany. The alternative was to use anthrax, then already in production. If the invasion of Europe had not proceeded satisfactorily, we may have witnessed in Europe the use of gas or biological warfare in desperation.

Today, the trials and fears involved in the research and experimentation relating to gas and chemical matters during the 1939–1946 period may seem remote and minimal to many. But to Moira and all those who worked in that field, there were real problems and real dangers, some known, some unknown. Moira performed her tasks with dedication and perhaps with more courage than fearlessness.

4

Moira's brother, RAAF Flying Officer Alan Shelton

Moira was in hospital at Bowen, recovering from a jeep accident, when she received an urgent telegram: 'Be Brave My Darling Tragic News Received Alan Lost In Action Over England Love Daddy.'

On 11 March 1945, June Shelton wrote to her sister:

> Dear Moi,
>
> I do not feel I can write much today, but know how you must be feeling up there. Mummy asked me to drop you a few lines. It is indeed terribly hard on you and Val to be so far away from home at such tragic times. We all loved Alan didn't we? And it is hard to understand why such a good spotless boy should be taken. Everyone loved him.
>
> Daddy got the news on Thursday about 5:30 p.m. and this is what the telegram said:

"Deeply regret to inform you that your son 428602 Flying Officer Alan Percy William Shelton lost his life on fourth March 1945 as result air operations. Known details are your late son was member of crew Halifax aircraft which crashed near Sutton on Derwent Yorkshire England. It is presumed that aircraft crashed as result of being struck by fire from enemy intruder aircraft. The Minister for Air joins with Air Board in expressing profound Sympathy in your sad bereavement."

Don't fret Moi dear. Alan would not want us to. It was his wish to fight and there is no doubt that he is in Heaven now. Daddy found out that four of his crew were saved—three of them uninjured, one with a sprained ankle but three were killed. Roger Johnson was killed.

I arrived down yesterday and have leave till Tuesday week. There may be a chance that Val can come down but haven't heard definitely yet. I am so pleased to be home with Mummy and Daddy. They are simply marvellous. David has to go back on Wednesday so will be here for the Requiem Mass at St Kevin's on Wednesday.

I won't upset you by writing any more now Moi dear—will write in a few days. Be brave although it is so hard and you cannot realize it. Hope you are getting better.

Love June[19]

MOIRA'S BROTHER, RAAF FLYING OFFICER ALAN SHELTON

The Catholic Archbishop of Melbourne offered his sympathy:

Dear Dr Shelton

I have just returned home and have heard of your great sorrow. I wish to assure you that you and your family have my deepest sympathy and that your son will often be remembered by me at the Holy Sacrifice. Tomorrow I will offer the Mass for the repose of his soul. Praying God, who gave him and took him away, to give you and all those who mourn for him the grace of courage and resignation in your grief and bereavement.

I am sincerely yours
+ D. Mannix[20]

On 12 October 1980, four years after the death of Moira, I had the opportunity to speak with Pat Hogan who was the navigator in Alan's aircrew. He had his Flying Log Book, which helped to clarify details. Pat told me about Alan's life in the Air Force in the United Kingdom, their earlier operational flights and the events on the night of 3–4 March 1945.

Pat Hogan's edited account

I first met Alan Shelton in July 1944. We had been sent to an RAAF Operation Training Unit at Litchfield. All the trainees were addressed after lunch on the day we arrived. We were told we would be there about ten days and that we were to mingle with other trainees and, by the end of ten days, the pilots were to form crews with people who were all individually compatible. Naturally the pilot was to be Crew Captain. Within an hour or so, a pilot approached me and introduced himself as Alan Shelton. We had a chat about our origins, background, families and interests. We soon got on to Aussie Rules and Alan's interest in South Melbourne. He asked whether I would like to join his crew as his navigator as he was sure we would have no worries in getting along together. I readily accepted and Alan took me to meet Roger Johnson whom he had known at Melbourne University. Roger was to be the Bomb Aimer. We met several Wireless Operators and we all agreed that the diminutive and likable Greg Dixon from Chatswood, Sydney was the one for us. Roger Laing from Adelaide was to be the Mid-upper Gunner. Our first tail gunner was not medically fit and we got a real bonus when he was replaced by the big and friendly Bill Bullen.

I think Alan probably commenced learning to fly a twin engine Wellington (Wimpey) at this stage, doing take-offs, circuits and landings ('circuits & bumps') until going solo. The rest of us were attending lectures, escape duties etc. We were then posted to the satellite station at Church Broughton, Derbyshire. Our flight commander was at that time the highest decorated Australian flying in the RAAF in England, Squadron Leader Dave Shannon, DSO & Bar, DFC & Bar. He was a veteran of over 100 operations at the ripe old age of 22. Dave got the direct hit that broke the wall of the Moehne Dam with the 'skip' bombs of the Dambusters. His right leg was encased in plaster. Our imaginations ran wild and we were somewhat disappointed to learn it was as a result of some frivolity in the Officer's Mess on pay night at Litchfield.

We did intensive courses, lectures and simulated training sessions in our own categories. We came together flying as a crew in all sorts of exercises, designed to give each of the crew the facility to improve his particular skills. This boosted the morale and confidence of each member of the crew working as a team and drove home the complete interdependence we had on each other under the quiet but firm leadership of Alan Shelton.

Our relaxation periods, outings and social evenings were also a very important factor in the 'getting to know you' process. On time off (48 hours leave pass), Wally, who joined the crew later, would head for home, the gunners had undisclosed plans and the other four of us usually headed for Leeds. On the first occasion, we stopped at a large hotel built over the main railway terminal. We were told we could not go near the fourth floor as the whole floor was occupied by an Indian Maharajah and his entourage. We came home about 1 am to find the doorman asleep at his post and the lifts were out of action. We started up the stairs and, when we got to the 4th could not resist a look. There was no one about and we were intrigued by the variety of shoes and knee boots, some with ornate silver and brass fittings, outside the doors for cleaning. We all looked at one another and grinned with the one idea in mind. We spread the Indian boots and shoes on all 12 floors, as also all those of other guests, including our own. Alan was up early, dressed and in socks and demanding the poor frustrated 'boots' man immediately find his new officer issue shoes—thence down to reception to join the queue of protesting guests.

Leeds was a favourite spot for us as it was easy to get to on leave at short notice. Also, by this time we had found an 'old' widow, Mrs Ackeroyd, who lived close into the city and would give us accommodation for a very nominal amount in return for a few food coupons. Apart from shows, Leeds was the Black Market town of the North. Whilst we did not smoke, the four of us always took our weekly ration of a carton of American cigarettes at a nominal fee. On one occasion in Leeds, we were able to barter (in a pub) two cartons of Camels for a tin of mushrooms, a tin of tomatoes and two Australian peaches (wrapped in cotton wool). For a couple of days, we dreamed of a magnificent feast on these delicacies. Off duty back at Riccall, we got on the bikes and toured the farms buying eggs. It was highly illegal, and the price was exorbitant at three pence each, but we eventually got 14 eggs. We obtained a loaf of bread, but how would we ever get butter? Alan said, 'Leave it to me'. Next day he got up early, went to the Officers Mess, read the morning paper, folding part on his lap, put the half-pound of butter on the paper and put the empty butter container at the end of the table. When English RAF officers arrived, he ordered his breakfast. When breakfast arrived, he politely asked one of the RAF Officers to pass the butter, please. As there was no butter, the Englishman called the stewardess and ticked her off for not putting butter on the table. After she produced more butter, Alan ate his breakfast and departed. When he turned up with half a pound of butter, he was almost hysterical telling us what happened. As a crew, together we cooked our meal on the pot-bellied coal heater in the middle of our hut and further cemented our crew relationship.

Alan, Roger, Greg and I spent leave time also in London and one night we went to a stage play. At first interval, we went into the crowded bar and had one drink when the bell rang. The barmaid said to us, 'A gentleman has just paid for another drink for you'. Around came Robert Newton and said, 'That's a bloody awful play. You might as well stay here and enjoy a few quiet drinks while the audience squirm in their seats'. With a deadpan face, he told us lots of stories about London, his dark eyes rolling and moving the whole time—just as they did when he later played Bill Sykes in Oliver Twist. We were in high spirits when we went down to the underground to make our way back to the Red Cross Club where we were staying. We were horrified to see the whole platform covered with people who had been bombed out that night. They were all so cheerful and making cockney cracks: 'Watch it, cock, don't stand on me. Stand on the missus, she's got more padding.'

On another occasion, we went to Edinburgh and stayed at the Victoria League Club in Princes Street. When we got in one evening, the hostess asked could we please stay in until lunchtime the next day as the Royal Family were coming and wished to meet all Dominion airmen staying there. With tongue in cheek, Alan told her that would not be possible as we had arranged an escorted trip over the 'Bass' brewery next morning. As it was only available once a week, we were sorry we would have to decline the kind invitation to meet the Royal Family. The hostess got on the phone to the manager of the brewery and arranged a private tour the following day. Whilst we were waiting for the Royal Family, Alan introduced me to a Flight Sergeant Ken Groves from Mordialloc. Just then, we were asked to form a circle around the room and Alan and I were on either side of this chap. We were wearing name tags and the hostess introduced us all to the King, the Queen, Princess Elizabeth (in A.T.S.[21] uniform) and little Meg and we shook hands with each. Because of the King's impediment, the Queen spoke to each third bod. She asked Ken, 'Where do you come from, Sergeant?' 'Melbourne, Your Majesty'. 'Which suburb?' 'Dudley Flats,* Your Majesty'. 'A lovely area, isn't it, Sergeant?' 'Delightful, Your Majesty'. It was hard to control our mirth until they were out of earshot.

While we had to take serious risks, work long hours and take enormous responsibilities on young shoulders, we were also fun-loving boys at heart.

I first flew with Alan on 4 August 1944 in a twin engine Wellington ('Wimpey') with a crew of six. On 25 November 1944, we had our first flight in the type of aircraft we would eventually fly on operation—the Halifax MK III ('Halibag'). This was at the Heavy

---

* Dudley Flats was the popular name for the waste-grounds in West Melbourne. According to Wikipedia: http://en.wikipedia.org/wiki//Dudley_Flats; [Accessed 4 January 2020]. 'During the Great Depression of the 1930s (and also possibly from an earlier date), the site was visited and then occupied by Melbourne's poor and homeless who scavenged for scrap and rags from the tips, and built humpies out of discarded rubbish such as old timber and corrugated iron, even lino and hessian sacking. By 1935, over 60 humpies had been erected along the waterways and around the rubbish tips.'

Conversion Unit at Riccall, York where we welcomed the seventh member of our crew—our new Flight Engineer, Wally Welsh, a tall, thin, shy, gangling, fair-haired 18-year-old youth from Devonshire, who integrated very well in the crew of Australians.

Alan got on with the inevitable 'circuits & bumps' in learning to fly a four-engined Halifax. We all had long sessions day and night, attending lectures and learning new procedures to master new equipment. As a crew, we all had 'circuits & bumps', whilst Alan practised three-engine, two-engine and single-engine landings. Then on to bombing practice, gunnery practice and cross-country flights of long duration, both day and night.

One night exercise was designed to take us virtually around England and Scotland. As we approached Land's End in heavy cloud we were tossed about in a violent electrical storm. Alan had to fight hard to maintain control. When we got on top he asked me for a course to take us up about NNE off the Cornish coast to cross into Wales. When a break came in the clouds, Alan saw the coast coming up at the estimated time. We all got quite a shock when anti-aircraft flak started to burst around us for the first time. We realised we were over the small pocket of resistance still holding on to Dunkirk. Our compass had gone haywire in the electrical storm. We came down to low level and 'unflappable Alan' flew over the heavily fortified Southampton with Alan using the distress call 'Mayday' and Wally firing Red Verey Cartridges and we map-read our way back to Riccall.

By mid-January 1945, we had been deemed a crew fully trained and ready for Operations. We were sent to fill a vacancy on 466 Squadron RAAF Driffield. Driffield had been a pre-war 'drome and Bulldust Castle'. On arriving, we had a great feeling of humility, expectation and awe, knowing we were the only crew on the Squadron which had not yet experienced an operation over enemy territory.

Our fifth operation was the most memorable. Our aircraft, K for King, had oil pressure problems and we were quickly transferred to the best aircraft—L for Love which belonged to the Commanding Officer. As it turned out, the boffins (planners) goofed on this one. The idea was that the main stream was to bomb a section of the Dortmund-Ems Canal. We were in a small group which flew over the main target about 15 minutes before the main stream to give Jerry the impression the target was further East. We flew on past our own target, a synthetic oil refinery at Reisholz with an 8,000 lb bomb load. After about 60 miles, we turned back and approached our target. As we came in on our bombing run, from the comments of those looking, we were flying into the moon. We were in a line of four aircraft, almost wing tip to wing tip—two on our left—one on our right in bright moonlight. We were attacked by ME109 fighters, being beautifully silhouetted for them. The bomber on our left took evasive action to starboard and the one our right dived to port, and both came underneath us. To avoid collision, Alan had no option but to calmly continue, straight and level and drop our bombs and cop it sweet. We got a lot of shells. An oil line was severed on the starboard outer engine and Alan had to feather it. Shortly after, the starboard inner also gave up the ghost and Alan had to work frantically adjusting trim etc. Bill Bullen reported that a shell had gone right through his turret, front and back, about half an inch above his head. The turret would not turn hydraulically but, 'not to worry', he would turn it manually.

Greg Dixon and I saw out for the first time on an operation as a shell had grazed down the port side of the aircraft taking a 6-inch strip off the fuselage. Wally went on an inspection tour and reported the Elsan (toilet-can) had been blown to bits and the interior of the aircraft would scarcely pass examination by a health inspector. Roger Johnson reported there was a 1,000 lb bomb stuck in the bomb-bay; the hydraulics weren't working and we couldn't open the bomb-bay doors. Wally Welsh got busy transferring fuel from the starboard tanks to the port tanks. Alan kept coaxing L for Love along as we gradually lost altitude. Over the North Sea, the port inner seized and had to be feathered.

There was a crash drome near Flamborough Head but not one of us questioned Alan's decision to return to Driffield or his ability to land on one engine with a 1,000 lb bomb. He also found the hydraulics would not operate the oleo legs (landing wheels). Control asked us to circle whilst more ambulances and fire carts were lined up. Keeping Wally to assist him, Alan ordered the rest of the crew into the centre of the aircraft and to brace themselves against struts and bulkheads as firmly as possible to avoid breakage of limbs. He put her down beautifully on her belly on the tarmac and, seeing the sparks flying, I wondered whether the bomb would blow or the fuel ignite and we all made a hasty exit.

At this stage, Alan Shelton was regarded around the squadron as a quiet, friendly, likable young pilot, improving with experience. After this incident, his stocks improved considerably and everyone on the base became aware of him as they all went to have a look at the wreck. Air crew and ground staff—fitters, cooks, riggers, drivers, armourers, clerks—came and shook us all by the hand. Certainly, Alan took a bit of ribbing for writing off the C/O's aircraft but the friendliness and admiration were gratifying.

Alan had ten operational trips over Germany, the last being on 3–4 March 1945. On the night of 3 March, we set off on a successful raid on an oil refinery. It started with the usual joint crew briefings, explanations of target, hazards that might be encountered, type and weight of bombs to be carried, met, intelligence, etc. Then back to our Sections to plot and plan our course; to the Mess for eggs and bacon and bar of chocolate. Eggs and chocolate were a strict ration, available only to air crew on a trip, and expectant mothers. A rush to collect our parachutes and the cheerful lasses pointing out the large wall sketch: 'It won't mean a thing if you don't pull the string.' Near the parachute section was the Chapel, and Father Baron, our Chaplain (from Lancashire), always waited in case we had the time to slip in. On this night, Alan, Roger Johnson, Wilf Tobin (also shot down that night), several others and myself slipped in for less than a minute, received a General Absolution and Holy Communion.

The trip itself was to be the easiest of operations so far. We had to bomb an oil refinery at Kamen, north of the Ruhr Valley. We had been there before. We took off at 1823 hours. The mission was completed. We encountered the usual flak at and around Kamen. The journey back was uneventful and, when we crossed the coast returning to England, we were very surprised when the gunners reported a heavy barrage of anti-aircraft fire from our own Coastal Batteries. We immediately correctly assumed that there were intruders in our midst and I gave Alan a course to take us directly back to Base at Driffield. We were the second aircraft of our Squadron back to Driffield. Joe Moss, the pilot of the first aircraft in, had already landed but one of his engines caught fire as we were approaching to land. We were about to touch down when we received a call from the tower 'Braemar to Rudkin Charlie Overshoot'. We overshot and Alan gunned the motors to full revs, replying 'Roger Braemar'. As we gained height, Joe Moss reported 'Runway Clear' and we went into circuit with other planes of the Squadron. Some of the others landed and we were instructed to prepare to land. As we got down to about 200 feet, the lights went out on the drome and we got the message from Control 'Braemar to all Rudkin Aircraft Scramble—Intruders'. Intruders were shooting up the tower and aircraft on the ground. So we had to stay in the air. When the order came from the tower to scramble, Alan asked me for a course to another drome. I moved back quickly to my navigation table in the nose and gave him a course to another drome.

Whilst on a mission the Navigator, Bomb Aimer and

Wireless Operator are situated in the nose under the Pilot. Roger, Greg and I always had to come back to benches in the centre of the aircraft for landing. This was called the 'rest position'. When Alan asked me to return to my position and give him a course, in my haste I left my parachute in the rest position—a mistake which undoubtedly saved my life.

We were flying west, the first drome was in darkness. We flew to three other dromes in that direction; they were all blacked out. Obviously, intruders were still about. Then Wally said, 'We're low on fuel'. We had a quick conference and aimed to gain height to a safe 4000 ft, head east for the coast to avoid any houses or towns, bail out on land and let the aircraft crash in the sea. As we turned to 90 degrees, we were unfortunate enough to fly head on into the firing line of a Junkers 88 night fighter. Roger reported an attack from the port bow just as the first burst struck our aircraft. The radial engines of a Halifax present a lighted circle from the front at night. It was relatively easy for the Hun to shoot out our four engines, a target rarely presented to him. The fuselage behind Alan caught on fire and the aircraft shuddered and lost height. Alan immediately gave us the order to bail out. He called out very calmly, 'Emergency jump; jump and go for your lives and the best of luck'; he said he would try and control the kite. Under my chair was the front hatch through which those in the nose normally get out. I didn't have my parachute with me. I had to climb past two bulkheads to retrieve it; all the way back, the port side was blazing. The middle upper hatch was already open as the mid-upper gunner Laing had gone out. Wally Welsh was standing there with flames all about him. I pushed him out and followed immediately, pulling my rip-cord as I went. Theory is that you count to 10 before pulling the cord. I pulled my cord as soon as I jumped because we were so close to the ground. Bill Bullen had caught his foot trying to get out at the rear. He was a big fellow for a gunner, ex-infantry, size 10 boots; he got his foot caught under the chair. He had flames all about him. He decided to pull his parachute cord in the hope that this would free him. It did, leaving his boot behind.

It was a relief in the darkness to feel the jolt as the parachute filled with air and I found myself sitting in the harness. I was looking up and saw other aircraft and ammunition exploding everywhere. Our two gunners had both got out at the same time and were able to talk to one another on the way down. They were descending quite close to me. We saw our aircraft spiral to the ground and explode. Eye witnesses later told the enquiry that 40 seconds elapsed between the time we were hit and the time the aircraft hit the ground.

Alan Shelton, Roger Johnson and Greg Dixon were my closest mates. They went down in the blazing plane. I don't know why they failed to leave the aircraft. I had tested the forward hatch before take-off and found it quite in order. I can only think it may have jammed when we were hit and that the fires at the nose may have been too intense or the gradient too steep. Mercifully, they would have died on impact and would not have suffered.

I hit the deck reasonably gently, as I was in a fallowed paddock. Roger Laing and Bill Bullen also survived. Wally must have waited to ensure he was clear of the tail-plane. His parachute had opened but did not break his fall. I had to go to the site the next morning and identify him. We were hit at around 0100 hours and the aircraft crashed at Fridaythorpe, nine miles WNW from Great Driffield. Seventeen aircraft from the Squadron took part in this mission. Only one other plane of the Squadron was lost that night but all of its crew got out.

Alan was calm in everything he did, even in his last moments. It was a pleasure to work with him and under him, as it was to enjoy his companionship. He was a great personality. He was always quietly confident in his own ability and let each of his crew feel he had complete confidence in them. There was magnificent cooperation and spirit within the crew—confidence in the pilot and in each other. My final tribute to Alan Shelton is to suggest to his family that, instead of praying for him, they pray to him.[22]

David Shelton, the youngest of the siblings, shared some memories of his brother Alan and the war years:

[The] final years at school [1939] coincided with the rising threat of war. As 'a sickening precursor of what lay in store for Europe', the Spanish Civil War and its horrors featured prominently in the minds of educated young Catholics like Alan. In October 1938, the army conducted searchlight and gunnery practice in Caulfield Park, not far from the Shelton residence. The exercise sparked concerns about air raids among a community still troubled by the bombing of the Basque town of Guernica eighteen months earlier. Pessimistic press reports heightened such fears, so that, by early 1939, local councillors 'were giving more and more of their time to plans and preparations for a time of war'.

As Alan followed in his father's footsteps by commencing medical studies at Melbourne University, Caulfield had already sent its first troops off to war, and the army had established an encampment at Caulfield Racecourse. On October 16, 1941, with the end of his second year approaching, Alan signed a Mobilization Attestation Form...and joined the Melbourne University Rifles...Alan was clearly one of many undergraduates who now viewed the MUR as a means of 'undergoing basic training before departing for full-time service'. From December 15, 1941 until January 18, 1942, Private Shelton was encamped with the Rifles at Bonegilla, in north-eastern Victoria. Australia was then enduring the worst crisis in its history. HMAS Sydney had been lost with all hands on November 19, 1941; the Japanese had attacked Malaya and Pearl Harbour on December 7–8; with the fall of Singapore on February 15, 1942, the Eighth Division of the AIF was lost; four days later, Darwin was bombed. Australia was now confronting two nightmares which it had long dreaded: the 'Yellow Peril' was on the march, and the very basis of British power in the Far East was gone. Christmas 1941 therefore found Australia 'grim and determined; at bay against a new and treacherous foe'. The Shelton household soon received a council circular explaining how to make a backyard slit trench. By February 1942, Caulfield had been blacked out, with glass in public buildings removed or covered. In the same month, the Prime Minister, John Curtin, announced the conscription of all of Australia's resources, human and material, for 'the purposes of war'.

Alan Shelton was one of 12,984 aircrew trainees to pass through Somers as part of the Empire Air Training Scheme between 1940 and 1945. Sadly, more than 7,000 of them never returned from their active service.[23]

SOCIAL LIFE AND MARRIAGE

5

Moira's post-war social activities and her newsworthy hats

After the war, Moira worked at the Commonwealth Serum Laboratories in Melbourne. At first, she was appointed Head of the Penicillin Assay Department. Later, at her request, she was transferred to Research Bacteriologist, working on penicillin and streptomycin. Moira and AG Matthews from the laboratories published a paper titled 'A Streptomycin Sensitivity Test' in *The Medical Journal of Australia*.[24]

In February 1948, Moira was appointed Officer (Female) on Staff at the Council for Scientific and Industrial Research at the head office in East Melbourne. Here she worked for Dr HC Forster and Sir Ian Clunies Ross.

Moira's social activities attracted the interest of Melbourne newspapers and magazines.

> **Demobilised** A jolly party on Saturday at Dr. and Mrs. Percy Shelton's home in Glenhuntly rd. was given by daughter, Moira, who, after a distinguished career

in the WAAAF as flight officer, is demobilised and working at Commonwealth Serum Laboratories. Sisters, Valda, out of the WAAAF, and June, just released from the WRANS, assisted the hostess.[25]

A Topping Topper "WHERE DID you get that hat?" Moira Shelton had this question fired at her from left and right at Helen Webster's cocktail party on Saturday night—from girl friends lost in admiration and from boys who for a second—only a second, mind you—glanced higher than the attractive face beneath THE HAT. A real top hat it was, but it was not the shape so much as the material which made it exciting—tropical red flowers and gold lame on black slipper satin. Moira told me she bought the material in Sydney and had it made up in Melbourne, so, for once, two rival states share the honours.[26]

Government House Party For Royal Navy To enable junior officers of the visiting Royal Navy Squadron to meet some of Melbourne's young people, and country visitors who are in town, the Governor (Sir Winston Dugan) and Lady Dugan entertained 200 guests at a late afternoon party at Government House yesterday... Most of the young girls present wore smart cocktail hats, but a few featured Alice-in-Wonderland ribbons or a flower spray tucked in their hair. The most outstanding hat was that worn by Miss Moira Shelton. It was a modified "topper" in black, embroidered in glittering gold, red and green embroidery. With it she wore black, with a velvet neckband and an orchid pinned at one shoulder.[27]

Oaks Day 1947 A full-backed royal blue coat was worn by Miss Moira Shelton with a royal blue felt hat, the crown of which was covered with pink roses.[28]

Small Crowd at Flemington Races...Miss Moira Shelton looked attractive in a cyclamen suit piped with blue to match her flower-pot hat.[29]

INTERESTING engagement announced today is that of Moira Shelton and Kevin Coleman.[30] Moira, who is wearing a solitaire diamond engagement ring surrounded by eight square-cut sapphires, is at present working at the CSIR. A Melbourne University science graduate, she was a WAAAF officer during the war and served with the chemical warfare section. Kevin, at present doing final year law at Newman College was an officer in the 9th Division.[31]

Caulfield Cup eve cabaret ball at the Palais Royale for St Vincent's Hospital, with over 800 people attending. Miss Moira Shelton was one of the hostesses.[32]

PARTY AT CLUB FOR FRIENDS So that she could greet her friends in 1950, Miss Moira Shelton entertained at a late afternoon party at the Lyceum Club yesterday. Among the guests were her parents, Dr. and Mrs. Percy Shelton; her brother, Mr. David Shelton; her sisters and their husbands, Dr. and Mrs. Charles McCann and Mr. and Mrs. Bill Martin; her grandmother, Mrs. Margaret Johnston; and her cousin, Dr. John Shelton and his wife, who recently returned from England. The hostess wore a ballerina frock of white, dull satin, patterned with a large floral design in pastel shades.[33]

Engaged Today: A beautiful three-diamond engagement ring is the choice of Moira Lenore Shelton, eldest daughter of Dr. and Mrs. Percy Shelton, of Glenhuntly Road, Elsternwick, whose engagement to John Francis Dynon is announced today. Moira is a scientist at CSIRO. John, the second son of Mrs. M. Dynon, of The Righi, South Yarra, and of the late Mr. J. Dynon, is an Old Xaverian and a law graduate of Melbourne and Oxford Universities. Moira and John will be married at Xavier College Chapel on December 2.[34]

Cherry Red: A frock and jacket of cherry-red crepe, with which she wore a small hat of matching straw, trimmed with self-coloured velvet, was chosen by Miss Moira Shelton when she was guest of honour at an afternoon party which Mrs. Ernest Rodeck gave at her Hawthorn flat yesterday…[35]

Pre-Wedding: Miss Moira Shelton was guest of honour at a party which Mrs. James Dynon gave for about 80 young people at her home in South Yarra on Saturday evening…A ballerina-length frock of grey cyclamen and silver lame brocade was chosen by Moira, whose parents, Dr. and Mrs. P.G. Shelton, were among the guests. Yesterday afternoon Moira was entertained at an afternoon tea party which Miss Joan Gaffney gave at her home in Caulfield.[36]

Household Hints Tea: A pre-wedding party with a difference, in the form of a household hints tea, was given for Miss Moira Shelton by Miss Margaret Crosbie at her home in St. Kilda yesterday afternoon. The guest of honour…chose an aqua angora frock with a matching jacket trimmed with white piping.[37]

Gift tea: Mrs. William Calanchini will give a handkerchief tea at her home in Ascot Vale Road, Moonee Ponds today, for Moira Shelton...[Wedding] guests will include mutual friends from the University, where Moira graduated in science. Mrs. Calanchini is an Arts graduate of Melbourne University.[38]

For Bride-To-Be: At her flat in St. Kilda-road yesterday afternoon Mrs. Charles McCann entertained a few friends in honour of her sister, Miss Moira Shelton...Among the guests were Moira's other sister, Mrs. W. Martin, who will be her matron of honour at Xavier College Chapel, and bridesmaid-elect, Miss Maude Murphy. Both will also be pre-wedding hostesses.

Pre-Wedding: An afternoon tea party at her home in South Yarra given by Mrs. Andrew Bird yesterday, wound up a round of parties in honour of Miss Moira Shelton...Moira topped her afternoon frock of floral silk in various blue tones, black and white, with a picture hat of fine black straw.[39]

6

Wedding and honeymoon

I met Moira for the first time in February 1949 on the occasion of an engagement party at my mother's home at 7 The Righi, South Yarra. Despite this, my cousin Joan O'Collins maintained that she had first introduced me to Moira at a party at Rock Lodge, Frankston. Joan's sister, Mary Lewis, wrote to my mother in 1950:

> Dear Aunt Margaret,
>
> I felt I must write and tell you how thrilled we all are at John's engagement. Joan feels she has a special interest as she introduced them at Maeve's 21st party. Moira is a lovely girl—plenty of brains plus charm. They were down to dinner last night. It was very cheery. John is so happy and she, so fond of him.

I saw Moira a number of times before returning to Europe in May 1949. Finally, back in Melbourne in May 1950, Moira and I became engaged on 21 August and were married less than four months later. Moira was later to describe this, probably accurately, as a 'whirlwind romance'. From that time on, our lives ran together until her untimely death.

Saturday morning, 2 December 1950, was warm and sunny. My brother Jim officiated at our marriage in the Xavier College Chapel, with the assistance of my good friend Father Jeremiah Murphy and Father O'Mahoney. I remember standing at the altar rails (donated by my mother in memory of my father, James) with Moira beside me. She was radiant and calm whilst my hands were trembling. *The Herald* reported the event:

> **Bride in Blue At College Chapel**
>
> The marriage took place this morning at Xavier College Chapel of Miss Moira Lenore Shelton and Mr. John Francis Dynon. The bridegroom's brother, the Rev. James Dynon, assisted by the Rev. J. Murphy, Rector of Newman College and the Rev. M. O'Mahoney, celebrated the wedding with Nuptial Mass.
>
> The bride, eldest daughter of Dr. and Mrs. Percy Shelton, of 'Illawarra', Glenhuntly Road, Elsternwick, wore a gown of ice blue French brocade, with a slight train, long sleeves and square neckline. Her ice blue tulle veil was held with a coronet of ice blue satin leaves, and she carried white orchids. She was attended by her sister, Mrs. William Martin and Miss Maud Murphy. They wore ice blue satin frocks, with bands of pleating at the necklines and hems. Their ice blue satin cloches had tiny brims of pleated satin, and they carried cyclamen pink peonies.
>
> The bridegroom, younger son of Mrs. James Dynon, of The Righi, South Yarra, and of the late Mr. Dynon, had Mr. Richard Buxton as best man and Mr. Richard Marron as groomsman. Ushers were Mr. David Shelton, Mr. John Mornane, Mr. John Crosbie and Mr. Douglas Buxton. The reception was at the Delphic.[40]

The 'getting to the church on time', the marriage ceremony, the signing of the papers, the taking of the photographs, visiting Mother Bernard and other Presentation Sisters at their Windsor convent and the reception at The Delphic, all went smoothly and enjoyably. It was as if in a dream.

That evening we flew to Sydney and stayed at the Hotel Australia. Sunday morning Mass was at St Mary's Cathedral. From there, we proceeded on our way with stops at Darwin, Singapore and Karachi for nights, before arriving in Rome. We loved Italy and the Vatican City. The Holy Year was coming to a close. Our journey took us to Pompeii, Amalfi, Sorrento and Capri. On our return to Rome, we had a special Papal audience at the Vatican; then on to Portofino, Florence, Genoa and Turin. From Italy, we went to France, Spain, Belgium, England, Ireland, Scotland and the Netherlands. We returned again to Rome in May for the last time and were honoured with a small special Papal audience before returning home via the United States of America.

I do not intend to give my description of events or my impressions. I have chosen instead to quote from Moira's letters.

On 3 December, Moira wrote to her parents:

> Dear Mummy & Daddy,
>
> Before we leave Sydney tomorrow I thought that I would like to write to tell you both how much John and I appreciate the wonderful day you gave for us yesterday. We thought that the day was perfect and you need have no doubts that everyone enjoyed it. The Delphic certainly rose to the occasion and we are both not forgetful of the fact that had you both not been so

wonderful and so generous the wedding and reception could not have been so good. Certainly John and I shall never forget the day and your kindness to us both.

We had a smooth trip to Sydney and at the hotel a beautiful box of red roses, blue cornflowers and gardenias awaited our arrival—sent by Mrs. Dynon. It was sweet of her and the flowers are lovely.

I am enclosing a telegram which also awaited us here from Mary Lewis, Ellie McGullicuddy & Dympna Glynn. Could you please send one of the thank you cards to each of them, when they are available. The address of the two former are in the "blue" book. I suggest that Dympna Glynn's is sent care Mary Lewis. We are both pretty tired today and spent a lazy day. We struck High Mass at St Mary's at 11 a.m.

John said to tell Mummy she is still beautiful. He objected to Dr. Body saying "used to be beautiful". We thought that his speech was excellent as was Daddy's reply. Don't you think all the speeches were good?… We were both thinking of you all today and we did not forget that it is David's birthday. Wish him all the best from both of us. Our address in Rome is Hotel Dinesen, Via Porta, Pinciana 18, Rome. We will be there until 29th Dec. After that you will not be able to contact us until early February when our address is c/o Union Bank of Australia. 6 Albemarle St, London W1.

Please give my love to David, Grandma, Val, June & not forgetting Tot and Les. They were marvellous also to me in the last few hectic weeks. Again my thanks to you both for everything and with love to you both.
Moira

> PS 4th Dec. Have just seen Melb papers. Could you arrange for copies of photos in Herald, Argus, Sun & Age. We liked the Sun & Herald the best. Ask Daddy are these more to <u>his</u> liking.

On 10 December, Moira wrote to her mother:

> We arrived safely in Rome on Friday evening. It was raining but rather warm and humid. We later heard that the humidity is due to the fact that Mt. Etna in Sicily is playing up. Rome is absolutely a wonderful city. Yesterday morning we went for a walk around some of the main streets. In the afternoon we took the bus to St. Peters, which is indescribably beautiful and far surpasses anything that I have heard or read about. The journey back in the bus was also indescribable but in a different way—Melbourne strike crowds have nothing on it. The Italians seem to have a 'bus mentality' all of their own.

> Today we took a glorious trip to St. Lawrence outside the walls where Sts. Stephen and Lawrence are buried. Then we went 25 miles out of Rome to Tivoli. There is a very old (400 years) mansion home with glorious grounds, over 400 fountains and trees and shrubs are just wonderful.

Still in Rome on 21 December, Moira wrote again to her mother:

> It was lovely to receive your letter today and I wish to thank you very much for it and also for the news. John and I are very happy to know that you are all well. We were interested to hear all the tit bits re the wedding and to know that everyone seems to have enjoyed it so

much. Personally we cannot see how they could have done otherwise. John tipped it was Auntie Eileen who remarked that the wedding was 'a fitting ceremony for a charming couple'. We are both well and still loving our stay in Rome.

On Saturday we visited the Basilica of St. Maria Maggiore which contains a miraculous image of the Madonna, one of the earliest in existence and also relics of the Holy Cradle. In the evening we went to the Opera and saw 'Cosi Fan Tutti', which was lovely, though we did not like it as much as 'Masked Ball'. This week we have also seen St. Pauls outside the walls which basilica contains two altars of the precious malachite and lapis lazuli stone. They were gifts from Czar Nicholas of Russia. We have also been to the English Protestant Cemetery and saw amongst other things the tombs of Keats and Shelley.

Yesterday we went to the general Papal audience at St. Peters and took up our very good positions about 10 a.m. Colonel Boyle had arranged this for us. I was next to an Argentine lady and a French Nun and the former was particularly kind and gave us a lot of information about what was going on. She said that she had met the present Pope when he was in the Argentine as Papal Secretary in 1934. From 11 a.m. till 12 the whole congregation took part in prayers and hymns in all languages. Just before 12 all the lights in the Basilica were turned on and the Pope was carried in his usual Papal chair amidst enthusiastic cheering. He was carried to the foot of the steps below the Papal throne and he ascended the steps jauntily like a 2 year old. The Pope looked well and he addressed the assembly first in Italian and then in French, English, Spanish and German. He then gave the general blessing to all present and this was applied also to all relatives at home. He descended the steps and moved among the crowd speaking to and blessing adults and children including several Arabs. It was a most impressive and unforgettable experience. The basilica holds 60,000 and was packed, and the doors were locked at 11 a.m.

After a quick lunch we just had time to make an afternoon tour which included the Colosseum, St. Pauls and St. Callisto catacombs: 10 miles of these catacombs have been unearthed and they are in 3 tiers. These are only one of 42 catacombs encircling the Roman walls. That night at 9.30 p.m. we went to the Argentina Theatre to hear a concert conducted by Ernest Bom with the American pianist Franceschi.

This morning by arrangement of the British Consul, I went to see the Director of the Italian National Research Council, Conte Aluffi. He was very helpful and it turned out that he was one of the main attendants of the Pope at the audience yesterday. This Council is similar to CSIRO. After that I went to see Mr. Callow at the new International Antibiotics Research Centre —a beautiful building costing ½ million pounds and not yet quite completed. Professor Chain and Mr. Callow, both of Oxford penicillin fame, are in charge. This Centre is to commence in full swing on 1st January and it would seem that some good work should be done there if one can judge from the personnel and facilities. Mr. Callow was very helpful and showed me around.

> This afternoon we went by bus to Frascati in the Alban Hills calling at Castel Gandolfo the Pope's summer residence. It was a lovely trip and we had the unique experience of having a guide and the whole bus to ourselves. The scenery was glorious and we saw some snow. The rain in Rome seems to have stopped and the weather is sunny and fresh. We leave here next Thursday and as we are now thinking of going to Spain, may not arrive in U.K. until the last week in February.

Moira wrote her last letter from Rome to her mother on 2 January 1951:

> I was terribly thrilled to receive your letter of the 17th and also letters from Val and June when we returned to Rome last night. It is lovely to know that you are well and we hope that by now the heat wave has left Melbourne.
>
> John and I were very upset to hear that June has not been well and we do hope that after her short stay with you she is feeling better. Will you give her our love and say that we join with Charlie in saying that she must take things as quietly as possible until her big day. I have sent you our London address and as we expect to reach London about the expected date, could you please cable us when the baby arrives. As you can imagine we shall be anxious to hear the news and we shall not forget to say a prayer that all will go well for her.
>
> I received a long letter from Nancy McDonald telling me the news and all the interest taken in the wedding by friends at CSIRO. She enclosed the cutting from Woman's Day which we rather liked. I shall make a

point of looking up Mrs. Lawrence. If you could send to England the address of the girl who looks after Alan's grave, I would like to see or telephone her when we are in Harrogate.

You probably know that John sprained his ankle (the carpet slipped on the polished floor when he got out of bed on the 24th Dec.) and he spent the 25th, 26th in bed and has had it bandaged until today. Fortunately it is now all right except for the remnants of the bruises.

On 25th I attended the first Mass of an Australian priest (Father Gallagher) with Jim Peters' sister (Mona Molony) her husband, Bill, and Father John Molony. I met several of the Priests and trainee Priests at the College (Propaganda College) and they included every race and colour. The Mass was most impressive, the choir wonderful and it was interesting to meet the various Priests. One was an Indian whose father has 40 wives.

On the 26th I visited the Blue Sisters Hospital 'Calvary' and was given a wonderful cup of tea (rare here) and then shown over the hospital by a Sydney Nun, Sister Dominic. She was young, charming and very broad minded. The hospital is new and extremely modern in design. It has every possible device and some of the equipment is marvellous. The Chapel is particularly lovely and is the centre of the hospital, which is built in the shape of a cross.

On Wednesday we went to the Vatican Picture Gallery which contains some wonderful pictures and tapestries. I loved especially Raphael's 'Transfiguration'. That evening we had drinks with the Boyles and a

Mr. Geiseking (a New Zealander) who came over in the same aircraft as we did. On our return to the hotel we were greeted by a telegram saying that the car had not been unloaded at Naples and had gone on to Genoa. However we did not alter our plans to visit Naples and Sorrento.

We left Rome by bus on 27th and arrived in Naples for lunch stopping ½ hour en route at Formia. The drive was very pleasant and the scenery lovely. We looked around Naples in the afternoon and made arrangements for John to collect the car in Genoa on 4th Jan. That evening we saw 'Don Carlos' at the San Carlo Opera House. It was a wonderful performance and the house was packed. There were approximately 100 in the orchestra; the 3rd and 4th Acts were especially outstanding and I shall never forget them. We returned to our hotel in a carrozza.

The next morning we left Naples and called at the Cameo and Tortoise shell factory (Capa Corallo) en route to Pompeii; was interesting to see the old shops, houses, streets, baths, theatres etc and almost impossible to believe that the city was covered by pumice and mud in 79 A.D. and dated from that time. There are excavations still in progress. In the museum I was interested to see knitting needles, bread, gold rings & bracelets of that time—not terribly different from present day design.

We then drove to Amalfi where we had lunch and then continued the magnificent drive to Sorrento. That drive is a little like the great Ocean Road but is even more rugged and here and there on the mountain cliffs there are villages. It was wonderful. We arrived at Sorrento where we had a nice room in the hotel with a beautiful view overlooking the sea and Vesuvius.

On the Saturday we went over to Capri. It was a glorious day and the water was very blue. On arriving at Capri, we went in a smaller boat to the famous Blue Grotto; that also was a lovely trip and the water was a real navy blue. To enter the Grotto we had to transfer into a small rowing boat and even then had to lie flat when going through the rocky entrance. I have never seen anything like the Grotto. The water is a true silvery turquoise and if you put your hand into the water it also looks the same colour.

That night there was a storm and the next day I was delighted to see Vesuvius and the Apennines were snow capped. After Mass that morning we were taken to see a shop which stocks the most wonderful hand made inlaid wood work (tables, musical boxes, book ends, etc.) linen and laces. They were exquisite and cheap but we have not the lire to do any shopping now that we are hoping to visit the south of Spain and also Holland in addition to France and Belgium. The Italians just delight in showing off their wares and the more we admired these goods, the more we were shown. They are very friendly and excitable people and go to no end of trouble to help in everything. There was a party for New Year at the Hotel that night and we all drank Champagne at midnight. We were both thinking of you all. Yesterday we reluctantly left Sorrento at noon and reached Rome last night.

Today we had a delightful lunch with a friend of John's, Dr. Vaccari of the Association of Christian Industrialists in Italy. He is a delightful person; he gave me an inscribed book on Rome, John a bronze medal and talked us into going to Turin. In the evening we had the Boyles and Father Kelly for tea. On Thursday we go to Florence and then to Portofino, Turin and the Riviera before going to Spain. We shall be on the move from now on so do not worry if you do not hear from us for a while.

Moira's next letter was to her mother and father from Avignon on 14 January:

Last weekend John wrote to Mrs. Dynon from the delightful spot on the Italian Riviera, Portofino, and so I shall continue the news from there. On Tuesday morning we went to Genoa where we saw the 31 storey building and had tea at the restaurant on top of it. From this restaurant there is a glorious view of Genoa, and Professor Pisetti, who was with us, pointed out the famous land marks of the city including the old house of Christopher Columbus. About midday we left Genoa for Turin. That was a wonderful drive—perfect roads, lovely views and there was plenty of snow both on the mountains and in the fields. In the winter the roads are swept to keep them open and it is funny to drive along a clean road with snow all round.

Turin is a beautiful city and I loved it. The shops there have to be seen to be believed. It was very cold but bearable and of course all the buildings were heated. Turin is the centre of fashion in Italy and is the 'Paris' of Italy. Scarcely had we arrived in our hotel when the door opened and in came a huge parcel of literature on Turin for John and a magnificent bunch of roses for me—gifts from Dr. Ottonello whom we later met. He is a friend of Dr. Vaccari, whom we told you about from Rome. Dr. Ottonello was really wonderful to us and he ensured that we enjoyed our stay in Turin. We were shown over the Salesian College founded by St. Don Bosco, and there met a Priest whose brother is head of the order in Victoria. We visited the Cottolengo where literally thousands of poor, ill and destitute are looked after. This is a huge place and is maintained entirely by charity. John was able to visit the huge Fiat works; we were taken for a drive to see a wonderful panoramic view of Turin and the 'Superga' church on the top of the hill about 10 miles outside the city. Outside this church there was a large memorial stone to the champion Italian Soccer team which was killed in an air crash in 1949, and I noticed that the date was 4th March. Amongst other things there was a dinner party for 12 in Turin where we sampled the social side of the town. The dinner lasted from 8 p.m. till 11 p.m. after which we all adjourned to a cafe for liqueurs. It would take pages to tell you all about our visit to Turin and so I shall merely say it was wonderful.

On Thursday afternoon we drove to the coast (about 90 miles of much climbing of mountains covered with heavy snow) and arrived at Savona on the Italian Riviera. The next few days we spent going through the Italian and then the French Rivieras, which are lovely. The scenery is gorgeous all along the coast.

We called at Monte Carlo where we visited the famous

Casino and watched the games. The buildings at Monte Carlo are beautiful and we saw the steps, balcony and bridge with the rail line below, which you will recall having seen in the film 'Red Shoes'. We thought that Cannes with its palatial hotels, lovely beaches and exclusive shops, was outstanding. We saw the Riviera in wet and later in sunny weather and it is good at any time. We spent one night at a hotel La Tour de l'Aiguillon which is built on a high rocky peninsula and which has a superb view from every angle.

Yesterday we reached Marseilles where we stayed last night. We visited a church 'Basilique de Notre Dame De La Garde', built on a high mountain outside the city and from where was had a wonderful view. We were able to see the island with the prison 'Chateau D'If' where the man in the iron mask was imprisoned. We are both well and having a wonderful time. Fortunately there have been no mishaps and the car is going like a dream.

On 20 February Moira wrote to her sister Valda from Roubaix:

My dear Valda,

John and I had 11 glorious days in Paris and I shall never forget them. Of course, I saw the Louvre with its wonderful paintings, the Tuileries gardens and the Arc de Triomphe. The Paris shops are simply divine and one could spend weeks just looking at the windows.

A friend of John's, Henri Rollet, was able to arrange (at least his Mother arranged) an invitation for me to attend a parade at the salon of Jacques Heim. The suits, ballerinas, and evening frocks and furs were very lovely and it was a wonderful experience to be able to attend one of these parades. Christian Dior was not showing the week we were in Paris but another friend of John's also arranged for me to attend his parade. Unfortunately, that was today and I am about 200 miles from Paris. We hope to have another 4–5 days in Paris before we come home and I may be able to visit Dior's salon then.

We saw the opera 'Aida' in Paris and it was superb—voices, production, orchestra, everything. I shall never forget that performance. We also saw the ballet which was better than any I have seen. The girls are so graceful, so lovely and the performance was wonderful.

One afternoon we visited the famous Carnavalet Museum, which was very interesting. Here we saw relics of Napoleon, the Revolution (including clothes etc. worn by Marie Antoinette and Louis XVI when in prison before they were guillotined), old signs that were on the shops in the days before people generally could read or write, frocks etc. of the different centuries. We also visited the old house of Victor Hugo, which is now a Museum. Yesterday morning we left Paris very early taking Monsieur Harmel with us, and proceeded to Rheims. Incidentally, action is being taken to have his grandfather, Leon Harmel, canonised as a saint.

Near Rheims we spent a delightful day visiting le Val des Bois Warmeriville wool spinning factory, after a delightful lunch with M. Harmel. It was a very interesting afternoon seeing the dyeing and spinning of the wool a great deal of which is Australian. We spent the night at Rheims and this morning visited the Pommery and Greno Champagne factory and cellars.

The cellars are 100 feet below the ground and over 12 million bottles of champagne are stored there as it is made. We drank some of the product, before leaving the factory, with one of the senior officials.

Moira wrote to her parents from Brussels on 24 February:

> We had a delightful day at Roubaix on Wednesday despite the weather which was typically Melbourne-like with alternate sunshine and rain all day. We saw Phillipe Bayart (a friend of John's who is in Moral Re-Armament) and had coffee at his home, where we met his wife and some of his young family. Mr. Bayart conducted us on a tour of the city and we were very impressed with the thousands of lovely new houses which have been, and are still being erected as part of the new housing scheme. On returning to Brussels we drove around and looked at the King's palace and the Courts of Justice. I am told that the latter is the largest building in Europe.
>
> Later that night we struck our first real misfortune. About midnight John became ill, suddenly with what we thought was a bad tummy upset. This continued and when about 2.30 a.m. he commenced to vomit blood I was very alarmed. With the assistance of the hotel porter I was able to contact a good doctor and one who spoke English reasonably well. He said that he would come immediately. We were very relieved to know that the trouble was not surgical and was due to food poisoning (we still do not know exactly the source). Poor John had a bad time until about 6 p.m. last night when the trouble subsided a bit. Dr. Ledent prescribed several things and we were fortunate to find

a Pharmacy open at 3.45 a.m. not far from the hotel and where we got the requirements. Actually it was a friend of John's (Mr. Humblet) whom I had phoned and who insisted on coming in (he helped with the language difficulties) who went out for the medicine. He was very kind and helpful to us and we are indeed grateful to him. John is better tonight though still in bed and has just had his first cup of weak tilleul (like black tea only weaker.) However, Dr. Ledent said that he will improve now and should be well again in about 4–5 days. We have to re-educate his tummy slowly to food and keep on the medicines to get his strength and blood pressure back to normal. It was terribly bad luck for him but the main thing is that by the time you receive this letter, he will be well again.

P.S. The patient looks pretty good—sitting up in bed reading 'The Times' and surrounded by daffodils (gift from John Humblet and his lovely wife).

I suppose by now you have a new grandchild. We both hope that June is well and we know that the baby will be a lovely one. I wonder if it will be a boy or a girl. Please give our love to all the family, Grandma, Tot and Les. We think of you all a great deal and hope that all is well. I hope that Les' elbow is better.

By 3 March we had settled at the Cumberland Hotel in London. Moira wrote to her mother:

From Brussels we went to Bruges (the town bells there are lovely) and to Ostend and then back to France to Dunkirk and Calais. There is still much evidence of bomb damage in these towns and many people live in temporary, pre-fabricated huts. We visited the beach at Dunkirk from where the big British evacuation was made.

We crossed from Calais to Dover on 1st March. It was a good crossing, though a little choppy and rather cold. We both enjoyed it. From Dover we drove via Canterbury and Maidstone where we had a wonderful dinner, to London and to this hotel. The hotel is close to Marble Arch and our bedroom window looks over Hyde Park.

Yesterday we both attended to the 101 things, (luggage, bank, laundry, hair, etc.) and are now more or less organised again. Last night we were lucky enough to fluke excellent seats for the Covent Garden performance "The Sleeping Beauty" Ballet. It was divine and unforgettable. Tonight we attended the BBC concert. Moiseiwitsch was the guest artist with the BBC Orchestra and he is a superb pianist.

Today John started my tour of London and we covered a great deal. Trafalgar Square, Westminster, Bond Street, Oxford Street, Grosvenor Square, Berkeley Square, Big Ben, and a host of other places. This afternoon we visited the National Gallery and saw some glorious works. John joins me in sending love to you all. We are both very well, happy and having a wonderful trip but I wish the time would not go so fast. Hoping you all are well. Lots of love.

Moira wrote again to her mother on 5 March from London:

I was terribly thrilled to receive your letters today. Fancy June having twins! We are both thrilled at the news and happy to know that all is now well. She and

Charlie must be feeling very proud indeed.

Today I went into the Australian Scientific Liaison Office in London (CSIRO show) and had a long chat with Mr. Cummins. He has given me names and contacts all over England which will prove helpful in enabling me to see some research places…

It is good to know that you all are well. Sorry about the hot weather. Sorry too, that we are missing it!! It is rather cold over here. Yesterday we had a lovely day at Oxford (about 70 miles from London). The colleges are lovely and I saw Christ Church, where John was. Of course, it is the best. Tell Dad the flu seems to be under control in U.K. now. There does not appear to be much of it in London and we intend to dodge any areas where flu may be raging. We are both well.

P.S. Thanks for the rabbit news. That is a thrill for CSIRO and also for me! Am looking forward to hearing more about it when I return.

Two days later, Moira wrote to June:

My dear June,

Firstly John and I wish to congratulate you and Charlie on the twins. We were both terribly excited to hear the wonderful news and I am sure that you must be feeling terribly proud. I always did think that twins were wonderful and now that I have twin nieces, I feel I have something to boast about…

John and I are still having a wonderful time. London is simply glorious. There is so much to see and it is a wonderfully interesting place. We were lucky to see Ivor Novello in his show 'Kings Rhapsody' the night he died. It was a good show and he was superb. We were shocked to hear the following morning that he had died suddenly a few hours later.

We saw another good show last night "Who is Sylvia" by Terrence Rattigan. It is very good and amusing. Yesterday we continued to see some of London's spots and visited St. Paul's (saw here Nelson's Tomb), Tower of London and part of the British Museum. The last is terribly interesting and enormous. We went today to the Victoria & Albert Museum and saw lots of the ancient relics of 5th century England, some divine glassware and china, water paintings by Constable and Turner, and many original manuscripts of Mozart, Chopin, Schubert, Schumann, Shakespeare, letters of Nelson and very early editions of the Bible. We had a wonderful day. Whilst at the Museum we saw Queen Mary who walked right past us in the ancient English relics section. She looked lovely and very charming in violet. She looked well. That was a thrill for us.

I was sorry to hear that you had been so sick. That was really terribly bad luck for you and I do hope that you are well and strong again. The twins will keep you busy but they must be lovely. I am looking forward to seeing them. It was good of you to write and especially when you were so sick. It was lovely to receive your letter and to hear the news. Many thanks.

On 16 March Moira wrote to her mother from the Randolph Hotel at Oxford:

As you can see from the address John and I are now at Oxford. We had a wonderful time in London. Tussauds wax works are very interesting and the figures life-like. One day we visited the Kew Gardens and were shown round by Sir Edward Salisbury, whom you will recall came to Australia for that big CSIRO conference. He was interested to see me and to hear the news of his 'Australian friends', as he put it.

We also went to the Home Exhibition where 6 houses were on show (inside the enormous gallery) and some interesting household gadgets. While in London we saw some of our friends including Joan Gaffney, Gwen Moorees and Mr. and Mrs. Paul Kelly. Mrs. Lawrence was away the week we were there and we shall see her at a later date. We saw a very interesting dramatic opera (modern) called 'The Consul' produced by Laurence Olivier which was superb. One day we went down to Dover to visit John's sister, who is very well and lovely. She is like Father Dynon in appearance. We really had a lovely day with her.

We left London on Monday 12th and went to Cambridge. We saw the University and Colleges and in the evening went to a good play called 'Who Goes There'. At Cambridge I met Dr. Robin Hill (Bio-chemist) who showed me round the scientific departments and also the famous Cavendish Labs. CSIRO corresponded a great deal with Dr. Hill. From Cambridge we visited the Cathedral at Ely which is magnificent. I shall never forget its beauty. As there was some delay re our luggage we decided to come to Oxford until Sunday (18th) before going to Liverpool and crossing to Ireland on the 19th. We return to England on the 1st April and shall then proceed to Harrogate returning then to Oxford for John's conference.

From here we have done some very interesting trips; one to Stonehenge, the ruins of the 14th century old Sarum Castle, and Salisbury Cathedral, which has the tallest spire in the United Kingdom. We also saw the atom research place at Harwell that day. We have seen the lovely ancient manor house (in ruins) at Minster Lovel, some of the lovely villages in the Cotswold Hills, Stratford-on-Avon and the glorious home of the Earl of Warwick at Warwick. The state rooms and gardens here are very beautiful and there are some paintings by Van Dyck, Raphael and other famous artists among his collection. We saw a sketch of Anthony Eden's eldest sister, who is the mother of the present Earl of Warwick. Here also was a painting by Rubens of St. Ignatius of Loyola, which was originally done for the Jesuits at Antwerp (Belgium). We visited Kenilworth and saw the ruins of the castle of Queen Elizabeth's day and also went to Coventry where we saw the statue of Lady Godiva. We have seen the grounds of the palace of the Duke of Marlborough (at Woodstock) 8 miles from here but have not yet seen over the palace. We shall do that later.

Moira's next letter to her mother was from Banbury, England on 3 April:

After a wonderful stay in Ireland, John and I returned to England on Sunday. Today we went to Harrogate and to the cemetery. We saw Alan's grave which is beautifully kept and which is situated in rather a lovely setting with gentle green hills behind it. It was a sunny day and the first violet on the grave was just about out. There were fresh daffodils on the grave as also there were on Greg's and Roger's graves. No doubt they had been placed there by Miss Vokes. I know that you and Daddy would be happy to see how well the graves are kept and I think that you would like the peaceful outlook over the country from the Air Force Section. You know, I think that there are many Canadian graves nearby. John took some snaps of Alan's grave and we shall send them to you after they are developed. I did not contact Miss Vokes as it was the middle of the day when we were there but shall try to get in touch with her when we go through again on our way to Scotland (about 20th April). It is kind of her to look after the grave so well.

From Harrogate we went to York and had a look at the glorious Cathedral. The stained glass windows are just superb. Tomorrow we go to Stratford and in the evening shall see Henry IV with Michael Redgrave at the Shakespeare Memorial Theatre.

The next day to Oxford for John's Conference (5th to 8th) and shall go to Paris for a few days on the night of the 9th. We hope to have a couple of days in Holland also. During the Conference we shall be staying at 'Oriel' College where Cardinal Newman was once a student. John wrote to Mrs. Dynon last week and told her something about our trip in Ireland. We went to Killaloe. Tell Daddy it is a beautiful spot. We met a Father Ryan there who said that perhaps he was a relation of ours. There are many families 'Ryan' in Killaloe. We had a lovely trip in Kerry which must be one of the loveliest spots in the world. It is so green and the lake and mountain scenery is divine. Whilst there we went to Killarney which is lovely, though I do not think the best part of that County.

We had a few days in Dublin where John bought me a watch. It is lovely and I am thrilled with it. It is a Rolex Tudor, gold and about ¼ inch square—tiny, dainty and lovely. In Dublin we had lunch with Mr. Paddy Glynn. We also saw Donald Tyndall, and Ursula and Mary Flynn and their husbands. Ursula's husband, Charles Brennan, took us for a lovely drive the afternoon we left. I visited Parliament House in Dublin which is the old House of the Duke of Leicester and is a gorgeous place. The carpets took my fancy—hand made Donegal carpets in lovely shades of deep blue, gold and a little white.

On Saturday night we crossed from Dublin to Liverpool and had a good trip. On Sunday we motored on to Preston where we went to Mass at the Jesuit Church "St. Wilfreda" and heard a very good sermon. From there we went through some of the lovely lake country and finally to Carlisle where we had tea with John's cousin, Carmel (nee McGinnis) and her husband Arthur Chessels and their two children. Carmel knew Uncle Len and you. On Monday we continued our trip through the lake country which was glorious. It was sunny and the lakes and snow covered mountains were lovely. In this area we went to Grasmere where we saw Wordsworth's grave and cottage.

I wrote to my mother from Rome on 9 May:

> My dear Mother,
>
> I am just starting to write this before going to have a drink at Col. & Mrs. Boyles. This morning we had a special—not a private—audience with the Holy Father. I am enclosing a cutting from L'Osservatore Romano of 10.5.'51 (Please do not lose it!). Arnold Lunn was next to us and we had a chat before the Holy Father arrived. He is very nice and was delighted to meet us. I told the Holy Father that I was working in Catholic Action and he blessed me and my work. I told him that we were expecting our first child in December and he blessed Moira and our marriage. He said quite a lot to Arnold Lunn on our right saying how much it was appreciated what Lunn was doing in his work. At the conclusion he gave us all in the room a blessing...
>
> I received Jim's letter for which many thanks. It has been a really lovely visit to Rome although it is a bit wet. I can't tell you all re. Holland except we had a hectic 5 days there. Dr. Albryts was charming to us in The Hague. We visited his home, met Mrs. Albryts again and their 7 children on Sunday—had drinks and lunch with them. He then placed his car at our disposal all day Monday and he came to say goodbye at the air terminal in The Hague at 5.30. Moira sends her love and she will be writing home by this mail. We are both well.
>
> Much love and hope to see you soon, John.
> Best to Jim.

Moira's last letter to her mother was from London on 14 May:

> Before we went to Holland I received your letters of 7th, 16th and 22nd April. It was a wonderful thrill to receive them and you are very good to have written them and told me all the news. I know how tired you must have been with Tot away.
>
> We really had a gorgeous time in Holland. It was spring and the weather warm and sunny. The bulbs were in full bloom and the whole countryside was a mass of multi coloured tulips. The sight was even more magnificent than I had thought could be possible. Some of the colours would have to be seen to be believed and we saw some tulips literally bigger than a good sized Australian lettuce. In the bulb area, a 17th century hunting lodge at Keukenhof has been turned into a 'show place' with its tulips, hyacinths, daffodils, etc and we loved our visit there. The huge pictures (composed entirely of flowers) are simply gorgeous and they must take hours to arrange.
>
> We paid a visit to Volendam where the people still wear their native costumes and the whole village (7000 people) is very picturesque. We had dinner at the hotel with a lovely view over the Zuider Zee and the view at sunset with the fishing boats, was beautiful. Whilst we were in Holland we were lucky enough to go to a Concert given by Yehudi Menuhin and the glorious Dutch pianist Kentner. It was a wonderful concert. The audience was extremely enthusiastic and Menuhin gave four encores. We were thrilled to have heard him and especially as we had missed concerts of his in London and Paris by a few days. It almost seemed as if we were dodging him until we got to Amsterdam.

We had a glorious time in Rome. John mentioned the wonderful special audience with the Pope that we were honoured to be granted on 9th May. He may also have mentioned the special blessing which was given to me. The Holy Father looked well. After the audience, Duc Arvio, who had driven us to the Vatican, showed us around the loggias and apartments. He is a member of the Italian Diplomatic Corps and was able to show us into sections of the Vatican not normally seen by visitors. The paintings, furnishings etc were wonderful. Later we had coffee with his wife, the Duchess, who is charming. I nearly forgot to mention that Arnold Lunn was also at the Papal audience and we had a long chat to him. He seems to have enjoyed his Australian visit last September. Rome was lovely the first part of our stay. It was sunny and the flowers in the Borghese gardens were gorgeous. We joined the people having tea in the open air cafes in the famous Via Veneto and watched celebrities go by. Unfortunately, it rained later, towards the end of our stay. Father Bill Dalton, who was at school with John, and Father Kenny had dinner with us one evening.

We spent the last of our travellers cheques and invested in a coffee set. It is simply gorgeous to look at and has a small inlaid design of silver and gold. We don't know what the china is like but at least it looks good and is guaranteed. I don't think I shall ever be game to use it but it will look nice.

We returned to London on Friday evening and went to see the film 'Tales of Hoffmann'. It is excellent. Moira Shearer is the ballet dancer. The background music is the London Philharmonic Orchestra conducted by Sir Thomas Beecham. Since our return we have also seen the Festival Ballet twice. The second performance with 'Sylphides' 'Beau Danube' and 'Impressions' was especially good. The first programme included 'Swan Lake', 'Spectre de la Rose', and 'Petrushka'. Tomorrow evening we shall see 'La Boheme' at Covent Garden and on Wednesday evening 'Fidelio'. This morning we went to early Mass at Farm Street Jesuit Church across the road and then at 10.30 to Westminster Cathedral (Catholic), not Westminster Abbey, to hear the Special Pentecost Sung Mass. The Cathedral was packed and the music glorious. It was impressive. In the afternoon we went out to see Hampton Court Palace and Grounds. It is lovely and the gardens were looking their best. The old Tudor (Henry VIII) kitchen was especially interesting though there were no works of art there.

As we leave on Thursday evening for New York this will be my last letter from overseas to you. We leave San Francisco on Sunday 27th May at midnight and shall probably stay a day in Sydney before coming to Melbourne. I have written to Pat Shelton and shall look her up in New York. In USA we spend 2 days in New York, 2 days in Washington, 3 days in Detroit and 2 days in San Francisco. Just enough for a quick look at the surface. It will be fun.

I was hoping, Mummy, that I would be able to keep the big news and tell the rest of the family myself when I return. However, one glance now and they will guess and so I was wondering whether you would tell

Valda & Bill, June and Charlie and David for me. Ask them, please, to keep it confidential for a little while yet. I do not want the news to be around Melbourne or my friends until <u>after</u> I return. I shall leave it to your discretion to do what you think re Grandma. I am very well, considering, and the only trouble has been one or two dizzy turns. I realise how lucky I am and hope it lasts.

Please give my love to Daddy and all the family and also to Mrs. Dynon and Father Dynon. We are both well and looking forward to seeing you all again.

lots of love,
Moira.

COMMUNITY ACTIVISM

7

The Spirit of Loreto Federation

When we returned from our honeymoon, Moira and I made our home at 29 Elizabeth Street, Malvern. Michele was born in December that year, Jacinta in 1953, John in 1954, James in 1955 and David in 1960.

Prior to John's birth, there was some conjecture as to whether we would have a girl or a boy. As the day approached, I was more than ever convinced that the baby would be a girl. Moira had gone into hospital and I was at home with Michele and Jacinta when the telephone rang at about 3 am. I had been asleep. It was Dr Lawson telling me to come in, adding: 'It's a boy.' I was so surprised that I asked: 'Are you sure?' to which he responded: 'I've seen enough of them to know.' I shot into The Mercy and there they were; both well and happy. He was named John, born on the Feast Day of John de Brito.

After James was born, we sold our house and moved to 7 Haverbrack Avenue, Malvern. Whilst making that move, the family stayed with my mother for a few weeks at her home in South Yarra.

During these years, Moira was deeply involved with the young children. In the early years, Gwen Webster, who lived nearby, was to become our faithful daily help in the house and with the children. There were also babysitters and a mothercraft nurse for short periods. Moira attended dressmaking classes at the Caulfield Technical College.

All the time, she kept up her association with the Loreto Old Girls' Association. Moira foresaw the wisdom of endeavouring to bring together all Loreto Associations in Australia to promote constructive debate on national and international affairs, and community and family matters. This would best be done, she thought, with the establishment of a federation. She discussed this with members of the Association and the sisters at Loreto from whom she received encouragement and support; in particular Mother Ursula Lyons IBVM, Mother Pauline Dunne IBVM (Sup Gen), Mother J Colombiere IBVM, Mother Assumpta (later known as Sister Ruth Winship) IBVM and Mother J Magdalen IBVM. She conferred with Mary Dobson, President of the Mary's Mount Loreto Past Pupils' Association, and went on to sound out all of the Loreto Past Pupils' Associations throughout Australia and won their support for the Federation, which came to fruition in 1955.

It was Mother Gonzaga Barry IBVM who, in 1897, perhaps caught up in the prevailing spirit of political federation, sowed the seed of Loreto Federation in Australia. She was the leader of the pioneer group of Loreto nuns who landed in Melbourne in 1875 and opened a school at Mary's Mount, Ballarat, known as the Abbey School. Mother Gonzaga Barry later became the first Provincial of Loreto in Australia. She kept in touch with her 'children'—both the school students and the past pupils—through her letters in the school magazine *Eucalyptus Blossoms*. On 8 December 1897 she wrote:

My dearest children,

Now would it not be a good thing for all Loretto [sic] Girls to Federate in a great league for a noble end, viz.: to work out patiently, steadily, faithfully, high and holy aims in the daily routine of life's duties...*Federate* to lend a helping hand to whatever is good and beautiful, noble and useful in the world around. It may seem to you that you cannot do much, but you will do much if you do all you can, and do it with a great and generous heart and a humbled mind, and do it for God's dear sake...Aim at something excellent; our life is largely influenced by what we aim at—our ideals often make our realities. Have enthusiasm for your cause. Be earnest, be persevering, be humble, and then with God's aid you will succeed.[41]

Moira, 58 years later, was to achieve the foundation of the federation of all the Loreto Past Pupils' Associations in Australia through her vision, courage and determination. At the time, there weren't exactly waves of enthusiasm for Moira's concept of federation. She did have loyal supporters but it was an idea which had to be worked on, worked for and worked out. As was her wont with all her commitments, she spent unseen hours in planning and preparing the ground for the establishment of the Federation. All through this period and beyond, she remained unaware of Mother Gonzaga Barry's letter. Moira's achievement would have been very dear to the heart of Mother Gonzaga Barry.

1955 was to be a memorable year for Moira. Already having three young children, she was expecting twins. In February, in giving birth prematurely, she lost one. Moira wrote to my mother who was overseas:

Dear Mrs Dynon,

It is now over three weeks since little James Newman arrived and I know that you will want to hear about his progress. John and I are really happy and truly grateful to have him alive, well and strong and he is doing very well. He now weighs 6 lbs 14 oz and Dr. Glynn White will be allowing him to come home probably early next week. Of course we are all looking forward to having him home. We have taken Michele into the Mercy to see James and she thinks he is just lovely.

I am sorry Mrs Dynon that we lost one little boy. It is sometimes hard to understand why God wishes these things. I do hope that you will not be too disappointed. At first I was very disappointed although I realized that, coming six weeks early, we were lucky to have one strong babe. I came home from hospital about 10 days ago and have been taking it quietly since. Leaving the baby in the hospital gave me the opportunity to pick up before having the responsibility of looking after another little one.

John has, no doubt, told you that we have had an Austrian girl for the past 4 weeks. She is good and is gradually picking up English. She and Mrs Webster have been a wonderful team and I have had a lovely rest.

You will be interested to know that this year Hiliary Dwyer is President of Loreto Old Girls Association. We have the Governor and Lady Brooks coming to the Ball, so it is a great honour for Loreto. I am staying on the Committee but am not an office bearer.

The children are all well. They seemed to grow while I was in hospital so you should notice a big difference in them. John is terribly strong and has bent all the hinges on the playground—Mr. Papworth will have to put on new ones for us. He is walking around the furniture but does not yet walk alone. He is a very placid child and cries only when he is in trouble. Jacinta is still the noisy one and will readily scream the house down if she cannot have her way.

We were hoping that you would be back in time for the baby's Baptism, which Father James is going to do for us, but if the babe comes home next week it looks as if that will not be possible. I would have to hold back the Baptism until you return, Mrs Dynon, but I agree with John that that would not be right. Pat Smith is to be God Mother and Glynn O'Collins God Father. After the Baptism we shall have the Christening party at Mummy's as we have not the room here now. We are still looking for a larger home but have not seen anything we like. Despite the girl in the den, the babies in the lounge and John's papers in the dining room, home is still far better than anything we have seen to date.

John and the children join me in sending love to you and we all hope you are having a good voyage. We are all looking forward to seeing you again soon.

Love from Moira.[42]

Later that year Moira suffered a major blow in the loss of her father whom she loved dearly. He was 64.

> The death occurred in Melbourne yesterday of Dr. Percy Gerald Shelton M.B., B.S. after a short illness. Dr. Shelton, a well-known medical practitioner and sportsman, resided and practised in Elsternwick for more than 40 years. Educated at South Melbourne College, he completed his medical studies at the University of Melbourne, taking up his first residency at Alfred Hospital. He was a surgeon commander of the R.A.N.A., a naval representative of the Red Cross, a member of the V.R.C., V.A.T.C., M.C.C. and South Melbourne C.C., and honorary medical officer to the Victorian Rowing Association...[43]

The first Federation conference was fixed for 6–8 November 1955 in Melbourne, four days after her father was buried. Moira spoke with me and wondered whether she could or should proceed. I said that I was sure that it would have been her father's wish that she carry on. With her sorrow at the time, it was courageous of her to carry through with the task which she had been called on to perform.

The first work accomplished by the Federation was the offering of a Spiritual Bouquet, praying for the Beatification of Mary Ward, the foundress of the Institute of the Blessed Virgin Mary (IBVM).

Mary Ward was born in 1585 into an England that was hostile towards Catholics. She established the congregation of religious women dedicated to active service, freed from the cloister. She set out to enable women to do for the Church what men had done for it in the Society of Jesus. With faith, courage and determination, Mary Ward established schools for girls across Europe, including a school in Flanders for the daughters of her exiled countrymen. In response to the unfortunate remark, 'When all is done they are but women', she said, 'There is no such difference between men and women that women may not do great things. I hope in God it will be seen that women in time to come will do much'. While receiving praise and support for her work she encountered sustained opposition and censure from influential quarters for her refusal to live in a cloistered community. In 1631, her Institute was suppressed on the order of Pope Urban VIII. Mary Ward was described as 'a heretic, a schismatic and obstinate rebel against the Holy Church' and imprisoned for a time by the Inquisition. Her faith remained strong: 'I had no other desire than to give myself over in all these difficulties and place myself with these uncertainties into the hands of God.' With characteristic felicity, she would say: 'If anyone gives you trouble, meet him with friendly words, for so you will soften both yourself and him.' [44]

The Spiritual Bouquet consisted of 13,120 Masses, 11,855 Holy Communions and 20,831 Rosaries. The bouquet was inscribed by a novice at the novitiate, Loreto Abbey, Mary's Mount Ballarat, on a beautiful parchment and was presented to the Holy Father at the Vatican by His Excellency, Mr Paul McGuire, CBE Australia's Ambassador to Italy in Rome. Paul McGuire wrote to Moira:

Dear Mrs. Dynon,

Forgive me for not writing to you before. I have delayed because I felt that you would wish to have a proper account of the presentation of the Spiritual Bouquet to the Holy Father. You will understand that my office as Envoy and Minister to Italy does not include accreditation to the Holy See. Hence Mrs. McGuire and I had to take the occasion of an Audience granted to us personally. We had that great privilege on Sunday morning last at the Vatican and before His Holiness entered on his Advent Retreat. It was a Private Audience; that is, His Holiness received us alone and sat at his working-desk.

He was most moved by your Bouquet. He read the document carefully and he remarked on its beautiful draftsmanship. He said that he would communicate his appreciation to you all. We took to the Audience a Cross which you might wish to use at your meetings. The Holy Father blessed it and attached to it an indulgence of 1,000 days for each time it is kissed and a plenary indulgence at the point of death for those who kiss it and utter the Sacred Name. I shall send it to you by surface-mail.

You will all be happy to know that His Holiness appears in such excellent health that one can readily believe in a miraculous intervention. Mrs. McGuire and I thank you and all your members for the privilege of conveying to His Holiness your offering which to him, he made plain, is most precious.[45]

The Provincial Superior of the Institute in Australia, Mother Colombiere IBVM, wrote from Loreto Abbey, Mary's Mount:

Dear Moira,

With great pleasure I am sending you a letter received from His Eminence Cardinal Dell'Acquin...The appreciation of our Holy Father will prove, better than any words of mine can do, how eminently worth while was all your labour in bringing this splendid effort to so successful an issue.

> I am very touched and pleased that this Spiritual Bouquet for the Beatification of our venerated Foundress should be the first work accomplished by the Federation. The spirit displayed by the representatives present at the November Conference was excellent. It is heartening to find that so many of our Past Pupils are prepared to do the work of Apostles in the world, thus loyally co-operating with the nuns who are trying to do that same work in our schools. I should like to thank you and all who have so generously and efficiently inaugurated this excellent movement from which I hope great things.[46]

The preliminary work had been done, the Federation established and the headquarters moving every two years from convent to convent and from State to State. Moira wrote and delivered papers for several Federation conferences, which were well received. In October 1965, at a time when Moira was deeply committed to Aid for India, she received a letter from Mother Assumpta from Loreto Convent, Claremont, Western Australia:

> My dear Moira,
>
> As the Loreto Federation Meetings continue gaily on their way I have been thinking of you and decided that you deserved to know at least how the Conference is progressing. It all stems back to you and to your early efforts to start the whole thing going and you are to be forever congratulated for what you have done.
>
> I am sorry that you are not here. Perth is a lovely easy place, and the people are kind and warmly hospitable. All the sessions have gone very happily and successfully...Mary England read her paper carefully

and with her usual dignity of bearing. I was proud of her and you would have been too...

I just wanted to let you know that you are not forgotten.

My fond love, Moira dear, & God bless you and all your good works.

Yours affectionately,
M.J. Assumpta, I.B.V.M.[47]

Mother Gonzaga Barry had written from Diego Garcia: 'Leave after you a something on which others may build.' Intrigued with the coral growth at Diego Garcia she wrote further to her 'dear children':

> be God's own little coral workers, building up with your tiny supernatural acts a solid foundation hidden in your own pure and loving hearts—a foundation so firm that all the waves of the world's sea cannot shake it, and on which God can raise a super-structure to last for all eternity.[48]

8

Australian Association for the United Nations Malvern Branch

In September 1951, a letter arrived from the Victorian headquarters of the Australian Association for the United Nations (AAUN). I was asked to call a meeting of people in Malvern to arrange a celebration for United Nations Day as a preliminary to establishing a local branch. These local branches were 'to ensure a continuous channel for the dissemination of UN ideals, as well as being centres to which people in the neighbourhood may look for information on the UN'.[49]

Moira, who was then six months' pregnant with Michele, agreed to help as Secretary with the assistance of her good friend, Nancy McDonald. Sustained by this assurance, I approached the Mayor of Malvern, Councillor John King, who offered his patronage.

On 23 October 1951,[50] 50 people gathered in the Supper Room of the Malvern Town Hall to celebrate United Nations Day when the Mayor announced the establishment of the Malvern Branch.[51] Our Branch aimed to bring a knowledge of the ideals and work of the United Nations to those who lived or worked in our municipality.

> The Committee believes that in our ever contracting world it is important that children as well as adults should be encouraged to turn their thoughts towards world affairs, and that they should be encouraged to take an increasingly intelligent interest in world events, particularly with regard to Asia.[52]

Our 1952 UN Day eve celebration[53] was a memorable occasion for our young branch. We were honoured by the presence of His Excellency, General Sir Dallas Brooks, Governor of Victoria[54] and Lady Brooks. The main town hall was packed, with many schoolchildren among the 1,200 present. Red, white and blue balloons decorated the hall and a guard of honour was provided by two officers and 50 rank and file cadets from De La Salle College. In the main address, Mr Paul McGuire CBE spoke on 'The Pacific' and Lauriston Girls' School Orchestra provided delightful support. His Excellency presented prizes for the competitions and spoke enthusiastically of the Branch and of the success of the evening.

Moira had organised the competitions for the schoolchildren. Melbourne newspapers carried articles inviting children living or attending school in the Malvern area to write an essay on 'Australia and the United Nations'. Girls under 15 were invited to dress their own doll in the national costume of any country. Newspaper articles included a photo of Moira holding two Lithuanian dolls that Mrs Zara Holt, the guest judge, had donated as examples. The competition was a great success with more than 60 dolls entered and on display. Moira had the children thinking about other countries and cultures.

She opened their eyes to a world beyond their own. Money for the prizes was raised through the private efforts of sympathetic and sincere followers.

The competitions were very popular. One school principal wrote to me after a winning essay had been published in *The Tribune*:

> Thank you for returning the Essay and more especially for getting it into print. You have no idea what that means for the school just at present.
>
> I take this opportunity also to offer you an apology for the impertinent request of the lad for the return of his paper. As the responsibility of final correction and despatch was left to the individual child it was interesting to see the response to the trust. I am endeavouring to stimulate the interest of the parents in your great work and to encourage them to attend the meeting on the 25th. [55]

The Malvern Branch was the largest of six AAUN's Victorian branches. We held evening meetings on the last Wednesday of each month, from March to October, in the Lecture Room of the Malvern Town Hall. The meetings were well attended. We often entertained the guest of honour at our home prior to the meetings. Michele told me recently that she recalled one such occasion: 'One evening, I remember standing in the lounge room. I was five or six years old. There was a lady sitting in the antique upholstered chair. She was vivacious and commanded the room with her conversation. She was using a long cigarette holder (and smoking). My parents were there, of course. I stayed for a little while but then I left because it was bedtime. The lady was Mrs Zara Holt.'

In 1953, we suffered a great loss in the tragic deaths of Mr Trevor Oldham MLA, one of our vice-presidents, and his wife Mrs Kathleen Oldham. They were both killed in an air crash over India whilst en route to attend the coronation of Her Majesty. They were travelling as the representatives of the State Parliament. At the time of his death, The Hon. TD Oldham was Leader of the Opposition. Moira and I felt we had lost two very good friends.

One of the notable initiatives of the Malvern Branch was the annual schoolchildren's rally. These were well attended by children from all schools in the Malvern area—public and private. The management of Metro Theatre Malvern generously made its facilities available for these occasions. The strong support we received from the schools was most encouraging.

A letter from St Catherine's School was typical of the feedback we received:

> On behalf of St Catherine's may I take this opportunity for thanking you very sincerely for the interesting program at the Malvern Theatre last Friday. For the last three years our school has been very fortunate in being permitted to attend these meetings, and it has become an event that all look forward to and enjoy. I am sure you have succeeded in impressing upon us the importance of the United Nations, and the part we can play in the world today. We always come out feeling slightly guilty that we have not really played our part as well as can be expected. However interest is not lacking, and there is quite a large and keen United Nations club here.[56]

On one memorable Friday morning in March 1958, over 1,400 schoolchildren and teachers[57] packed the auditorium of Metro Malvern for the fourth Malvern AAUN schoolchildren's rally. The Official Party included representatives from 14 countries.[58] The guest speaker was Mr Graham R Hall, US Consul-General in Melbourne, who addressed the gathering on 'The United Nations and International Cooperation'. Most of the participating schools had nominated a representative to come onto the platform and ask Mr Hall a question, of which the school had given notice. The questions were thoughtful and showed considerable maturity. They included: 'Why did America veto the inclusion of Communist China in the United Nations?', 'What is the opinion in the United Nations Organisation of Australia's treatment of her Aborigines?' and 'Can United Nations ensure that atomic power is used to help mankind?' Our daughter Jacinta, aged 5, presented a bouquet of flowers to Mrs Hall at this function.

During these years, many men and women of distinction came and spoke at our monthly meetings and schoolchildren's rallies. It was as early as 1953 that Mr Muni Lal from India spoke to the Branch on 'The India Five Year Plan'. On that occasion, Moira first obtained information from him concerning the sending of gift food parcels to people in India.

In September 1956, Dr M Jovy, Vice-Consul, Federal Republic of Germany, spoke to us on 'The Recovery of Germany'. On another occasion Professor Alan R Chisholm, Professor of French, University of Melbourne, spoke to the Branch on 'French Achievements and Commitments in Indo-China'.

Another well-received guest speaker was His Excellency, Dr Chen Tai Chu, Minister Plenipotentiary, Chinese Embassy, who addressed the schoolchildren on 'The East and the West – A new outlook'.

In March 1957, our guest speaker was Dato Nik A Kamil, the first Commissioner for Malaya in Canberra, who spoke on 'The Federation of Malaya'. In 1959, as Ambassador for Malaya, Dato Nik A Kamil moved a courageous resolution at the United Nations General Assembly, which brought to the attention of the world, reports that fundamental human rights and freedoms of the Tibetan people had been forcibly denied them.[59] This was the first international resolution supporting Tibet. The resolution called 'for respect for the fundamental human rights of the Tibetan people and for their distinctive cultural and religious life'. We sent messages of congratulations to the Malayan Government and to Dato Nik A Kamil for their magnificent support of the people of Tibet at the United Nations.

Our last involvement with these events was in 1966 when 1,269 students from 17 local schools rallied to Metro Malvern during the visit to Melbourne by His Excellency, Mr DN Chatterjee, the Indian High Commissioner in Australia. Mr Chatterjee spoke to the students about India and its rich history. He also spoke of the considerable development in India since Independence. Later, at our home, Mr Chatterjee received individually a number of distinguished citizens including Zelman Cowen.[60]

The AAUN work was rewarding, particularly as it reached schoolchildren and interested them and helped to alert them to the world outside Australia.

9

President and Secretary of Stonnington Branch of the Liberal Party

I recall early in 1953, around the time of the birth of our second child Jacinta in February, Moira telling me that she had renewed her annual subscription to the Stonnington Branch of the then Liberal and Country Party (LCP). The field officer called in for the renewal fee and Moira complained to him that she had received no notices as to meetings of the Branch.

I well understood her amazement when, some nine months later, a letter signed Alex A Rosenblum, Chairman, Malvern LCP Electorate Committee, appeared in *The Age*:

> SIR,—Mr. HOLLWAY has declared his intention of forming a new party under his own leadership, although surely on that point it would be more fitting to await the decision of his future supporters. He

informs the world that he is already assured of Labor support in various electorates at the next State election. Have the local A.L.P. branches been consulted?

If Mr. Hollway will consider what happened to his candidate in the recent Malvern by-election he might get some idea of the electoral prospects of his proposed party. In an electorate of approximately 20,000 voters, fewer than 4 per cent supported the Hollway policy— hardly enough to win elections. Mr. Hollway should also note that, despite all his efforts and the bitterness created by the Malvern campaign, there has not been a single defection from any L.C.P. committee in the whole Malvern electorate.[61]

To say that Moira was astounded by such a claim was to put it mildly and she wrote to *The Age*:

SIR, — Mr. ALEX. A. ROSENBLUM, chairman, Malvern L.C.P. electorate committee, states in "The Age" (6/11) that "in an electorate of approximately 20,000 voters, fewer than four per cent. supported the Hollway policy." I recollect that Mr. Dawnay-Mould polled approximately 4000 primary votes—something more like 20 per cent than 4 per cent...

Secondly, he states: "There has not been a single defection from any L.C.P. committee in the whole Malvern electorate." I have been a financial member of the Stonnington branch of the L.C.P. for 18 months. On payment of my renewal subscription in February this year, I complained that I had not received notice of any meeting or elections within the branch. Despite a verbal promise that this would be remedied, the position remains the same today. Is it any wonder that there has not been a single defection from any L.C.P. committee in the whole Malvern electorate, if other L.C.P. branches in Malvern are similarly conducted? Who votes for the committees in Malvern?

M. DYNON (Malvern).[62]

Moira had made her point clearly and publicly and with merit, and it was a matter for the LCP to take up and remedy, and a matter for the public to note and remember.

One wonders what went on at that time within the Malvern Electorate Committee and the branch committees and at the Malvern Convention within the Malvern electorate. In those days, high branch membership numbers were important at conventions. One vote for every 10 financial members in each branch was a power in the hands of those chosen members of the branch who attended the Malvern Electorate Convention. The numbers game at the time must have distracted busy executives from worrying over-much about the actual attendances of members at branch meetings. All that was necessary and essential was to have a high financial membership at the crucial time. In his public thrust at Mr Hollway, Mr Rosenblum had concentrated on his figures and deductions, passing over the most obvious weakness in the Party's organisation.

In his report on the campaign in Higgins after the 1955 Federal Election, Alec A Rosenblum, Chairman of the Higgins Electoral Committee noted:

> The following brief comments on the present Branches are submitted not with any desire to criticise or to dogmatise, but to provide a starting point for the discussions on branch development that appear to be desirable...

> **Stonnington**. This Branch, formerly one of the largest in the Electorate, is completely in the doldrums, with a barely three figure membership and an inactive Committee. Although it contrived to carry out most of its election time activities, there was less evidence of enthusiasm than on any former occasion. Moreover, although the Branch is reputedly (and certainly is potentially) wealthy, it was the only Branch that asked for its allocation of election expenses to be reduced and was the only Branch that, up to two months after the Election, had not forwarded even a preliminary contribution. All this points to extreme apathy which must be overcome if the Branch is to function properly. It appears desirable that an active Canvasser be appointed to this area to work up the membership to a more appropriate figure and to seek, in particular, active and enthusiastic recruits to the Committee. Stonnington definitely requires complete re-organisation.[63]

For the next couple of years, Moira was on the Stonnington Committee and besides participating in committee discussions, also gave faithful service in the various activities of the Branch. These activities usually related to elections in the State seat of Malvern and the Federal seat of Higgins, and included the tasks of canvassing, distributing how to vote cards and acting as a scrutineer on election night.

In 1957, the retiring President, George Crowther, and the Committee of Stonnington wanted Moira as Honorary Secretary of the Branch. I distinctly remember George Crowther telephoning her one night to make this request. She explained to him that it was difficult for her with a family of four very young children, but that she would be able to do it and prepared to do so if I was President. That is how I became President of Stonnington.

It was to be a challenge to attract interested new members so as to make the Branch more open and representative. The Branch Committee agreed to Moira's proposal of an annual social-political function with the aim of encouraging interest and genuine membership. We held three very successful annual receptions at The Bambalina, 119 Wattletree Road, Malvern. These functions had been Moira's brainchild and proved to be immensely helpful in bringing together interested people in a congenial atmosphere. In this respect, Moira played a most significant part in the development of the Stonnington Branch. Her personality and organisation together with a cooperative committee resulted in a healthy democratic operation.

After the 1958 Federal election, Mr Rosenblum reported on the campaign in Higgins:

> At the conclusion of the 1955 Election, some objections followed the circulation of the Chairman's report on that campaign, mainly based upon criticisms levelled therein at a number of the Branches in the Higgins Electorate. It is pleasing to report that in at least some instances, these criticisms, although unwelcome at the time, have been justified by improvements carried out by the Branches concerned...The Liberal Party, as a living organism, can continue to function successfully only for so long as it permits itself to grow and develop, and inactivity and complacency are the two greatest enemies to be feared by such an organisation...

> **Stonnington**. This Branch has very successfully emerged from the "doldrums" reported in 1955 and is not only active itself but has also established an active Women's Section. During the 1958 campaign, Stonnington set an example of efficient, willing work that proved an inspiration to the Electorate Committee.[64]

Membership and interest in the Stonnington Branch increased during these years. In 1956–57 membership was 157, in 1957–58 it rose to 222, and in 1958–59 it reached 308. Mr John Bloomfield MLA, the representative for the State seat of Malvern and Mr Harold Holt MHR, the Federal member for Higgins were appreciative of our efforts in building up interest in Stonnington and thanked us for our contribution to the Party's success.

Early in 1959, Moira and I encountered our first major controversy in Stonnington. A number of members of the Stonnington Committee approached me with concerns about the Richardson Report, which recommended increases in Federal parliamentary pay and allowances. The policy of the Party, made in September 1951, was that parliamentary salaries should be adjusted only after a determination by a Judicial Committee. In January 1959, the Government had appointed a Committee to review parliamentary salaries under a chairman who was not a judge. This was not a Judicial Committee. Moreover, in August 1958, the State Council had passed a resolution that it would strongly disapprove of any increase in parliamentary salaries at that time.

We called a special general meeting of the Stonnington Branch for Monday, 20 April 1959 to give members of Stonnington the opportunity to express their opinions concerning the content and implementation of the report.

Mr Holt advised us that he was unable to attend as he was at the AGM of East Malvern-Darling Branch that evening.

At the special meeting, the members of Stonnington passed a resolution:

> THAT this meeting deplores the timing and method of implementation of the Richardson Report, which has degraded the prestige of Parliament and of its members. Such implementation is likely to defeat one of the aims of the Report, i.e. to attract a higher standard of candidate offering for election. As a consequence the membership of the Branch has been affected adversely. It is the opinion of the Meeting that it could affect the result of the next election.
>
> This Branch objects to certain public utterances made by our Federal member (Mr. H. Holt) over T.V. which cast undue reflection on members of his electorate in-so-far as they inferred acceptance of the timing and method of implementation of the Report by the Members of Stonnington.[65]

Mr Holt was genuinely surprised when Moira telephoned his office the next morning with a report of the meeting and resolution. He wrote:

> Dear Mrs. Dynon,
>
> Thank you for having telephoned my office to convey the terms of the Resolution passed at the Annual [sic] Meeting of the Stonnington Branch on Monday last, and for your account of various circumstances associated with it.
>
> ...I would welcome an opportunity to meet the Branch and discuss the whole problem quite frankly with you

all. In the meantime, I offer some comments.

I note that the meeting "deplores the timing and method of implementation of the Richardson Report". Members of the Branch, when including that passage in the Resolution, were presumably aware that the Federal Executive of the Liberal Party, at its meeting on 6th April, unanimously adopted the following Resolution—

> "Federal Executive agrees with the procedure adopted by the Government of having an independent, competent committee to inquire into and advise in the matter of salaries, allowances and superannuation of members of Parliament. We agree that these matters should be reviewed periodically and believe that sufficient time had elapsed since the previous review. We are conscious of the fact that under the Constitution these matters are to be decided by Parliament and we believe that such is the proper procedure. We are confident that the present review can safely and quite properly be left to Parliament."

All State Executives of the Liberal Party are represented on the Federal Executive.

...I would like to deal at once with the objection taken to what are described as "certain public utterances" made by me in the "Meet the Press" session last Sunday, which are alleged to have "cast undue reflection on members of your Electorate..."

This statement puzzles me. My recollection is that I was making the point that wherever I had been able to come face to face with Branches in my own Electorate and discuss the Richardson Report with them, I had found a willingness to understand and accept, in the broad, the recommendations of the Committee…

Your account of the Stonnington meeting mentions a Resolution moved and seconded—"that Mr. Holt be not automatically re-endorsed for the next Federal Election." I gather that this was not widely supported, but the fact that you subsequently received an enquiry about it from the Melbourne "Herald" would suggest that some member of the Branch was so disloyal, both to the Branch and to myself, as to retail to the press, obviously with the intention of causing some political harm or embarrassment to myself, the substance of a Resolution which the Branch had not been willing to accept.

It has never been my desire, nor my expectation, that I should look for automatic re-endorsement. If the members of the Liberal Party in Higgins believe there is available a better representative, then they should endorse him. Frankly, threats of the kind implicit in that Resolution leave me quite untroubled. I am now in my twenty-fourth year of service in the Federal Parliament. The prospect of a break in that service, which would enable me to see a great deal more of my family and friends, enjoy some of the comforts of my own home, some respite from travel and greater peace of mind, is not uninviting, nor would it be unwelcome were it to arrive. Until that day, I shall continue to give the best service, both to Higgins and to Australia, of which I am capable.

Yours sincerely,
Harold Holt[66]

Mr Holt agreed to attend a further special meeting of Stonnington members fixed for Monday, 18 May.

The matter was given wide coverage in the Press, including the Sydney *Daily Mirror*:

Branch wants to Sack Mr. Holt

Canberra. Mon. — The Stonnington Branch of the Liberal Party wants the endorsement of the Federal Treasurer (Mr. Holt) withdrawn because of his part in the Parliamentary "salary grab". It has demanded that fresh nominations be called for the Liberal candidate at the next elections. Mr. Holt is Deputy Leader of the Parliamentary Liberal Party, and will be acting leader for two months from tomorrow, when the Prime Minister (Mr. Menzies) leaves for his world tour. He represents the blue ribbon seat of Higgins (Victoria) in the House of Representatives.

Seething

Chief opposition to him in the Stonnington Branch of the party, which is in the heart of the Higgins Electorate, are the "Ladies of Malvern", last remnant of the Australian Women's National League. They are reported to be seething with indignation at Mr. Holt's part in the "salary grab". [67]

Moira responded with a Letter to the Editor:

Dear Sir,

The Report in your newspaper of Monday, April 27, Page 24, "Branch wants to Sack Mr. Holt" has just been brought to the attention of our Executive. I have been instructed to write to you and to draw your attention to your misrepresentation of the facts.

Regarding your paragraph: "The Stonnington Branch etc." I wish to inform you that the Stonnington Branch has made no such decision. Regarding your paragraph: "It has demanded" etc., The Branch has made no such demand. Regarding the latter part of your paragraph. I wish to inform you that the "Ladies of Malvern", last remnant of the Australian Women's National League, are unknown to the Stonnington Branch. Our Branch has no knowledge that such women, if they exist, are seething in this life or sizzling in the next.

The members of the Branch are distressed that this untrue report has appeared in your newspaper which has circulated in Victoria also. I would like you to know that the members of the Branch have the highest esteem for Mr. Holt and for his service to the Nation. For you to report such damaging untruths is not in accordance with decency and our national interest. We feel that the least you could do is to give an apology to Mr. Holt and to this Branch.

yours etc.,
M. Dynon, Hon. Secretary.[68]

Notice of the special meeting for 18 May had been sent to all Stonnington members.

On Sunday, 17 May at 3.45 pm, Mrs Holt telephoned me to inform me that Mr Holt had gone to bed with the prevailing flu and had a temperature of 102 degrees and that he would not be able to attend the meeting arranged for the following day. I immediately told Mrs Holt that in the circumstances, I would postpone the meeting. I proceeded on the ground that the whole point of the meeting was to give Mr Holt the opportunity to answer the Resolution and to give our members the opportunity to question him with regard to the implementation of the report.

I went into the city and inserted in the Public Notice column of Monday's *Age*, *Sun* and *Herald* notification of postponement of the meeting with the reason given. *The Age* reported:

> **Mr. Holt Has Influenza**
>
> The Federal Treasurer (Mr. Holt) is confined to his bed with influenza. He is at his Toorak home. Mr. Holt was to have addressed the Stonnington branch of the L.C.P. in the Malvern town hall tonight on the Richardson report and its implementation but the meeting has been postponed. A new date for the meeting will be fixed after Mr. Holt's recovery. [69]

There was also mention over the radio of Mr Holt's indisposition. It was impossible to circularise in time to all our 308 members. In case members had missed the newspaper and radio notifications, a notice was placed on the door of the town hall.

In the meantime, I had received an invitation from Alec A Rosenblum, President of Malvern Branch LCP, addressed to me as President of Stonnington.

> Dear Mr. Dynon,
>
> In view of Press attacks, both in Victoria and other States, upon members of the L.C.P. Organisation in Higgins as well as upon the Member for Higgins, Rt. Hon. Harold Holt, and of published statements that he has lost the support of the Liberal Party Branches in his Electorate as a result of his support of the Prime Minister in the recent controversy over Parliamentary salaries, the Malvern Branch is organising a Rally of

Members in the Malvern Town Hall (Supper Room) on Monday 25th May at 8 p.m.

As President, I extend an urgent invitation to you, to members of your Committee and to other members of your Branch to attend as a means of demonstrating to Mr. Holt the measure of support we have for him and the confidence we repose in him. To ensure a bumper meeting, will you do your best to see that this invitation is extended to as many of your members as possible. [70]

I communicated Mr Rosenblum's invitation to the members of the Stonnington Committee, together with my comments:

My wife and I have had a number of long telephone conversations with Mr. Holt and his Secretary in Canberra and our endeavour, with their concurrence, has been to minimise the effect of the press reports.

In reply to Mr. Rosenblum, I objected to the method of calling this meeting and to the material, used in the invitation letter, which, in my opinion, principally and probably solely concerned the Stonnington Branch. I claimed that if Mr. Rosenblum wished to call a Higgins Electorate Rally, he should have called together the Higgins Electorate Committee to discuss the overall advisability of calling a Rally or Meeting, and if it was considered desirable, to work out what it was desirable to confine the meeting to.

Secondly, if he wanted to call a Malvern Branch Meeting then that was the affair of his Branch. But in the circumstances he should not have included in his invitation letter to other Branches matter which was the concern of Stonnington. Mr. Rosenblum stated that Mr. Holt shared his opinion <u>completely</u> and that also my wife (as Secretary of Stonnington) likewise shared his opinion. Mr. Holt has since twice replied to me that he had assumed that Mr. Rosenblum was calling the meeting in his capacity as Chairman of Higgins Electorate Committee.

In addition my wife whilst concurring in the holding of a Rally by Malvern Branch did not concur in the nature of the Rally proposed nor in the introduction of matters relating to Stonnington. Mr. Holt considers: "The important thing is that members of the various Branches and myself should discuss the issues raised by the Richardson Committee controversy."

In my opinion the nature of the meeting proposed and envisaged does not permit of the frank, constructive and calm discussion of the matters with which the Stonnington Branch has been concerned and is still concerned. I have twice objected to the meeting of the Malvern Branch to Mr. Rosenblum and to Mr. Holt. My belief is strengthening that Stonnington Branch should not be <u>officially</u> represented at this meeting organised by the Malvern Branch.

If you concur in my view or have some other suggestions to make would you please let me know <u>BEFORE</u> Friday, 22nd May. Otherwise I will be officially informing Mr. Holt and Mr. Rosenblum that the Stonnington Branch will not be represented <u>officially</u> at this meeting.[71]

In consultation with Stonnington Committee members, Mr Rosenblum's invitation was declined. Mr Rosenblum's separate invitation to the Chairman of the Stonnington Women's Section was also declined.

Mr Holt did not contact us later to seek another opportunity to speak to the members of the Branch and I believe there was no further approach to him on the matter by Stonnington. Many letters and telephone calls were received from members, all critical of the Government's timing and method of implementation of the report.

Moira wrote to the General Secretary of the LCP, Melbourne, seeking an explanation of the circumstances surrounding the April 1959 resolution of the Party's Federal Executive that Mr Holt had referred to in his letter. Moira also wrote:

> I enclose copies of the first two letters we have received from members who have now resigned. In view of the work and loyalty of members of Stonnington and of its financial contributions for the election campaigns last year in Higgins, Malvern and Gellibrand Electorates and Central Headquarters (£255), the method and timing of implementation of the Richardson Report has shocked members.[72]

Following the Federal Government's implementation of the Richardson Report (and the State Government's implementation of the corresponding Martin Report), there were 11 branch resolutions on this matter before the State Council meeting in August 1959. The first resolution was that the State Council express its strong displeasure for the manner in which its Parliamentary representatives adopted both the Richardson and Martin reports, in spite of the overwhelming wishes of Party members and the adverse reaction of the Australian people.

This resolution was carried by the State Council meeting. It was then decided that the State Council would not consider the other 10 associated resolutions. It was really a gentle rebuke, but nevertheless a warning.

The resolution of the Party's Federal Executive on 6 April 1959 in effect ex post facto approved the appointment of a non-judicial committee and agreed that the time had come for a review of parliamentary salaries. Thus it appeared that the Federal Executive outside Parliament and the Liberal Party inside Parliament ignored the 1951 policy and August 1958 Resolution of State Council.

Moira and I believed that the representatives of the Victorian Division of the Party, who voted at the April 1959 Federal Executive meeting in favour of the Federal Government's proposal and policy, should have been called upon to explain why they so voted. To my knowledge, this question was never answered.

Moira and I were drawn into this controversy on the request of a number of Committee members, and we took the appropriate steps required in accordance with democratic principles, even if Mr Holt and/or Mr Rosenblum seemed somewhat threatened and endeavoured to manoeuvre the position in another way.

10

Section 28 (m)

Before the 1958 Federal Election, Prime Minister Robert Menzies announced:

> We will introduce marriage and divorce legislation, allowing adequate time for study and debate on a matter which is not of a party kind.
>
> In the last Parliament, Mr. Joske introduced a Private Member's Bill for a Uniform Divorce Law. After it had passed its Second reading without a division, we examined the measure and decided that, with amendments and with suitable provisions for marriage guidance and other means of preserving marriages and safeguarding the interests of children, we could adopt it. For various reasons, important discussions with State Governments will have to occur, while in a matter which is of such social importance and on which there are sharp divisions of opinion, **not** on party lines, it is important that ample time should be given for the critical examination of the measure, in detail, by interested bodies. We therefore propose to introduce marriage and divorce legislation early in the new Parliament, and to afford adequate time for study and debate.[73]

The *Australian Constitution* empowered the Commonwealth Parliament to make laws for the peace, order and good government of the Commonwealth with respect to 'Marriage' and 'Divorce and matrimonial causes'.[74] Before 1959, each State had its own laws governing marriage and divorce. Sensibly, the Government decided to introduce national legislation regarding marriage and divorce that would apply throughout Australia.

Before 1959, the position in most Australian States was that a petitioner could seek a divorce only in circumstances where his or her spouse had committed a specified matrimonial offence, such as adultery, cruelty or desertion.

Of the 14 grounds for divorce in the *Matrimonial Causes Act 1959*, our concern was with only one—section 28 (m): 'that the parties to the marriage have separated and thereafter have lived separately and apart for a continuous period of not less than five years immediately preceding the date of the petition, and there is no reasonable likelihood of cohabitation being resumed.' This ground had not been in Mr Joske's Private Member's Bill but it was part of the Matrimonial Causes Bill presented to Parliament by the Attorney-General, Sir Garfield Barwick. During the passage of the Bill through the House, it was referred to as clause 27 (m). It became clause 28 (m) in the Senate.

Moira and I talked at length about this clause. We were both fundamentally opposed to the new principle of divorce based on the ground of separation, under which either party to a marriage could insist on divorce and under which a party who was guilty of a matrimonial offence could proceed against an innocent partner, and against that partner's will.

SECTION 28 (M)

The issues inherent in the Matrimonial Causes Bill came to a head in Stonnington on 28 September 1959 at a reception at The Bambalina when our guest speaker, Mr Percy Joske, MHR, spoke on the Bill. It was puzzling that Mr Joske did not consider his original Bill to be substantially different from the Bill presented by the Attorney-General when clause 27 (m) was looked at honestly.

No motion was put to the meeting on this matter and Stonnington Branch, as such, had in no way officially expressed a view one way or another. There remained freedom of expression on the matter. I wrote an open letter to the Party's Victorian President, which was published in *The Advocate*:

Liberal Party has No Mandate for Divorce Bill

Branch President Threatens to Resign

A strong protest against the Liberal Party's introduction of the Uniform Divorce Bill now before the Federal Parliament is made by a Liberal Party Official, Mr. John Dynon, President of the Stonnington Branch of the Liberal Party of Australia, Victorian Division, who threatens to resign from his office if the bill becomes law. Mr. Dynon's statement is in the form of an Open Letter addressed to Councillor John Buchan, President of the Liberal and Country Party of Victoria.

"Dear Councillor Buchan,

I note that the Federal Council is meeting in Canberra and that you are leading the Victorian delegation. In case the Matrimonial Causes Bill be on the Agenda, or in case it, or matters connected with it, should arise under General Business or otherwise, I wish to draw your attention to the following:

(i) The Liberal Party of Australia has no mandate from the Party or from the people for the Matrimonial Causes Bill now before the House, which changes the position with regard to divorce in every State of the Commonwealth and very extensively in Victoria.

(ii) The rank-and-file members of the Party in Victoria have not been given the opportunity to put their views on this matter before the State Council of the Party before next March.

(iii) It is public knowledge that our Party's State Council policy on 'Pay and Allowances' was departed from, at least at the Federal Executive level (and without any authority from the State Council representatives of the rank and file of the Party.)

(iv) At the last State Council I stated, with the full authority of the branch I represent, that there was blame for this action which must be shared by the Victorian delegate or delegates as well as by certain members of Parliament.

(v) I am aware that the vote on the Matrimonial Causes Bill may be "pressurized" in the House of Representatives and in the Senate so far as the Liberal Party is concerned.

(vi) Our Victorian delegates to the Liberal Council have no rank-and-file authority to commend or condemn this Bill, or any section of it, at this stage.

SECTION 28 (M)

My prayer and hope are that nothing will be done at the Federal Council or at the Federal Executive levels to compromise the members of the Victorian Liberal and Country Party at this stage.

For my part, I have considered this matter over many years and I have stated publicly, and I adhere to my statements: 'That if this Bill becomes law with Clause 27 (m) intact I could not continue to hold the position of office of Presidency of the Stonnington Branch in this Federal electorate of Higgins.' I could not continue to hold such office in a party which has sponsored a Bill which humiliates our predominantly Christian community, which clearly offends the Christian Churches and their adherents, and which legislates against the interests of the component States of the Commonwealth, and contrary to the well being of our national life.

Sir Garfield Barwick, who is in charge of this Bill, has held himself up as the Federal confessor who so well knows the little frailties and the decency of our people better than the respected churchmen of our nation. The Prime Minister's support, at this stage, for the Bill in toto appears to be more a friendly gesture of support for the error of judgment and poor secular approach of Sir Garfield, at all costs, rather than the sincere profession of an intelligent Christian politician and leader.

Further, the section dealing with marriage guidance, as amended, indicates the desire to promote a rigid Marriage Guidance Council system, in preference to the principle of diversity of such councils which would have been widely accepted.

Finally, I comment on the statement of Mr. Joske in the House: 'Divorce is not the disease; it is the remedy for the disease.' On the contrary, divorce is not the remedy. (Matrimonial Guidance in a diversified field, properly fostered, would, however, be a remedy.) Is it remedy (with particular reference to 27 (m)) to encourage and legitimate illicit unions?

Is it remedy for the all-powerful Government machine to strike at the innocent party and the innocent children per medium of the judges of our State Courts?

What provision is made in this legislation for the child and/or children to be represented by Solicitor and Barrister, adequately and independently of the legal representatives of the husband and wife—and who pays? Is any property settlement, approved by the Court, to serve as any proper safeguard of the real interest of the children's future?

Is Federal Parliament, in passing into law the Clause 27 (m) going then to wash its hands and leave it to the Judges in each State to make the best they can out of this clause? Have the State Premiers and Attorneys-General been consulted re. this Bill? Have the Supreme Court Judges of the States been asked their considered opinion as to the merits of the Bill as it stands at present?

Also, is the Government going to provide finance for the State Judges' Administration of such a Federal law, and also finance the provision of appropriate Divorce Court facilities to carry out the whole declared intention behind this Bill?

I call on you, at the Federal Council and Federal Executive levels of the Party, to see that the rank and file of the Party in Victoria is not compromised in this matter at this stage.

I am, yours sincerely
John F. Dynon[75]

This letter was never acknowledged or returned to me, and I did not receive any official indication of what transpired at Federal levels of the Party at that stage.

What was transparently clear to any interested observer was that Sir Garfield, who had taken over the Joske Bill, had moulded it and changed it to suit his purpose, and was intent on going ahead without any compromise, and at all costs. In Parliament, Sir Garfield Barwick explained the effect of clause 27 (m) referring to the case of an innocent party not wishing to be a party to a divorce:

> He may say, "I have some religious or sentimental reason for not wanting to be divorced". In speaking on this matter last night my proposition was that the interests of the community in ensuring that the other party to the marriage did not form an illicit union and was able to form a sound union would overbear those sentimental or religious scruples on the part of the respondent.[76]

Apart from Sir Garfield, the only other member of Cabinet who spoke on the subject in the House was Mr Harold Holt:

> I do not propose to canvass the merits of this legislation in any great detail. That task has been made unnecessary for me and for other of my colleagues of the Cabinet because of the brilliant exposition of the contents of

the bill, and the justification for its detail, given by my colleague, the Attorney-General (Sir Garfield Barwick). In making that presentation, the Attorney-General spoke for his Cabinet colleagues...

As time has gone on, there has been a disposition in some quarters to represent the bill as the child of the Attorney-General, and to present him as being out on his own in his advocacy of some of the more controversial elements contained in the legislation. I stress that that is far from being the truth...I have seen a suggestion in the press that the Prime Minister (Mr. Menzies), in announcing his support for the legislation, has done so as a friendly gesture to his colleague, the Attorney-General. No question arises about the friendship of the Prime Minister for the Attorney-General. But to suggest that the Prime Minister gives his support to legislation dealing with a major social problem that has exercised the minds of the nation's leaders since federation merely as a passing gesture of his goodwill is to do far less than justice to the right honourable gentleman...

In April, 1957, my friend and colleague, the honourable member for Balaclava (Mr. Joske), a great deal of whose expert and able professional career had been devoted to the legal side of this question of divorce, brought to the Parliament a private member's bill seeking to have the Parliament adopt uniform matrimonial and divorce legislation. Later that year this Parliament unanimously supported to the second-reading stage the legislation he had brought forward... The Government...decided that it should adopt the bill as a government measure...

Clause 27 (m) adopts in substance, although not in all its detail, a provision which has been in operation in Western Australia for some fourteen years…We gave a great deal of thought to it when we had our Cabinet discussions about it. Quite clearly, there is a dilemma so far as the parties to the marriage are concerned. On one hand, there is the position of the partner who does not seek a divorce, who, never having committed any matrimonial offence, does not want to find himself or herself in the position of being regarded as a divorced person…On the other hand, there is the other partner to the marriage who has been denied the normal human companionship and the normal human parental relationship to which his or her instincts would lead. Therefore, we have to weigh justice as evenly as we can between those partners to the marriage. Perhaps if we waver in our judgment—because there is a real dilemma presented to us here—then in my own view, having given this matter as much thought as I could, and with as much responsibility as I could bring to it, the scales must be heavily weighed by the situation of the children who will be the product of an irregular union unless relief of the kind proposed under the legislation is given.[77]

Mr Holt said that he felt as the children of the irregular union would otherwise lead a 'twisted, embittered existence because of the stigma' they felt attached to them, he must therefore come down in favour of clause 27 (m).

The 'brilliance' of Sir Garfield Barwick kept the Prime Minister and all other Cabinet members off their feet during the debate in the House (Mr Cramer being absent and Mr Casey being overseas). Garfield Barwick provided some interesting views: 'For my part, I feel that the community owes it to itself to enable either of the parties to have the initiative. Clause 27 (m) is designed to that effect.'[78]

That indeed was a very honest declaration.

One might fairly draw the inference at this point that Sir Garfield was being more frank than Mr Holt had been in his exposition in the House.

Sir Garfield had a special word for the bishops:

> The next thing that the bishops say is—
>
>> The acceptance of this ground would further undermine the sanctity of marriage in that far from discouraging illicit unions, it would encourage them, since those who enter into them would be "secure in the knowledge that, after the required number of years had passed, they would be free to marry."
>
> I want honourable members to understand what is being said. It is that a man or woman would leave the lawful spouse and deliberately begin a de facto or illicit relationship on this footing, "Well, it is all right; at the end of five years of this illicit intercourse, I will be able to get a divorce". If there is one thing that is not true of this bill, it is just that. For this statement to be circulated in this uncritical fashion, I think merits the criticism that I have offered. If that sort of wanton conduct were presented to a court, I would expect the court to say that it was not in the public interest and that it was against public morals.[79]

Mr Kim Beazley MHR, member for Fremantle, had this to say about clause 27 (m):

> clause 27 (m)...corresponds with the provision in the law of Western Australia. The provision means that if a husband and wife have been separated for five years they may have a divorce. Any one who knows the shoddy history of this provision in the Western Australia law knows that it was tailor-made to suit an individual case.[80]...[This provision] was wickedly introduced in Western Australia, has been wicked in its effects, has been sustained in the courts by perjury and has been characterized by gross injustice to wives and children.[81]

In the Senate Chamber, Senator Reginald Wright (Liberal, lawyer) also spoke about the Western Australian provision:

> Then the surprising, inexplicable thing to me is that, in Western Australia, which produced this provision, it was made an absolute bar, disqualifying any petitioner from getting a decree on this ground, if in the five years separation period he had committed adultery or if, at the time of his petition, he was in default with payment of maintenance for his wife or children, under any order in force or any agreement that he had entered into...Western Australia does require that before a petitioner can be successful on this ground he shall be up to date with his payments. Secondly, it disqualifies him if he has been guilty of adultery during the five years. Why, when we propose to make this provision applicable to the whole of Australia, do we degrade the disqualification of adultery from an absolute bar as it is in Western Australia, to a discretionary bar?...

> The Western Australian provision is bad and we should see that we strengthen the safeguards to ensure that a wife, at her own election, can deny a culpable spouse the right to dissolve the marriage. That is her right... The wife's right, from my point of view, is paramount in such a personal matter as this. She has committed herself to matrimony which, in all our conceptions of that institution, promises her lifelong protection. That promise is given in the interests of the wife and not less in the interests of the children.[82]

Barwick promised safeguards:

> Of course, there needed to be safeguards...By clause 27 (m) I have tried to provide that there shall be no injustice to the individual. I have said to the courts, "You must not give the guilty party a divorce in circumstances which would be harsh and oppressive." I could not express the idea of justice better. I have said to the courts: "You shall not give the guilty party a divorce in circumstances where it is against the public interest and where it is offensive to public morals."[83]

A number of members of the House of Representatives, in supporting the legislation, stressed the importance of the safeguards. EH Cox, Canberra correspondent for *The Herald*, wrote after the House of Representatives' vote on the Bill: 'Assurances by the Attorney-General, Sir Garfield Barwick, that the five-year separation clause in the Divorce Bill would operate under strict safeguards contributed to the big affirmative vote for it today.'[84]

Prime Minister Menzies spoke not one word on the Matrimonial Causes Bill in the House, although, it seems, he also had been reassured by the safeguards. He later wrote to me:

Dear Mr. Dynon,

I refer to your letter of 28th December, 1961, in which you wrote about section 28 (m) of the Matrimonial Causes Act, 1959.

Your views on the philosophy of section 28 (m) of the Matrimonial Causes Act, 1959 are now well known to the Government and they are respected. At the same time, I think that you are well aware of the views of the Attorney-General on the provision. Consequently I think that no useful purpose will be served by my traversing your argument.

I would, however, refer you to section 37 (1) of the Act...The purpose of this section...was to prevent the ground being made subject to abuse.

Yours sincerely,
Robert Menzies
Prime Minister[85]

So much for Sir Garfield's assurances and expectations. One wonders if he was later overly concerned that the courts did not live up to his expectations. At the time was he ignorant of what was to be the effect of this law, or was he naive?

Eight years later, the senior New South Wales Divorce Judge, Mr Justice Selby said he thought the intended legislative safeguards were 'more or less a dead letter'. Mr Justice Selby had refused a husband a decree on the grounds that it would be harsh and oppressive and contrary to public interest to grant it because of the husband's failure to comply with a maintenance order, the wife's religious beliefs and time factors. The Court of Appeal allowed the husband's appeal and Selby J then granted the separation decree at the direction of the Court of Appeal. *The Herald* reported Mr Justice Selby's comments: "There may be some circumstances where the court could say it would be harsh and oppressive to pronounce a decree...But since it is not in this case, it is hard to think of circumstances where it would be."[86]

So much, indeed, for throwing open the whole conduct of the parties for the consideration of the court.

During the Parliamentary debate, Senator Wright referred to the Morton Commission in England:

> ...we could look to England for some guidance. The Morton Commission considered this subject at length. Lord Morton of Henryton and Lord Justice Pearce, whose reputation in law and jurisprudence are well known to all lawyers in the House, subscribed to this statement—
>
>> If the principle that a marriage should be ended if it has irretrievably broken down is followed to its logical conclusion, then it must be accepted that a spouse who had committed no recognized matrimonial offence could be divorced against his will. In our opinion, this would be so plainly unjust as to be in itself conclusive against the introduction of any ground of divorce which had this result.
>
> ...Lord Morton, Lord Justice Pearce and another seven commissioners also said—
>
>> ...to give people a right to divorce themselves would be to foster a change in the attitude to marriage which would be disastrous for the nation.
>
> Those views were expressed by those eminent gentlemen and, with respect, I adopt them. They said also—

> The argument that divorce by consent provides a dignified and honorable means of release is perhaps the most insidious of all. There could be no subtler temptation to divorce than the belief that there was a wholly blameless way of terminating a marriage. In our view it is not the function of the law to provide such a means of release; its proper function is to give relief where a wrong has been done. To go beyond this and provide an easy way out would be actively to assist in what can only be regarded as a socially calamitous act.[87]

Obviously, the concept of the institution of marriage as so far understood throughout Christendom and recognised in our courts and the courts of England, was under threat in this dissolution legislation. It had become crystal clear why the Attorney-General considered it vital to introduce the divorce bill before the marriage bill. The divorce bill had to be put through Parliament before the members were to be asked to set their minds to discussing marriage and its significance. To her great credit, Senator Ivy Wedgwood brought this aspect to the attention of the Senate.

So far as Moira and I were concerned, the Government's determination to persevere with this Bill was the last straw. We had no real choice. It was not an issue on which either of us could compromise. I sent a letter at my personal expense to every member of the Stonnington Branch so that there would be no mistake about the issue involved, in so far as it concerned Moira and myself:

Dear Member,

Some nine months ago, following upon our Branch's strong protest against the timing and the method of implementation of the Richardson Report, our membership was decimated from 308 to 153.

Following upon the undemocratic, unreasonable and anti-social Divorce legislation recently sponsored by our Government and enacted, I have myself resigned from the office of President of Stonnington. This action is the only satisfactory expression of protest that I can make in order to emphasize, not only my complete disapproval, but also the disapproval of many thousands of citizens who share my moral and sociological approach, and who have directly supported me.

In any case I maintain that the Government did not have a mandate to enact the Divorce legislation which it did enact. Sir Garfield Barwick's Bill was fundamentally different from Mr. Joske's, when we consider the implications of Clause 27 (m)—which became 28 (m) in the Senate—providing the ground for Divorce of 5 years Separation…In view of my belief that the Government Parties were proceeding beyond their policy declared in the Joint Policy Speech of the Prime Minister in October 1958, and in view of my own belief that Clause 28 (m) of the proposed legislation was bad on moral and sociological grounds, I considered that I really had no other course but to resign from office.

This Divorce legislation introduced a new principle of divorce—on the ground of Separation—where there was no matrimonial offence by the party proceeded against. This new principle is supported by the Attorney-General and the Government on the basis of its supposed humanity. A vast number of Church and lay leaders and thinking citizens cannot help being appalled at this new 'modern' approach, which strikes at the high character of this most personal contract-status—the Institution of Marriage.

It is widely held that this new principle strikes at the whole fabric of society and will be a bad influence on the community, and also cause many injustices to innocent parties.

The special Royal Commission in England, during a period of four years devoted itself to the whole problem of Divorce (without considering any religious argument) and the associated problems of husband, wife, children and society, and came down entirely against such new principle which is now to be accepted in our first Federal Divorce Act.

In such a case the innocent party who has taken the marriage vows and wants to keep them is, according to Sir Garfield Barwick, affected by some sentimental attachment or "religious scruple", which is to be considered as equivalent to guilt, in order to justify the other party's bid for freedom to—in most cases—"make his or her relationship conformable with the standards of respectability of which the community approves" (to take a quote from Mr. Justice Barry's recent judgment) i.e. to seal in a State union this illicit association.

I cannot believe that it is true that our community has lost respect for the individuals who sincerely believe in

> their marriage vows—"for better or worse", "in sickness and in health", "till death us do part", and who want to keep them.
>
> It is indeed with profound regret that I vacate my position as President, as likewise has my wife from the position of Hon. Secretary. For our part, we have gladly chosen to place our love and loyalty for our country and our people in pride of place before the narrow interests of the political Party which we had thus far served faithfully.[88]

In addition to resigning from the office of Honorary Secretary of the Branch, Moira also resigned as Chairman of the Stonnington LCP Women's Sections:

> ...I have resigned because I consider Section 28 (m) of the Matrimonial Causes Act is objectionable on religious, moral and sociological grounds. It is authoritatively considered that under this Section women will be the greater sufferers...I could not continue to hold office in a party which sponsors such legislation.
>
> Would you kindly convey to Senator Wedgwood congratulations on her stand in the Senate on this Clause.[89]

A letter from Mrs Sylvia Blogg included an interesting reference to the legislation in Western Australia:

> My two dear Dynons,
>
> That was nice of you to send to me a copy of what you have posted to all members of Stonnington Branch. Very many people—like me—will be sad that you must go from this work that you have done so well—to work with you is to know how valuable is your

contribution to any cause. As you say—Clause 28 (m) was not in the original Bill drafted by Mr. Joske and I think that Western Australia must have pushed for its retention. It has been on the Statute books for 14 years during which time there have been 4 different Governments and none have thought it bad enough to take it off—on the other hand apparently none of the other States have thought it valuable enough to include in their own Legislation.

So there it is—you two must do what you must do, and I am sure it was no quick decision and I must stay where I think I can help in the best way to keep Australia part of Western Christian civilisation, which is what we all are working for anyway.

Again thank you both, God bless
Yours
Sylvia Blogg.[90]

Mr Steve Alley, Vice-President of the Stonnington Branch, urged me to reconsider my expressed intention to resign. After Moira and I placed our resignations on the Secretary's file, Steve commented that the Branch could ill afford to lose both of us and he was sorry that our views on the divorce bill had been so strong that we felt compelled to resign.

In January 1960, I received a letter from the Premier of Victoria, Mr Henry Bolte:

Dear Mr Dynon,

I have your letter of the 23rd ultimo, enclosing a copy of your communication of the 22nd idem to members of the Stonnington Branch of the Liberal and Country Party, concerning the Federal Divorce Bill, and desire to say I regret that Mrs. Dynon and yourself have found it necessary to resign from the Offices you held in the Stonnington Branch.

Your services in the past for the Party have been much appreciated.

Yours sincerely,
Henry E Bolte,
Premier[91]

11

The petition to Her Majesty

In February–March 1960, two events occurred. The first was, I suppose, the inevitable outcome, demonstrating the resentment amongst the members against the policies, attitudes and actions of the Party. The Stonnington Branch met for its Annual General Meeting and a report appeared in *The Herald*:

> The Stonnington branch of the LCP decided last night not to recommend that the Federal Treasurer, Mr Holt, be automatically re-endorsed for his electorate at the next election. The newly-elected president of the branch, Mr J.T. De Ravin, a Toorak chemist, said today that "some dissatisfaction" was expressed at the meeting over the Parliamentary pay rises and also over the Matrimonial Causes Bill.
>
> The decision on Mr Holt will apply also to Mr J.S. Bloomfield, MLA, State Minister for Education, and Mr Lindsay Thompson, MLC, the Assistant Chief Secretary.[92]

Moira and I were not present at the meeting and we attended no further meetings of the Branch. We were never again to work for the Liberal Party.

Secondly, being free of any official Liberal Party constraint, I convened a meeting in February 1960 of what was initially called The Association for the Advancement of the Family. The committee agreed that its first task was to seek the disallowance of the *Matrimonial Causes Act 1959* or the deletion of section 28 (m) by constitutional means. The Association decided to petition Her Majesty, Queen Elizabeth under section 59 of the *Australian Constitution*:

> The Queen may disallow any law within one year from the Governor-General's assent, and such disallowance on being made known by the Governor-General by speech or message to each of the Houses of the Parliament, or by Proclamation, shall annul the law from the day when the disallowance is so made known.[93]

The petition[94] was signed by 155,689 people, over a five-week period. Signatories to the petition came from every state in Australia and included bishops, deans, ministers of religion of various denominations, Justices of the Peace, mayors and councillors, members of the Press and other men and women of all walks of life. Despite the many pages of signatures, only a single page of signatures was forwarded to Her Majesty.

The Official Secretary to the Governor General wrote to me:

> I refer to your letter of 24th November, 1960, and your telegram of yesterday afternoon regarding the Association's Petition to Her Majesty The Queen praying the disallowance of the Matrimonial Causes Act 1959 or alternatively section 28 (m) of that Act.

> On receipt of the Petition the Governor-General submitted it to his Ministers for advice, in accordance with constitutional custom.
>
> Immediately on receipt of advice the Governor-General transmitted to The Queen by airmail one sheet of the Petition, your letter of 31st October, 1960, his Ministers' advice, His Excellency's own recommendation and advice to the effect that the Petition which His Excellency retained less the sheet mentioned, was said to contain over 155,000 signatures.[95]

In the end, the petition failed.

I appreciated the support of many people including Robert Moline, the Anglican Archbishop of Perth, who wrote to me:

> Thank you for your progress report about the petition which I received some time ago. Since then I have seen in the press that the petition has failed. That is a disappointment for which I am sorry even though it may not be surprising. I imagine that Her Majesty would only in very extreme circumstances intervene in the legislation of a self-governing member of the British Commonwealth. In any case I suppose that the invocation of Section 59 of the Australian Constitution must inevitably be beset by many difficulties, not least the constitutional requirement that the Governor-General should consult the Ministers of the Crown before taking action.
>
> However I think that your effort has been well worth while. It has at least registered the fact that a very considerable, and not wholly unimportant section of the public are gravely concerned about the Matrimonial

Causes Act of 1959 and in particular Section 28 (m) of that Act. If the operation of this Act is leading as I am told, to a great deal of confusion, we may still hope that it will be eventually amended. Meanwhile I congratulate you on what you have attempted.[96]

To complete this matter, I wish to quote from a lecture on 'The Divorce Laws' delivered by The Hon. Mr Justice Denning at King's College, London in 1947:

> No branch of the law is more important than that which relates to divorce…Before we consider divorce we must surely pause a moment to consider marriage, for without marriage there would be no divorce… Marriage is not a contract which the parties can mutually agree to rescind. It confers a status in which others besides the parties are interested. The parties to it bring forth children who have the strongest claim of all that the marriage should be maintained. In that claim society itself is interested. The future of society depends on the upbringing of the children. Society itself for the sake of the children, cannot allow the unity of family life to be broken by the consent of the parties. Hence in this country the fundamental rule that divorce by mutual consent is not allowed. Hence the whole of our divorce law which permits divorce only for grave causes prescribed by law.[97]

There was not even a 'pause for a moment' to consider 'marriage' within the Australian Federal Parliament, prior to the enactment of the Matrimonial Causes legislation. The concept of marriage was kept discreetly out of sight, so out of mind. When the Marriage Bill came to be discussed in the House of Representatives in March 1961, Sir Garfield

Barwick said: '"Marriage" is not defined in this bill, as such, but it is quite plain from the legislation, particularly from the inclusion of a provision against bigamy, that marriage is a union of one man and one woman for life to the exclusion of others.'[98]

Mr Whitlam asked the Attorney-General: 'Under the Constitution, we could pass bills on monogamous marriages only, could we not?' Sir Garfield replied: 'That is right. We are probably compelled constitutionally to confine ourselves to monogamous marriages.'[99]

In due course, the Family Law Act was enacted in January 1976 and the rot continued. One wonders whether our legislators really had any regard for Australia's adherence to the Universal Declaration of Human Rights Article 16(3): 'The family is the natural and fundamental group unit of society and is entitled to protection by society and the State.'

It must have been obvious to Menzies that Barwick was striking a blow for hedonism. I am sure that, ultimately, he was embarrassed by the outcome of this Barwick piece of legislation, the spreading malaise of broken marriages, the hurt done to faultless spouses and innocent children, and the resultant burden imposed on the taxpayers.

Menzies himself must have recalled the outcome of his visit to President Nasser of Egypt at the request of Sir Anthony Eden, then Prime Minister of the United Kingdom. Menzies had reported to Eden on Nasser's assertion of his unfettered right to nationalise the Suez Canal. Nasser had said: 'We had the right to do what we did and if we have the right to do something we can't understand how people can take exception to it.' Menzies reported: 'This will explain the kind of logical mess which exists in his mind. It is just as if one said that, as the Parliament of the United Kingdom has power to pass any laws it thinks fit to pass, nobody would ever be at liberty to complain about it, to resent it, to seek to alter it.'[100]

Today we witness the chasm which exists between the belief that valid Christian marriage is permanent and the modern legislative approach that divorce is for the asking. The middle ground where State and Courts following the spirit of Christendom, at least had recognised 'justice' to the faultless spouse as an impediment to divorce, has now crumbled away in a hedonist society.

12

Australian-Japanese children in Kure

In 1960, Moira and I were actively engaged in the Australian-Asian Association of Victoria, which was dedicated to friendship, understanding and good fellowship between the peoples of Australia and Asia. The work included receiving and entertaining guests and delegations from Asian countries and helping Asian students in Australia with accommodation, study, health and a variety of problems. Moira was a member of the Executive Committee headed by the President, His Honour Sir Charles Lowe of the Supreme Court of Victoria.

In January 1960, Denis Warner[101] had written some articles in *The Herald* highlighting the plight of the Australian-Japanese children living in Kure, Japan.

Kure was a former Japanese naval base. After Japan's surrender in World War II, Kure was transformed into the headquarters of the British Commonwealth Occupation Forces. Virtually all Australian troops who went to Japan between 1945 and 1956 landed in Kure. Australian warships used its naval facilities and Australia was primarily responsible for its logistical support. After Japan regained independence in 1952,

Australians stayed in Kure because it was the main supply base for all Commonwealth forces in Korea. The last Australian troops left Japan in mid-1956.

In the first years of the Occupation, Australian troops were under strict orders not to fraternise with the Japanese and marriages between Australian servicemen and Japanese women were not recognised by the army authorities. Despite this ban on fraternisation by the Occupation authorities, a number of Australian members of the British Commonwealth Occupation Forces married Japanese girls before Japanese registrars and/or by Shinto rites and/or by Christian rites or entered into Japanese Informal Marriages. As Australian troops left Japan, they were denied permission to bring their wives and children to Australia.

The Herald reported that a number of these children and their mothers or guardians were living in impoverished conditions. Moira brought this issue to the attention of the Executive Committee and the Association appointed a Special Sub-Committee, comprising Sir Albert Coates, Dr EE 'Weary' Dunlop, Mr S Dimmick, Mr RR Buxton and Moira as Chairman, to investigate and report.

Moira prepared a detailed report,[102] which highlighted the dire position of 52 children of Australian paternity living in Kure, whose ages ranged from six to 13 years:

> These children are living in extreme poverty and all are in need of material help for their maintenance and for their education and vocational training... The members of our Sub-Committee believe that there is a moral responsibility for Australia to do what it can to help the Australian-Japanese children, who through no fault of their own were abandoned by their

Australian fathers and are living in conditions of great hardship and extreme poverty.

The last paragraph of Moira's report threw out a challenge:

> We must not ignore the plight of these children—rather let us give an example of charity. We contend that our Christian, Democratic civilisation here is a precious heritage in the Pacific area of the world. To help these children is a golden opportunity for us to demonstrate the practice of our convictions.

Sir Charles Lowe had said of these children: 'Australians cannot as a matter of national honour simply evade helping them by ignoring their existence. Their plight must appeal to our deepest humanitarian instincts.'[103]

The Australian-Asian Association of Victoria launched an appeal 'For the Maintenance and Education of the Australian-Japanese children in Kure' that raised over £8,500. In addition, a large consignment of donated new woollen clothing and toys was sent to the Australian Ambassador in Japan for distribution to the children. On the recommendation of the Ambassador, International Social Service (ISS), a voluntary organisation, was asked to accept and administer the fund and to arrange the distribution of the clothing and toys.

Prime Minister Menzies acknowledged in Parliament that the Australian Government had been asked to contribute to an appeal to raise funds for the education of the Australian-Japanese children and also for the relief of the mothers and guardians of these children who were living in Japan in impoverished circumstances. His response was: 'The Government decided that it was unable to provide any financial assistance for this purpose.'[104]

There seemed to be a policy on the part of Australian Government spokesmen to group all the children together as 'illegitimates' as if to belittle them. In March 1960, the Minister for Immigration, Mr A Downer, had spoken of 'these illegitimate children in Japan'[105] and 'the identifiable illegitimate children supposedly of Australian servicemen'.[106] On the information available, at least 20 per cent of the children were the offspring of marriages legally recognised in Japan.

On the matter of adoptions by Australian couples, there were obviously some difficulties. However, with regard to children who were living with persons other than their mothers, it appeared that the true interest of at least some of these may have been best served by adoption into Australian families. The Federal Government was clearly against any such adoption. In the House of Representatives as far back as October 1959, in reply to a question touching on the matter of adoption, Mr Downer had said: 'On the question generally, however, I must tell the honorable gentleman that I do not favour, in principle, Japanese migration to this country, nor do I think that it would be acceptable to public opinion or desirable in any respect.'[107]

Mr Downer was not alone in his views on Asian immigration. In 1958, whilst we were heavily involved in the Liberal Party, Moira and I formulated a resolution (supported by Steve Alley, Vice-President of the Stonnington Branch), seeking to broaden marginally the immigration policy. We brought the matter to the Victorian State Conference in 1958. The resolution was:

> THAT, in the name of humanity and charity and pursuant to our obligations to our fellow citizens and to our neighbours in the Asian area of the world, the

> Federal Government be requested to consider further a modification of its present migration policy with regard to the Asian peoples, who make application to settle permanently in Australia and who have the capacity to contribute to our way of life and to our security.[108]

At the conference, a male member of the Central Executive, with old-time emotional oratory from the platform, warned of the 'menace of the Chinese hordes coming down on us with their swords'. He received a thunderous applause from the males and females in the Assembly Hall that afternoon, and 5/8 of the representatives raised their hands to give thumbs down to the resolution. It was an almost unbelievable public performance—firstly, by the speaker, and secondly, by the majority of the official representatives present from all the Party branches throughout Victoria. The entrenched racism so enthusiastically displayed was both startling and sickening.

In 1961, in her concern for the Australian-Japanese children, Moira sought the support of Senator Frank McManus, who raised the issue in the Senate during a debate on Government grants in aid:

> I regret that there has not been included in this section a grant for the assistance of Japanese children. When I refer to Japanese children I mean children of mixed parentage, the children in most cases being those of Australian soldiers who were stationed in Japan during the occupation. Those soldiers fathered these children and then failed to continue to support the mothers or the children...Their plight was brought to the notice of the Commonwealth Government by a number of

church organizations but I regret that after investigation the Government decided not to make a contribution. The matter was then taken up by voluntary bodies, one of which is the Australia-Asia Association in Melbourne. This association...made a further approach to the Government asking it to reconsider its decision.

I regret that again the Government decided that it could make no contribution to the support of these children...I do not desire to labour the point, other than to say that I think an opportunity was lost to create goodwill. Further than that a contribution by the Government would have helped these unfortunate children for whom we have some responsibility in view of the fact that their fathers, in most cases, were Australian members of the armed forces.[109]

Senator Vincent responded:

I wish to refer very briefly to the remarks of Senator McManus about the children of Australian soldiers in Japan. I join issue with the honorable senator on this matter. I do not believe there is a firm obligation on the part of Australia to advance money in a somewhat vague way to assist these children. I agree that there is a problem in relation to them. No one will deny that that is so, but I do not agree that an overall grant of money should be handed to some authority in Japan for the assistance of the children.

There is, of course, an obligation on the fathers of the children. Our Australian law recognizes that there is an obligation on every father to support his child...I suggest that the people who are now clamouring for funds from the Government for this purpose...could better assist in solving the problem by endeavouring to help the mothers of the children to enforce the law in Australia. There is a perfectly good law in Australia which renders the father of the child in these circumstances responsible, and it is not very difficult to implement it...We have a law that is applicable. It should be enforced. We could well concern ourselves with its enforcement.[110]

After reading Senator Vincent's suggestions for the Japanese mothers, Moira wrote to him:

Dear Senator Vincent,

It was with great interest that I read in Hansard your speech in the Senate...concerning the Australian-Japanese children in Japan.

...May I refer now to what you said with regard to the obligation on every father to support his child and your suggestion that it would be better to help the Japanese mothers of the children to enforce the law in Australia...

We would be indebted to you if you would assist us by indicating the appropriate the practical way that any such aggrieved wife and, or mother could approach the Court in Australia to seek maintenance for herself and/or her children, taking into consideration the fact that these Japanese women are living in dire poverty, and have very little knowledge of the English language and our laws and were told by Australian authorities that their marriages would not be recognized in Australia. In addition, what facilities does the Immigration Department provide for the coming into Australia of a Japanese woman and/or her children solely for the purpose of seeking maintenance in our Courts of Law against an Australian man whom she claims is her legal husband?

If you think that it is wise to approach the problem in the way you have suggested, could you ascertain if the Government would be prepared to finance a case in our Courts to test the validity of a marriage between a Japanese woman and an Australian serviceman, which took place in Japan in accordance with the local legal forms under Japanese Law at a time when there was an Army ban on such unions.

It seems to us that after all this time it would be unwise to approach the problem in this way...I feel that it is particularly unfortunate in all the circumstances that the Federal Government has consistently refused to help these children and their mothers.[111]

Moira, as Chairman of the Special Sub-Committee, reported that the Association was receiving regular reports from the Japanese Branch of ISS on the implementation of the project and was confident that the money was being used for the maintenance and education of the children. A trained social worker (Miss Yone Ito) had been assigned to assist the children. In her report, Moira thanked the people of Victoria for their generosity and pointed out that the Federal Government gave no help whatsoever to the Association's appeal, either by way of donation or tax deduction. The problem could not be solved by a voluntary association alone. 'I believe that there can be no real solution for these children until the Federal Government faces up to the problem and formulates a realistic and charitable policy. Much more money is needed to give these children better living conditions and some hope for the future.'[112]

Melbourne journalist Keith Dunstan, after returning from a visit to Kure, commented:

> It's easy to pick out these Japanese-Australian orphans at Kure. They're different. They speak hardly a word of English. Like everyone else, they wear these ugly, black Japanese school uniforms, yet it's obvious that they are almost Australian. They are taller, their skin is paler, their hair not jet black and they are wide-eyed. There was one I shall never forget—Yoshio Shimizu, aged 12. His face was covered in freckles. Now freckles in Japan are extraordinary, an object of real curiosity. They called the orphans 'Specials' or 'Mixed bloods'. Being a mixed blood at a Japanese school is not easy to live down, but that is not the only problem. It goes deeper than that. They know these children are even more different. They have no respectable ancestors.[113]

The Kure children were starting to grow up. They needed money to further their education. Education was a fiercely competitive business in Japan. Unless you had some form of specialised training, you didn't have a chance.

In October 1962, Moira asked Prime Minister Menzies to receive a delegation to discuss the issue and he nominated the Minister for Immigration, Mr Downer. The delegation, consisting of Dr EE Dunlop, the Reverend Frank Byatt (representing the Australian Council of Churches) and Moira, was received by Mr Downer at Parliament House, Canberra on 15 November 1962.

Moira reported the delegation's interview with the Minister:

> The interview lasted a little over 1¼ hours during which time the members of the delegation discussed with the Minister many aspects concerning the children and in particular asked Mr. Downer for:
>
> 1. A Federal Government grant spread over 5 years to help the children. It has been estimated that the cost of maintaining the children and providing secondary education or vocational training for them is £85,000 Australian.
>
> 2. Tax deductions on donations for the children.
>
> 3. No Immigration Restriction to prevent the entry to Australia of any of the children whose interests would best be served by adoption by Australian families.
>
> With regard to this third matter, Mr. Downer promised to give sympathetic consideration to any application for entry to Australia of any of the children whose interests would best be served by adoption here providing—it was in the best interest of each child involved; all Child Welfare authority requirements were met; legal difficulties of inter country adoption to Australia could be overcome; and the prospective adoptive parents and the child concerned could be suitably matched. Since the youngest child is now eight years old, it is apparent that at this stage only a few children may be able to benefit from this sympathetic consideration by the Minister.
>
> In addition, Mr. Downer stated that any Australian ex-serviceman, who claimed paternity of any of the children, would not be prevented by immigration restrictions from bringing that child to Australia.[114]

Mr Downer issued a Press statement:

> The Government would grant £20,000 towards the administrative costs of the International Social Service in its work among mixed blood children in Japan...

> "As a general rule," Mr. Downer said, "I do not consider that proposals to permit the children to come to Australia for adoption would be in their own interests, even if that were practicable. I would be prepared, however, to consider sympathetically all the circumstances of any request by an Australian ex-serviceman for the admission of his child, provided he acknowledged his paternity."

> Although illegitimate children born abroad of Australian servicemen was not a matter for which the Government accepted responsibility, it had been concerned to find means of assisting the children in a way that would be in their best interests. This was the guiding consideration.

> "Since 1957 the Japanese Branch of International Social Service has been engaged in attending to the welfare of mixed blood children in Japan, regardless of paternity", Mr Downer said.

> ..."The Government, in recognition of the value of the work which International Social Service is doing in this way in Japan, has decided to grant a sum of £20,000 towards the administrative costs of the organisation, in its work among the mixed blood children in Japan...to be available for expenditure over a five year period," Mr Downer said.[115]

In announcing the grant, the Government was careful not to commit itself to giving financial aid to 'Australian-Japanese' children preferring to use the words 'mixed blood' children. Not surprisingly, the Minister's statement drew a critical response from Moira:

> The Minister for Immigration, Mr Downer, was strongly criticised today for his statement on the entry of Australian-Japanese waifs to Australia. Commenting on the statement, Mrs John F. Dynon said:
>
>> "It is incredible that a generous Government grant should be linked with an unfortunate statement raising the children's legitimacy and excluding them from Australia."
>
> Mrs Dynon is chairman of a special sub-committee formed by the Australian-Asian Society of Victoria to investigate the plight of the waifs. She said that much of the good will gained by a grant of £20,000 to the International Social Service organisation would be lost by Mr Downer's comments.
>
> On Friday, Mr Downer said...that the Government did not accept responsibility for illegitimate children of Australian ex-servicemen born abroad. Mrs Dynon asked today: "Will Mr Downer say why the Government is not accepting any responsibility? Is it because they are allegedly illegitimate, or because of their skin colour and race?" Mrs Dynon added that to class all the children as illegitimate would be untrue and unfair to about 20 per cent. She said some Australian servicemen contracted marriages which were binding under Japanese law but which the Australian Army would not accept.[116]

Moira was also concerned that Mr Downer, in his lengthy Press statement, failed to mention his undertaking to give sympathetic consideration to any application for entry to Australia of any child whose interests would best be served by adoption here. In the House of Representatives, Dr JF Cairns MHR reminded him:

> I ask the Minister for Immigration a question about the proposal to bring children from Japan. Did he receive a deputation from the Australian-Asian Association of Victoria...? [and] Did he undertake to consider favorably the requests made by the deputation, and has he now rejected those requests, refusing permission for the children to come here?[117]

Mr Downer then confirmed the assurance he had given to the deputation:

> ...The deputation said...that there might be two, three or possibly four cases in which it would be in the child's best interests to come to Australia. For my part, I said that if this could be established in some specific case I would consider it sympathetically, in spite of all the very great legal difficulties that are involved. I have nothing further to add.[118]

At this time, Moira had formed a very happy association with the Consul for Japan in Victoria, Mr M Nomoto and Mrs Nomoto, whom we first met during our AAUN work. Keen to learn more about Japan, the people and culture, Moira was attending a series of studies at the University of Melbourne on 'Japan Today'. She also organised an afternoon tea at our home [119] to meet Misses Satoyo Abo, Fumiko Adachi, Kazuko Fujii and Makiko Yamanishi,—graduates of KOBE College Japan who were on a goodwill tour of Australia.

It was also about this time that Moira joined the Australian Labor Party. After the 1963 Federal election, Moira wrote to Dr Jim Cairns congratulating him on his re-election as the Member for Yarra and offering her assistance towards a Labor victory in the future. She became a member of the ALP and, for three years, was Secretary of the ALP Hawthorn Branch.

In April 1964, the AJ Ferguson Memorial Appeal for Australian-Japanese Children in Japan was launched.[120] Moira spent much time and energy promoting this appeal, arranging functions and giving talks[121] and interviews. This Australia-wide appeal was dedicated to the late Alex Ferguson, who had championed the cause of these children up to the day of his death in October 1962. It was acknowledged that he did more perhaps than any other Australian to focus public attention on the plight of the waifs. His son Noel Ferguson carried on the work of his late father.

In the House of Representatives, Sir Robert Menzies made the Government's position clear: 'In view of the grant which the Government has already authorized towards the welfare of the mixed-race children generally in Japan, it does not propose to subscribe to the A.J. Ferguson Memorial Appeal.'[122]

Four months later, Moira wrote to Hubert Opperman MHR, who was then Minister for Immigration, requesting additional Federal help. He responded: 'I would not propose to recommend that the Government should consider making a further grant towards the welfare of these children...I do not see that there is a case for further Government intervention at this stage.'[123] No tax deductions were allowed on donations for these children.

Following the Tokyo Olympics, 20 members of Australia's swimming team visited Kure and staged a special carnival for the Australian-Japanese children. Senator Fitzgerald spoke of this in Parliament and asked the Leader of the Government in the Senate what assistance the Australian Government was giving to help these unfortunate children.[124]

Senator Paltridge replied:

> On request, some time ago, the Government gave consideration to the matter of the waifs in Japan who are alleged—and I emphasise the word "alleged"—to be the children of Australian servicemen. The decision taken then was that the case was not one which could appropriately be supported by the Australian Government. The decision was made after full consideration of the facts and I do not see that there is any case for re-submission to the Government.[125]

The Leader of the Government in the Senate thus confirmed the attitude behind the Australian Government's grant made at the end of 1962. The Government had in fact turned its back on the specific cause of the Australian-Japanese children in Japan and had donated funds to a worthy international organisation for all 'mixed blood' children in Japan.

The Australian Government was prepared to let the dust settle and hoped that the question would not arise again. The Government may have wished to save face for the Australian nation but the Australian people do not need such cushioning from the facts of life. The cold and mean reactionary spirit behind the Government's thinking is a sorry page in the history of this nation.

The 1964 appeal had been launched in favourable circumstances as Miss Ito was visiting Australia. When the appeal was discontinued at the beginning of 1965, the net receipts were approximately £20,000. The Appeal Director, Mr Rodgers, reported that it had not been a 'popular' appeal. It involved money going out of the country; there was a reluctance from many organisations and individuals to be associated with a cause they felt to be unpopular in Canberra, and the negative attitude of the RSL did not help.

In January 1966, Mr LS Reid MLA, on behalf of the trustees of the fund,[126] travelled to Japan at his own expense and to Kure, where he personally presented the Mayor of Kure with a cheque for £4,500. This represented the first contribution from the Australia-wide appeal. Subsequent donations were made, including a cheque that Moira delivered personally to the Consul-General of Japan in Melbourne in April 1969. The Mayor of Kure was very grateful:

> On the 11th of May I duly received a cheque for U.S. dollars $6,052.32 donated by your Appeal through Mr. Consul General Imajo of Japan, Melbourne, and lost no time in handing it with your donative word to Miss Yone Ito, Senior Social Worker of International Social Service, Kure.
>
> As Mayor of the City of Kure, I beg to tender my most sincere thanks to your Appeal for the very significant and invaluable donation for the care of Australian-Japanese children which your Appeal has so kindly made four times. Truly, no words can give utterance to the sentiments of gratitude I owe your Appeal in the execution of the humanitarian and worthy undertaking, and I highly appreciate your human approach with untiring patience very much indeed.[127]

I am sure that Moira would have loved to have heard the broadcast on ABC radio on 13 November 1977 when Miss

Yone Ito spoke about her work. She had studied in the United States for five years before returning to Japan in 1958 and going to Kure in 1959. She worked on the Kure project with 130 children and prevailed on some influential local people and also local government to help in her operation of this ISS project.

She said that 1960 onwards were the crucial years and ultimately it had been the education programme that had done so much for the future of the children. The financial help received from the Australian Government and from private sources had been the basis for its success. Early on, many of the children wanted to go to Australia. She had to tell them that it was not possible as, in 1960, the Australian Government opposed the immigration to Australia of any of the children as a solution. Although they spoke Japanese, she realised that they all felt they were Australian. In fact, the main obstacles to their advancement in Japan were first, emotional and secondly, their Caucasian appearance. Yone Ito was convinced that the education programme had been both essential and successful.

13

Italian welfare

It was during our United Nations work that Moira first became associated with the Italian community and the Consul-General of Italy in Melbourne.

In 1960, there was a downturn in the Australian economy and many immigrants—especially recently arrived Italians—were unable to find work. Dedicated members of the Italian community and friends cooperated in fund-raising efforts. Moira had a sympathetic concern for the plight of the families of unemployed Italians. In 1961, not long after our youngest son David was born, Moira was asked to become President of the Women's Division of the Italo-Australian Welfare Association and she accepted.

Two of the fund-raising events readily come to mind. The first was a wonderful concert given by the celebrated Italian tenor, Luigi Infantino, who gave his services gratis and performed to a packed house at the Palais Theatre, St Kilda.[128] The second was a party at our home.[129] It was a beautiful Sunday evening and an extra-large marquee was erected on the front lawn. I recall the entertainment by the choristers of the Australian Boys Choir who performed under the direction of Vincent Kelly and the songs beautifully sung by

Mrs Borsari. Amongst those in the large attendance were Arthur Calwell, the then Leader of the Federal Opposition, and the members of the Italian Davis Cup team who had been playing at Kooyong. Our son John sang in the choir, and our daughters Michele and Jacinta, who had attended a function at Loreto that evening, joined us later.

We attended many lovely Italian consular gatherings and came to know well both Dr Vittorio Strigari, the Consul-General, and Mr M Jacobucci, the Vice-Consul. In December 1962, Mr Jacobucci wrote to Moira:

> Dear Mrs. Dynon,
>
> Recalling our recent conversation, I have much pleasure in introducing to you Mr. Ignazio Fontana and his sons, Salvatore and Giovanni...I warmly recommend them to your kind attention towards having reviewed the situation concerning the issue of Entry Permits in respect of the members of the family still in Italy: Angela, Rosario and Agrippino.
>
> Thanking you for anything you may do for the Fontana family.[130]

Subsequently, Mr and Mrs Fontana and their two sons came to our home and we had a four-hour preliminary interview. It appeared that there had been a prolonged struggle over 11 years by the Fontana family who were seeking to bring the other members of their family to Australia. The Department of Immigration had repeatedly refused the applications for Angela, Rosario and Agrippino to come from Sicily to Australia. The Italian Consulate had tried three times to get the Immigration Department to change its decision. It was clear that what had been done so far, had been of little avail.

Two weeks before Mr Jacobucci wrote to Moira seeking her assistance, Mr Downer had said in the House of Representatives:

> The honorable member refers to one of the rather unhappy and unfortunate cases that come before me from time to time. I have informed one or two honorable members, by way of a confidential letter, of the reasons why Miss Angela Fontana was not allowed to come here. There are very substantial health reasons why she should not be allowed to come. These reasons apply also in the case of two of her brothers who are still in Italy. I would ask the honorable member not to press me to tell him and the House publicly what the reasons are, out of respect for the feelings of the young woman concerned and her family.[131]

This gave me the opportunity to call on the Minister to be more open on the issue and to re-investigate fully. I put it to the family that I was prepared to call a Press conference and put the facts openly, to see if we could obtain definite answers publicly. I had to be sure that the Fontana family did not object to the publicity necessarily involved. The family agreed.

At the Press conference,[132] I showed the medical reports[133] to the Press representatives. Dr GF Bruno of the Health Department of Catania had certified that Angela had curvature of the spine but was in 'perfect good health', 'lacking sickness of any kind, including either infective or contagious diseases'. He certified to Rosario's 'healthy and strong constitution', that Agrippino was physically fit, and that both were 'lacking physical deformities including diseases either infective or contagious'.

It is a matter of history now that Alexander Downer, the then Minister for Immigration, was prevailed upon to reverse all previous decisions, ministerial and departmental. In June 1963, he wrote to me:

> I have now had an opportunity to study carefully all of the relevant reports and have decided that Miss Angela Fontana and her two brothers, Rosario and Agrippino and their wives and children may come to Australia.[134]

After 12 years of battling and disappointments, the family separation was finally over. Of the three-hour plane delay at Essendon airport, Mr Fontana said, 'Three hours is nothing. I have been waiting a lifetime. Nothing can spoil my happiness today'. The report in *The Herald* captured the family's joy that day:

> When the plane taxied to a stop in front of the terminal at Essendon, Mr and Mrs Fontana stood waiting at the gate with their two daughters-in-law, Tina and Maria and Tina's two children, Ignazio (3) and Ross (15 months). Scores of passengers disembarked, but there was still no sign of Angela or Rosario. Mr and Mrs Fontana became more anxious as the minutes ticked past. Then Angela appeared, smiling and waving in the doorway of the plane, and Mrs Fontana made her 50-yard dash to the plane steps. Soon the whole family group was milling around the foot of the steps, hugging, kissing and crying. With Rosario and his wife Maria were their four children, Agrippino (9), Salvatore (5), Giovanni (3), and Ignazio (12 months).[135]

In the following years, I was to deal with quite a number of similar cases. These came to me as a matter of last resort when apparently no one else could help. I made representations to a number of different Ministers for Immigration and to the Secretary of the Immigration Department.

One aspect that made it particularly difficult for applicants was the Department's policy of not giving reasons when refusing applications. In October 1965, Mr Opperman, the Minister for Immigration, stated in Parliament:

> It is not a matter of Government policy. These decisions are made as a result of departmental consideration. It is not the practice to give reasons for rejection of applications in confidential letters to the applicants or in letters to members of Parliament...Because certain matters touching upon health, security and character, may, if disclosed openly, cause embarrassment to the applicants or to their relatives.[136]

In 1964, the Australian Government introduced compulsory National Service for 20-year-old males. Conscripts were selected by lottery, based on their date of birth. Harold Holt, who became Prime Minister when Menzies resigned in February 1966, decided to increase conscription for Vietnam and to include foreign nationals resident in Australia in the conscription ballot. This extension of conscription to foreign youth to serve in Vietnam ignored the views of Mr Holt's predecessor, RG Menzies[137] and also Mr William McMahon, who, when Minister for National Service, was reported as saying that under the rules of international law aliens are not and should not be liable to service in the armed forces of a country other than their own without the acquiescence of their government.[138] Mr EH Cox wrote in *The Herald*: 'By international tradition, one country does not conscript the nationals of another to its defence forces.'[139]

Moira, as President of Italo-Australian Welfare Association, Women's Division, together with James M Galbally, President of Italo-Australian Welfare Association, issued a joint statement voicing their protests against the Government's proposed policy.[140]

On 9 September 1967, at a function in the Royale Ballroom, Exhibition Building, decorations from the Republic of Italy were awarded to a number of Australians. Moira was included among those named but as she was in India at that time, the award was conferred on her some months later at a special function at the Italian Consulate in South Yarra. The decoration was the Cross of the Star of Italian Solidarity and the citation, in translation, was:

> CONSOLATO GENERALE D'ITALIA
>
> Conferment of the Decoration All'Ordine Della "Stella Della Solidarietà' Italiana"
>
> on Mrs. Moira Lenore Dynon née Shelton.
>
> Mrs. Moira Lenore Dynon in her capacity of President, from 1961, of the Ladies' Committee of the "Italo-Australian Welfare Association", always did all she could to organise functions making it possible to raise funds to be used for charitable purposes within our Community.
>
> On the occasion of the measures of the Australian Government on the obligation of military service for foreigners, in numerous declarations published in the Press, she opposed the project, thus supporting the action of the Italian Government.

For her meritorious services, the Cross of the "Stella della Solidarietà Italiana" has been conferred on her.

At the Royale Ballroom function, I was honoured with the award of Cavaliere Ordine al Merito della Repubblica Italiana (Knight of the Order of Merit of the Italian Republic) in recognition of my work in re-uniting families in Australia.

I prepared a few words for this occasion:

Italian Honour

Deeply moved by your Government's kindness. Truly, sir, I am quite overwhelmed by your Government's generosity in recognising in this way the little that I have been able to do to re-unite Italian families in Australia.

Naturally, as an Australian subject, I love my country; as a husband and father, I love my family. My conviction and the conviction of those associated with me in the Association for the Defence of the Family is that love of family transcends love of country and knows no national boundaries or barriers, and especially so should this be on the subject of immigration. The re-uniting of families takes pride of place; *compassion* must be a compelling influence on those who bear the responsible role of sitting in judgment. To me this is not merely a matter of emotion—it is a cold fact that must be faced.

One happy family will bring to our shores other happy families; our future as a nation may well depend on how good an account we can give of our stewardship in relation to our approach to immigration. If we open our hearts to welcome those who desire to migrate here to share in our good things of life and to work for them, and if we keep firm in our resolve to put the family first and make the family happy, and to treat associated migrant matters with respect for the dignity due to man, then I do believe that Australia will grow in strength and stature, in numbers and in the quality of its citizens.

I would like to assure you, sir, that I, as a private citizen of this country which I love so much, will continue to do whatever I can to assist migrants in problems concerning the re-uniting of their families. With God's will, I want to live to see the growth and development of Italian migration to Australia.

I well recall the occasion on board the ship when migrants were being specially welcomed. The Consul-General Dr Strigari, smiling broadly, introduced Moira and myself to the Minister for Immigration Mr Alexander Downer as 'his right and left hand'.

14

Catholic Women's League

During the last days of her life, Moira held in her hand a badge engraved with three words—Charity, Work, Loyalty. This was the badge of the Catholic Women's League (CWL).

I am not sure of the exact date Moira joined the Catholic Women's Social Guild.[141] Miss McBride often telephoned our home in the late 1950s requesting her to join the State Executive. I spoke with Miss McBride a number of times and endeavoured to delay the inevitable for Moira was so busy with the family, schools and her other interests. She always said that she preferred not to join an organisation if she felt unable to 'pull her weight'. Eventually, she succumbed to the invitations and commenced her association with the Guild.

At the time, Moira and I were unaware that my father's sister, Abigail, had been the inaugural President of the first Australian branch of the CWL.[142]

Moira regularly spoke out on the matter of justice for all children in education. She also took a prominent part in the Guild's campaigns, including the campaign to have railway stations manned at night. Moira attended a conference at

Unity Hall, Bourke Street, Melbourne and prepared a statement on behalf of the Guild, which was discussed in State Parliament.[143]

Moira's participation in such campaigns often involved her working alongside men and women in the unions and other groups who fought on the same issues. In doing this, she exposed herself to the criticism of some reactionary activists who considered any association with communists or with people working alongside communists, anathema. There were those in the community who saw 'RED' in everything with ease, and there were those who did not want to know or listen, as well as those who did not care.

As a Catholic and as a member of the Australian Labor Party, Moira would not have consciously appeared on a platform with an avowed communist. This was in accordance with what she understood to be the view of the Catholic Church and, as I understand it, of the Australian Labor Party.

In her public work performed on behalf of the CWL, Moira had a kind and wise adviser and confidant in Bishop Moran of the Archdiocese of Melbourne, who fully supported her good works.

Moira enlisted the support of the League in her efforts on behalf of the Australian-Japanese children in Japan. Mrs Gertrude Bray was on the Executive of the 1964 public appeal for these children. Moira also gained support in the League for her work for the needy in India. For many years the Guild had been already helping in certain areas in India.

Moira was frequently called upon to address CWL gatherings. In 1965, she prepared a paper on 'Friendship in the World'. The thoughts in this address and in addresses that Moira gave on other occasions were thoughts that she often wrote about, discussed, propagated, believed in and put into practice. She wrote:

> If we are sincere in our desire to promote friendship and understanding in the world, let the seeing see, the hearing hear and those who are able, act. Let it be known that we, the people of Australia, join with those who seek to advance their human dignity and to claim their legitimate rights as human beings.
>
> And I think that it is particularly appropriate that we, the women of Australia, should heed the muffled calls of the poor, the sick, the hungry and the destitute. Let us work towards our objective step by step and side by side with all those of goodwill who strive to make a better and a peaceful world. And let us be inspired by the words of the late President John F. Kennedy:
>
>> The war against hunger is truly mankind's war of liberation. There is no battle on earth or in space more important for peace and progress cannot be maintained in a world half fed and half hungry...If we can all persevere, if we can in every land...look beyond our own shores and ambitions, then surely the age will dawn in which the strong are just and the weak secure and the peace preserved.
>
> Friendship in the world can be promoted by co-operation and understanding. Let us do all in our power to demonstrate the supreme value of Christian love, justice, truth and peace.[144]

'Cooperation' was a recurring theme:

> Speaking in the General Assembly of the United Nations on 10th November, 1961, the late Prime

Minister of India, Jawaharlal Nehru, after having reviewed the urgent problems facing the world, said:

> 'I cannot suggest any rapid or magic ways of dealing with the problems of the world. But I find that perhaps the worst difficulty we have to face is to fight something you cannot grip: an atmosphere, the imponderables of life, how people suddenly are filled with fear, passion and hatred. How can we deal with them?... The essential thing about this world is co-operation, and even today, between countries which are opposed to each other in the political and other fields, there is a vast amount of co-operation...A great deal is said about every point of conflict, perhaps it would be a truer picture if the co-operative elements in the world today were put forward and we were made to think that the world depends on co-operation and not on conflict.'

Mr. Nehru then went on to suggest that the General Assembly resolve to call upon all countries of the world to devote a year to the furtherance of

> 'co-operative activities in any field—political, cultural and whatever fields there may be, and there are thousands of fields. That perhaps would direct some of our energy and some of our thinking to this idea of co-operation, which would create an atmosphere for solving the problems more easily. That by itself will not solve any problems, but it will lessen this destruction and conflict which now afflict the world.'[145]

Moira was on the Executive Committee of the CWL for several years and was General Vice-President in 1967 and 1968. She often told me how pleasant and rewarding it was to be working with such a dedicated Executive.

In April 1968, Moira issued the League's Statement on Abortion.[146] I personally remember the long hours she spent preparing that statement in draft, reading and studying the issue, and the discussions with Dr John Billings, Dr Evelyn Billings, Davern Wright, Dr Haydon and others. I believe that in her mind, she was uncertain as to when the human embryo became a person with a soul, but with the Executive she was emphatic that if there was any doubt, due respect must be given to the embryo at all stages.

Moira was totally dedicated to the work of the CWL and gave talks and addresses to various organisations and groups into the early 1970s. It was through the CWL that Moira was asked to address a gathering on Women's World Day of Prayer at Corowa, New South Wales. The title of her talk was 'Be of Good Courage'.

> What do we mean when we say "Be of Good Courage"? The Oxford Dictionary defines courage as "that quality of mind which shows itself in facing danger without fear or shrinking". And from where do we draw the inner strength to be of good courage? We draw it from love. Love is the most potent factor in the world—love of God and love of our neighbour. As the illustrious Indian Rabindranath Tagore wrote:
>
> "This is my prayer to Thee, My Lord,
> strike, strike at the root of penury in my heart.
> Give me the strength lightly to bear my joys and sorrows.

Give me the strength to make my love fruitful in service.

Give me the strength never to disown the poor or bend my knees before insolent might.

Give me the strength to raise my mind high above daily trifles.

And give me the strength to surrender my strength to Thy will with love."

(GITANJALI)[147]

AID FOR INDIA

15

Milk for India

Over the years, Moira had been concerned about the hardships endured by the people of India and particularly by the children, the elderly and the disadvantaged. India suffered from time to time, indeed in every year, some form of disaster—fire, flood, famine, drought or cyclone. The bitter existence for so many was then made more bitter.

In our United Nations work, we learned more about other countries, including India. Moira saw that in Australia, individuals and voluntary organisations did what they could in their own way, and the Government sometimes helped. However, the assistance given seemed so little whereas the needs were so great.

Early in November 1964, items appeared in the Australian Press drawing attention to the serious famine in India. One such item reported that the 17 million people of Kerala State had no rice:

HUNGER RACKS INDIA

Children faint in school from lack of food

NEW DELHI, Sun.—Children so hungry that they can't go to school, others who faint at their desks from lack of food...ration shops that haven't any rations...

> The Indian Government is making frantic efforts to divert 63,000 tons of rice...to feed Kerala's hungry millions...The sober and usually reliable Times of India said on Saturday: "Distress reports from all over riceless Kerala indicate that the people are getting panicky and their patience is at breaking point. Unless immediate food supplies are rushed the situation will get out of control."[148]

Previously, such information had not been given wide publicity in the Press here, but this time there was a note of special urgency. The Editor of *The Herald* took up the subject:

> Reports today of rioting and looting of food stores in southern India are only the violent fringe of a great tragedy. Among the many millions facing starvation in India, most are suffering passively. But their acceptance of famine and disaster as part of their fate must not stop the outside world from caring.[149]

The pressing needs in India appeared to be increasing and Moira felt a compulsion to do what she could, in her own way, to bring immediate aid to those, particularly the disadvantaged, who needed help at once, even though these very people were not calling out directly to us for help.

I recall Moira in her concern speaking to Denis Warner at a function at the Southern Cross Hotel. It was in November 1964 and the function was, I believe, in connection with the 'Miss Pacific' event. She told Denis what she thought about the situation in India and of the failure of the Australian Government to comprehend the immensity of the problem and the urgency of the need. Denis told her that he thought she was the person to push forward the concept of Aid for India. I remember, after this discussion with Denis, Moira asking me if I felt she would be able to do what was necessary. I told her that I had no doubts but that her involvement would or could be an immense commitment. I told her that if she did decide to take up this cause on behalf of the people of India, I would help her all I could.

It indeed proved to be a lifetime commitment. That night at the same function, Moira mentioned her concern to Gough Whitlam, who was one of the guests, and received his sympathetic support.

In July 1977, I wrote to Denis Warner asking him if he recalled that conversation with Moira and he replied:

> Yes, indeed, I remember my discussion with her about Aid to India…the meeting did take place at the Southern Cross. She talked at length about the situation in India and the difficulty of doing anything meaningful within the framework of government aid. I thought she was the ideal person to take on the job and to start things moving. She had the interest and genuine concern and also the strength of character, the dynamism, to get things moving. I don't recall whether she had given any thought to taking such a personal role before we spoke. But I do remember very vividly her excitement—and her determination—at the prospect of doing something really worthwhile.
>
> So far as I can remember this was the only time that we sat down and talked about what she <u>might</u> do, because the next time we met—or spoke on the phone—she had taken things in hand and things were moving.[150]

Moira lost no time putting into action her Aid to India. At short notice, she called a meeting for 23 November 1964 at the Australian-American Centre, 120 Exhibition Street, Melbourne. Its purpose was to focus the attention of the Commonwealth Government and the public on the need for immediate and long-term aid to India. Some 200 people attended, including representatives from 43 organisations who were interested in doing something of a practical nature to help. Many distinguished citizens addressed the meeting.[151] Moira was appointed Chairman and opened a public appeal calling for gifts of dried milk to be left at our home for eventual shipment to India. The meeting recommended that the Commonwealth Government be requested to provide free air transport to India for these donations. It also recommended that the Commonwealth Government be requested to make immediate and further gifts of food to the Indian people and to allow tax deductions on donations for immediate and long-term aid to India.

Moira conveyed the recommendations of the meeting to the Prime Minister, Robert Menzies and sought the Government's support.[152] Moira then wrote to the High Commissioner for India in Canberra, Mr BK Massand, with news of the appeal:

> The purpose of the meeting was to focus the attention of our Government and of the Australian people on the reported food shortages in certain areas in India... Admiration and respect for the manner in which India is developing her economy in a free and democratic way was strongly expressed.
>
> It is our wish that the Australian people will be able to send a useful gift of food to the Indian Government or

to an organisation nominated by your Government... We desire such a gift to be made in the spirit of friendship and to bring closer together the Indian and Australian people.[153]

Almost immediately, a large amount of tinned milk arrived at the family home in Malvern. Adults, children, even pensioners, came bearing tins of milk. These were stacked in the sunroom which Moira had by then set aside for the tins. The cartons were stacked inside the entrance in the hall. Cartons and tins were left on the front porch when no one was home.

For Moira, there was no turning back. She wanted to get the milk to India speedily where it was needed urgently and was seeking cooperation from all parties.

From the outset, instantaneous goodwill, understanding and cooperation was established between Moira and the Indian representatives in Canberra and the Prime Minister of India. The Indian High Commissioner was very grateful for Moira's efforts to promote and strengthen friendship between the peoples of Australia and India: 'It is more important today than ever before that our two countries should come closer to each other on the basis of understanding. This is a common hope which we equally share.'[154]

A week before Christmas, *The Sun* newspaper published a photo of Moira with our five children in the sunroom surrounded by tins of milk. The headline was: A family with 2600 presents for India. The subheading was: No reply yet from P.M.[155]

Moira arranged for the first consignment of 5,000 lbs net weight of tinned milk to be shipped from Melbourne on board the P&O Orsova on 1 January 1965, some five weeks after the initial meeting. The consignment was addressed to the Secretary, Department of Food and Agriculture, New Delhi. P&O Lines of Australia Pty Ltd offered generous charity rates, which were met by private sponsors. Young's Travel Agency cooperated in this effort and gave their services free of charge.

Moira sent a telegram to Lal Bahadur Shastri, the Prime Minister of India:

> This Christmas on behalf of people in Victoria Australia who have donated tinned milk to my Aid for India Campaign I wish to express goodwill and friendship to India and to the Indian people STOP I have received five thousand pounds net weight tinned milk for the poor STOP I wish to advise you and through you the people of India that arrangements have been made to transport the milk by P&O Orsova leaving Melbourne first January STOP Milk is expressly donated to Indian Government for distribution
>
> Moira Dynon Chairman Aid for India Special Meeting[156]

The Indian Prime Minister was deeply grateful:

> Prime Minister Lal Bahadur Shastri deeply grateful to you and people of Victoria for despatch of five thousand pounds tinned milk for the needy people in India STOP Prime Minister sends New Years greetings to all of you STOP Kindly send Bill of Lading STOP...
>
> Joint Secretary to the Prime Minister India Foreign[157]

Lal Bahadur Shastri had been elected Prime Minister of India in June 1964 following the death of Jawaharlal Nehru. Frank Moraes, in *Nehru – Sunlight and Shadow*, noted that Lal Bahadur assumed office at a time when the food grain crops were being affected by bad seasons for the third year in succession. Moraes described him as a devout Hindu: 'Shastri shares some of the Mahatma's traits, notably his pragmatism, his humanity and gentleness and his sense of service.'[158]

When Lal Bahadur responded with New Year greetings to the Campaign's Christmas gift of tinned milk, one sensed that he understood well the depth of feeling and sincerity inherent in this gift, small as it was.

On the morning of 30 December, as the first consignment of tinned milk was being loaded onto a truck at our home in Malvern to be conveyed to the P&O *Orsova*, a telegram from Prime Minister Menzies was delivered at our front door addressed to Moira:

> Thank you for your telegram 22nd December concerning Milk for India STOP Government has considered request for airlift of gifts but felt it was not justified STOP However £1250 has been allocated to help meet shipping costs STOP Full reply to your letters of 23rd November and 11th December follows...R.G. Menzies[159]

Moira replied immediately:

> Thank you for your telegram 30th December concerning Milk for India STOP Overjoyed and grateful for Government decision to allocate £1250 to help meet shipping costs of gifts for needy people in India... Moira Dynon[160]

The advice from the Prime Minister of the allocation towards shipping costs showed at last that the Australian Government acknowledged that non-governmental aid was needed by India and was encouraged by the Australian Government. This was a step forward, but it did not go far enough. Moira was concerned that the Government did not fully appreciate the urgency of the need in India. The subsequent letter from Prime Minister Menzies, whilst confirming the grant 'to help meet the shipping costs of processed milk sent to approved organisations in India', advised that tax deductions would not be extended to gifts that provide relief for persons outside Australia. He also wrote:

> We have no reason to believe that the immediate food situation in India warrants special emergency action on the Government's part, including an airlift of food to that country. Certainly no such action has been sought by the Indian Government.[161]

Moira replied:

> Dear Sir Robert,
>
> ...May I again draw your attention to the fact that India's chronic food shortage has been worsened by floods and many millions of Indian people are hungry. Many poor people in India are dying the slow agonising death of starvation. Internationally, this is a well known fact. Further, I would point out that many Australians share my conviction that India should neither be expected nor allowed to ask for a gift of food, which should have been offered months ago early in the crisis period. A gift of food to the people of India would be a friendly gesture and a practical expression of understanding, which could only strengthen and promote the bonds of friendship and good relations between our two peoples.
>
> May I thank you for the assistance which the Government has agreed to give to our efforts to send gifts of tinned powdered milk to needy people in

India…The allocation of £1,250 to help meet shipping costs…is most welcome.[162]

Once the Menzies policy regarding transport costs was announced, the response of the people grew. The milk aid, first provided by the people of Victoria and soon after in ever-increasing numbers throughout Australia, was being moved on to India with the blessing of our Prime Minister, the Department of External Affairs, the Prime Minister of India, the High Commissioner for Australia in Delhi and the High Commissioner for India in Canberra. Our Prime Minister provided the funds to cover transport of the milk by ships to India, the use of the Department of Supply trucks, storage, packing and administrative facilities in Australia and insurance. The Indian Government arranged for distribution of the milk to the people in need in India, free of all charges. This made it an all-round cooperative gift.

This position had been achieved through the initiative and perseverance of Moira and by the voluntary labours of herself and of those who were helping her, and that included her family.

I well recall, early in 1965, the visit to Australia by The Hon. C Subramaniam, Indian Minister of Food and Agriculture. Moira had a long discussion with him at the Windsor Hotel in Melbourne. On that occasion—and on many other occasions—Moira made doubly sure that powdered and processed milk was the most valuable, useful and appropriate gift for the citizen campaign. She was advised that gifts of whole-milk powder and skimmed-milk powder would be of great help.

In July 1965, a telegram arrived from the Office of the Prime Minister of India:

Mrs Moira Dynon,

> The Prime Minister has greatly appreciated the donations of processed milk that are so kindly being sent by Aid for India Campaign STOP He has desired me to convey to you and through you to the donors his grateful thanks for this generous help STOP
>
> Joint Secretary to the Prime Minister Foreign[163]

Many more consignments of processed milk, ever-increasing in quantity, were shipped to India by the Campaign. Mr Smithies of the External Affairs Department telephoned Moira one day to advise her that the Indian Government had expressed the wish for an official handing-over ceremony in India of one of the consignments. Accepting an offer to send a message for the occasion, Moira wrote:

> On behalf of the Australian citizens and children who have donated this gift of processed milk I wish to convey their message of friendship to India and the Indian people. The processed milk is expressly donated to the Government of India. It is the wish of the donors that this milk be distributed to those most in need. This gift is offered in the spirit of friendship and co-operation and it is our desire to strengthen and promote understanding between the Indian and the Australian peoples.

Mr Mahavir Tyagi, Minister for Rehabilitation, New Delhi, wrote to Moira after the handing-over ceremony:

> I was extremely gratified to learn that the Aid for India Campaign in Australia under your Chairmanship has been collecting donations of milk and milk powder...for distribution among the people of India, who might be in need of it.

The Government of India felt that these gift consignments could be made use of by my Ministry, which has to look after a very large number of migrants (about 788,000) who have been coming over from East Pakistan to this country in the hope of finding refuge. These migrants have had to leave their homes after immense sufferings. The stresses and strains to which they have been subjected have left their mark on them and many of them have been suffering from severe malnutrition. The Government of India have spared no effort or resources to give them adequate relief and rehabilitation.

Nearly a hundred camps were set up for them and at present we have about 53,000 families comprising about 223,000 persons in these camps. This naturally imposes a heavy burden on us. We have to arrange for their food, clothing and shelter, provide them with facilities for education and medical care and at the same time we have to settle them on land or in other vocations. While engaged in this stupendous task of giving relief to the people rendered homeless by the circumstances beyond their control, I am heartened to learn of the goodwill and sympathy which the people of Australia have for the people of India.

You will be glad to know that we held a small function on the 26th August 1965 at which your High Commissioner in India, His Excellency Sir Arthur Tange presented me with a token consignment of the milk powder which had been sent by the Aid For India Campaign. Sir Arthur read the message that you had so kindly sent for this occasion.

As I told His Excellency, we are extremely gratified to receive your message and to note that this gift is offered in a spirit of friendship and cooperation and that it is your desire to strengthen and promote understanding between the peoples of our two countries. The gesture is all the more welcome, as it has been made in a free and informal manner. We hold your assistance in high regard, particularly as it has been proffered directly and not on a Government to Government basis.

I also explained to His Excellency at the function that during my visits to the camps, I was struck by the change in the health of the migrants, who have been given the milk powder. We have taken care to ensure that this milk and milk powder is given mainly to patients in hospitals and to others suffering from severe malnutrition. The change among the women and children, who were suffering from rickets, anaemia, debility and other ailments was remarkable…I can assure you that these gifts would be put to the best use possible. May I express my thanks to you and to the donors once again for this friendly gesture. We appreciate it very much.[164]

As the Milk for India Campaign gathered momentum, Moira's involvement increased but still she found time for her other interests. I interpolate here 'Profile by Florence Hagelthorn',[165] which appeared in *The Advocate*, to make the point that Moira had been actively engaged in other pursuits prior to and during her involvement in Aid for India.

"Friendship in the World"

I NEVER cease to marvel at the effortless grace and efficiency of Mrs. Moira Dynon. I first met her a few years ago when I conducted a mail-order service for a Catholic bookshop, and she used to come in with lists of alumnae whom she considered should be kept *au fait* with good literature. She looked little more than a school girl then, although she was the mother of a young family, and yesterday, some years and one or two children later, she didn't look more than a couple of months older.

"The challenge of the century," she said, "is for Australian people to realize that our neighbour extends beyond Darwin, to Japan, South-East Asia and India." Particularly India. Ever since she went on a world tour as a bride and saw the stark and terrible poverty in India, Moira Dynon has felt deep compassion for the under-privileged people of the rapidly developing nation where a third of the world's poorest people are living. She never forgets that, within one day's flight from Australia, sixteen hundred million people go to sleep every night sick and hungry, and that nearly half the children born in India die before they reach the age of five, not from neglect, but from malnutrition.

Last November Moira Dynon made up her mind that she would try to do something to bring immediate help to the hungry ones. For some time she had helped in every possible way the efforts of Freedom from Hunger, and all the good work done by the Australian-Asian Association, of which she was an executive member, but she felt the need was for something more definite and practical. So she called a meeting of two hundred people, representing forty-three organizations, the Churches, the medical profession, the University, and both State and Federal Parliament. No one wanted to take the chair, so she took it herself. (She is an excellent platform speaker; I sometimes think she is a potential parliamentarian in the making.)

The meeting soon brought results, and it is still bringing them. The resolution that Federal Parliament be asked to make a gift of food to India sent 150,000 tons of wheat, valued at nearly £4,000,000 to Bombay last February. Another resolution called for the opening of an appeal for tinned processed milk, and the response from every Australian State, particularly Victoria, has been magnificent. No less than twenty-two tons of processed milk have been sent to India since last December, and the Federal Government, in response to Mrs. Dynon's urging, has made £1,250 available for the cost of transport. The State Government, by courtesy of Mr. Bolte, is providing free rail transport from anywhere in Victoria for processed milk consigned to Mrs. Dynon, c/o Caulfield railway station.

The co-operation of everyone, little people in every walk of life, children, dairying associations, milk processing companies, local carriers, shipping companies, has been remarkable. Only that morning, Mrs. Dynon told me, she had received two cases of milk from Sacre Coeur Convent, another from Mandeville Hall, and yet another consignment from Geelong. It has been a revelation of the fundamental goodness of human nature, she said, the way people of all creeds and classes, all political parties and none at all, have united to help the under-privileged and hungry. The gratitude of the Indian people was evident in the letters she has received and from two cables sent by the Prime Minister, Lal Bahadur Shastri.

My friend and predecessor, "Veronica", has recounted the story of Mrs. Dynon's life, so I will not go back over the past, save to say that she was educated at the O'Neill Presentation Convent and Mandeville Hall. Before she married Mr. John F. Dynon, old Xaverian and Oxford graduate in law, she took her Bachelor of Science at Melbourne University and worked on scientific research in the Air Force during the war, and afterwards at the C.S.L. and the C.S.I.R.O.

She will tell you now that her primary interests are her husband and her children, "in that order", and you can quite believe this when you see the happy faces of the five children and sense the serene, homely atmosphere of the lovely house in Malvern in which they live. I gathered she has been Mr. Dynon's right hand in the Association for the Defence of the Family, of which he is president.

Her other activities include the Italo-Australian Welfare Association, which has done so much to help in the assimilation of Italians. In this field she has also assisted many Malaysian students. Another interest has been the A.J. Ferguson Memorial Appeal for Japanese Waifs. She is currently a trustee of the funds which are being used specifically for the maintenance and education of these children. Her commitments nearer home include the Loreto Federation of Australia, and the Kostka Hall Parents' Association. (Two of her sons go there, and the two girls go to Mandeville Hall).

Besides all this there is her work for the C.W.S.G., which she represented at the International Co-operation Year Conference in Canberra last May. She is preparing to attend the biennial conference of the Australian Council of Catholic Women, being held in Hobart from 22 to 29 August. At this she will report on the Canberra visit, and she has also written a very fine paper which will be read on behalf of the Guild by the Victorian State President, Mrs. G. Bray. Appropriately, it is entitled "Friendship in the World." [166]

I do not propose to traverse the details of the ensuing consignments of milk shipped to India by the Aid for India Campaign. The Campaign's milk aid had been increasing through the great generosity and concern of the Australian community. The milk was most welcome in India; it was preserving life, it was accepted with gratitude, and was distributed to those most in need, including refugees, without regard to race caste or creed. And it was producing goodwill.

16

Feeling sorry won't help—milk will

The response from the Australian people was overwhelming. I have selected a handful from literally thousands of donor letters that Moira had kept and filed.

> 'In response to your appeal for Milk for India we will be sending 4 cartons of powdered milk via rail today. This contribution is small, I know, but there again, every little bit helps. The children have gained much during this appeal as they are now more aware of others' needs.'

> 'We have enclosed a postal note for 7 shillings—the Christmas pudding money—for the Food for India appeal and hope it will buy some little child some tins of milk.'

> 'I heard you discuss your Milk for India work on 3AW and was greatly impressed. Until hearing of your campaign I considered the task of easing world hunger beyond the scope of ordinary citizens.'

'Enclosed is a cheque for $20 from this Union as a donation towards the Milk for India appeal.'

'I am enclosing $2 being my donation for March and April. I am always thrilled to see month by month the increase in the tonnage of powdered milk being forwarded, at the same time, of course realizing that it is very little in the light of the tremendous need of the babies there. God bless your work and all within it.'

'Enclosed is a cheque for $36 for your Milk for India appeal, proceeds from the morning coffee party held at my home.'

'My wife & I appreciated your broadcast address on India at P.S.A yesterday. After your fine talk, we would like to send the enclosed $10 extra contribution to the relief of hunger in India.'

'Please find enclosed a cheque for $10 for the Milk for India Campaign. We, several Melbourne University students, hope that we will be able to submit similar contributions throughout the year. Wishing you every success.'

'As a result of your invitation to attend the public meeting re Food for India, approx. 60 of our senior girls were present and we made a special effort for this cause. By means of lunchtime talent quests and other fund raising the girls collected $299.37.'

'I am enclosing a cheque for $64 collected from a mixed group in the Taxation Department on behalf of your Aid for India Campaign. Hoping your wonderful work will meet with every success.'

> 'On behalf of our Brownie Guides I have forwarded per rail a carton of tinned milk for the Milk for India appeal. The girls who collected the milk (in exchange for small jobs) have signed their names.'

This donation, as with all donations, was receipted with thanks:

> Dear Girls, On behalf of the Committee for Milk for India, I would like to thank you for the wonderful gift of milk that you collected for the poor and needy children of India. We were very thrilled to receive your collection and to learn that you worked for these tins of milk, which makes your effort a very special one to us. I was particularly thrilled to know that Brownies had worked so hard for others, as I was a Brownie when I was a little girl. The children in India who will drink this milk that you have sent will be most grateful to you all. Yours sincerely Mrs Leonore Ryan Hon. Secretary

Dr Val Noone, who was assistant priest at Sacred Heart parish, St Albans from 1965 to early 1968, put a lot of energy into Milk for India with Moira. He recalled the enthusiastic response of the local community following the publication of his article, 'What can we do?' in the parish magazine in February 1966:

> The St Albans branch of Milk For India was amazing, post-war European refugees, Mrs Bankowski from Poland being a good example, Councillor Eric Alan put in a lot of effort, Mayor of Keilor Cr Rex Webb took the lead, Catholic, Anglican and Methodist parishes and the local paper, the council, as well as youth groups, all backed it actively.[167]

Mentone was another municipality that galvanised local support for Milk for India. Mrs Pat Mutimer, a member of the Milk for India Victorian Committee, was Chairman of the Mentone Milk for India Drive, which in 1966 collected over 10 tons of processed milk. This was strongly supported by all sections of the local community.

Milk for India was organised on an Australia-wide basis with committees operating in six states. Moira was heartened by the warmth and generosity of the Australian people:

> Recently a pensioner walked 8 miles to my home to deliver 3 tins of milk, the 3rd being possible because he walked and did not have to pay for transport…My warmest thanks go to the people of Australia who have responded so warmly and so generously to this call for help for the immediate needs of the people of India. Every person who contributes a tin of powdered milk for a needy family in India through this Appeal, can be assured that the contribution will enter India duty-free and that it will be transported by the Indian Government to where it is most urgently needed and distributed free to the needy. A donation of $5.50 will buy a 56 lb bag of skimmed milk powder which will provide a pint of milk for 400 hungry Indian children.[168]

17

Reconsidering the policy of Prime Minister Menzies

I come now to the events which took place and the decisions taken by the Australian Government, which reversed the initial Menzies policy. The facilities offered by Sir Robert Menzies and provided through the Department of Supply were to be withdrawn from the Campaign and no more monies would be provided to ship the milk to India.

Milk for India appeals were underway. The Australian people were responding warmly and generously. Milk donations were arriving daily. To now place the burden on the Campaign, which was wholly voluntary, of raising the money directly from the Australian people to pay the freight costs from Australia to India of large quantities of processed milk, was a blow that normally would have crippled the operation of any entirely voluntary organisation. The reversal of Government policies, at a time when the Campaign was in full flight, imposed a great strain on Moira and her stalwart helpers.

Maybe the Government justified its change of policies on the ground that the benefits gained for Australia were not worth the dollars the Government spent on shipping costs and in departmental expenditures; or perhaps that there was allegedly no need for this kind of aid for the people in India. The fact remains that, at the very time when the Campaign was proving to be a magnificent aid programme producing magnificent results measured in humanitarian and goodwill terms, as well as life-sustaining, the Australian Government 'pulled the plug'.

Moira was now feeling the pressures involved in the extent of her commitment, and the commitment was increasing day by day. It so often seemed to Moira that Australia was officially drawing away from developing a worthwhile understanding with India, and that the attitude of the United States towards India was contributing to Australia's lack of warmth, officially. It was as if the United States did not wish Australia to move too close to India and our Departmental officers were thus guided. USA regarded India as too close to the USSR for comfort.*

Despite messages of praise and assurances as to the importance of the Campaign's work for the needy in India, restrictions were imposed and lengthy delays in Governmental and/or Departmental decisions nearly crippled the Campaign's efforts. The necessity of having to fight incessantly to retain

---

* Dr Val Noone, who worked closely with Moira on Milk for India and with John in the anti-conscription movement, commented: 'Moira and John's work for better relations between Australia and India brought them into conflict with the Liberal Country Party government which, in line with its slavish support for American foreign policy, criticised India's non-alignment in the Cold War and gave priority to cooperating with the American war in Vietnam.'[169]

assistance from the Australian Government to defray shipping costs added to the already heavy administrative demands. This cast an increasing burden on the voluntary campaign organisers, especially Moira, who bore the brunt of the responsibility.

Correspondence identifies a clear beginning of the restrictions imposed on the Campaign. On 7 June 1965, Mr Smithies, for the Secretary, Department of External Affairs, wrote to Moira, summoning her to Canberra to 'discuss some of the problems that have arisen in the administration of the Government grant'. The Department's 'main concern was to minimise some of the less desirable side-effects of the granting of government assistance', in particular: 'if further publicity is given to the Government grant, more shipping companies may withdraw concessions,' 'the difficulty the small staff of the Procurement Directorate is experiencing' and 'the Department's duty...to assure itself that the grant cannot...lead to a charge of "favouritism" to members of any particular faith'.[170]

Five weeks later, Mr LJ Arnott, Assistant Secretary, Department of External Affairs, informed Moira that the Department had 're-considered its policy':

> I am directed to inform you that in the new financial year this Department has re-considered its policy on this matter and the following rules now apply:
>
> For the present, the Government will consider freight assistance on gifts of food to India only if: —
>
> (a) they are consigned to the Government of India for distribution; and
>
> (b) donors have applied for freight concessions from shipping companies.

> ...You will appreciate that it is necessary to apply these rules...from now on, because of the alleviated famine conditions in India and the small amount of funds we have left for this kind of relief of the Indian people.[171]

On receipt of Mr Arnott's letter, Moira in her concern wrote to Arthur Calwell, Leader of the Opposition:

> In a letter which I received today from the Department of External Affairs...it would appear that the Department has "re-considered its policy" and changed its attitude on matters relating to the Commonwealth subsidy for shipping of processed milk to India. The present rules are quite different to what I was led to believe they were likely to be during my conversations with Department representatives...The whole position would now appear to be quite different from the Prime Minister's undertaking of 29th December.
>
> I am taking the matter up with the Department in the hope that the position will be rectified without it being necessary for me to again approach the Prime Minister. I would like to feel that I could again call on you for help should this be necessary.
>
> The whole tenor of this letter received today is disturbing and unfortunately worded to say the least.[172]

Moira replied to Mr Arnott:

> As no doubt you are aware, it was the Prime Minister, Sir Robert Menzies, who advised me by telegram and also in his letter to me of 29th December 1964, of the Government's decision to make available £1,250 for shipping costs of processed milk sent to approved organizations in India...When you state that "this

Department has re-considered its policy on this matter", am I to understand that your Department has altered the undertaking given by the Prime Minister, or that the Prime Minister has changed his mind?[173]

In her letter to Mr Arnott, Moira pointed out that most of the gift consignments were already being sent to the Indian Government for distribution but that she had received a number of urgent requests for milk from charitable institutions, orphanages and hospitals. Moira also considered that the Department's new condition placed the donors in the position of seeking freight concessions from shipping companies on behalf of the Commonwealth Government, which she regarded as 'improper'. And, not for the first time, Moira needed to point out that any suggestion of 'alleviated famine conditions in India' was at variance with the reality. She also wrote:

> You refer to "the small amount of funds we have left for this kind of relief for the Indian people". You do not indicate whether or not the greater part of the allocation of £1,250 for the freight costs has, in fact, been spent. If so, I would appreciate your advice accordingly so that a submission to the Prime Minister for a further allocation can be made without delay.[174]

If the new policy of the Department of External Affairs was designed to avoid a bottleneck hold-up in the working of the Campaign, it certainly failed.

The Campaign did appreciate that in July 1965 the Menzies Government, without receiving any application or request, made another allocation of funds similar to the initial allocation. But four months later, the Department of External Affairs warned Moira:

> At this stage I feel that I should remind you that funds to meet the shipping costs of processed milk gifts for India this financial year are limited to £1,200. £625 has been spent to date and we can hold out no prospect of additional funds being made available by the Treasury if and when the allocation is exhausted, nor can we anticipate a similar appropriation for the financial year 1966–67. [175]

Meanwhile, the food situation in India was dire. In December 1965, Moira sent a telegram to Prime Minister Menzies:

> As our democratic leader I implore you to give a lead to the world—particularly to the food producing nations—to grant immediate food aid to the people of India now suffering from the great scourge of famine because of drought and failure of crops STOP Even if such aid calls for denial of food to our usual market purchasers the present crisis on humanitarian grounds alone—apart from friendship and ties of Commonwealth—demands bold and imaginative measures STOP India must not be allowed to starve STOP Our national conscience demands immediate and substantial assistance STOP
>
> Respectfully and sincerely Moira Dynon [176]

A week later, Moira sent another telegram to the Prime Minister:

> With regard to grain sales to India the Australian Government has remained silent and apparently inactive since the drought and crop failures in India STOP Grave concern is now being expressed in view of the BBC announcement Saturday disclosing proposed grain aid by Australian Government ostensibly

on humanitarian grounds to certain southern African countries STOP This aid is now proposed whilst the Australian Government has apparently done nothing, since the present grave famine in India, towards satisfying the immediate food needs of the people of democratic India STOP

It is submitted that whilst the proposed aid to southern African States may be welcomed by these States and commendable on humanitarian grounds, the timing of this aid could be interpreted in Asia and in Africa as a move by white Commonwealth countries to stave off criticism of certain British policies at the forthcoming conference at Lagos STOP

When it is remembered that the President of the United States of America in December, 1965, set the stage for one of the largest famine relief programs in history, by calling on all grain producing nations including Australia to make available supplies of grain on humanitarian terms to India, the now proposed Australian Government priority aid to South African States could fairly appear to the USA as a rebuff, and to India, an unfriendly act by an unsympathetic and disinterested Commonwealth Member Government

Sincerely, Moira Dynon[177]

Prime Minister Menzies replied:

Reference to your telegrams on matter of assistance to India STOP As regards food sales the Australian Wheat Board has been selling wheat to India on generous credit terms and doubtless would be prepared to continue doing so STOP

> As regards aid the Government is deeply concerned over the food situation in India and is examining what forms of assistance Australia might be able to give STOP
>
> As regards drought relief for Southern Africa including Rhodesia Mr Wilson has made a proposal to which the Commonwealth Government is sympathetic STOP The extent of any Australian assistance to that area would depend however on an assessment of the areas requirements and Australia's ability to assist in the light of available supplies and our other commitments. R.G. Menzies[178]

Moira responded:

> Thank you for your advice that the Australian Government is deeply concerned over the food situation in India STOP It is noted that no Australian Government decision in principle to supply Australian grain to India on humanitarian terms has yet been made STOP
>
> In the context of India's foreign exchange position and bearing in mind the functions of the Australian Wheat Board your reference to commercial arrangements concerning any sales entered into between India and the Board evades our plea STOP
>
> You imply doubt with regard to the availability of supplies STOP This is not surprising in view of this years reduced Australian wheat yield and recently announced sales of Australian new crop wheat to Communist China despite Mr. McEwan's statement in Parliament on 3 December that Communist countries are not our regular customers STOP

> Internationally and at home the inference appears to be that Australia prefers to sell wheat to Communist China whilst ignoring democratic India's emergency needs and also ignoring President Johnson's clarion call to all grain producing nations including Australia to make grain available to India on humanitarian terms STOP
>
> Sincerely Moira Dynon Chairman Aid for India Campaign[179]

Moira also sent a telegram to Mr Averell Harriman, US President's Envoy to Australia:

> On behalf of Aid for India Campaign I request you to convey to your President our great appreciation for the continuing efforts by United States of America to assist the people of India with their immediate food needs—especially resulting from the present drought and crop failures STOP There is profound goodwill amongst the Australian people for the people of democratic and freedom loving India STOP We earnestly trust that the warmth of feeling at present being expressed by the people of Australia for the people of India will soon be reflected in Australian Government action on a massive scale in line with your President's recent call to all grain producing nations to make supplies of grain available to India on generous terms STOP Sincerely Moira Dynon[180]

Averell Harriman replied:

> I am gratified to learn that the people of Australia share the deep concern of the American people and Government over the serious food shortage in India STOP As you know we have already taken emergency

action to help alleviate the situation with more to follow STOP I will be happy to convey your message to the President STOP

With all best wishes Averell Harriman[181]

It was not long before there was a change of leadership in Australia. Prime Minister Robert Menzies retired from office in January 1966 and was succeeded by Harold Holt. Although the Australian Government had paid the freight costs on all of the Campaign's milk consignments to date, the decision to do so for each new consignment was becoming increasingly protracted. In February 1966, the Department of External Affairs informed Moira that pending a decision of the Prime Minister, 'it will not be possible to anticipate that Commonwealth funds will be available to assist with freight charges on further supplies of powdered milk'. [182]

India was still in the grip of a severe famine because of crop failures. The Australian Government had not yet made a decision as to how it would be prepared to help. Individuals and groups dedicated to helping India came together under the banner of 'Food for India' and two public meetings were held in the Melbourne Town Hall.[183] At the invitation of the cooperating groups, Moira chaired the crowded meetings. The meetings were called so that the facts concerning the position in India could be presented to the public. The Australian people were at that time showing a great warmth of feeling and compassion for the people suffering in India. Following the meetings, a Memorandum[184] regarding Australian food assistance to India was sent to Prime Minister Harold Holt, who had declined to receive a deputation from Food For India but had requested that the views and suggestions be submitted to him in writing.

Shortly after receiving this Memorandum, Prime Minister Holt advised Moira that, after considering the special merits of her organisation's request, the Government had decided to provide additional funds for the purpose under similar arrangements to those which previously applied.[185]

In May 1966, Mrs Vijaya Lakshmi Pandit[186], visited Australia. At her first press conference in Australia, she said:

> The battle we face today is infinitely more important than the struggle for independence. It is a fight for living standards—a far harder fight than that for freedom. There is no glamor. It is hard and ugly work.[187]

Mrs Pandit interrupted her planned itinerary to visit us at our home in Malvern. There she met a number of Moira's supporters in her work for the people of India. This visit indicated warm support for Moira and her 'team' and for the concept of fostering mutual understanding and goodwill between the peoples of Australia and India. Mrs Pandit thanked the Australian people for their gifts of processed milk. She said, 'Milk is needed to build up our people and we are very grateful for this beautiful gesture made by the Australian people.'

Meanwhile, the milk donations kept coming and Moira's running correspondence with the Department's officers, Ministers and the Prime Minister continued. God knows where her strength came from. She was under pressure from all sides.

In July 1966, with 100 tons of milk awaiting shipment, Moira sent a telegram to the Prime Minister, Harold Holt, c/- The Prime Minister of the United Kingdom, 10 Downing Street, London:

Today Friday 8 July in Canberra I had prolonged discussions with representatives of External Affairs Department in the presence of one Treasury Official regarding Australian Government continued payment of freight costs of shipments of Australian citizens contributions of processed milk to the Government of India for the needy STOP Discussions revealed External Affairs officer unsympathetic and critical of a certain Indian policy STOP Afterwards I spoke to Mr Deane of your Department STOP I then learnt for the first time that you had instructed the Ministers of The Treasury and External Affairs to work out details of assistance to be given to this voluntary emergency campaign STOP Food Situation in India is critical STOP Some 100 tons of processed milk awaits shipment to India STOP Apparently no arrangement whatsoever can be made until you or your delegated Ministers decide STOP Respectfully request your immediate intervention in view of the Departments apparent obstruction of the smooth implementation of enlightened policy of your predecessor and yourself.[188]

On her return home from Canberra that evening, Moira told me that when she saw Mr Deane, he was surprised that Moira had not been informed of the arrangements the Prime Minister had made. Moira then sent telegrams to Paul Hasluck, Minister for External Affairs, and to William McMahon, Treasurer, pleading with them to work out the details so that the 100 tons of milk could be shipped.

I implore you to treat this matter with the urgency it deserves STOP I cannot believe that any Government would reverse the earlier decisions which made possible this practical expression of humanitarian concern of the Australian citizens for the presently hungry needy people in India[189]

The Treasurer ultimately provided funding for this shipment but pointed out that this was without prejudice to the outcome of the Government's review of the 'whole question of Commonwealth assistance towards voluntary aid schemes in Australia'.[190] The Minister for External Affairs also warned Moira: 'I should mention that it is probable that a limit will need to be placed on any funds made available in the course of any one year.'[191]

Later in 1966, more consignments were held up by Governmental delay in providing funding for shipping costs.

18

A Pleasant Sunday Afternoon

Mid-1966 was memorable for an altogether different reason. What started as a Pleasant Sunday Afternoon for Moira very quickly changed.

This episode illustrates the oft-made remark these days: 'Life wasn't meant to be easy.'

On Sunday 12 June 1966, by invitation in her capacity as Chairman of Food for India, Moira spoke at the Wesley Church on the *Pleasant Sunday Afternoon* broadcast programme. She received congratulations from many quarters for her talk on India. There were several musical items prior to Moira's address. There was one hymn sung, the Our Father was recited and at the conclusion the national anthem, *God Save The Queen*, was sung. The address was reviewed on the front page of the Catholic newspapers, *The Tribune* and *The Advocate*.

On Saturday morning, 18 June, I received a letter.[192] The author indicated an intention to publish a statement in the Melbourne Catholic newspapers. Moira and I studied the statement. We took this as a proposed public rebuke to Moira.

I wrote to Monsignor Clarke, Vicar General, St Patrick's Cathedral, Melbourne:

Dear Monsignor,

I write to acknowledge receipt of your letter addressed to me and dated 17th June, which I have received this morning.

I cannot understand why you wrote such a letter to me for it was quite clear from the review in "The Advocate" that it was my wife speaking as Chairman of the Food For India campaign who gave the address last Sunday on the Wesley Church P.S.A. (Pleasant Sunday Afternoon) broadcast over a period of 30 to 33 minutes.

In view of the contents of the letter, which was obviously meant for my wife, I have handed the letter to her to reply. However as this correspondence was sent to me it is obvious that I could not ignore or wish to ignore the contents of the letter.

I was interested to read in your letter that His Grace Archbishop Simonds personally himself wrote to a Catholic man[193] who had been asked to speak at a P.S.A. broadcast and pointed out that he would not grant permission to any of his subjects, lay or clerical, to act as guest speaker at "P.S.A.s or services in non-Catholic churches". Prior to giving the broadcast address my wife had not been given this information although the fact that she was to be the Guest Speaker was well publicised in advance in every Victorian paper, Herald, Sun and Age.

The question uppermost in my own mind is—is it compulsory under pain of sin or ex-communication for a Catholic lay woman, fulfilling a public service, as Chairman of a widely based humanitarian campaign for the needy and sick in India and requested by the authorities in charge of the Wesley P.S.A. to speak, to seek and obtain prior specific permission from the Archbishop to speak on the Wesley P.S.A. broadcast?

I would be pleased to have the reply to this question in writing from the Archbishop personally or from his named representative at the Cathedral who has been authorised by a Bishop to make such a pronouncement.

I must say that I am truly amazed at what you say in your letter. With regard to the statements which you say that you are having inserted in "The Advocate" and in "The Tribune" there are several points which I want to make quite clear now.

1. As my wife is, so far as I am aware the only lay or clerical Catholic of the Archdiocese who has spoken recently at the Wesley P.S.A., the publication of the proposed statement is understood by us as a clear public rebuke to her. That the Archbishop personally has taken the decision to do this is beyond my comprehension. It seems to us that His Grace is obviously unaware of the nature of the work being carried out by my wife, and apparently unaware of the nature of the P.S.A. gathering.

2. May I refer to the second paragraph of your letter where you write "to act as guest speaker or preacher at P.S.A. or services in non-Catholic churches". I then refer to the text of the statement which you say is to be inserted in The Advocate and The Tribune, where you write "some Catholics have acted as

guest speakers at <u>P.S.A. services</u> at Wesley Church". I respectfully suggest that to call the P.S.A. broadcast from Wesley Church "P.S.A. <u>services</u>" is straining the cause of truth beyond endurance.

For my part I want to make my position quite clear. I appreciate the fact that you have written to me to advise me in advance of the proposed course of action which you have referred to in your letter. However in the climate of the world spirit of ecumenism and in the light of the Holy Father's appeals to feed the poor people of India, which appeals are world wide and do include Australia, I am quite unable to understand His Grace's apparent decision.

The clear and unconditional answer to the question which I pose at the commencement of my letter will place me in a better position to let you know my own thoughtful response to the proposed public rebuke of my wife.

I can only now say that I hope that the proposed statement will not be published at all. However if His Grace sees fit to have a statement published in The Advocate then I hope that he will refrain from doing so at least until the question which I have put has been answered and communicated, and until His Grace has had the opportunity to hear my wife's representations. In this respect I accordingly request that His Grace grant an interview to my wife and myself so that this matter may be clarified, before any further damaging action is taken.

I am, yours sincerely and respectfully,
John F. Dynon[194]

Moira also wrote a letter:

> Dear Monsignor Clarke,
>
> John has passed on to me your letter of 17th June concerning an address delivered on the P.S.A. Programme at Wesley Church on Sunday, 12th June. As John has pointed out in his letter, it was I, in my capacity as Chairman of Food For India, who delivered the address. John has shown me his reply to you in which I concur.
>
> Whilst working with people of goodwill of all denominations, I have seen the wonderful uniting force of love of our hungry neighbours actively promoting Christian unity and understanding.
>
> It has come as a complete shock to me to learn from you that His Grace, The Archbishop, Himself, was other than happy with all that I have done to obtain help for the starving needy in India. As you are aware, Food For India is a widely based public campaign and we are deeply grateful to Church leaders of all denominations for their support of our efforts. As you are aware, it was His Holiness Pope Paul who called on mankind to send supplies of food for needy people in India.
>
> At the time of my address at P.S.A., I had no idea that His Grace The Archbishop had specifically made any pronouncement such as is referred to in your letter. In fact, in view of the nature of the P.S.A. Programme, it did not occur to me that there could be any objection. When speaking to His Lordship Bishop Moran at a Reception at the home of the Italian Consul General on 2nd June, I told him that I was giving this talk and

also mentioned that I had given the P.S.A talk in Adelaide on 17th April.

It seems to me that the ban, as is referred to in your letter, would frustrate the objectives envisioned by the Popes, particularly in view of the Papal exhortations to men and to women of the Church to go out and work with others, and in view of the basic Christian principle of helping the poor, the needy and the destitute. If such a ban is to prevail, it seems to me to be incompatible with any Catholic woman assuming a position of leadership in Public life and in public and mixed organisations.

In view of the implication of the proposed Statement to be inserted in 'The Advocate' and 'The Tribune', I can only take the view that this is a public rebuke to me and that I am to be publicly branded a sinner. Before His Grace takes such irrevocable action, which I consider damaging to my good name and reputation, I hope that His Grace, Archbishop Simonds will grant John and me an interview.

Yours sincerely,
Moira Dynon[195]

I delivered both letters to the Cathedral on Sunday afternoon.

In the end, no statement appeared in *The Advocate* or *The Tribune* or elsewhere. We were very grateful for the assistance of Mr Justice McInerney. I wrote to him:

Dear Murray,

I hesitate to write to you on this matter, but after due reflection I felt that I must request your help and your intervention, not only in the interest of my wife, but in the interest of His Grace the Archbishop of Melbourne and the Catholic community.

On the 18th June I received a letter from Monsignor Clarke, a copy of which is enclosed. On the 19th June my wife and I each wrote a letter to Monsignor Clarke. These letters were delivered by me by hand to the Presbytery at St Patrick's Cathedral at approximately 1.30 p.m. today. Copies of these two letters are enclosed...

My wife and I are gravely concerned at the damage that will be done by the publication of the proposed statement mentioned in Monsignor Clarke's letter. In our opinion this statement amounts to a public rebuke to my wife which is completely unmerited. It is also our opinion that at some time recently, maybe at the time when a letter was written to a Catholic man referred to in Monsignor Clarke's letter, there was a change of policy, apparently and allegedly by the Archbishop himself.

For some reason or other I feel sure that His Grace the Archbishop does not presently understand the extent and nature of my wife's work for the needy in India...

We are concerned that the contemplated action by Monsignor Clarke will spark off recriminations which could do irreparable damage to the whole Catholic community, and I fear that this would include the Hierarchy.

In the interest of the good name of the Church in Melbourne and in the interest of the needy people in India I request you do whatever you can to persuade the authorities of the Church in Melbourne of the folly in pursuing the course proposed. I must say that I am not at all happy about the letter which His Grace is said to have 'personally' written recently. The blanket ban seems to be based on this letter...[196]

One thing I refuse to believe was that His Grace, himself, would take the proposed action in all the known circumstances. He was obviously, if making these decisions, unaware of the nature and extent of Moira's public work and also of the nature of the Wesley PSA. I was later given to understand that at the time of this correspondence, His Grace was hospitalised.

Following this episode, Moira sought the permission of His Grace Archbishop Simonds before speaking at functions in non-Catholic churches in Melbourne. Monsignor Clarke then notified her that the Archbishop had granted permission.

Not long after James Knox took over as Archbishop of Melbourne, Moira made an appointment to speak with him about her works. He placed no impediment in her way should she be invited to speak in churches within the Archdiocese, in connection with her public activities. This included all churches.

19

Politicians, politics and resilience

On 15 October 1966, Moira wrote to His Excellency Mr E Clark, Ambassador for the United States of America, requesting him to hand to the President a letter on his arrival in Canberra:

> Dear President Johnson,
>
> <u>The Price of Freedom is Not Cheap.</u>
>
> On behalf of Aid For India Campaign and its Milk For India Committees and supporters in the various States of Australia, I extend to you and Mrs. Johnson a warm welcome to Australia.
>
> As you know, Mr. Averell Harriman, your special envoy to Australia in January this year, was asked to convey to you our great appreciation for the continuing efforts by the U.S.A. to co-operate with the people of democratic and freedom loving India.
>
> We are vitally interested in the future of India for reasons which include the following three: —

1. India, the world's largest democracy, most realistically represents the cause of freedom and democracy on the Asian mainland.

2. As no doubt India holds the key to the future of Asia, the destiny of Australia as a democratic nation is inevitably linked with India.

3. It is important to Australia and to Asia that China be flanked by a strong secure and independent India. India indeed is Australia's shield against any Chinese expansionist ambition whether economic, ideological or military.

We are aware of the serious dangers and problems in Viet Nam. However, for Australians the outcome of the struggle in Viet Nam fades in importance when compared with the outcome of Indian endeavours to build a strong, secure, independent and self reliant nation by democratic methods.

It seems that the importance of the success of Indian ideals is not always fully recognized by freedom lovers in the West. You, Mr. President, have given world leadership and the Government of the U.S.A. has given generous assistance to India. However, in view of the urgency for rapid economic progress and development, it is surprising that on a per capita basis, India ranks so low as a recipient of international aid.

There is profound goodwill amongst the Australian people for the people of India—our neighbour and friend. We hope that this warmth of feeling will soon be reflected in a decision by our own Government to enter into a strong, firm and substantial Australian economic commitment to India by way of trade and aid.

Geographically, Australia lies between the world's two largest democracies, India and the United States of America. We Australians desire to look both ways and we must look both ways.

U.S.A., India and Australia have so much in common—our love of freedom, democratic ideals, our multi religious societies, parliamentary institutions, free press and the rule of law. The widespread use of the English language in Indian official and parliamentary spheres provides a unique opportunity for close understanding between the peoples of our three countries.

The price of freedom is not cheap. India today is in the early industrial revolution period. Her territorial integrity is threatened by neighbours at a time when she is making heroic sacrifices to raise the living standards of her people and to progress in freedom. This presents a challenge to Australia and indeed to all freedom lovers in that we must recognize that the price of freedom is not cheap.

With every good wish,
yours sincerely,
Moira Dynon
Chairman, Aid for India Campaign.[197]

As supplies of wheat were urgently needed in India at this time, Moira called on our Federal Government to respond generously. Moira sent a telegram to the Prime Minister of Australia, the Leader of the Opposition, the Leader of the

Country Party and the Leader of the Democratic Labor Party:

> The new food crisis in India endangers the lives of seventy million Indian children and adults and threatens to undermine the democratic structure of India STOP It has been announced that India urgently requires Australian wheat on generous trading terms STOP Aid for India Campaign implores you to give an undertaking forthwith to implement or support a policy providing for the sale of Australian wheat to India on more generous trading terms than are granted to Communist China STOP Australia must not let it be inferred in Asia that our great democracy drives a hard bargain with suffering humanity[198]

In November 1966, the Australian Press reported that President Johnson had banned food aid to India. Moira immediately sent a telegram to Senator Robert Kennedy, The Senate, Washington, USA:

> Australian people alarmed at Press announcement that President Johnson has banned food aid to India STOP New crisis in India calls for immediate food supplies by all countries which profess love of freedom STOP India must not be allowed to starve STOP Survival of India's democracy vital to Australia and World Peace STOP We believe suffering humanity must not be held captive to political ransom STOP Implore your sympathetic and immediate intervention on humanitarian grounds[199]

Senator Kennedy replied:

Dear Mrs Dynon:

Enclosed please find the correspondence I received from the inquiry I made in your behalf. I hope this information is helpful to you. If I can be of assistance to you in the future, please feel free to contact me again.

Sincerely,
Robert F. Kennedy[200]

Enclosed was a copy of a letter from Douglas MacArthur II, Assistant Secretary for Congressional Relations, Department of State, Washington:

Dear Senator Kennedy:

I have received your communication of November 28 regarding the concern for the Indian food situation conveyed to you in a cable from Moira Dynon, National Chairman of the Australian Aid for India Campaign. I share Mrs Dynon's sympathetic concern for India's current food problem and agree on the necessity for an international effort to help India confront this problem. The United States has not "banned food aid to India" and there is no basis for the reports to this effect cited by Mrs Dynon. We have shipped some 44 million tons of grain to India over the past ten years and have already made very large shipments of grain to India this year.

The entire question of additional food for India is under urgent consideration within the United States Government. We are following India's developing food crisis, both from Washington and from the field, very closely. This already complex matter is further complicated this year by our own food production problems, for our wheat crop was below that of last year and our stocks have been drawn down substantially.

Some quantities of United States supplied grain and foodstuffs are regularly distributed, on a donation basis, by such American voluntary agencies as CARE, the Catholic Relief Services, and the Church World Service. These agencies have now placed special emphasis on the drought-stricken areas and we are backing them in their activities.[201]

Moira responded:

Dear Senator Kennedy,

Thank you very much for your letter of 15th December and enclosed letter dated 12th December from Mr. Douglas MacArthur II Assistant Secretary for Congressional Relations. I thank you sincerely for your representations following receipt of my cable and for your kind offer of further assistance.

You will be interested to learn that Press reports in Australia yesterday (21st December 1966) claimed that "Australia had given 150,000 tons of wheat to India as a result of considerable diplomatic pressure from the White House". As an example of these reports I am enclosing the clipping from "The Age".

There is profound goodwill amongst the Australian people for the people of India—our neighbour and friend and such reports have created a feeling of resentment amongst Australians. Such reports, whether true or false, do not foster friendship and goodwill between the people of Australia and of the United States of America.

The gift of wheat and flour by the Australian Government has been made unconditionally in the spirit of friendship and understanding. It is the third such gift of food made by our Government to India in less than twenty-two (22) months. In addition, numerous voluntary organizations throughout Australia are doing what they can to strengthen the ties of friendship between the peoples of India and Australia in a practical way, either by contributions of processed milk (see enclosure) or by the supply of money and equipment for long term development projects.

With regard to the letter from Mr. Douglas MacArthur II dated 12th December, I wish to make the following comments:

1. It is a fact that millions of people in India are facing starvation due to drought and crop failures consequent on the failure of the monsoon rains.

2. It is a fact that India has serious foreign exchange difficulties and the new food crisis has placed a heavy strain on her financial resources.

3. It appears to be a fact that some high authority in the U.S.A. has delayed the signing of the proposed new Agreement providing for the supplies of grain to India.

4. In the Indian Parliament on 29th November, the Indian Minister for Food and Agriculture (Mr. C. Subramaniam) stated:

> "In the case a new agreement with the United States Government on food supplies is not finalized in a few days, there will be a break in the shipments resulting in a shortfall in January... The Government also has to provide for imports from February onwards...in view of our extremely difficult foreign exchange position we cannot naturally embark on any large scale imports of wheat on a commercial basis and we are hoping that a new agreement with the U.S. Government will be possible very soon."

5. It has been announced that on 26th November, the Prime Minister of India, Mrs. Indira Gandhi, said at the Press Club that the "suddenness with which the United States freeze on food imports had come has thrown us out of gear...If India had been told of the American difficulties in sending supplies earlier—the request for two million tons was made as early as August—we could have adjusted our own programmes accordingly". (India News, Information Service of India, Sydney, N.S.W., Australia 29th November 1966).

6. It is a fact that the date for the next Indian General Elections has been fixed for 14th February to 20th February, 1967, in all the 17 States of India for the Lok Sabha (House of the People) as well as the State Legislative Assemblies.

7. If the shortage of grain supplies in the U.S.A. is the reason for the delay in the Agreement referred to, what can be the objectives of the U.S. field survey team?

8. If the high U.S. authority is concerned whether India is doing enough to help herself, the information concerning India's progress and development is readily available and there should be no reason for delay. As no doubt you are aware, in June 1966 in New Delhi, the U.S.A. Ambassador, Mr. Chester Bowles said "India has made more progress in the past fifteen years than during two centuries under foreign rule".

9. It would appear that the sending of the U.S. survey field team to India is a delaying tactic.

10. If it is intended that the aim of the U.S. field team should result in an international co-ordinated effort for emergency supplies of food to India, it would seem appropriate that the field team should include representatives of other nations.

11. In Australia and elsewhere, it is being suggested that President Johnson is using the situation as a political lever on the Indian Government in an effort to persuade her leaders to approve of certain foreign policies of the U.S.A. Of course, I myself am not in a position to know whether this allegation has any substance of truth.

12. There can be no doubt at all that the United States Government and people have given generously to help not only in India but also in other countries throughout the world. However, the present world situation and the present Indian famine call for substantial and immediate food assistance to India on pure humanitarian grounds leaving no room for suspicion of political pressure.

It has been reported that India has asked our Government for the supply of a large quantity of wheat on deferred payment terms. Our Campaign has called upon the Australian Government to enter into the necessary arrangements providing for the sale of Australian wheat to India on more generous trading terms than are granted to Communist China. It is hoped that our Government will be able to make such arrangements even if it means changing the present systems of wheat sales by the Australian Wheat Board. Our Campaign feels that this may be in line with what President Johnson has in mind. However, if widespread starvation in India is to be avoided decisions must be made now before it is too late.

As you are aware, India, the world's largest democracy, most realistically represents the cause of freedom and democracy on the Asian mainland. As no doubt India holds the key to the future of Asia, the destiny of Australia as a democratic nation is inevitably linked with India. The new food crisis in India not only endangers the lives of seventy million Indian children and adults but also threatens to undermine the democratic structure of India.

I am sure that Australians would appreciate your further intervention in an effort to expedite the early decisions and action required if mass starvation and tragedy are to be avoided in democratic India.

With every good wish,
I am, Yours sincerely,
MOIRA DYNON,
Chairman Aid for India Campaign.[202]

At the end of December 1966, on the occasion of the Davis Cup encounter at Kooyong tennis courts between India and Australia, the visit to Melbourne of the High Commissioner for India and his family was a most pleasurable interlude. His Excellency and Mrs Chatterjee stayed at Government House and their children stayed at our home in Malvern.

In January 1967, Moira reached out again to Senator Robert Kennedy:

> Australian people profoundly disturbed B.B.C. news 22nd January quoting Prime Minister of India announcement that United States food aid to India is now offered subject to political conditions STOP In view of India's food crisis and forthcoming Indian election such proffered aid must shock World opinion STOP United States food aid subject to political conditions appears inconsistent with Douglas MacArthur II letter 12 December expressing sympathetic concern for India's current food problem STOP We believe suffering humanity must not be held captive to political ransom STOP Implore your sympathetic assistance to clarify position and rectify apparent administrative lapse[203]

Senator Kennedy replied:

> Dear Mrs. Dynon:
>
> Thank you very much for your fine letter and the clippings from *The Age*. I just recently received the copy you sent and I apologize for not answering sooner. I am always pleased to receive your thoughtful views and suggestions.

You are probably aware that the day after you mailed your original letter the United States agreed to ship 900,000 tons of food grains to India during February and March.

Last week the President authorized an emergency shipment of 2 million tons. He also asked Congress to approve of 3 million additional tons to be shipped in the near future, with the condition that appropriate amounts also be given by the other developed countries of the world.

As you know, I share your sincere concern for the people and democracy of India. I was very pleased to see our government take these much-needed steps.

Thank you again for writing. I hope I will be hearing from you again concerning matters of mutual concern.

Sincerely,
Robert F. Kennedy[204]

Moira spoke with the Reverend Maurice Carse SSS, Superior of St Francis Church, Lonsdale Street, Melbourne with regard to prayers for India. Subsequently he arranged a special Mass for India and the Indian people. This was celebrated at St Francis on Monday, 16 January 1967 at 1.15 p.m. before a packed congregation.

I know that Moira was very grateful to Father Carse for arranging this special Mass. I believe that it was this occasion that inspired Moira that night to write to the Federal Treasurer.

Dear Mr. McMahon,

I am writing to you because I am deeply concerned at the delay in the decision concerning the continuation of the original policy providing for the allocation of funds to meet freight and insurance costs to ship to the Government of India the processed milk contributed by private donors through my 19 Milk For India Committees.

...The January ship, S.S. Lombok, is now in Melbourne Port and no decision from the Government is yet to hand. Now it is a practical impossibility for the processed milk currently held to be shipped on this ship to Bombay. To me it seems inhuman that the despatch of powdered milk, urgently needed for the Indian Government's relief programmes for children, pregnant mothers and the sick and infirm, and donated in the spirit of friendship by thousands of Australian people, should be delayed.

...I hope and trust that you will continue to support our humanitarian gesture of friendship to the people of India.[205]

Treasurer McMahon was unmoved by Moira's letter. He replied:

As you know, the Government has recently undertaken a comprehensive review of the whole question of Commonwealth assistance towards voluntary aid activities undertaken by private organisations in Australia. This review has been made necessary by the increasing number of requests of this nature which the Government has received over the past year or so and it embraces the activities of a great many voluntary aid organisations, apart from your own.

Although no decision has yet been taken on the general policy which the Government should adopt in this field in the future, I thought it only fair to let you know last year that you ought not to anticipate that funds would continue to be made available for this purpose once the review mentioned above has been completed...

Moira's reply gave the Treasurer something to think about:

Indian Government the recipient of our processed milk is aware of delay in forwarding substantial quantity of milk currently held here for distribution in India through Government official relief programmes STOP...Campaign proceeding New South Wales where people would desire the same Federal Government assistance to the scheme as has been provided in Victoria South Australia and Tasmania STOP

As you are aware my husband was contemporary Oxford University with Mrs Indira Gandhi STOP If it would help understanding between Australia and India he is prepared to write personally to her explaining the reasons for the Government delay in deciding whether it will continue the policy initiated by Sir Robert Menzies STOP Await your early advice regarding proposed action[206]

The Treasurer responded:

I regret that you should have adopted the attitude which you did towards my letter of 20th February. I can only confirm what I said in that letter, namely, that when the Government has decided upon the general policy which it will adopt in future towards requests for official assistance towards voluntary aid schemes in Australia, including your own, you will be informed.[207]

Meanwhile, Moira continued to press the Prime Minister:

> Dear Mr Holt,
>
> As you are aware, since 4th December 1966, this is the fourth occasion on which I have approached you concerning the continuation of the policy of the Government regarding allocation of funds to cover shipping costs and insurance of the consignments of processed milk sent by our Campaign to the Government of India…As a woman and a mother I am appalled at the procrastination especially at a time when millions of Indian children and adults are suffering acute hardship.[208]

On 14 March 1967, the Leader of the Opposition, Mr Gough Whitlam, asked a question in the House of Representatives.

> Mr WHITLAM—I ask a question of the Prime Minister. I preface it by pointing out that six months ago the Government suspended the assistance it had given over a period of about twenty months to the Aid to India Campaign in transporting powdered milk to India. It did this on the ground that it was undertaking a comprehensive review of its assistance to voluntary aid schemes. I ask the right honourable gentleman: is this an example of the policy expressed last Thursday by the Minister for Defence that a civilian agency or organisation which undertakes a thoroughly good work of this kind should go the second mile and itself

arrange for the transport of the supplies that it has assembled? Since tons of powdered milk have now piled up in Australia at a time when millions of Indian children are suffering from starvation, will he intervene in this matter as promptly as he did last Thursday in regard to the transport to Vietnam of generators by another voluntary organisation?[209]

Mr HAROLD HOLT—This matter is in the hands of my colleague the Minister for External Affairs.[210]

Mr HASLUCK—...I would ask the Leader of the Opposition to appreciate one or two points of difficulty on the broad question before I refer to the particular case he has mentioned. When a group of persons decide to open a fund for something and those persons prosecute the fund with the utmost goodwill, of course whether that is the form of aid that is most required or can be of best help to the receiving country is a matter entirely of their own decision.

In our governmental aid the forms of aid we give are as the result of consultation with the receiving country and a request by the government of that country. So I am sure the honourable gentleman will appreciate the point that we do have to make sure that before public funds are expended the form of aid is the result of a decision in which the receiving countries join rather than a decision that has been made ad hoc by a group full of good intentions but perhaps not always with close local knowledge of the circumstances it is trying to relieve.

...if people choose, as they have every reason to choose, to assist in one particular direction, they should complete the assistance themselves rather than look to public funds to complete the job for them...

> Turning, in conclusion, to the particular case that the honourable gentleman has mentioned, we are of course in sympathy with the objective of this group of people. On previous occasions we have assisted them. On the last occasion, when we assisted them by helping to provide shipping for the transport of the milk that they had obtained, we told them that in future they could not count upon Government expenditure of public funds to provide shipping to the receiving country. Australia is providing very substantial aid in meeting the food shortages in India. This aid comes from governmental sources. We believe that this private fund should complete its own job to its own satisfaction from its own means.[211]

Dr Jim Cairns MHR also spoke on the matter in Parliament:

> Dr J. F. CAIRNS—...We believe there is evidence to indicate that for quite a long time the Government has put Vietnam well ahead of India and that it is not taking very seriously the important job of aiding India in the problems that that country faces...are we to understand that the Government has refused to give assistance to the Milk for India campaign? Has the Government refused to give assistance by helping to pay the freight on the many tins of powdered milk which, if it gets to India quickly, will no doubt save hundreds of lives in that country? Is that the meaning of the reply given by the Minister for External Affairs on 14th March or is it not?[212]

After reading the Hansard Report of the House proceedings, Moira wrote to the Prime Minister:

> It is clearly implied that Mr Hasluck appears to be unaware that the careful investigations carried out by my Committee revealed that gifts of processed milk by Australian citizens were most desirable and most acceptable to the Indian Government for use in Indian Government official relief programmes. From the outset, the wisdom of the decision to send processed milk to the Government of India has been confirmed from both Indian and Australian representative specialist authorities.[213]

On 17 March, the Minister for External Affairs wrote to Moira:

> It has been decided that the Government will not be making any further funds available to the Aid for India Campaign this year...When the Prime Minister wrote to you in November last he warned that the Campaign should not anticipate the availability of funds for shipping costs on milk to India and so any buildup of milk which has occurred since then should be regarded as the Campaign's responsibility to be met from the Campaign's resources.[214]

Moira then sent a telegram to Prime Minister Holt:

> Received Mr Hasluck's letter this afternoon STOP He advises firstly Government will not make any further funds available this year for the freighting Aid For India Campaign milk gifts to Government of India for needy and secondly he holds Campaign responsible to meet shipping costs of the milk presently

held for famine relief in India STOP

I remind you firstly the Department of External Affairs initially encouraged this Campaign Secondly the Government has never made funds directly available to the Aid for India Campaign and thirdly the Campaign has no funds at present in existence for payment of freight costs STOP Do you as Prime Minister of Australia confirm this decision referred to by Mr Hasluck STOP I request your early reply [215]

The Prime Minister replied:

I am taking up the contents of your telegram with my colleague the Minister for External Affairs who has the administrative responsibility for aid matters this kind [216]

On 28 March at 1 a.m. Moira sent another telegram to the Prime Minister:

Our Campaign hopes and prays for early favourable decision STOP As you know processed milk urgently needed for famine relief in India [217]

Five weeks later, the Prime Minister gave Moira his answer:

Dear Mrs. Dynon,

...I regret that my absence overseas has prevented me from replying before this. I have now, however, had an opportunity to discuss this matter with my colleague and I confirm that the Commonwealth's position is as explained to you by him in his letter to you of 17th March.

Yours sincerely,
Harold Holt [218]

The Government's decision to withdraw its support from the Campaign did not come as a surprise to everyone. In early January, Moira had written to the Prime Minister:

> Dear Mr Holt,
>
> On Friday, 6th January in Sydney, certain information was brought to my attention in the presence of others. Because of the nature of this information, I am writing to inform you and respectfully request that you take any action you may consider appropriate.
>
> It was stated that Dr. Beermann, United Nations Representative in Sydney alleged that he had been informed prior to Christmas by an unnamed, highly placed Australian Government departmental officer that a "policy decision" had been made by the Australian Government that no further funds were to be made available by the Australian Government to transport to India the processed milk collected under my campaign.
>
> Needless to say, I am shocked and alarmed that a highly placed person, who is not an Australian, should hold himself out to be in a position to pass on information concerning an alleged policy decision of the Australian Government regarding the shipment of processed milk donated by the Australian people to the Government of India for free distribution to the needy.
>
> In view of [letters from the PM's Private Secretary and Minister for External Affairs] I find it incredible that such an allegation could have any substance of truth.

In addition, I am deeply concerned that a United Nations representative in Australia who is not an Australian appears to consider that he is in a position to make claims which concern arrangements entered into between the Government of Australia, Aid for India Campaign and the Government of India.[219]

Prime Minister Holt replied 'that no policy decision has yet been taken by the Government on the matter of Commonwealth assistance towards freight costs in relation to voluntary aid schemes'.[220]

On 14 March, Mr DN Chatterjee, the High Commissioner for India, wrote to Moira:

My dear Mrs Dynon,

Thank you for sending me the articles in the Melbourne Herald. I have passed them on to Moulik in Sydney.

It is almost a hopeless task to get some journalists to write with some objectivity on India. One can do little with those who are mean of spirit. Practically anyone can now insult India pretending to help her at the same time.

Yesterday, I recorded a programme with the A.B.C. (Get to Know your Asian Neighbours) which will, probably, be broadcast some time in June. The transcript will be printed and distributed to secondary schools. I was glad to be able to say in that programme what you have been doing.

Kindest regards,
Yours as Ever,
Dwarka Nath Chatterjee[221]

A month later, an item appeared in *The Herald*'s 'In Black and White' column on page 3:

> AFTER E.W. Tipping's grim reports of starvation in India, this story seems almost incredible. Tragically it's true. A Melbourne woman charity worker recently collected 400 lb. of dried milk. She arranged for an airline to freight it to Calcutta. Now both she and the airline have been told that the entire shipment was destroyed on the order of the Indian Customs because import duties were not paid.[222]

Moira telephoned Andrew McKay at *The Herald* office the following morning and pointed out that this item was damaging to her Campaign and that the alleged incident had nothing whatsoever to do with her Campaign, but that since the publication of the item many people had told her that they understood that she was the 'woman' referred to. Mr McKay did not offer to clarify the position in his column. Moira wrote to the Editor of *The Herald*:

> **India gets our milk**
>
> IN BLACK AND WHITE (Herald, 13-4-67) reported that 400 lb. of dried milk a Melbourne woman air-freighted to India was destroyed because import duties were not paid. As national president of the Aid for India Campaign and chairman of Milk for India Victorian Committee, I wish to point out that this dispatch of dried milk had no connection with my campaign or any of its Milk for India Committees or their program.
>
> I wish to make clear the following points:
>
> - All the 762 tons of processed milk sent to India by my campaign has arrived safely and has been

distributed free to the needy, regardless of race, caste or creed.

- Before any of our consignments of processed milk are shipped from Australia, adequate and appropriate arrangements are made for duty-free entry to India and for the reception and clearance of the gift consignments at the port of entry.
- Landing costs of the consignments are met by the Government of India.
- First-hand reports from Australians in India and from Australians who have visited that country confirm the value of the processed milk in the relief programs and the efficiency of the handling and distribution of our gifts of processed milk.
- Numerous letters and messages received have expressed gratitude and appreciation.

Recently I received a letter expressing the "sincere and grateful thanks" of the Indian Prime Minister, Mrs Indira Gandhi, and asking that this appreciation be conveyed "to all those who are helping in this cause".

At this critical time when so many millions of Indian children and adults are facing starvation and suffering terrible hunger, hardship and privation in the States of Bihar and Uttar Pradesh, the Press can be of inestimable value in letting the Australian people know of the great need and what can be done to alleviate it.

Moira Dynon, national president, Aid for India Campaign and chairman Milk for India, Victorian Committee, Haverbrack Av., Malvern.

> [The Herald has been in the forefront of newspapers reporting the grim facts of the famine in India. It has given, and will continue to give, unstinted support to the Aid for India campaign.] [223]

This 'In Black and White' story was of the 'Melbourne woman', who was not identified by name. The airline was unnamed. The source of the story was also unnamed. There was no confirmation of the alleged destruction of the 'entire shipment'. This was indeed an 'incredible' story, but the fact remains that *The Herald* reported it as being 'true' and gave the story wide publicity.

The Acting High Commissioner for India, Mr JS Gill, investigated the matter and wrote to the editor of *The Herald*, advising that he had made enquiries and found that no such consignment had been received in Calcutta or destroyed.[224] *The Herald* still did not publish any retraction of its story.

During the life of the Campaign, there were references in some of the Australian Press to unsubstantiated allegations. It became patently clear that such allegations were of a mischievous nature made for dubious reasons. It was this kind of opposition that increased the work and strain on the volunteer workers in the Campaign.

In one of her many letters to the Department of External Affairs, Moira wrote:

> May I also thank you for your comment that "The continued interest and activity of the Campaign in helping India is greatly appreciated by the Government". The reception of a friendly word of encouragement from you has moved me deeply. However, I would be less than honest if I did not say that I do not

know one Indian or Australian person who would share your expressed opinion as to the present attitude of the Government towards the efforts of the Campaign. In fact I think it is no exaggeration to say that the widely held opinion is that the present attitude of the Government and of your Department is quite the opposite to that expressed by you.

As possibly you are aware, for some considerable time a number of rumours damaging to the Campaign have been spread throughout Australia. Some of these rumours have been brought to my notice. My Campaign's investigations of these revealed that some of these rumours allegedly originated from departmental sources.[225]

It is true that the more opposition and misrepresentation Moira encountered, the firmer was her resolve to meet all such challenges. She never relaxed in her efforts to fight for the cause which she believed was good.

20

Offer from Shipping Corporation of India

It was towards the end of May 1967 that Moira received a telephone call from the shipping agents, George Wills and Co. Instructions had been received from India that the Shipping Corporation of India was standing ready to freight the Campaign's processed milk to India, free of charge.

Before receiving this welcome news, Moira had written to Gough Whitlam, who had announced his intention to visit New Delhi as part of a forthcoming overseas journey. Moira invited him to a presentation ceremony and she also gave him the latest information about her Campaign.

> With regard to Shipping Costs—as you know, the Australian Government has given no help whatsoever since the consignment of 60 tons which was shipped from Melbourne on 2nd December.
>
> I have been advised by the Indian High Commissioner in Canberra that "We have written to the Government of India to explore the possibilities of free transportation of the consignments of milk powder from Australia to India by the Shipping Corporation of India's vessels plying between Australia and India..."

I understand that this matter is at present under consideration by the Government of India. I would like you to know that my Campaign did not seek or ask for this action. The Campaign has always held the view that its gifts should be without conditions and should be delivered free to India. However, in view of the unfortunate reversal of policy by the Australian Government (with regard to the provision of funds for shipping costs and insurance and the use of the facilities of the Department of Supply), any offer of help by the Government of India at this stage would be greatly appreciated and would give great encouragement to the donors.[226]

On 8 June, on board the *Vishva Mahima*, a presentation of the milk gift to the Government of India was made to Mr R Axel Khan, Indian Trade Commissioner. Guests at the presentation included members of Federal and State Parliaments, representatives from the Indian High Commission and also representatives from religious organisations, charities, banks, businesses, community groups and education. The Federal Government had indicated that it would not be represented at this ceremony. At the last moment, Moira advised Mr McMahon's office that Mr Whitlam would be attending. The Campaign was then advised that Senator Anderson would attend representing the Australian Government. As the guest list had already been prepared, the name of Senator Anderson had to appear as the last name on the list.

This was a wonderful event in the life of the Campaign. Particularly as the Indian Government had demonstrated in the most definite way possible its wish that the milk campaign continue with its work for the people of India. I know Moira was deeply grateful to the Indian authorities for this most gracious and helpful gesture, which so clearly indicated both confidence in her work for the needy in India and also the need for the milk in India. At the same time, she was saddened by the Australian Government's withdrawal of all funding and facilities.

The implication in the answer by Mr Hasluck to the question in Parliament on 14 March that the Campaign's milk aid was or could be inappropriate, misguided or worse, showed that the Minister was not properly informed by his Department and/or by the Prime Minister's Department, or was misleading the Parliament and the people of Australia as to the position of the Campaign. With all the glowing reports that Moira received from all quarters, what shows up is either that there was a complete double-face by the Department and/or Government or a complete lack of understanding of the impact the Campaign was having on the good relations between the Australian and Indian peoples.

The Indian Government's approval of the Campaign from the beginning and its offer to ship the milk to India free of charge after the Australian Government had withdrawn all assistance, gave the lie to all insinuations made in the Parliament and elsewhere with regard to the Campaign. Goodwill, understanding and care for the underprivileged in India during times of ordeal and disaster dominated the giving so far as Moira, the Campaign, the donors and the Indian authorities were concerned. Frankly, I do not know what motivated the Australian Government or the Department of External Affairs. Maybe the Australian Government was acting on instructions from some outside party. For some time, the Government's support appeared to have been given grudgingly.

Whatever the real reason for the termination of its assistance to the Campaign, it remains incomprehensible that the Australian Government failed to follow the policy lead initially given by Prime Minister Menzies.

Following the withdrawal of all facilities by the Australian Government, the Campaign organisers had to work even harder and for longer hours. The Campaign had to draw more and more on its supporters to help cope with the new situation. There was the sorting, packing, steel-banding and marking of every carton of milk, much of which was carried out at our home in Malvern. There was ongoing contact with captains of the various Indian Shipping Corporation's ships and the transporting of the cartons within Australia to the ships. Moira also dealt with all the necessary correspondence, administration and documentation associated with each shipment. Expenses increased inevitably, especially with the extra transport within Australia and the special packing which involved making protective crates, which is a tradesman's task. Such expenses made inroads on funds which would otherwise have been available for the purchase of milk.

Moira did not give up on the Australian Government. Following an announcement in July of its gift of 150,000 tons of wheat to India, Moira wrote to Prime Minister Holt:

> I wish to congratulate you and the Government on this timely gift of wheat to India. With very great pleasure I note that Mr. Hasluck is quoted as saying that "India has made great efforts to help itself". Unfortunately, this fact is not well publicized in certain sections of the communications media in Australia.

OFFER FROM SHIPPING CORPORATION OF INDIA

...I believe that it is more important than ever before that Australia and India should come closer together on the basis of friendship, co-operation and understanding.[227]

21

Eight weeks in India

Early in 1967, Moira received an invitation from Air India to join its inaugural flight to Teheran. On her acceptance of the airline company's offer, Moira was asked by the Central Government in New Delhi, and subsequently by a number of the State Governments, to be their guest.

Moira left from Sydney on 16 August and after visiting Iran she returned to India. In Delhi, she had a private meeting with the Prime Minister, Mrs Indira Gandhi. Moira said that it was a wonderful joy to meet and talk with Mrs Gandhi, who was dedicated to the cause of peace and of raising the living standards of all the people of India. 'She is a lovely person—gracious, feminine and cultured. Despite her enormous problems, she retains her wonderful charm. It is obvious that the people just love her. Wherever she goes, they turn out and line the streets.'[228]

Throughout her travels in India, Moira was aware of being in a country that was suffering from food shortage. Visitors staying in hotels had enough to eat, but to prevent waste there were restrictions on the number of courses served at a meal. At a formal reception for which Mrs Gandhi was hostess, the guests were served fruit juice with a few nuts. The Prime Minister herself told Moira that, for some considerable time, she personally had refrained from drawing on her cereal ration and had simply learned to eat other things.

After New Delhi, Moira visited the Taj Mahal in Agra and then flew across Uttar Pradesh State, then heavily flooded, into Bihar where she visited some of the worst famine areas. Moira witnessed many aspects of the 'Food for Work' programmes in Bihar, the best-known feature of which was the well-digging. The Central Government had a big programme for this. Also, land was being cultivated, which only a year or two before had been considered unsuitable. She saw women carrying soil in containers on their heads as they worked to level new fields by hand.

Moira was greatly impressed at the vast, efficient cooperative effort and the nature and scope of the relief programmes operating throughout Bihar. She commented later:

> India's success in keeping more than 500 million people alive despite acute drought and food shortages merits the admiration and respect of the whole world. It is one of the great achievements of the century. In the State of Bihar alone, the vast co-operative effort between Central and State Governments and both Indian and international voluntary agencies has provided relief or part relief feeding for thirty million people for some twelve months. I travelled through Bihar and other drought affected areas by car, by jeep and on foot, and I saw so much evidence of these programmes and the food for work projects. On numerous occasions I helped to mix, cook and distribute relief food and I felt so proud that the Australian Government, by its gifts of wheat, and the people of Australia, by their gifts of milk powder, were sharing in this work.[229]

Despite this effort, there was still terrible hardship and suffering, particularly among the poorer people.

Moira was also impressed by the agricultural development and food for work programmes at the Hazaribagh headquarters of the Australian Jesuit Mission. The Jesuits were running courses for primary school teachers on how to implement the modern methods of agriculture that were appropriate to their area. The teachers in turn went back to their villages and passed on the information.

In one small hospital, St Columba's in Hazaribagh, the matron told Moira that before the milk powder started coming, they were feeding the babies on water that wheat and rice had been cooked in and they weren't getting any better. The babies were now being fed on milk powder gifted from the Campaign. It was making a big difference.

During her visit to Bombay, Moira was a guest delegate and speaker at an international seminar on 'Long-term Educational and Training Programmes for the Advancement of Women in Asia'. The seminar was sponsored by the National Council of Women of India in conjunction with UNESCO and was attended by 250 women from all parts of India as well as by international delegates. Moira appreciated the opportunity to meet the delegates and to learn of their dedicated work. Later she wrote: 'Certainly, I now have a deeper understanding of the difficulties confronting the women's organisations. I greatly admire the courage, the spirit and the determination of these Indian women leaders.'[230]

Moira told *The Advocate*:

> I was tremendously impressed by the way in which these Indian women are facing up to such problems as

illiteracy among villagers and rural people. They show great determination and patience in trying to co-operate in various plans and programmes aimed at raising the living standard of the people. It is not simply a question of making them literate, but how do you get to them?

One newly literate woman from a rural area in Maharashtra State addressed the seminar and told how twelve months ago she had attended a class organized by one of the voluntary women's organizations—in this case, the Maharashtra State Women's Council. Within four months she had learned to read and write and now she was teaching her women neighbours to do the same.[231]

In India, the rate of population increase was a matter of concern. This was one of the topics discussed at the Bombay seminar. The central issue was communication—how to persuade illiterate villagers that curbing the population growth was a necessity.

Moira was keen to see the developments in science and agriculture. During her visit to the Atomic Energy Research Station at Bombay's Bhabha Institute, she saw some of the research being done on the use of radiation and radio isotopes to increase agricultural production. This work was aimed at producing high-yielding varieties of seed and the elimination of pests and diseases in various types of wheat and rice seeds. At the time of Moira's visit, 13 million acres were under production with high-yielding seed developed by the researchers.

Moira also found a fierce demand for education in India. While many colleges and schools were run in much the same way as Australian schools, there were numerous occasions when travelling by road from one township to another she saw classes being conducted in the open air. She was told that since Independence, 40 million more children were attending school.

Moira noticed that the Church was playing an important role in the national life—especially in schools, hospitals and social welfare. In Kerala, Moira commented that the Catholic churches were packed to overflowing—'just crammed'. One of the highlights of Moira's trip was her private meeting with Cardinal Gracias, Archbishop of Bombay. He gave Moira a memorial volume of the Bombay International Eucharistic Congress (1964) on which he had inscribed: 'In grateful appreciation of your help for India.'

One of the chief aims of Moira's tour was of course to view the 'other end' of the Aid for India consignments. During her visit, three of the gift consignments sent by her campaign arrived. Moira was in Calcutta on 14 September when the *State of Orissa* docked, carrying a consignment. She was able to see the milk unloaded and follow it through to its distribution. Moira said that scrupulous care was being taken to see that the milk reached those in greatest need—mainly babies, small children and nursing mothers. She went to many of the relief feeding centres which had received milk powder, and on several occasions she helped to mix this milk and distribute it. She said that it was a deeply moving experience to give a glass of milk to a needy child when you knew that the milk had come from Australia.

During her visit to one of the villages in Bihar, Moira was very moved by the 'hero's welcome' she received. The whole population turned out to welcome her. The village had been razed by fire and the first food to get through to the villagers had been powdered milk from the Aid for India Campaign. Moira said that every time they stopped, the people cheered. When she enquired about this, the officer escorting her told her that the people were grateful for the help but quite overwhelmed that Moira had shown a personal interest in their welfare by her visit.

Moira's travels took her from Kashmir in the north to Kerala in the south, and from Bombay on the west coast to Calcutta in the east. Moira was later to write: 'Despite the tremendous difficulties created by the worst drought in living memory, I found it an India in which the most wonderfully dedicated work is being carried out by both public and private organisations.'[232]

Moira enjoyed the warm friendliness that she encountered everywhere. She also appreciated the beauty and colour of the places she visited. Even Calcutta, for all its stark poverty, had much beauty. The most memorable scenery of the whole trip was in the two 'Ks' at the northern and southern extremities of the sub-continent—Kashmir and Kerala. Although completely different from the other, Moira said each in its own way was 'breathtaking'.

> My overall impression was of a country, freedom-loving and democratic, multi-religious and multi-racial, vigorous in its intelligent development and in its industrial and agricultural progress. One cannot but observe and admire the strength of the family and respect for the family and the deep spirituality of the people.[233]

Moira identified poverty as the central problem facing India, not only the provision of food but also employment. When, as in Kerala, you had a combination of a relatively high literacy rate and widespread unemployment, one of the consequences was the kind of frustration that had led to the democratic election of a communist government. This was unique in the free world and it had occurred in a region where one-third of the people were Christians.

Unfortunately, Mother Teresa was not in Calcutta during Moira's visit, but all around the country she heard about the famous nun's work. In Calcutta, Moira noted the inescapable evidence of unemployment's consequences with enormous numbers of desperately poor people in that city, and there was serious political unrest. Moira commented: 'I think that Calcutta and the whole of West Bengal need a lot of prayers and a lot of help.'

Although the worst of the famine was over at the time of Moira's visit, there was an enormous amount of malnutrition in the country. Doctors were worried about the danger of protein deficiency causing brain damage in very young children. In every state Moira visited, programmes were being introduced to provide milk for children. Unfortunately, there was a shortage of supplies. 'But it is a beginning,' Moira said.

Shortly after returning home, Moira wrote to the Australian Prime Minister, with news of her trip:

> Dear Mr. Holt,
>
> Since my return to Australia, I have been visiting many centres in Victoria and New South Wales to deliver addresses concerning my impressions of India.
>
> During my eight weeks' visit, it was a wonderful joy to meet and talk with Mrs. Indira Gandhi, the Prime

Minister of India. I visited ten States and met a cross section of the people. I was impressed by the fact that there was so much goodwill for Australia.

In every State I visited, Government and private social welfare agencies were introducing programmes to provide milk for school and pre-school children. The Mayor of Bombay, Dr. L. De Souza, has introduced a vast programme whereby as many as possible of the needy children are given a daily cup of milk. Throughout India, the provision of milk to needy children is a relatively new programme aimed at combatting malnutrition and protein deficiency diseases. At present, the programmes are limited owing to shortage of milk powder. I feel that Australia could do a vast amount to promote goodwill by offering to assist in this scheme for children on humanitarian grounds.[234]

Despite having much to do after eight weeks away, Moira made time to write to the many people who had looked after her in India, including the Chief Minister of the Government of Jammu and Kashmir:

Dear Mr. Sadiq,

I wish to express to you my gratitude and appreciation for the very warm welcome which you so kindly extended to me in India. I shall always retain very happy memories of my visit to India, which has been one of the most memorable episodes in my life. Some of the things which were indelibly impressed on my mind were the kindliness, the friendliness and the courtesy of all sections of the Indian people, whom I had the pleasure and the happiness to meet.

With very great pleasure I remember my visit to your breathtakingly beautiful State, Jammu and Kashmir. The highlight of my visit was meeting you; it was wonderful of you to entertain me for dinner and with pleasure I recall our discussions concerning Indian affairs. It was a privilege to hear a Session of Parliament from the Speaker's Gallery and I really enjoyed this.

During my stay in Jammu and Kashmir, I very much appreciated all the facilities that were made available for me to see so much and especially in the fields of social welfare, education and scientific development and research. Mr. Dhar, Mr. Zutshi and Mr. Madain took very great care of me and their efficiency and minute attention to detail made it possible for me to see a vast amount in the time available. Please convey my grateful appreciation to them.

It was a privilege to stay at the lovely State Guest House in Srinagar. The colour slides which I took from the verandah of the views of the Jhelum and the houseboats have given very great pleasure to my family, my friends and Meetings which I have addressed on my return to Australia.

Enclosed please find a cheque for the equivalent of two hundred Australian dollars. This gift is offered in the spirit of friendship and co-operation for children in the Batmaloo Reconstruction Project. Supporters of my Campaign have been very interested to hear from me of this wonderful work being carried out by you and your Government. It is the wish of the donors that you be asked to utilize this gift to provide some small treat, which you may consider appropriate, for the children at Batmaloo. I shall always remember my visit to this project, the happy smiling faces of these children and their warm regard and friendship for Australians.

With kind personal regards,
Yours sincerely,
Moira Dynon[235]

22

The ABC 'Noises Off' Affair

When Mr Chatterjee informed Moira in March 1967 about his positive reference to the Campaign in the forthcoming ABC radio programme for secondary schools, this was very welcome news. Milk for India was the approved appeal in NSW public schools in 1967 and Mr Chatterjee's comments would show that the Campaign's work was valued and appreciated by the Indian authorities.

On 13 April, Moira asked the ABC in Sydney for broadcast details and a copy of the transcript when it was available. Mr BA Kent replied:

> The programme recorded by His Excellency is to be part of a series, "Getting to know our Asian Neighbours" to be broadcast to schools in N.S.W. in the second school term and in Victoria in term three. This series is being compiled in Sydney at our Head Office; …we have forwarded your letter to our Director of Education who will provide you with the required information and transcript.[236]

Three months after Moira had requested the broadcast details and transcript, a letter arrived from Dr John Challis, who had interviewed Mr Chatterjee:

> Yes, Dr. Chatterjee did make a generous reference to your work in the interview I taped with him for this series. Unfortunately that particular section of the interview (and others) was spoiled by loud background noises which we have been unable to eliminate, so we have not been able to include the segment in the series. I am enclosing a brochure of the programmes for your information. You may like to listen to the very interesting contribution of Dr. Chatterjee to the whole problem of Australian/Asian relations.[237]

Moira's responded by sending a telegram to the Prime Minister:

> Reference Australian Broadcasting Commission Series Getting to Know our Asian Neighbours and taped recording interview then Indian High Commissioner Mr. Chatterjee STOP
>
> A.B.C. now advise me that segment of recording concerning Mr. Chatterjee's generous reference my Campaign has been deleted STOP Understand Mr. Chatterjee's remarks concerning Aid for India Campaign also deleted from transcript for distribution Australian Secondary Schools STOP In view India's food needs and Milk for India programmes in schools both State and private such deletion appears inhumane and unfriendly to India and unfair to Campaign STOP In addition please refer to radio programme number seven of series[238] STOP Aid for India Campaign was not invited to participate STOP Above deletion linked with omission Campaign's participation series seven

undermines goodwill between Australia and India STOP

I treat the matter with grave concern as to damage Indian Australian relations and because of apparent lack of justice to the Campaign which has already gifted over 800 tons processed milk to Indian Government for the needy[239]

Moira replied to Dr Challis, expressing her concern that the Campaign had not been included in the ABC series and she asked for the text of Mr Chatterjee's remarks concerning the Campaign. She also commented:

Thank you for sending to me the copy of the brochure of the programmes for the series "Getting to know our Asian neighbours". I note that the map on the front of the brochure does not include India.[240]

Dr Challis sent Moira an extract from the transcript of interview between Mr Chatterjee and Dr Challis.[241] This extract was marked '(Copyright reserved)'.

High Commissioner: We are not thinking of Australia in this particular context [capital aid for India] I think what Australia has given, is giving—well we are more than satisfied and we are grateful because it is spontaneous; because we haven't asked for anything—that is the thing that touches me so deeply—this feeling of concern; this is not just the government. Take for instance Mrs. Dynon's Milk for India campaign—she has sent about 800 tons of milk—she and some friends—and I was very, very distressed to hear that the Chairman of the Milk for India campaign in Tasmania, Mr. Blacklow—he was very badly affected by the fire; we are trying to do something for him.[242]

The ABC's decision to ignore the Campaign in the ABC series and to omit Mr Chatterjee's comments from the broadcast for schoolchildren was disappointing, but Moira was more concerned that not enough was being done for India during its worst drought in living memory. She wrote again to Senator Robert Kennedy regarding US shipments of food grain to India and he replied:

> Dear Mrs. Dynon:
>
> Enclosed is a copy of the report I received in response to the inquiry I made in your behalf. I hope this information is helpful to you, and that if I may be of assistance in the future, you will feel free to contact me.
>
> Sincerely,
> Robert F. Kennedy[243]

Senator Kennedy enclosed a copy of the report that he had received from William C Gibbons:

> [The report included details of the considerable U.S. assistance to India]...The above actions plus the concentrated efforts of the Indian Government itself have helped to contain a possible widespread disaster in Northern India. The situation is much improved than five months ago and if the summer wheat crops proves as good as current indications project, we believe Northern India will weather the drought of the past two years.[244]

This was the last occasion that Moira sought the help of Senator Kennedy. Less than 12 months later, Robert Kennedy was shot down by an assassin in the Ambassador Hotel in Los Angeles. President Johnson, who had stepped into the presidential shoes of John F Kennedy, declared a national day of mourning. The United States had lost another great son.

From mid-August until mid-October 1967, Moira was in India. On 26 September 1967, Prime Minister Holt replied to the telegram that Moira had sent to him in July. He wrote:

> On receiving your telegram of 20th July concerning the A.B.C. programme "Getting to Know our Asian Neighbours", I arranged for the matters you raised to be referred to the Australian Broadcasting Commission. I understand that officers of the Education Department of the Australian Broadcasting Commission have since had discussions with you and I trust that the points raised in your telegram have now been explained to your satisfaction.[245]

A month later, Sir John Bunting, Secretary, Prime Minister's Department, informed the NSW Teachers' Federation that 'officers of the Education Department of the A.B.C. have already had discussions about this matter with Mrs. Dynon, the National President of the Aid for India Campaign, who, I understand, has expressed her satisfaction with the explanation offered'.[246]

On her return from India, Moira was shown a copy of Sir John Bunting's letter and she wrote immediately to the General Secretary of the NSW Teachers' Federation to advise that she had no such discussions, nor had she been given a satisfactory explanation.[247]

Moira also replied to the Prime Minister:

Dear Mr. Holt,

Thank you for your letter of 26th September concerning the A.B.C. programme "Getting to know our Asian Neighbours". I appreciate the fact that you referred the matters, which I raised, to the Australian Broadcasting Commission.

You refer to "discussions" between myself and "officers of the Education Department of the Australian Broadcasting Commission". There have been no such discussions concerning this matter but there was some correspondence.

...With regard to the deletion of Mr. Chatterjee's remarks from the broadcast, the explanation given to me by the officers of the Education Department of the Australian Broadcasting Commission was unconvincing for a number of reasons including the following:

1. The recording was made over a month in advance of Mr. Chatterjee's departure from Australia.

2. Dr. John Challis of the Education Department of the Australian Broadcasting Commission advised me in writing (17th July) that Mr. Chatterjee had made a "generous reference" to our work.

3. On 13th April 1967, I asked the Australian Broadcasting Commission for a copy of the transcript and it was not until the letter dated 17th July that I was advised of the deletion of the remarks owing to "loud background noises".

4. Enclosed with this letter was a brochure of the programmes for the series 'Getting to Know Our Asian Neighbours'. The map on the front of the brochure excluded India.

5. In reply to my request, on 10th August Dr. John Challis forwarded to me an extract from the interview, marked "(Copyright reserved)"...

At no time have I expressed satisfaction regarding this whole matter. On the contrary...I was profoundly disturbed to learn that the reference to the Campaign had not been included in the series in any way.

As you are aware, this was a series of ten programmes for Secondary Schools and was broadcast when Milk for India Appeals were being conducted in schools both State and Private, throughout Australia. It seems particularly unfortunate that the generous reference concerning Milk for India made by the then Indian High Commissioner was deleted from the text for the school children.

Recently in India, I have seen the arrival, unloading, transportation and distribution of some of the Campaign's gifts of milk powder. Scrupulous care is taken to ensure that the milk is used to maximum advantage and distributed without delay on a priority basis to needy babies, children and nursing mothers. Some of the milk powder is utilised in the preparation of the food provided under the relief feeding programmes—crushed wheat and milk powder cooked into a kind of porridge.

All the evidence points to the fact that the milk powder gifted by Australian children and adults has saved countless lives and is combating malnutrition and protein deficiency diseases. I have seen children whose health has been restored as a result of these Australian gifts of milk powder. I am sure that their gratitude will be everlasting. In addition to these benefits, milk powder gifts (as also is the case with wheat gifted by your Government) are creating enormous goodwill for Australia.

With every good wish,
yours sincerely,
Moira Dynon[248]

Sir John Bunting later advised Moira:

> The decision as to what material can be used in a programme must depend in the final analysis on the professional judgement of the broadcaster. In the present instance, the matter must rest with the Australian Broadcasting Commission.[249]

On 17 December 1967, Prime Minister Harold Holt disappeared in the surf at Portsea. The Country Party leader, John McEwen, took over as Acting Prime Minister temporarily and made it clear that the County Party would not accept William McMahon as Prime Minister. Senator John Gorton obtained Liberal Party endorsement for the electorate of Higgins (Harold Holt's seat), became Prime Minister, was elected to represent Higgins in the House of Representatives in a by-election and retired from the Senate.

Mr Holt, I believe, was respected by the people of his electorate of Higgins. The electors certainly maintained their vote for him. He was perhaps best remembered in his roles of Treasurer, Minister of National Service and Minister of Immigration and for his fair and tolerant approach on immigration policies. He was approachable and recognised the right of every man and woman to stand up and put his or her case.

Moira paid tribute to Harold Holt:

> I am sure that our late Prime Minister, Right Honourable Harold Holt, will be remembered in India with everlasting gratitude for the response by the Australian government and people in India's hour of need and for those outright gifts of wheat, milk powder and other assistance including well drilling equipment.
>
> It was a courteous and significant gesture of esteem for Mr. Holt and Australia that Mrs. Indira Gandhi, the Indian Prime Minister, sent a special representative to be present at the Religious Service at St. Paul's Cathedral in Melbourne on 22nd December last.[250]

23

Making a difference

During these years, the Aid for India Campaign responded to each new crisis that confronted the Indian sub-continent. Letters to Moira pleading for milk arrived in increasing numbers as did letters of thanks and gratitude. The Campaign was helping where it could and was making a difference. At the same time, Moira never tired of singing the praises of the leaders in India, both government and non-government, for their extraordinary efforts and achievements in the most trying of circumstances and with very limited resources, who were making a difference to the lives and welfare of their countrymen.

On 27 July 1968, the Prime Minister of India, Mrs Indira Gandhi, wrote to Moira:

> Dear Mrs. Dynon,
>
> You have helped us in the past. Now I learn of your latest gift of milk powder. I appreciate your genuine humanitarian concern and thank you on behalf of the many to whom you have brought succour.
>
> It was a pleasure meeting you again in Australia. I have pleasant memories of my visit.
>
> With good wishes, Yours sincerely,
> Indira Gandhi[251]

Mother Teresa MC[252] was always grateful for every shipment from the Campaign. She wrote:

Dear Mrs. Dynon,

This is to express our sincere thanks for the shipment of 169 cartons, 1 teachest and 1 bag milk powder and 230 boxes condensed milk sent to us ex s.s. VISHVA KALYAN and which reached us in good condition on 12.11.69. I am very sorry I could not write earlier as I was away from Calcutta and also I was busy with the retreats of the sisters and preparations for the Christmas Tree for the children and Christmas hampers for our poor people. Over 2000 families received a hamper of rice, dhal, potatoes, tea leaves and milk powder and on Christmas Day itself we served out a nice hot Christmas meal to about 1000 aged and starving people.

Wishing you a happy New Year with God's blessings.
God bless you
M. Teresa M.C.[253]

Brother Andrew MC[254], the first Superior of the Missionaries of Charity Brothers, founded by Mother Teresa MC, wrote to Moira:

Dear Mrs Dynon,

Yesterday we received the shipping papers for the milk that you have sent. And it was a very pleasant surprise. It will be a very great help in our distribution for the babies and children. It is especially valuable at this time, since the supplies of milk powder from America have stopped, and we just don't know what will happen. It is wonderful how something unexpected comes along just when it is needed.

Calcutta is in an awful mess at present, and we don't know what will happen. With all the uncertainty supplies, jobs, etc are also uncertain. And it is the really poor people who are the first to suffer. So your gift will be of help to people who really need it. Kindly thank all those who have a part in this gift for us.

With all best wishes and a prayer for you all.
Yours sincerely,
Andrew, M.C.[255]

Miss Nama Ajgaonkar, Superintendent, Dadar School for the Blind, Bombay, wrote:

Dear Mrs. Dynon,

Enclosed please find a photograph of our children taking milk which you have so kindly sent us through your organisation.

You may perhaps be aware that there are 4.3 million blind in India and most of the children get blind due to malnutrition. The effects of malnutrition often lead to blindness and some of them are suffering from T.B. The donation of your organisation is really very helpful for us to give the children substantial milk which is so necessary for healthy growth. We would therefore be grateful if you would arrange to send us this donation of milk powder annually.[256]

During her visit to Bihar in 1967, Moira had met Bernadette Keans from Melbourne, who was working as an Australian Volunteer Abroad at St Columba's Hospital in Hazaribagh. Bernadette later wrote to Moira:

My dear Mrs Dynon

As promised here are the photos taken at the hospital famine relief kitchen. We feed 200 daily. The people are given milk & bulgur wheat, made into a sort of mushy porridge. Not very palatable, but then hunger doesn't breed choice.

The volunteer workers who supervise the feedings, are boys from the local college. Each person is required to bring a stick of wood, which is used for cooking fuel. This is our only method of guarding against encouraging a beggar mentality. Expect that this free feeding scheme will continue until the rice is harvested. Say about early November.

Thank you so much for your support and interest. Without your supplies of milk we would never have embarked on this programme. Kindly extend to the other Committee workers and helpers how much the milk powder has been appreciated here. I did enjoy meeting you during your brief sojourn in Hazaribagh.[257]

Mrs TG Hymavathy from Stree Seva Mandir, Women's Tutorial Institute, Madras, wrote:

Dear Mrs Dynon

We met at the seminar in group discussion and you accepted my invitation to visit our institution. You are so nice...this is what you have written in our visitors book:

> 'I am very happy to have had the opportunity to see the wonderful work being conducted at this institution for children and the training of girls. The work is impressive. Congratulations, also, on the very happy atmosphere in the institution.'

We train women in book-binding, needle work and embroidery, weaving, wood working, wood carving, doll-making, painting...The children are provided with educational facilities. We request and appeal to you to try to extend your help to our institution.[258]

Dr KB Grant of the Poona Medical Foundation was very appreciative of the Campaign's gifts:

Dear Mrs Moira,

Your letter of 7th December, 1970 has indeed thrilled me to know that you have again sent us the valuable gift of 40 tins of powdered milk, for the use of poor and deserving patients of our Hospital. Your last year's gift of milk helped the institution quite a lot in nourishing the poor patients and I can assure you that this gift will also be utilised for the betterment of poor deserving patients...

Kindly accept my most grateful thanks for your gift. It is encouraging that you are appreciating whatever humble and little work our Institution is doing here... With my renewed thanks and warm regards.[259]

R Chittiak of Rangaraya Medical College, Andhra Pradesh wrote to Moira after a devastating storm:

Dear Mrs J.F. Dynon,

Probably you would have seen in the papers about the serious havoc created by cyclonic storms and rains in the coastal districts of Andra Pradesh. The disaster came at a time when the farmers were very jubilant about their crop and were preparing for harvest. For many everything was lost. I am sure you will do your best to alleviate the suffering of thousands.

Numberless humans and cattle lost their lives. Many are rendered homeless. I need not elaborate and hope that you will do something and come to our aid. Always praying for your welfare.[260]

The gratitude extended beyond the gifts of milk. The Indian Minister for Rehabilitation, Mr Mahavir Tyagi, wrote to Moira:

I would like to convey grateful thanks to you for the new consignment of milk supplies which will be utilised as carefully as the previous one. More than the gifts we value the sentiment behind these gifts and particularly your sentiment that truth and justice will prevail. It is one of the greatest pleasures in the world to be understood correctly.[261]

In October 1968, Moira received news of the catastrophic floods which devastated West Bengal, including this copy letter from Father Peter Ranger of Maria Busti Parish in Pedong, who had written to the local bishop:

A boy is travelling over the landslides to take this letter about the terrible calamity in the parish—the loss of lives, houses and crops…11 were killed in Maria when one house collapsed—three others miraculously survived. Almost everywhere enormous landslides have occurred & still are. Of 100 odd families none have escaped loss of land & crops. 21 houses collapsed.

People are taking refuge in our school and dispensary and the wounded are being cared for by M. Anne Mary. Many have lost all possessions and starvation is facing us as no supplies can get to us. No more water to drink no bridges left I don't know if this letter will get to you but I hope runners will get through. We dig the bodies out and bury them on the spot as there is no way of moving them to the cemetery. I performed the burial ceremonies through the loudspeaker from the presbytery & a proxy blesses them.

Please bless us all.[262]

Sometimes, all you can do is pray.

24

The Prosecution

What happened next was an episode we simply did not see coming.

On 21 August 1968, two officers from the Commonwealth Police, in the persons of Mr Veitch and his colleague Mr Kennedy, called on me at my home office in Malvern. I well remember that day. All the furniture had been removed from my office and the old floor coverings taken up in preparation for the laying of new carpet. The task of the Commonwealth Police in this exercise appeared to be to ascertain whether I had written certain letters of representation to the Immigration Minister. Even though it was not clear to me what this was all about, I quite readily acknowledged the letters, which were produced to me, as mine.

From the time of the 'Fontana Affair' in 1962, I had been making representations to the Minister for Immigration (Downer, Opperman, Snedden), the Prime Minister, various members of Parliament, and the Secretary or other officials of the Department of Immigration, concerning families who came to me, generally as a last resort, after all else had failed. They sought my help to bring to Australia members of their families who were still residing in foreign countries after being refused permission repeatedly by the Australian authorities to migrate to Australia.

At no time during that period of almost six years did the Prime Minister, the Minister for Immigration, any other Minister, the Secretary of the Department of Immigration, or anyone else ever advise me that before making such representations I was required by law to give notice in writing in certain form to the Secretary of the Department in Canberra. I was not aware of that requirement. I made the representations quite openly in writing to Ministers and to the Department on paper headed 'The Association for the Defence of the Family' together with my full name, address and qualifications—M.A. (Oxon.); LL.B. (Melb.).

In December 1962, Moira asked me to take on the Fontana family case after she had received a letter from the Italian Vice-Consul. Some seven months later, Mr Downer reversed all decisions made over the previous 11 years and decided to permit Angela Fontana and her brothers, Rosario and Agrippino and their wives and children, to join the remainder of the family in Australia. Many hours were devoted to that case and also to a whole series of other cases which were brought to me by families who had suffered rejection by the Australian Immigration Department. I recall some of the family name cases—Pronesti, Troise, Wee, Suraci, Ruberto, Catanuso, Jayagopal, Mastrioanni, Pakabuth, Baronessa, Gentile, Garofalo and Salafia.

In 1966, Moira received a letter from India from Mrs Mary Howard:

Dear Mrs. Dynon,

Some time ago, I read your appeal in the Statesman for Aid to India, and the human way you spoke I felt that here was a kind lady that would, I felt sure help if it were in her power, to give a family the happiness they would attain, if their wish was fulfilled.[263]

The Immigration Department had not approved her family's application and Moira asked me if I could help. I pursued this matter entirely by correspondence and happily the outcome was successful. More success followed in several other Indian cases.

I treated each case carefully, and sought and insisted on being given the truthful facts. As part of my representations to the Minister, I enlisted the support of various responsible citizens and politicians. In many instances I charged no fee. As time went by, I was unable to devote so much time to the work without making some appropriate charge. Success in cases led to Ministers overruling Departmental decisions and even Ministerial decisions, which had been unfavourable to the families. Unfortunately, in certain Departmental quarters, I gained no friends. I fear that my approaches and successes were unhealthy for me.

When Mr HA Veitch first called on me, he asked whether I had been acting as an immigration agent. I replied that I could not answer that question as I did not know the definition of 'immigration agent'. I pointed out to him that I was at a disadvantage by reason of the fact that he was referring to an Act which I had not studied in particularity.

Mr Veitch later showed me sections 46 and 47 of the *Migration Act 1958* (Cth.). Under these sections, a person was deemed to be an immigration agent if he received a fee or reward for his services relating to an application or representation to a minister, department or authority of the Commonwealth for a person to enter Australia as an immigrant. Before acting as an immigration agent, he must give notice in the prescribed form to the Secretary of the Department of Immigration. The penalty for failure to comply was £200 or imprisonment for six months.

The next day, I wrote to the Minister for Immigration:

> Dear Mr. Snedden,
>
> I wish to advise you that I had a visit yesterday afternoon from Mr. Veitch of the Commonwealth Police enquiring into my immigration representations to you.
>
> I was surprised to learn—and it was pointed out to me—that to charge any fee in respect of such immigration representations as I made to you, made me an 'immigration agent', in which capacity I could not act without apparently forwarding to you or to your Departmental Secretary a 'prescribed form'. I asked to be informed as to what law was said to be breached, and I was referred to sections 46 and 47 of the Migration Act which sections I had never read or heard of.
>
> ...I am writing immediately to assure you personally that I was quite unaware of any such provisions requiring the submission of a 'prescribed form'. If I had known it would have been quite simple to complete such requirement. I trust that my quite innocent ignorance on this matter will not prevent the continuation of my work in this important field of human national development in Australia.

I wish to regularise the position immediately in accordance with whatever laws and regulations apply so that I may proceed with this work.

In this regard I would request a 'prescribed form' for completion by myself, if this is the only way in which I can carry on with my work for migrants.

yours sincerely,
John F. Dynon.[264]

I was advised that the matters I raised were being examined and that I would shortly receive further advice.[265]

Mr KJ Smith, Commonwealth Director of Migration for Victoria, then sent me a copy of the prescribed form that I had requested.[266] He also advised me of Regulation 29 of the Regulations under the Migration Act:

> The maximum amount that may be charged by a person for all services rendered or to be rendered by him in relation to an application or representation, [to a Minister, Department, or authority of the Commonwealth for a person to enter Australia as an immigrant]... (not being a service of a legal professional character rendered by a legal practitioner) is Two Dollars.

I wrote immediately to the Minister on 9 October:

> Dear Mr. Snedden,
>
> ...I have now received a 'prescribed form' from Mr. K.J. Smith, Commonwealth Director of Migration for Victoria. Mr. Smith also advised me [of] Regulation 29 of the Regulations made under the Migration Act...

According to my interpretation of this Regulation and section 46 of the Act, it is permissible for me as a practising Solicitor to render services to my client, including representations to any Minister of the Commonwealth, and in so doing do not act as an 'immigration agent' within the meaning of the Act, and therefore do not need to submit the 'prescribed form' to the Secretary of the Department of Immigration.

If I am wrong in this my present understanding of the Act and the appropriate Regulation, since the whole question concerns migration matters I would like to be advised, as, naturally I do not wish there to be any misunderstanding.[267]

As I had received no response to this letter, I wrote again to Mr Snedden:

Dear Mr. Snedden,

I refer to my letters to you dated 22nd August and 9th October 1968.

I am writing to advise you that an Information was laid against me by an Officer of your Department on the 22nd October 1968 in two matters: one regarding Guiseppe Adamo and the other regarding Sebastiano Breci on whose behalf I made representations to you. These matters are returnable at the Court of Petty Sessions in Melbourne on the 29th November.

In view of the fact that I have been informed that you gave instructions for the laying of these informations, I am forwarding to you, with this letter a copy of a voluntary statement which I gave to Mr. Veitch. This letter I am posting Air Mail and registered post to you

> by way of 'Advice of Delivery' service.
>
> ...So that I will be aware of your opinion as to my dealing with fresh matters as from 21st August I would appreciate your early reply to my letter of the 9th October concerning the interpretation of the Regulations and Act, in view of the exclusion '(not being a service of a professional character by a legal practitioner)'.[268]

I then received a letter from the Commonwealth Director of Migration, Melbourne:

> I acknowledge receipt of your letter to the Minister dated 9th October, 1968. I have been instructed by the Minister to inform you that he has referred the matter to the Crown Solicitor. After reviewing the case, and considering all the circumstances, the Crown Solicitor will institute proceedings if he considers this action is warranted.[269]

By the time that letter was written, two Federal Informations had already been sworn out against me and had been served on me by Mr Veitch. Mr Veitch said to me then that he was surprised that the prosecution had been initiated, but it appeared to him that the Minister had seen fit to take the action. I replied that I too was surprised and that there appeared to me to be something definitely political about the proceedings.

After the summonses had been served, Dr Jim Cairns MHR told me that he had asked Mr Snedden about the matter. Mr Snedden had said that he was taking no part in it as he considered it as purely a Departmental matter. Mr Snedden also indicated that, to his knowledge, there were no other similar prosecutions recently or currently. Mr Snedden in fact

THE PROSECUTION

had refused to accept my letter of 26 October 1968. It was returned to me unopened through the post office on 23 November 1968, six days before the hearing date.

On the day of the hearing, 29 November 1969, outside the court, Mr. Veitch, in the presence of Moira, again expressed his surprise that the matter was proceeding.

There was a Mr RH Mooney, apparently of the Special Investigation Branch, Canberra, who attended the proceedings. He told my counsel that 'the Minister had given express instructions that the proceedings were to go ahead'.[270] My good friend Charles Francis[271] was my counsel in these legal proceedings.

At the hearing, the Magistrate, Mr N Thompson SM, ruled that the requirement regarding giving of notice applied to 'any person'.

The first witness was Mr Kelly of the Immigration Department in Melbourne. He had been with the Department for 21 years. He had the authority to institute proceedings, which he did on the instructions of Mr KJ Smith. He agreed that I was the first lawyer investigated under the Act and the first lawyer to be prosecuted under the Act. Mr Smith had given him no reason as to why the charges were to be laid. He said that he could not recall anything about the Fontana case, but the Department would have been embarrassed if the Minister had been given false instructions. He knew that I had made representations, and in many cases had obtained change of decisions.

The second witness was Mr HE Parslow, the Officer in Charge, Operations Branch, Immigration Department Melbourne. He produced in evidence a bundle of blue cards, which were said to bear the names of those persons who had given notice in accordance with Section 47. He said: 'I have no record that Mr Dynon is an immigration agent. Mr Dynon is not recorded on these cards.' Under cross-examination, Mr Parslow said that there was only one card which bore the name of a solicitor with a city or metropolitan address. His name was Woodhouse. Charles Francis told the court that he had known Woodhouse personally and that Woodhouse had been dead for over two years. Every living person recorded on these cards was in the country.

It seemed to me that Counsel for the Prosecution was not impressed by the way the Department or Minister had gone about the prosecution. He told my counsel that it was obvious to him that the Department had 'got it in' for me and that I had been 'too good', and that the Department wanted 'to get the knife into [me] and to turn it'.

On 1 March 1969, two months before the Magistrate handed down his decision in the matter, Mr and Mrs De Brass came to see me. They asked me to take up the case of their good friend in India who had applied for immigration to Australia but had been refused admission by the Department of Immigration. I explained to Mr and Mrs De Brass that, because of the Department's prosecution and because of the Migration Act, I could not act for them at that stage. I also told them that I could not effectively recommend any particular solicitor to take on this assignment since I knew as a fact that, as at 29 November 1968, according to the Departmental records, there was not one living solicitor in Melbourne who was permitted to perform immigration work.

On 6 March, Mrs De Brass telephoned me. She had contacted the Immigration Department in Melbourne and had spoken to a senior official, Mr A Barber. She asked him if there was any solicitor in Melbourne who was permitted to take on the immigration matter. He told her that he did not know of any solicitor in particular who was specifically authorised to do this work; he did not know of any reason why a solicitor could not act; there were many letters coming in all the time to the Department from solicitors concerning immigration matters. She could go to any solicitor.

This confirmed what had become obvious to any interested observer. There were numerous Melbourne solicitors doing immigration work at this time, none of whom had given notice in the prescribed form under the Migration Act. The authorities had no interest in any other solicitor. I had been singled out for prosecution.

During the course of my various representations to the Minister on behalf of many families, I had received valuable support from *The Herald* and in particular from its experienced and reliable representative in Canberra, Mr EH Cox. When I told him of this matter, he advised that if the prosecution was against me alone, or if I was the only professional person being assailed, then the prosecution was surely being done with malice. That was his opinion.

When the Court reconvened on 2 May 1969, we found, on arrival, three Press representatives in the particular Court— from *The Truth*, *The Age* and *The Herald*. It is not difficult to imagine that someone in or on behalf of the Immigration Department tipped off the Press in anticipation of a 'kill'— plenty of adverse publicity for me and damage to my professional career and to my work for immigrants.

Mr Thompson SM said that he remembered the matters which came up on 29 November and that 'when the defendant learned that there was a provision in the Act relating to notice he wrote to the Minister seeking elucidation. In reply he received a summons'.

The Magistrate said he was satisfied the charges had been made out. He could dismiss, discharge or adjourn the matter. Mr Bergin for the Commonwealth stated: 'If you dismiss, it is not a conviction.'[272] The Crown urged that the adjournment practice be adopted. The Magistrate made an order dismissing the charges, there being no conviction.

The Age reported:

> In dismissing the charges Mr. N. Thompson, SM, said he believed Dynon had acted in ignorance of the regulations. He said he doubted neither Dynon's character or his integrity.[273]

I do not level any charge at higher or lower authority when considering the motivation for this prosecution. I will, however, make some comments.

First, the Liberal Party was never pleased that Moira and I had quit our Branch positions in the Party following the Matrimonial Causes Act and had eventually quit the Party. Secondly, Mr John Gorton, who was Prime Minister at the time of the prosecution, had previously taken little pleasure from a strong letter that I had written to him, criticising his leaving Australia on the summons at short notice from US President Johnson, whilst Mr Gorton's Guest of Honour, Mrs Indira Gandhi, Prime Minister of India, was still in Australia in 1968.

Also, there were those who viewed with disfavour Moira's promotion amongst Australians of friendship with, and aid for, India. Although Prime Minister Robert Menzies had supported her work by granting transport and shipping assistance, some Liberal Ministers later effectively belittled the Campaign and some Departmental officials appeared to lack sympathy and understanding. I recall vividly the occasion when William McMahon, in conversation at an Australian-Asian Association dinner at the Hotel Australia, Melbourne, saying to Moira that the Indians were not grateful.

Also, Moira was a member of the Australian Labor Party and was receiving 'too much' support from Labor leaders and others in the Labor Party throughout Australia in her Milk for India Campaign.

Those who were aware of the prosecution and the attendant circumstances at the time were convinced that the move was calculated to discredit the Dynons through me, in the past, present and future.

Amongst other things, certain matters were not viewed favourably—our stand on the question of race and colour; our attitude with regard to immigration of those, other than of European extraction; and my role in bringing about the re-uniting of families in Australia, especially as it questioned many Departmental decisions. Mr KJ Smith,[274] Director of Australian Immigration Department in Melbourne, would not have forgotten my many letters to him during the Fontana affair. On 6 December 1962, Mr Downer had advised Dr Jim Cairns that extensive enquiries about the Fontana matter had been made by Departmental officers. Mr Downer felt sure that the comprehensive report by his Department included all the details necessary for him to arrive at his decision. Mr Downer was to think otherwise by May 1963, and the Department felt the sting of reversal.

Moira was most upset by this prosecution of me. She considered the way in which I was treated was most unfair and she felt involved because she had asked me to help in the first case—the Fontana family and, later, the Howard family. That was not her fault. However, she sensed that my technical omission provided an opportunity to assail her through prosecuting me. She was concerned for me. I was not so concerned for myself but I was concerned that the prosecution had all the earmarks of a dirty trick and that it had hurt Moira. Jacinta told me recently that this was the only time she ever saw her mother cry.

My brother had written to me on 6 January 1969: 'It does seem rather strange that the usual method, which is to give a strongly worded warning, was not used. This is very difficult to understand.'

My last word on this subject is to thank Mr Howard who prayed for me to St Jude, the Patron Saint in apparently hopeless causes. His prayer requesting intercession was granted.

25

India revisited—Letters between Moira and John

In January 1969, Moira travelled again to India. She had been invited to speak at the National Seminar on Human Rights in Madras, organised by the Guild of Service in collaboration with UNESCO. She was also invited to present a paper and chair a section of a seminar in Poona, organised by the National Council of Women in India, with the theme, 'Comparative Studies of Women's Progress in the East'.

Before leaving, Moira received a letter from Nancy Dobson, Hon. Secretary of the Australian-Asian Association of Victoria:

> Dear Moira,
>
> It surely would be a great understatement to say I was pleased to receive your letter of 14th January...It would give me the greatest of pleasure to have attended that Seminar, as I know what a splendid contribution you will make with that lively mind of yours ticking over at about 1,000 seconds a minute.

I am also so very pleased at the high honour that has been accorded you in being invited to speak on "Women and Social Welfare in Australia". I feel sure you are the right person to present our women as they are, and the magnificent contribution they make towards social welfare in the country...

With love to you, and wishing you every success in this great opportunity to show your ability as a very representative Australian woman.

Sincerely,
Nancy.[275]

Early Saturday morning on 25 January 1969, the children and I farewelled Moira at Essendon airport. Two days later I wrote:

Dear Moira,

Your plane took off from Essendon pretty much on time—hope the subsequent journey to Singapore and Calcutta went smoothly. Did you finally have a sleep in Singapore? I had a few hours extra sleep on Saturday morning whilst the others busied themselves in various jobs.

We set off for Sandringham at about 12.15. It was a very boisterous day—overcast. The waves were rough and the beach deserted. They eventually persuaded me to go in and it was quite warm. Unfortunately biting rain came—David said it was hailstones. We took shelter under the water. After an hour we concluded with fish & chips in Sandringham.

On Sunday Jacinta & John redid any squashed boxes

for markings—all 295 boxes are now 'set' to go. All the family are exceptionally well.

Engagement has been announced between Dame Zara and Mr Jeff Bate, M.H.R., 63, Liberal Member for Macarthur, N.S.W. The Sun writes he has been member there since 1949. He was married twice & was divorced last year by his second wife, Mrs Thelma Bate CBE.

Professor Ronald Henderson, Director of Melbourne's Institute of Applied Economic Research has said some 42,000 Melbourne children are growing up in 'acute poverty'. A survey revealed that the poorest people were large families, women bringing up children without a male breadwinner, the aged, the sick and accident victims. (Sun 27/1/69)

Lord Casey said: "Australians have a special responsibility in Asia, an area that needs much development, security & political stability…we're the closest to Asia and Asians look to us for aid more than they do elsewhere." The fact that Australia could still be regarded as "underdeveloped", he said, made it easier for Australia to see the world's problems from the point of view of both the developed and less developed countries. (Sun 27/1/69)

The Age (27/1/69) quotes Mr J.E. Menadue, Federal President of the Australian Natives Association "Australia is not geographically connected with South-East Asia—although we are told the dingo originated there". "It is absolutely ridiculous to say our destiny is tied up with countries of South East Asia. It is the other way around." "As Governor Phillip said on January 26th 1788 "We hope not only to occupy and rule this great country but also to become the <u>beneficent patron</u> of all the nations of the Southern Hemisphere."

This morning is quiet and fine to warm. We will be setting off at about 1.30 for Sandringham probably.

I'm sending this to Bombay rather than to Calcutta, because I feel sure that it would just miss you in Calcutta.

Keep well and try <u>not</u> to do the extra bits which would make you over-tired. All send their love. Nothing to report. Our prayers and thoughts are with you always.

Love John[276]

Moira wrote from Singapore:

Dear John

We arrived in Singapore about 10 p.m. local time last night after a pleasant trip. The plane was two hours late leaving Sydney. Father James very kindly came out to the airport and waited with me. After talking with him I am making a few alterations in the papers as follows—Madras paper line 6 political (correct the spelling); line 17 after "discrimination" insert "many of the "apartheid" laws"—apartheid to go in inverted commas. In the Poona paper Page 9 delete blue eyed—I want blondes to appear to be either gender. Should it now be blonds?

A girl from S.M.H.[277] interviewed me at the airport and a photographer took my photo. They were supposed to be used in Sun Herald today. I was very tired at the time, so hope the Report is not too bad.

At Perth, the Howards & Jeewas were there to meet

me. The Howards are both very bright and alert—even better than the letters. He is waiting to hear from you what he can do to help in that matter[278]. He talked about all the work involved on their behalf and I gather has all your letters etc. He mentioned organising some of the people you have helped into doing something. Meanwhile his family is praying daily for you and all of our family. Mrs Jeewa and Elizabeth are very nice. Mrs J. is very worried about her brother in Burma.

Singapore appears to be very wealthy. There is much evidence of new buildings (hotels, offices, flats etc). The shops were all closed today being Sunday. I attended Mass at St Bernadette's Church—a very modern, huge church. The congregation was quite large. Mass was in English. I returned to look at Raffles Hotel, Raffles Square etc. It does not appear to have changed at all except for a new coat of white paint on the Hotel. The harbour was full of ships.

Father gave me addresses of two of his friends. So far I have not been able to contact them but will try to telephone them later. It is hot and humid—typically tropical. The hotel has a glorious swimming pool which is well in use. After I have seen so much evidence of wealth here in Singapore, could you kindly add on page 5 of Madras talk line 3 after "non-white" for me, "in many areas". It would be more accurate and I have altered my copies.

It was lovely of you and the children to get up early and come to the airport. I could see you all from the plane and David also on the upper deck. I do hope that you were not too tired or that the very early rising did not spoil the children's day.

As you can guess I was very tired when I arrived. The hotel is comfortable and I slept until about 9.30 a.m. It is air-conditioned and the food excellent. Today I have been well looked after and have seen many of the sights of Singapore.

With my love to you and to Michele, Jacinta, John, James and David.

Love from Moira[279]

I wrote next with news of correspondence:

Dear Moira

Letter, dated 21/1/69 received today from Mr Sapru, Hon Sec Delhi Branch, Red Cross. He had just returned to Delhi after 3 weeks in the South—thanking you for arranging gift which 'helps to revive our milk feeding programme for the children which had to be suspended a couple of years ago. They will arrange what you requested & ask you to book consignment at Bombay port addressed, Secretary-General Indian Red Cross Society New Delhi and forward shipping documents to them—most grateful to Aid for India Campaign for generous gift. "One hopes that the shipping charges will be met by the Aid for India Campaign as it is difficult here to procure foreign exchange."

Letter, dated 24/1/69, received today from J.N. Douglas Pringle[280] thanking you for letter "and the very interesting information in it. I am glad you are going to India again. When you return I would be glad to consider a letter from you refuting allegations that the Campaign's milk gifts have been misused."

Letter dated 21/1/69 at Brisbane from GV Thumbunkel forwarding Dairy. Vishva Vibhuti he said is expected to call at Melbourne in the first week of February. "would be delighted to meet you & would be happy to carry back your good wishes to Mr Mehta".

It is another sunny day today. Yesterday afternoon we spent about three hours at Sandringham & are off again this afternoon. John has gone to get his books at Halls this morning. Michele has gone into the City with Patricia to see The Charge of the Light Brigade. Jacinta rang Wilsons and Shipping Company in reverse order this morning & cancelled for Wednesday & has asked Wilsons to keep in touch with the Shipping Company.

Some more milk arrived about midday today. A pre-school centre, I'm not sure from where, is bringing some milk this afternoon. Had a very nice letter from Howard this morning. He also said that you had been speaking to a lady from Burma & her daughter.

Love from all, John[281]

With further news, I wrote the next day:

Dear Moira,

I had a letter from Mrs Jeewa this morning saying how happy they were to meet you. She said: "I understand that Mrs Dynon will be visiting New Delhi; & from the conversation, I gather that Mrs Dynon has not met Mrs Violet Alva personally. Should you be writing to

Mrs Dynon before she goes to New Delhi, I am giving you the address of Mrs Violet Alva. She is a very nice lady & will be very pleased to meet Mrs Dynon...

Had letter from Father this morning & am deleting the adjective on page 9 of Poona paper & inserting "many of" before the apartheid laws on line 17 page 5 of other paper. Have just done corrections of copies that are to go to Thomas and will do the others when I finish this letter.

Letter today from Sarla Shar from Bombay saying she is "eagerly looking forward for your arrival at Bombay..." and "I will be very glad if I will be of any help to you during your stay at Bombay please. On your arrival at Bombay contact me..."

Jacinta went off to Halls to purchase her school books today. Tonight we will be going to the Toorak drive-in to see the "High Commissioner".

The External Affairs material came through the post this morning—the letter was <u>actually</u> <u>signed</u> by <u>Freeth</u> and dated 20th January. It had West Australia cancelled postage stamps 23c, but the date of despatch could not be read.

All are well. No further news.
Love from us all, John[282]

Moira wrote to me of the five wonderful days she spent in Calcutta:

Dear John

Thank you for your letters of 28th and 29th which I received on arrival at Bombay today. It is good to know that you all are well. I shall especially be thinking of John, Jacinta and James on their birthdays next week. Thank you for the news re Mr Sapru. I shall telephone him in New Delhi. Also I was happy to hear of the nice offer by Mr Pringle.

Calcutta was so interesting, so busy and so wonderful. I hated leaving there this morning. You know, I always feel so at home with Bengalis. The atmosphere in the city was considerably improved from what I saw in 1967. The elections are due on 9th Feb and it will be interesting to see the results. Mr Mehta very kindly placed a car and driver at my disposal and I was able to do three weeks work in the few days there. Some of the highlights were meeting Mother Teresa and seeing some of her work. It was an honour and pleasure meeting her—likewise Brother Andrew. Mother T is coming to Australia late in February. Regarding the books for her children could you kindly send to me, preferably at Delhi if time permits, two or three copies of letter head (National P. A for I.C.). As we thought, there will need to be a special permit and after my talks with her, I want to get things moving before I leave India. Also, would you kindly telephone the Secretary to Archbishop Knox and advise him that I had the honour and pleasure of meeting Mother and that we are proceeding with the formalities for duty free special certificate.

Brother Andrew likewise is doing wonderful work—at his Home I gave undernourished children milk and New Zealand milk powder biscuits and fed a baby with a bottle of milk. The poor little things are in dire need. Also I visited Loreto Convent and also the orphanage at Entally—the latter also is in need of help. The officers at Food Corporation are so helpful and co-operative. After what I have already seen and heard I feel so ashamed that Australians should spread those malicious rumours. Certainly from what I have seen the exact opposite is the truth. It seems incredible that the milk can be made to go so far and to do so much for so many needy children, women and refugees. I think we shall have to extend our activities to cover gifts of flour also. Time and again, it is obvious that milk, flour and egg powder are required. At Loreto House Sister Caroline and several of the nuns down from Darjeeling all asked after Father James. Brother Andrew also wanted to hear about him. They all sent kind regards etc.

The show "Glimpses of India" and the S.C.I. dinner party were fabulous. On Wednesday evening, I went to a gathering at Mrs Pathak's home (you remember Captain Pathak from State of Orissa). This was all arranged by Captain Bhoot and it was all very pleasant. Last night, after having drinks with Mr & Mrs Mehta at their home, we went to a dinner party at Mr & Mrs Chatterjee's home—another lovely evening. A very talented Indian entertained us with some glorious music. Mr and Mrs Muthachen (friends of H. E. and Mrs Thomas) entertained me for lunch at their home at Belvedere overlooking the Botanical Gardens. They were lovely to me. In between visiting the numerous social welfare projects and talking to officers, I was able to see many of the sights and places of interest, such as Indian Museum, Hindu temples, Schools,

University, Victoria Memorial, new buildings, bridges etc. This must wait until I come home.

I hope you received my cable regarding the Seminar papers. Regarding Madras, the Chief Minister there is critically ill. If anything should happen to him, I feel it could possibly affect the Seminar and I think it wise that you do not release the paper until I advise you further. I shall keep you informed.

Regarding the Poona paper, I am amending page 9 in another place. (I take it you received my letter re blonds). Line 16 "<u>I would describe a policy</u> based on the <u>so called</u> "H..." principle as a h...etc." I hope you understand what I mean. The paper will be more consistent if that word "present" is deleted. (The underlining is to help you—it is not in the paper). I am aware that I slightly altered the sense but I am anxious that "easing" should be the message. I think it is better that way and more accurate.

The flight to Bombay was good. Mr Mehta came all the way out to the airport to farewell me—so kind of him. Mr Maluste of Reserve Bank of India whom I met at the party last night was on the same plane. Everyone is being so kind. I shall have to curtail some of my Bombay plans so as to be fresh for Poona. With my love to you and to the family and hoping you are all well.

Love from Moira

(over)

P.S. Fancy Zara!! Thank Jacinta & John for boxes etc. Very proudly I have told of their efforts—and of the help you and all the children give. M

I have a lovely room at the hotel overlooking the sea and "Gateway to India". At the moment some children in the street below are playing musical instruments and singing—it is all so lovely. I wish you could be here too. M[283]

Moira's next letter was from Bombay:

Dear John,

This is just a brief note to accompany the press clipping. I thought you would be interested to read about Mr Sen. Thank you for your letter of 29th which I received yesterday afternoon. I am having dinner with Mrs Shar this evening.

I have been busy in Bombay and have done much and seen many people. Everyone is so kind to me. Yesterday afternoon I went to Regina Pacis and saw the bags of milk powder we sent. All of the remaining ones are in excellent condition. The Sisters there have an orphanage, a school for poor children and a training centre for girls. They are doing wonderful work. Mother Superior took me around and the teachers and the girls made me so welcome. In the senior classes, I was surprised at how much the girls knew about Australia—they asked me many questions.

From what I have seen in social welfare projects both here and in Calcutta I think that the saddest cases are those who have no one—orphans and abandoned children. In places I have visited this time, I have met many such children who speak some English. I am "Auntie" to hundreds of such children.

I have met and talked with officers of Food Corporation of India and Regional Director of Food. Also, the Shipping Corporation of India is just wonderful to me. As in Calcutta, their officers here in Bombay are so kind and there never seems to be enough time to talk about all the things we want to. Tomorrow I am having lunch with some of their officers before I leave for Poona.

Mr and Mrs Fernandez came to see me this morning. Both are well and it was lovely to see them again. Mr F. has had much to do with rehabilitation of Koyna earthquake victims. Mrs F. gave me a beautiful sheath of roses and tuber roses from her garden. The perfume is lovely. Last night I saw Dr Nagarajan and we talked for ages. His daughter Usha, to whom I sent those books, gained first class honours in her Masters Science degree. I spoke to Usha on the phone and will see her on Thursday evening when I am having dinner with them. On my return from Poona I shall be visiting the Bhabha Atomic Research Centre to see more of the recent developments. It is expected that electricity generated at the plant and its sub stations will provide power for Gujarat and Maharashtra State by next May.

Mr Sathaye and Mr R S Mehta (no relation to our Calcutta friend) of S.C.I. are just wonderful to me. They have provided a car for me which means that I can see so much in a short space of time. Also, they have very kindly "teed up" by telephone on my behalf many of my appointments which is such a great help. I am so grateful to them. I saw Mr Harris, Aust Trade Commissioner in Calcutta but have not yet seen Mr Melhuish here. I expect to do this in the morning.

Yesterday I had tea at the home of Mr and Mrs Maluste and met their family. Mrs Maluste is a very talented lady and a very active social worker. Their daughter is studying M.A. in foreign languages. She has her B.A. and last year studied at the Sorbonne in Paris. She is such an interesting person—and very pretty.

It may not be possible for me to write again for a few days so don't worry if you don't hear from me. I am feeling nervous at the thought of the Poona Seminar with so many talented Indian ladies attending.

Love to you and the family.
Love from Moira

P.S. Holy Name Cathedral where I went to Mass this morning is really lovely. It was packed.[284]

On 2 February, Moira sent a postcard to our son John:

Dear John

This picture is of the Chowpatty Beach—the site of many famous and historic meetings. It is not far from the hotel where I am staying. In Oct 1967, I went to a rally at this Beach at which Mrs Gandhi spoke and which was attended by over 300,000 people. The place is even more picturesque than this card.

Happy birthday on 4th
Love from Mum.[285]

My next letter to Moira was filled with family news:

Dear Moira,

On Friday, 31st January, today, we had a lovely day all at the beach at Dromana. It has been hot all day between 80 and 100. We had our meal at Mornington on the way back, and bought icecreams to have at home later. Got home just after 8 p.m.

Yesterday afternoon I went to see both Form Masters at Xavier, and everything went alright. Saw Hiliary there when she was waiting to talk to Mr Hingston. She was asking for you. I told her that you had gone to India. She asked was it the Milk. I said yes it was; but that principally you had gone because you had been invited to deliver papers at two Seminars. She said 'Moira has certainly dug her heels in'; in which of course we would all concur.

Letter arrived today from Frank Moraes saying 'I look forward to meeting you when you come to Delhi from February 9 to February 14.'

Mon (3/2) Your telegram arrived this morning. I am holding all papers until further notice. We went this afternoon to Sandringham—extremely hot & sticky—then a thunderstorm & lightening—however it was very refreshing.

David is off to School tomorrow and I believe he has a half day for a start. He is all ready to go and will be going by tram & bus. On last Saturday night—after a few hours at Sandringham—I went to the Law Institute Reception 5-8 at the National Gallery & enjoyed the evening. Met John Molomby & Frank Williams, also Sir John Barry and was introduced to Mr Haymanson, Secretary of the Institute; Arthur & Julie Adams, Mary & Roy Dobson and some others. I explained to Leah Molomby about the Entry Free Certificate.

Newman Ros. rang this morning. Adelaide had been injured in a car accident last Thursday & is in Cabrini. He asked to speak to you & I told him where you were. He asked me about the other matter and I said that so far as I know at the moment the matter was proceeding. He said he had understood that it was to be withdrawn. He asked me to let him know of any developments. After the reception I went straight down to Luna Park. John had taken David there. I took him on the Scenic Railway and Big Dipper. Michele wrote to you today to Delhi to which I will write too, as I may miss you at Bombay.

Letter came in this morning from S.K. Sen, 29 Jan 69. He had been away up to 28th. He writes "It would give my wife and me great pleasure to have an opportunity of renewing our acquaintance. I shall be most happy to receive you on your arrival at Delhi if you let me know your plans. In the alternative, if you could kindly let me know where you would stay in Delhi. We could call on you..."

All the children are well and we go to the beach almost every day. Your mother rang this morning re the boys shirts—re sleeves. She also said Margaret McCann got a scholarship for Arts & Crafts.

Children all send their love
John[286]

Moira wrote to our daughter Jacinta, after the Poona conference:

Dear Jacinta

Thank you for your lovely letter which I received on

my return to Bombay last night. It was wonderful to hear from you and to know that you are spending some happy times at the beach. I am sorry that you have had so much trouble with the "milk".

The Conference at Poona was an outstanding success. They liked my paper. It was attended by many distinguished people including Mrs Violet Alva (Dad will tell you about her). She is a lovely person. The whole time we were very busy—from early morning until late at night. The Poona ladies looked after us beautifully. I stayed with Mr and Mrs Sangtani who are delightful people and really "spoilt" me. They have a superb new home and I was very comfortable there. I was made "Chairman" of Section 2 "Women and Social Welfare" which kept me very busy. I had to make several speeches which (all) were well received.

Poona is a very pretty place about 120 miles from Bombay. The weather there was cold at night but hot and dry from about 10 a.m. to 4 p.m. The Mayor gave a Reception in our honour and we were entertained in several homes. The Seminar was inaugurated by His Excellency The Governor, Dr Cherian who together with Mrs Cherian remembered me from our meeting in 1967. The inauguration was in a huge hall and I was one of the speakers. At the Reception following, I had the pleasure of meeting Archbishop Gomez who is a friend of Archbishop Knox.

Today I have had a busy day seeing various people. Please tell Dad that I am staying privately at Madras so would he send any letters either to Air India or to

Mrs Jadhav there. The hotel booking has been cancelled for Madras. The Seminar there will take place as State Mourning will finish on 11th Feb. Also, will you tell Dad that he may release the paper as arranged subject to the alterations which I wrote to him from Bombay (my letter 2nd Feb).

With love to you, Dad, and to Michele, John, James and David and again thanking you for your letter

Love from Mum

P.S. Thank you for the prayers which I greatly appreciate. Don't forget to say some more for the Madras Seminar.[287]

Moira's next letter to me was from New Delhi:

Dear John

Thank you for your letters of the 31st and 3rd which I received on my arrival here today. It was good to hear the news of you and the family. I had hoped that by now there might have been some favourable action regarding "that matter". So far I have not mentioned it to anyone but intend to do so this week in appropriate quarters.

Following on a letter by H.E. Mr Thomas, Mr Dias has asked Mr Gera, whom I met on my last visit, to arrange a programme for me. Mr Gera is extremely nice and is taking an immense amount of trouble on my behalf. He told me this afternoon that an appointment has been made for me to have an interview with Mrs Gandhi at 12.30 on 12th. Needless to say I am very excited about this. In addition, a number of very important people are graciously making their time available to see and talk to me.

I was interested to hear about the Institute Reception and am so glad that you went and enjoyed it. Regarding Adelaide Rosenthal—I am so sorry to hear of her accident. Would you ask Lela florist (Mrs Menzies) to send some flowers and charge to my account and would you word an appropriate message? It would be nice to phone Rosie and ask about her progress. I know he would appreciate it.

I have noted your comments re Mr Moraes. Mr Sen has gone to Assam unexpectedly following on the sudden death of his father. He left a message for me. During the week I shall contact Mrs Sen. This afternoon Mr and Mrs Vinayakam, friends of Mr Dias, came to see me. They are charming people and we had an interesting conversation. Their son, a doctor, is at present studying in Moscow on a fellowship. Mrs Vinayakam works for the Government in Cabinet Secretariat. Very kindly, they have invited me to have dinner with them on Tuesday. Words are inadequate to tell you how kind and how friendly everyone is to me.

Press people at the Poona Conference told me that reports of my paper had gone to A.A.P., Reuter and some press here. They told me New directions A, B & C were all of interest. I think, at least in my Section, that a vast amount was achieved at Poona. The Report of the Section was very well received and the 6 resolutions arising out of our Section were all carried. There was an election for the new President of N.C.W., which, after a secret ballot, was won by an Anglo

Indian lady from Calcutta—in my opinion, another triumph for multi religious India.

Tonight after making a few phone calls, I intend to go early to bed. I am well but tired after an exciting but exhausting week.

With love to you and to all the family.
Love from Moira[288]

On her arrival in Madras, Moira wrote:

Dear John

This is just a brief note to let you know that I arrived safely at Madras today where I am staying with Mr and Mrs Muthiah. They are so kind to me. Their beautiful home overlooks the Bay of Bengal and the views are glorious. The Conference starts tomorrow morning and judging from the programme, it is going to be very busy.

My stay in Delhi was most enjoyable and I met many interesting people. Unfortunately, at the last minute, due to sudden events, it was not possible for the P.M. to grant my interview. Naturally I was disappointed but it could not be helped. I saw many of my friends in Dept. of Rehab. They have given me (I did not ask) masses of details re milk powder distribution which should keep the critics quiet. As I said in an earlier letter, it is amazing how far the milk powder gifts are stretched and the "unconditional" offering is helpful and most appreciated. On Tuesday I was taken by road to Karnal in Haryana to visit a home for destitute women and children Bengali refugees. It was a moving and unforgettable day. The rehabilitation work for the women is most impressive. It was a long but memorable day.

Mr and Mrs Dias, Mr and Mrs Nanjappa and many others were wonderful to me. They entertained me in their homes and looked after me in a multitude of ways. The weather, especially at night, is quite cold and I am now enjoying the warmth of Madras. On my arrival here at Madras airport, Mary C.J. greeted me with the largest glorious garland of tuber roses I have ever seen. Also a representative of Shipping Corporation of India kindly came to the airport and greeted me with a lovely silver garland. My welcome here was lovely.

I received Jacinta's letter at Delhi. Please thank her for it and for all the news. Thank you all for the prayers which I greatly appreciate.

As it is now late and I have an early start in the morning I shall save the rest of the news till I return except to say that I handed over the A-N-A cheque in the office of Mr Ramdas of Social Welfare Dept to the appropriate lady from the Retarded Children's home. She will be writing direct to Dick Buxton.

With my love to you, Michele, Jacinta, John, James and David

Love from Moira[289]

After returning home, Moira wrote to Mrs Mary Clubwala Jadhav, Chairman of the Guild of Service:

Dear Mrs Clubwala Jadhav,

I want you to know how much I enjoyed the Guild of Service National Seminar on "Human Rights" in collaboration with U.N.E.S.C.O. held at Madras. It was an honour to Australia and to me personally to have been invited to participate in and to be the Chairman of Section 1 of the Seminar dealing with "Education and International Understanding".

May I congratulate you and all those concerned on the outstanding success of the Seminar. I am aware that this success was achieved following much organisation, hard work, detailed planning and minute attention to detail. The "Human Rights" Seminar at Madras was a tremendous achievement and I am sure that you and the Planning Committee must be very happy with the outcome. For me, the deliberations, the sessions, the discussions and the exchange of ideas were most valuable. To have participated in this Seminar was a wonderful experience that I shall always remember.

It was so very kind of you to welcome and farewell me at the airport. I know that there are many demands on your precious time. May I also say how very much I enjoyed staying with Mrs Murugappa Chettiar. It was a great pleasure to have stayed in the home of this charming and distinguished lady.

Thank you for your kind letter of 18th February and your generous comments which I greatly appreciate.

With kind personal regards,
Yours sincerely
Moira Dynon[290]

26

Surplus Australian wheat for India

In 1969, Moira's attention turned to the wheat surplus in Australia. Press reports had disclosed that millions of bushels of surplus wheat were piled up on farms around Australia:

> Angry Wimmera and Mallee farmers say they have already harvested enough wheat to fill their quotas for the next two years. Mr. Bill Kelly of Culgoa, stands beside a 6000-bushel stack of wheat which he can't sell. And why? A record season has already filled Victoria's 1969–70 quota of 65 million bushels.

> ...farmer Kelly summed up the feeling of thousands of Victorian wheat farmers: "We might as well take a bloody long holiday. The game has gone dead flat and here we are right in the middle of the best season in years. I've already harvested 9000 bushels to fill my quota and I've got just as much again sitting in the paddock. The Wheat Board can't sell it and I can't do a thing about it."[291]

In October 1969, the Aid India Campaign initiated a 'Wheat for India' programme with the objective of purchasing surplus

Australian wheat at fair prices for gifting to Indian Governmental and non-governmental social welfare projects. Within a month, the Campaign had dispatched two shipments of wheat and flour and further consignments were sent in January 1970.

Moira wrote to the Prime Minister, John Gorton[292] and *The Herald* picked up the story:

> The president of the Aid India Campaign, Mrs Moira Dynon, wants the Federal Government to subsidise the immediate buying of surplus wheat and give it to India. In a letter to the Government this week, she said: "Australia cannot afford to adopt the attitude that because India cannot afford to buy our surplus wheat, millions of under-privileged children and adults deserve to starve. We don't ask Australian farmers to give wheat away. Many of them are facing enormous economic difficulties and hardship."[293]

The Herald quoted 'an official of the Primary Industry Department' as saying that Australia will give India 70,000 tons of wheat, worth $3.5 million, this year.[294]

The Herald also reported that Dr Jim Cairns MHR 'supported a call by the president of the Aid India Campaign, Mrs Moira Dynon, to send surplus Australian wheat to India'.

> "The Government official who yesterday listed our wheat gifts to India was simply excusing Government failings and issuing Government propaganda," he said. "Australians should demand that the surplus wheat in this country be shipped to the starving people in Biafra and India. Our national conscience insists that action be taken. The Government must organise a systematic,

regular way to provide wheat to countries that need it, to raise our contribution in overseas aid to one per cent of the gross national product," Dr. Cairns said.[295]

Moira commented:

> The Statement by "an official of the Primary Industry Department" helps neither the needy people in India nor the wheat farmers in Australia. If the Official is trying to suggest that India could not use a gift of surplus Australian wheat for needy people, his suggestion is ridiculous. From all parts of India, numerous social welfare organisations have asked Aid India Campaign for wheat and flour...
>
> It is no answer to our plea for assistance with wheat purchases for the Official to congratulate the Australian Government on the proposed gift of 70,000 tons of wheat to India this year under the terms of the International Grains Agreement. The economic compulsion taints the humanitarianism. The Prime Minister of India, Mrs. Indira Gandhi herself has questioned this approach. Speaking in New Delhi on 31st October, 1969, she said: "The issue is whether international aid is to remain primarily an instrument of national policies of donor countries or whether it becomes part and parcel of genuine international co-operation."[296]

One of the grateful recipients of Australian wheat was Mother Teresa MC:

> Dear Mrs. Dynon,
>
> On behalf of the Missionaries of Charity and our Poor, especially the leprosy patients, I take this opportunity

of thanking you for sending us 33 bags of wheat ex s.s. VISHVA KALYAN under B/L No: 4 of 6.6.70 which reached us in good condition on 6.8.70.

You will be very happy to hear that these 33 bags of wheat reached us just in the nick of time to help us tide over a crisis. As you know our leprosy patients receive each week very strong medicine, which requires them to take plenty of nourishment to complement it, otherwise they may become very weak and even face death. Divine Providence came to our rescue and helped us clear this consignment to give each of them sufficient ration for the week. Thanks to your generosity and the trouble taken. God reward you a hundredfold for your kindness for the Poor of India.

Assuring you of our prayers and in return requesting yours.

God Bless you
M Teresa M.C.[297]

27

Twenty-five million pints of milk

By mid-1970 the Campaign had sent processed milk sufficient for 25 million pints of liquid milk to India. The Minister for Education, Lindsay Thompson MLA, said in opening the 1970 Milk for India Victorian Appeal that Australians had donated enough powdered milk to Indian relief programmes to fill milk bottles stretching between Melbourne and Brisbane. Mr Thompson said he hoped we 'are developing a generation of Australians who feel they have a genuine relationship with their counterparts in India'. Person-to-person aid campaigns like Milk for India encouraged him to have a real optimism for the future of the world.[298]

Bishop John Cullinane, when offering the support and good wishes of the Catholic Education Office and Catholic schools, had said earlier: 'Important as the material aspects of the Campaign are, the spiritual and psychological aspects are of even greater value. Programmes such as the Milk for India Appeal do good in expanding awareness of the real dimensions of neighbourliness.'[299]

At the 1970 launch, Moira reflected:

> Tonight, just briefly, I look back to the past. The inaugural meeting of this Campaign was held on 23rd November, 1964. At the time there had been failure of the monsoons in India and drought and potential hardship were in sight. A number of those who spoke on that occasion are with us tonight.
>
> I look back to the contribution by the then Prime Minister, Sir Robert Menzies, who made the decision to provide funds specifically to meet the shipping freight costs of processed milk to India and made available the facilities of the Department of Supply. Sir Robert, although not able to be with us tonight, recalls his interest in the work and he has made a generous donation to the Campaign.
>
> I look back to the decision of the Victorian Government under Sir Henry Bolte to provide free transport on the Victorian Railways of milk consignments gifted to the Campaign. This practical support for our work demonstrates a belief in its beneficial results and is recognized with gratitude as help from the Government and people. Likewise, we thank the Victorian Education Department which, for the fifth successive year, has approved the Milk for India drive and has given permission to the Committee to approach the schools in Victoria.
>
> I look back to the Malvern City Council decision to arrange transport by Council truck from Caulfield Railway Station to our depot here. This transport of the heavier consignments joined with the transport provided by our voluntary workers is most valued and

appreciated. In the last three years this lead by Malvern Council has been followed by other Municipal Councils, Shires and local Government authorities, who have given us assistance in many ways.

I look back to the spontaneous and gracious offer made to the Campaign by the Shipping Corporation of India to provide free shipping transport on its ships to India of the milk powder despatched by the Aid India Campaign. This offer came early in 1967 at the time when our Federal authorities under another administration were re-considering Sir Robert Menzies' policy decision. We are personally very grateful indeed to the officers of the Shipping Corporation of India for their continuing sympathetic and invaluable assistance.

I look back to the enthusiasm and co-operation of officers of C.S.I.R.O. Division of Dairy Research which resulted in gift consignments for under nourished Indian children of the Australian High Protein Milk Biscuits. I look back to the assistance and generosity which we received from A.J. Ferguson & Co. Pty. Ltd. and Vulcan Australia Ltd. with regard to the gifts of electrical equipment which we sent for special training purposes in Madras.

Lastly and certainly not least, I look back to the kindness and co-operation of the Prime Ministers of India, Mrs. Indira Gandhi and the late Mr. Lal Bahadur Shastri, and of the authorities in India and their representatives in Australia for their courtesy to myself and the officers of the Campaign.

So much has happened in the intervening years that it

is impossible to relate these events in the space of time at my disposal on this occasion. So much has been done by so many not only throughout Victoria but throughout Australia. It is obvious on all sides that the voices of the people in Australia have been heard and there is practically a demand for the promotion of deeper understanding between the peoples of Australia and India.

Tonight, I want principally to speak of the present and the future. There is today in India a continuing need for powdered milk to combat protein deficiency diseases particularly in children and nursing mothers. Naturally, our Campaign cannot alone meet this need, but it is well to emphasize that it plays a part and can continue to play a part in the fight for health of many in India. Milk is destined to play an important role in India's battle against malnutrition. The supplies consigned by the Campaign have not only helped to heal and preserve the health of countless children and people in India, but have also built up a great fund of goodwill.

The Campaign wishes to continue its humanitarian work and wishes to extend the areas of goodwill, understanding and co-operation across the Indian Ocean. The Campaign appeals for the practical assistance in any way possible from all people of goodwill. The Campaign is extending its help even now—it is filling gaps in aid in certain areas in India where international agencies have withdrawn help for various reasons. Instances which immediately come to mind are Milk Feeding Centres for poor children which previously received their vital supplies of milk powder from U.N.I.C.E.F. and C.A.S.A. (Christian Agency for Social Action).

I have often been asked how and why the Campaign began. I believe that love of humanity and the fostering of goodwill between the peoples of our two large countries bordering the Indian Ocean are the prime motivations. In addition, I believe there are other compelling factors which can be assessed as we will. I personally believe we owe a special duty to our neighbour, India, the world's largest democracy—and I believe it is a simple exercise in political wisdom.

So we believe these things—what more can we do about them? The objectives of Aid India Campaign are to promote friendship, co-operation and understanding between the peoples of India and of Australia. These objectives are being implemented by five programmes:

1. Education Programme – new Information bulletin "India's Atomic Energy Programme"
2. Financial assistance (to specific projects in India)
3. Advisory services (open to all Australians)
4. Wheat for India
5. Milk for India –Points

Milk is needed to combat malnutrition in underprivileged children, nursing mothers and refugees, and to alleviate hardship following natural disasters such as floods, drought, earthquakes, etc. In the spirit of friendship and co-operation, processed milk sufficient to provide 25 million pints of liquid milk, have been gifted to Government of India social welfare projects and approved relief programmes for free distribution to the needy regardless of race, caste or creed. The Campaign is a "person to person" goodwill gesture. This year in addition to consignments to Department of Rehabilitation, we hope to be able to maintain supplies to 62 social welfare projects including hospitals, orphanages, schools and milk feeding centres. At present 20 Milk Feeding Centres are dependent on the Campaign to maintain their programmes of one cup of milk a day per child.

Two weeks ago in Canberra through the courtesy of the Prime Minister of Canada, The Right Honourable Pierre Trudeau, I had discussions with officers of his Government. The officers expressed interest in the aims and work of the Campaign. The Campaign is greatly encouraged by their interest. As a result of these discussions it is now my deepest hope that whilst our two Governments may well develop a useful dialogue at Government or Departmental level, our respective peoples through voluntary organisations dedicated to help India may come to seek and find avenues for co-operation.

The co-operation and generosity of Australians in the past has enabled the Campaign to continue the flow of life-giving supplies of processed milk for Indian children in dire need.

Please, will you help again?[300]

28

Disasters in East Pakistan

On the night of 12 November 1970, a new disaster struck the Indian sub-continent. A great cyclone in the Dacca area and devastating tidal waves inundated East Pakistan, causing countless deaths and immense destruction. At the time, it was described as 'the greatest natural catastrophe this century'.[301]

Despite the enormity of the need, Mr B Hayes, Director of the Foreign Affairs Aid Council advised Moira that the voluntary aid bodies would not be running an appeal. In view of this, Moira called together a group of citizens and formed an ad hoc Committee for East Pakistan Disaster Relief. Moira asked Sir Robert Menzies if he would accept the position of President of this Committee. He replied:

> Dear Mrs Dynon
>
> I have always admired your energetic efforts on behalf of good causes, and am delighted to know that you are proposing to make a special effort to help the Pakistan Relief Organization.

It is kind of you to ask me to accept the position of President of the Committee but I am afraid that I must say "No". I am already committed to sufficient enterprises. My vigour is not what it was, and I would not care to accept such a position knowing that I could do nothing active about the matter. I am glad to see that you have Sir Edward Dunlop interested; he, of course, is a great name and enjoys widespread respect. I am sorry to have to disappoint you on this matter but I really have been forced to make a resolution about accepting future positions.

I enclose my cheque for a modest donation towards your fund.

With kind regards,
Yours sincerely,
Robert Menzies[302]

Sir Edward Dunlop and others at the meeting declined to accept leadership of this committee, so in order to get the appeal 'off the ground', Moira agreed to accept leadership of the committee[303] and, inevitably, all the worries and problems that went with it.

Mr Len Reid MHR was in Dacca following the disaster and he knew first-hand how bad it was, as did Mr Allen, Deputy High Commissioner for Australia in Dacca. Foreign Affairs Department officers approved the appeal going ahead and offered to transmit money raised by the appeal to Mr Allen to be used for relief at his sole discretion. The Department also offered to pay for and facilitate the transport by sea or air of a first consignment of foodstuffs, and a second later consignment.

Moira appealed to all Australians:

> In the past, at times of emergency and natural disasters, Australians have responded with warm-hearted generosity. Now when millions of people in East Pakistan are facing a calamity of a magnitude unprecedented in living memory, I appeal to your readers—please will you help again?[304]

Moira was distressed at the time by the delay of the Foreign Affairs Department in sending the first donation cheque for $3,000 to Mr Allen in Dacca, and again when a second cheque for $3,000 was initially mislaid in the Department's office in Canberra.

I remember well during this appeal Moira was exhausted. All the family knew of the great stress she was under, not only with the Aid India Campaign but with the additional problems of the East Pakistan Disaster Relief Appeal. The workload on Moira was overwhelming.

The Campaign, over a period of some 12 months, had been having problems with deliveries of mail between Australia and India, and indeed within Australia. Moira used to work constantly into the early hours of the morning. Despite the many difficulties she encountered, despite all her other duties, she persevered with courage and determination to carry through the work involved in serving others.

We booked a family holiday at the beach at Mt Martha for January 1971. Although she was desperately tired, Moira gave up this holiday to try and get her correspondence up to date. She did get away for a short time for a break and tried to think through some of the problems she had encountered.

Then in the midst of it all, the Pakistan military machine commenced its attack and onslaught on Dacca and East Pakistan. The Government of Pakistan had refused to transfer power to legally elected representatives and had arbitrarily prevented the National Assembly from assuming its rightful and sovereign role. Pakistan sought to suppress the people of East Bengal by the use of naked force: by bayonets, machine guns, tanks, artillery and aircraft.

The Prime Minister of India, Mrs Indira Gandhi moved a resolution condemning the actions of Pakistan and supporting the people of East Bengal.[305] This resolution was passed unanimously by both Houses of Parliament in New Delhi.

The direct result of the military onslaught from West Pakistan on East Pakistan was a great flood of refugees into India.

Moira was shocked and revolted at the genocide that took place in East Pakistan. The best information Moira had was that the greatest single need of the refugees was food. The Aid India Campaign was sending food supplies to aid these refugees specifically.[306]

Moira wrote to the Indian High Commissioner Mr AM Thomas:

> I want you to know of my deep sorrow at the suffering and hardship of the defenceless and poverty stricken refugees from East Pakistan. Please be assured of my whole hearted support in the noble work which your Government and people are undertaking to provide relief and rehabilitation for these adults and children in dire need.
>
> The fact that I am uncertain as to what further steps I can take to help in the present situation intensifies my anguish.[307]

The Indian High Commissioner replied immediately:

> The number of the refugees coming over into India is in the vicinity of two and a half million and if they continue to flow in at present rate, influx could be five million or even more. The Government of India are trying their very best to provide all help and succour, but the magnitude of the problem is getting to be beyond their unaided capacity. The Government of India have requested international agencies for assistance and relief supplies.
>
> Your organisation has ever since its inception shown commendable lead in organising assistance for areas and sections of population whenever it became necessary to do so. Your assistance would be most welcome at the present juncture where this man-made disaster has overtaken millions of poor and defenceless people.[308]

Moira sent telegrams and letters to both the Prime Minister William McMahon, and Deputy Prime Minister Doug Anthony, urging the Australian Government to assist these refugees. Seeking the support of other nations, she wrote to various consul officers including the Italian and Japanese Ambassadors in Australia. Moira also approached church leaders including the Catholic Archbishop of Melbourne:

> Your Grace,
>
> Moved to compassion at the plight of the suffering refugees in India and in the spirit of love for the poor and needy, I am writing to you in the hope that you will, on your own initiative, take steps in an effort to obtain assistance by the Australian Government for

these children and adults in dire need. I am aware that in the context of the current international scene, diplomacy and tact are required. With your outstanding qualities of Christian leadership, your experience in international spheres and your knowledge and understanding of India, I feel that an initiative by you could be of immense help.[309]

Prime Minister McMahon responded to Moira's letters and telegrams:

> Your proposal that Australia should provide food for the East Pakistan refugees is understandable and appreciated. There is, of course, an undoubted need for food and this will continue on a very large scale. At present, however, the food problem is mainly one of distribution and diet rather than of inadequacy of Indian supplies. India's stocks will need replacing in due course and, as a traditional donor of food aid, we expect to provide further assistance of this sort later in the year.
>
> ...our current aid allocation is being spent in the light of advice received from the Indian authorities...At present the most urgent needs, so far as supplies from overseas are concerned, are for shelter materials, medical supplies and ambulances and we are concentrating on meeting these requirements. To date the Government has delivered over $750,000 in emergency aid to the refugees. This has consisted of cash, vaccines, mass injection guns, antibiotics, anti-diarrhoeal drugs, intravenous administration units and solution, vitamins, baby foods and shelter materials. The latter have consisted mainly of woven and laminated plastic sheeting

> for protection against the monsoon...So far we have provided enough shelter material for over 330,000 people and will eventually provide enough for about 800,000 persons.[310]

Moira left for India in August 1971 to examine the position of the refugees from East Bengal into India and to follow up on some consignments. She found a refugee problem of gigantic proportions. Refugees from East Bengal were streaming into India at many places on the frontier. Moira saw men, women and children with bullet wounds. She saw a boy of 12, his leg shattered with gunshot wounds and later amputated; she saw a 72-year old man carried in with bullet wounds in the back. She also saw countless cases of severe malnutrition, mainly children under eight. But Moira said that one of the saddest sights she saw was a full-term, new born baby who weighed only two pounds. Everything she witnessed confirmed reports that hundreds of thousands of refugees would die of hunger and disease by the end of the year if adequate food and shelter were not provided.

Moira became unwell during this trip and was compelled to cut short her stay. But with remarkable resilience, she renewed her activities not long after her return home in September. *The Advocate* reported:

> Memories of starved bodies and frightened faces of Pakistani refugees have haunted Mrs Moira Dynon, of Malvern, since her visit to India this month. She is just back from a 25-day stay, during which she inspected refugee camps and spoke with numerous social workers and Government officials.
>
> "I talked to many people and even those who were not showing signs of starvation still had terror in their

faces. In all the places I visited there was abundant evidence that the Indian authorities and private agencies were doing everything possible to help the suffering people...I drove out to Salt Lake City, a refugee camp that makes the best of what it has, and on that five-mile drive I couldn't help noticing the poverty of the area and thinking what a heavy strain was being forced on the West Bengal economy." [311]

Moira sent a telegram to Nigel Bowen at the United Nations headquarters, New York:

> Against the background of history culture religion and democracy and in context of aspirations for Independence by people of East Bengal I implore you to
>
> 1. Support human rights and democracy
>
> 2. Condemn Pakistan genocide in East Bengal
>
> 3. Emphasize with revulsion that West Pakistan colonial military junta has ruthlessly effaced democratic vote of people of East Bengal
>
> 4. In the interest of world peace abhor supply of arms to bolster up military junta in Pakistan
>
> 5. Excoriate military junta for secret trial Mujibur Rahman the leader of democratically elected representatives of East Bengal
>
> 6. Plead for urgent massive aid to Indian Government to assist in temporary care of millions of refugees
>
> 7. Initiate recognition and autonomy Bangla Desh[312]

At 2 a.m. on 14 October, Moira sent a telegram to Prime Minister, William McMahon:

> Massive aid for refugees in India is urgently needed STOP In the interest of peace political settlement repeat political settlement acceptable to the people of East Bengal is imperative STOP Respectfully remind you of statement by Prime Minister of India 29th September Quote Basic issues involved and real threat to peace and stability in Asia are being largely ignored unquote STOP I implore you and your Government to provide massive aid and to take appropriate steps for political settlement STOP If I can be of assistance please advise accordingly [313]

Moira spoke to a well-attended public meeting at the Melbourne Town Hall.

> The situation in the Indian sub continent compels Australians to jolt our Government out of its complacency. More than 9 million refugees have been forced to leave their lands. These are just some of the survivors of the terror unleashed in East Bengal by the Pakistan military machine. The cruel barbarity is almost unbelievable.
>
> By its caring for the refugees India has shown respect for their human rights. At the same time her own people suffer more. And still the flow of refugees into India continues—25,000 and more each day. The care of these refugees is an international responsibility. But so far, outside India, generally speaking, this responsibility has been accepted by most Governments only to a token degree. On moral grounds massive aid is needed now. Millions of refugees are in danger of death through malnutrition.

> Typical of the technique of the Pakistan military junta was its action in arresting Sheik Mujibur Rahman, the leader of democratically elected representatives of East Bengal, throwing him into prison and announcing a secret trial for treason. The savagery has unleashed Bengali Nationalism. The seething ferment of Bengali Nationalism has now erupted. Bangla Desh independence is now inevitable. Unless there is a political settlement acceptable to the people of East Bengal, Pakistan's actions will continue as a threat to stability in Asia and endanger world peace...
>
> In the context of Australian democracy it is for us to let the Government know that we expect from it action and compassion. How many more Bengalis have to die before the Australian Government is moved from meanness to generosity?
>
> I urge the Australian Government to take its head out of the sand and publicly affirm that a political settlement in East Bengal is fundamental to stability and peace. The situation demands massive aid and a political settlement.[314]

Moira recalled the pertinent comments of Victorian Premier Sir Henry Bolte, as President of the Victorian Committee for World Refugee Year (1 July 1959 to June 30 1960):

> If thousands of refugees were pouring across our borders as the result of some terrible disaster, surely none of us would hesitate to help. We would set up emergency relief centres. We would share our homes and arrange food services. We would give time and money. A lucky accident of geography has saved us from all this. I am thankful to say that most of us know

nothing first-hand of the terrors of political oppression or the miseries of a refugee camp. But our responsibility to help others does not diminish with distance. Rather, our own security depends on the solution of refugee problems in other parts of the world.[315]

Moira sent a telegram to the Australian Prime Minister, then in Washington having talks with the US President, Richard Nixon:

Mindful of events concerning Panama in 1903 and in context of publicly reported United States request for Australian intervention in Cambodia respectfully suggest you request that United States join with Australia in collective intervention to protect human rights of the people of East Bengal STOP Against background of history and by reason of public opinion being horrified at the cruelties inflicted by West Pakistan authorities on Bengalis suggest co-operation of Great Britain France and U.S.S.R. should be included in your approaches.[316]

Prime Minister McMahon replied:

As you will be aware, the Government has decided to give an additional $2.5 million as aid to the East Pakistan refugees, thus bringing its total aid since May to $5.5 million. This additional aid consists of $500,000 as a cash grant to the United Nations High Commissioner for Refugees and $2 million for the provision of urgently needed items. We are in close consultation with both the local and United Nations authorities. The need for relief aid will continue and I can assure you that we will maintain a constant review of the situation.

> We are aware of the need for a stable political solution and have been active in diplomatic exchanges to this end. When in Washington recently I took advantage of the presence of the Prime Minister of India, Mrs. Gandhi, to have a full discussion with her on the situation in the east of the sub-continent. After this meeting I sent another message to President Yahya Khan urging upon him once again the need to deal with the elected representatives of East Pakistan and with Sheikh Mujibur Rahman. Until a solution is reached, however, we will continue to play a full part along with other governments and international bodies, and will keep a close watch on all aspects of the situation.[317]

Shri SN Sapru, Hon. Secretary of the Indian Red Cross Society, Delhi branch, wrote to Moira:

> It is a great pleasure hearing from you and especially to see the press comments on the excellent work you are doing in organising aid to this country and helping to strengthen the already subsisting friendly relations between our two countries. Your work in mobilising aid for Bangla Desh refugees and also in projecting the true image of India to your countrymen has evoked our great admiration. God bless you for the good work you are doing.[318]

The Australian Deputy High Commissioner in Dacca, Mr Allen, gave Moira an account of the heroic life-saving work done for refugees in Nagori using the money Moira sent for cyclone relief, 'though not connected with the Cyclone, was every bit as urgent'.[319]

In October 1972, Mr Len Reid MHR in the House of Representatives, had this to say:

> In emergencies we fail badly, and I wish to quote 1 or 2 instances with which I have had first hand experience. The first is the great cyclone which ravaged the offshore islands and coastal regions of East Pakistan on the night of 12th and 13th November 1970...now claimed to be the greatest natural catastrophe this century and there is no doubt about that...To the victims...all we provided was $425,000.
>
> This time last year we had the refugee problem in India, mainly in West Bengal. The Government provided $5,500,000, but of course $2m of that was not used because India's invasion of East Pakistan quickly brought an end to the refugee problem...There are still some 20 million people homeless in Bangladesh and large scale assistance is urgently needed to avert famine conditions at the present time. For almost 2 years I have been endeavouring to get the Government interested in a rehabilitation programme. However it has shown little interest to date.[320]

WINDING DOWN

29

Winding down the Campaign

In March 1971, India held general elections for the fifth time since Independence. Moira spoke about this:

> Voting in India is on the basis of universal adult franchise regardless of race, caste, religion or sex. For this coming election, more than 270 million voters, speaking 14 distinct languages and hundreds of dialects, will be eligible to vote. They will cast their votes, freely and by secret ballot, in a network of some 300,000 polling stations all over the country. They will cast their votes for candidates representing 10 major political parties and a number of smaller parties and independent candidates. The policies and platforms of the candidates range through the whole political spectrum. The administrative machinery required for an Indian election is staggering.
>
> Whatever might be the positions of the respective parties after the election, whether power at the Centre is held by one political party or by a coalition of parties, it is important that we in Australia adequately recognize the importance of democracy in India.

> In Asia, democracy of any sort is a rare jewel. When the people of the largest nation in the world are forced to live in accordance with the thoughts of Chairman Mao, we should be truly grateful that the second largest, thinking what thoughts it chooses, goes freely to the polls. Especially in this region of military and princely dictatorships, and rubber stamp parliaments, India merits the respect of all those who value freedom for her faith, amply demonstrated in the past, that the basis of power is not force, but the free will of the people. The people of India are aware of the power of their vote.[321]

Under Mrs Gandhi's leadership, the Indian National Congress won a landslide victory. Mrs Gandhi wrote to Moira:

> Dear Mrs. Dynon,
>
> I am grateful to you and the members of the Aid India Campaign Committee for their message of congratulations on our recent elections. The task before us is indeed complex and immense. We shall need the understanding, not only of our own people, but also of well-wishers abroad.
>
> Yours sincerely,
> Indira Gandhi[322]

At a Special Meeting of the Campaign Committee in April 1971, Moira spoke of two matters. The first was:

> Today it is my sad role to speak of the late Mr. Frank Keating—our late Hon. Treasurer. It was in November 1964 that I first turned to him for help. In truth I really cannot recall whether I asked first or he offered first—

the result was the same— Frank became Hon. Treasurer of the Campaign. His guidance sympathy and dedication were such real pillars of support for me and I wish to emphasise the part that he played in the progress and solidarity of the Campaign. I myself and the members of the Committee owe a deep debt of gratitude to him. His compassion was extended to me when I needed the help of his invaluable services, and his compassion was also directed always towards those whose lives and welfare we were affecting in India. Frank will be long remembered in our hearts for his generous unselfishness, for his good advice and for his painstaking care of the records of account. He was a very good friend to me, to the Campaign and to the people of India. On this occasion may I extend to Mrs. Keating our deep sorrow for her and the members of her family. I would like her to know how much we respected Frank and how much he meant to us and to the Campaign.[323]

The second matter concerned the future of the Campaign.

> I want to put you right in the picture. There is no doubt at all that our work, and especially the Milk for India programme is of tremendous help for Indian children in dire need. In many of the social welfare projects for which we are supplying urgently needed processed milk and other assistance, we are the only group out of India that is helping. Over the years there has been wonderful support from thousands and thousands of men, women and children throughout Australia who have compassion and wish to support this Campaign.
>
> However, we also have to consider the climate of opinion in this country which overall is not only

negative but in certain important influential places hostile to our campaign's protein food aid and work for the Indian people. In saying this, I have in mind a number of instances including:

a. A Minister of the Crown[324] recently speaking strongly against such aid and in a place where it did considerable harm. He has not retracted his remarks and I know that by some people both in India and in Australia his comments were interpreted as Federal Government policy.

b. Representatives of organisations who belittle and almost condemn food aid.

c. Influence of individuals whose views are unfair and antagonistic to India and whose views are given considerable publicity.

d. Some Australian Federal Departmental officers who either knowingly or unknowingly undermine the Campaign. There is considerable evidence to indicate that the Federal Government in contrast to the State Government does not want this Campaign to operate successfully.

Dissemination of incorrect rumours—such as, Indians don't drink milk; Milk makes Indian sick; the Campaign's powdered milk is burnt by the Indians; or it is left to rot on the wharves; the Campaign's powdered milk is sold on the black market; Indians don't care; Indians aren't grateful. I suppose there might be some who would say that all these things are sheer coincidence. A constant barrage of erroneous rumours, which appear to be directed against our work, has had to be combated.

This prevailing climate increases the work load and it increases the costs. All the time these attitudes are making it increasingly difficult for us to carry on.

It is against this background that I think we have to give very serious consideration as to whether this Campaign should continue to work. I am aware of the significance of the decision—stated quite simply it is—the health, vision and lives of needy children depend on the continuation of our work. We have sufficient resources to meet the shipments which we have undertaken to send to India within the next few months.

At the present stage, I am not prepared to recommend the continuation of this Campaign. I feel that we must think this through very carefully during the next few months and then take a final decision. In the coming weeks, I would like to talk individually with each of you and have your views on the question. I would like you to be as fully informed as possible so that when next we all meet we will all be in a position to make a wise decision.[325]

After the meeting, Rohan Rivett wrote to Moira:

Dear Moira,

I was away from Melbourne so missed notice of the April 2 meeting. However I have since read the minutes and your report. It would seem we have gone on far longer than we expected—but are running into opposition from bigger bodies as well as natural inertia here.

In all the circumstances one would believe that having an organisation intact, we should suspend operations until some new and drastic emergency arises when the present members can be called together to consider if action is fitting. Nan and I would like to pay personal tribute to the wonderful work of yourself and John over six years. It is greatly appreciated you know—in India—where it matters.

Yours sincerely,
Rohan[326]

During 1972, the decision was made to gradually scale down the Campaign's activities. There were no new appeals after this time. For several years, milk continued to arrive, either to the front door at our home or by rail to Caulfield Station where either Moira or I collected it. Moira arranged to have these goods packaged and transported to the Indian ships, which continued to take the milk to India free of charge.

Letters from India continued to arrive. With limited resources, the Campaign Committee had to prioritise as it was not possible to assist all causes. Assistance was given where the need was greatest and where the practicability of getting the aid to the needy was high. From March 1971, the greater part of aid given was to refugees through the Government of India and refugee organisations whilst endeavours were made to keep up some of the more long-standing activities of the Campaign in helping specific organisations, including Maharashtra State Women's Council, Red Cross India and West Bengal Council of Women.[327]

During the early 1970s, Moira noticeably slowed down. A diagnosis of cancer was followed by treatment at the Peter MacCallum Clinic.

In the last years of her life, Moira realised that she just could do no more. It was such a cruel moment for her to arrive at the understanding and realisation of this because, although she wanted to continue, she found it impossible to cope with the demands made on her for aid and the work involved. She said simply: 'I can do no more.'

I know Moira would want to thank everyone who helped in any way to provide the aid which was given through the Campaign. There were so many in Australia and India and other parts of the world and I could not possibly single them out. Thousands who were children at Australian schools, particularly during the period 1964 to 1970, would have memories of gifting tins of processed milk. In the community, there existed a genuine love of giving to this cause.

30

Into Eternity

When Moira died, I was numbed with shock. Despite Moira's hope, I was expecting the end, yet not despairing. If there could have been a miracle, I longed for it, but it was not to be.

Moira had just turned 56 when she died. Her Requiem Mass was concelebrated at St Joseph's Church, Malvern, and the sung items were prepared by Loreto for a 'Mass To Celebrate The Entry Into New Life of Moira'. Michele wrote down her thoughts the night Moira died: 'Today the Lord took unto Himself my beloved mother. He transported her gentle spirit out of an existence suffused with pain and distress; he guided her safely into his eternal kingdom of Divine Joy. We know too that we shall leave this transient earth to join her in Love.'

Moira seemed to have been interested in the whole human race, with a deep understanding of the concept of 'neighbour'. She was a tender and loving person; loyal, courageous and compassionate; and had tremendous powers of memory, persuasion, perseverance and organisation. She did not sit down and pontificate. She tended to her family and went out and forward into the stream of life, to help foster a spirit to serve the people of God and to care for the needy. Moira had reached her time, her strength being spent, and her earthly life faded and her spirit passed into eternity.

Moira was a practising Christian, believing in a common God of us all. She comprehended that people found God through diverse religious beliefs. She believed in the sacredness of human life, from the moment of conception, and that love was the all-pervading force in the world. She had tremendous compassion and a burning zeal for justice. She fought for those who often could so little help themselves. Moira devoted her married life to her family and to many causes, and drew to herself, by her magnetism, tenacity, gentleness and sincerity, diverse personalities to help her in her endeavours.

Whatever Moira did, she endeavoured to do well. Her standards in all things were those of excellence. If she set herself a task, she considered that it should be done well. Moira had many talents; she used them well. Recalling the parable of the Master who called on his servants to use their talents and not to bury them, Moira was a shining example and a heroic victim.

Moira put aside so many activities and interests and gave her maximum available time to the Aid for India Campaign. From the very start, she gave it high priority. She knew the good it was doing. She travelled throughout Australia, driving home the message of the need to help India and her people. She was made welcome. She was rebuffed. She was helped. She was opposed. Moira worked for others in deep realistic charity, which is sheer love for others. She not only held out her hand to those in need, she worked for peace and for social justice. She regarded people as human beings, not as economic individuals. She abhorred tyranny and the 'grinding down' of humans, socially or economically.

Moira was an inspiration to our family. To our children, she was more of a mother than anything else. They all enjoyed her cooking. She kept the kitchen a showpiece of cleanliness. The girls went to her for dresses and frocks. Her love for all the children was deep. All along she watched over their health and education and she gave an amazing example of industry and devotion. In her long-term wisdom, she never endeavoured to make them dependent on her. Full credit must be hers for inculcating the habit and system of good study, something which has stood them in good stead as the years have rolled by.

I believe that the real uniting family quality was based on love and respect for one another. Did not Pierre Teilhard de Chardin say: 'Love alone is capable of uniting living beings in such a way as to complete and fulfil them.'[328] And 'Love is the most universal, the most tremendous and the most mysterious of the cosmic forces.'[329]

Only six years before her death, Moira had given the address at Corowa, 'Be of Good Courage'. This was at a time when her courage and faith and metal were being severely tested by the strain and stress involved in her intense and passionate concern for the people of the sub-continent of India. The strength that Moira burnt up in all her works, she gave to the Lord through those she helped.

I received many letters following Moira's death and I quote from a few.

Murray McInerney (later Sir Murray), Justice of the Supreme Court of Victoria:

> Dear Jack,
>
> I was saddened at the reading of the death notice today concerning Moira. You and your children have lost a wonderful wife and mother and your and their loss and sorrow must be endured. Please accept my heartfelt

sympathy with you all. I will remember Moira as a most vital personality, courageous and determined patient and persistent with the politicians in her Milk for India campaign. Yet I remember how at a function at your home, full of political leaders etc, she turned aside with motherly solicitude and love to put her arm around one of her younger children and dealt with the problem then uppermost in that child's mind. She was indeed a valiant woman with a tender loving heart. May God grant her a special welcome in heaven and console her family here on earth.

yours sincerely,
Murray McInerney[330]

Sir Edward Dunlop:

Dear John

I went away overseas shortly after seeing Moira last, and her brave spirit rather haunted me. I talked over her case with Don Lawson and realised how inevitable the end of a long courageous fight. She was one who truly lived with passionate intensity and knew true compassion. I always felt something close to shame watching the calls she made on her frail body and burning spirit. I feel sure that the saints had that sort of zeal. Her name was a legend in India, and I am sure that she did more for Australia's name in that teeming Continent than any of our political leaders or High Commissioners. With my deep sympathy and a prayer for a brave soul.

yours sincerely,
Weary.[331]

Dr Martand S Joshi, President, Australia India Society of Victoria:

Dear Mr. Dynon,

It is with regret that we learned about the untimely demise of your wife Moira. A person of her calibre never really dies. She has left behind a wealth of contribution to humanity. Her efforts in procuring milk for the needy Indians will never be forgotten.[332]

D Henry Thiagaraj, Madras, Deputy Director of Tourism, Government of Madras:

Dear Mr. John Dynon,

It was with sadness and a sudden shock I read the announcement in "The Hindu" Daily the news of the death of Mrs. Moira Dynon, your beloved wife—whom I have known for the last 8 years. Whenever she visited Madras we met and discussed several subjects of mutual interest. During her last visit I was able to host a dinner and my wife and son enjoyed her visit. We still have her thanks letter and some gift book on Australia she presented to my son and to our home. Her concern on problems of developing nations like India was so sincere that she was willing to make any sacrifice for the distressed people—especially children. We cannot forget her great service to India through her Aid India Campaigns especially when drought afflicted our country. My wife Philo and son Gerard join me in expressing our very sincere condolences to you and to the members of your bereaved family... Please be assured that because of the goodwill of Mrs. Moira Dynon you have friends all over India.[333]

Sir George Reid, retired former Attorney-General of Victoria:

Dear John,

I have only recently heard the news of your great sorrow and I am writing to say how deeply grieved I am. Moira was a wonderful example of Christian living. She will be remembered for her unselfish and untiring devotion to good causes and for her great ability to inspire others in her charitable works. At this sad time you will no doubt find some consolation in the knowledge of Moira's devoted and courageous life.[334]

Brother Andrew MC:

I am sure Moira is now beyond all pain and suffering, and is enjoying the fullness of life and joy with God—after all she did to feed Christ in His hunger in so many in India. Hers was surely a wonderfully fruitful life-giving life. And we can all expect God's blessing to continue in us through her. As I go on I feel more and more the pain of peoples' lives in all places. And yet the pain leads us somehow to a deeper and richer appreciation of life. I suppose this is the mystery of Jesus.[335]

Mark Shelton (aged 12):

Dear Uncle John, Michele, John, Jacinta, James and David,

Our deepest sympathy on the passing of a wonderful woman, from this life into 'Eternal Glory'. Aunty Moira was loved dearly by all of us because of what she was and what she did for others. About 99% of her time was devoted to her family and friends and the people in India. She loved everyone and she was full of the good things in life.

Right at this moment I'm sure she is pouring down grace and love on each of us. She was always active and wanting to help and find out about others. Now she has met the Lord and she is happy so why shouldn't we be. She may not be here with us physically but I can assure you in Spirit she is very much here and helping us about our business.

I too was close to death but the Lord preserved me and I hope he is going to make me someone very much like Moira Dynon. I couldn't think of anything better in life. I hope you will all look after Uncle John and help him and each other. This will make your family a very united one and I hope you stay this way. Once again our deepest sympathy to you all and look after yourselves both physically and mentally and we hope to see you in the near future.

Yours lovingly, Mark Shelton, Jill Shelton, Carol, Katrina xxxxxxxxxxxxxxxxxx[336]

Pat Hogan:

Mr. John Dynon & Family,

I was deeply shocked to read the item in Tuesday night's "Herald" announcing Moira's death. Having been closely associated with her late brother Alan, both as a close friend and dependant crew member, I was well aware of his admiration for her and his pride in her early achievements. Meeting her confirmed Alan's opinions, & in more recent years, I followed with interest and a certain amount of pride, her original and compassionate "Milk for India" campaign…

"Lest We Forget" May she rest in peace,
Pat Hogan.[337]

R. Verma, Acting High Commissioner for India, Canberra:

Dear Mr. Dynon,

I am writing to express our deep sense of shock and sorrow at the passing away of Mrs Moira Dynon. Not only did Mrs Dynon feel for her less fortunate fellow humans in distant India but she also took positive action to contribute towards improving their lot. Hers was, indeed, a rare and inspiring example of selfless service for the poor and the needy. I know that I speak for the very large number of my countrymen who benefited from Mrs. Dynon's work when I say that we shall always cherish the memory of her association with India even as we mourn her loss.[338]

Denis Warner:

Dear John,

I was away from Australia last October and was dismayed to learn of Moira's death when your letter arrived. She was such a dynamic character that it is difficult to think that she isn't turning her hand to something to make life better for those less fortunate than ourselves. I am indeed sorry to know that Moira died. She was a loss not only to you and your family and to the community but in a real sense to the world. Too few people have her compelling desire to help the underprivileged.[339]

Bernadette Smith:

Dear John,

I learned with shock of Moira's illness and death only in the last few days…I have been thinking of her a lot, as I knew her, and you may be surprised, but the Moira

I knew was in the R.A.A.F. (not the WAAAF as in my case). The only time we were together was, very briefly, in Bowen, where she was a RAAF officer (even to the male cap) in C.R.U. —Chemical Research Unit. I remember it was all quite "hush hush" and Moira used to have to wear a special rubber (?) suit completely insulating her from whatever stuff they handled. It must have been very hot work.

I remember Moira's reputation at Melbourne University as "the girl with the bows". She was always very feminine while still being quite a brainy student! At Bowen she landed in Hospital briefly with an injured spine and I had to carry up her calcium tablets which she always took in war-time. She had been out for a "burn" in after-working hours, in a jeep, with a lively group and they turned over—as was their wont (jeeps). She was very serious about her work, but happy and gay as well. One air crew wrote a signal in flags spelling out her name around the top of the wall of the dining room—the mess. This was just one of those little light hearted interludes, I remember.[340]

Alice Langenbacher:

Dear Mr Dynon,

May I offer to you my sincere sympathy in the death of your dearly loved wife Moira. During my term as General President of the "Catholic Women's League", I came to know Moira for what she really was. She had an outstanding ability for the work of the League, and furthermore a personality that endeared her to all members of the Executive Committee.[341]

Babette Francis:

> When I first came to Australia in 1954 the White Australia policy was in operation, and I was somewhat apprehensive as to how I would be accepted. Moira was one of the first to invite me to her home and her spontaneous friendship did a great deal to reassure me. Friendship and co-operation were the keynotes of Moira's personality—her assistance was never offered in a patronising way, and this spirit also pervaded her "Milk for India" campaign. She will be very much missed by her relatives and friends and mourned by many mothers and children on the Indian sub-continent who survived because of her concern.[342]

Australian-Asian Association of Victoria newsletter:

> This delightful member of the Australian-Asian Association contributed greatly to its work in its formative years. Of the women who were ever ready to contribute to the organisational or field work, or both, Moira Dynon's name would be high on the list. We will miss the integrity and courage of this member.[343]

St Joseph's Record, Malvern:

> Moira was a member of our parish community, and we are grateful to her for the example of dedicated Christian service that she has left us. In her outlook and activity she was genuinely in line with the spirit of the Second Vatican Council and the recommendations of Popes John XXIII and Paul VI. As we extend our sincere sympathy to her family we also rejoice with them at the wonderful memory she has left and the example she has given us. Requiescat In Pace.[344]

On the first anniversary of her death, following a special Loreto Federation Mass, Moira was remembered in a reading at the Memento for the Dead:

> In the true tradition of Mary Ward and fulfilling her maxim: "Women if they would be perfect might do great things", Moira used her gifts of mind and heart and her frail body to bring past pupils and friends of Loreto together every two years, to scrutinise the changing times and Loreto's response to them, to study matters that called for attention, to search for and take courses of action that conscience discerned. The search led Moira beyond Australia at times and in India particularly her concern found expression. To and fro she journeyed there distributing vast quantities of powdered milk that she and her helpers had collected for the starving poor. Social justice was being betrayed and Moira sought to right the wrong.
>
> To the end Moira Dynon lived a life of faith for others in her role as wife and mother and in her universal role as a Christian in a changing world. In our Mass today Moira will be affectionately remembered at the memento for the dead. Let us all unite in prayer especially then that Moira's glory in heaven may be great and her influence long felt on earth.
>
> **At Memento:** Remember...Moira Dynon, first President of Loreto Federation. She accepted your call to serve and inspire your people to a Christian way of life and bore with faith and hope the cross of illness and death. May she have the eternal happiness of union with you.[345]

At the same time, I received a letter from my brother, Father James Dynon SJ:

> The Loreto Federation are preparing to hold their meetings in Perth this year and one of their committee phoned and asked me to concelebrate with Bishop Healy on Sunday 23rd October. She also mentioned that she knew of Moira's work in the early years of the Federation's existence. I told her that I had said the Mass at Mandeville and had been asked to preach on the new Federation that was coming into being that day. I remember taking the text that "they all may be one" and applying it briefly at the end to all the Loretos in Australia. Moira told me she was waiting breathlessly for the punch line and was glad when it came. God blessed her work here also, as the Federation is still thriving. Moira's idea that Loreto in Federation would strengthen one another's Christian ideas has borne fruit also. One example would be a greater knowledge of the abortion issue—and of Christian marriage.
>
> I won't forget her and you all on October 23rd—her anniversary to Heaven, and your own birthday, 22nd.[346]

Over the next few years, Father James read some early drafts of my manuscript and he commented:

> I think Moira was a politician in Aristotle's sense of one who concerned oneself with the common good, the welfare of society, rather than a party politician, who may find self pressure to vote against one's conscience.

Moira's reputation extended beyond Australia. Her standing internationally was recognised with the inclusion of an entry in *The Blue Book 1971–72: Leaders of the English-Speaking World*[347].

Moira is buried at the Melbourne General Cemetery, Section KL (Catholic), and her tombstone is inscribed:

> In Memory of
> Moira Lenore Dynon
> (Shelton)
> Born 4.9.1920 Died 23.10.1976
> Wife of John Francis
> Mother of Michele Jacinta
> John James and David.
> Our love for you is everlasting.
> REQUIESCAT IN PACE

Above the stone is a Celtic cross in white marble. At the top of the cross is inscribed the sacred Indian symbol 'Om' (ॐ) signifying eternity.

Appendix A

Reports, documents and letters

A1. *Table Talk* report of wedding of Lily Johnston and Percy Shelton, November 1919 — 365

A2. Flight Officer Moira Shelton's war service account — 367

A3. Petition to Her Majesty under Section 59 of the *Australian Constitution* seeking disallowance or amendment of *Matrimonial Causes Act 1959* — 385

A4. Special Report on Australian-Japanese Children in Japan, July 1960 — 388

A5. Joint Statement concerning Proposed Policy of the Commonwealth Government of Australia to Conscript a Minority of Aliens Resident in Australia for Military Service including Service Overseas by James M Galbally & Moira Dynon, 15 August 1966 — 397

A6. Statement on Abortion prepared by Moira Dynon and released by National Executive Committee Australian Council of Catholic Women, 30 April 1968 — 399

A7. Letter to Moira Dynon from M.W.B. Smithies (for the Secretary) Department of External Affairs, 7 June 1965 — 404

A8. Memorandum to Prime Minister Harold Holt regarding Australian Food Assistance to India, February 1966 — 406

A9. Letter from Moira Dynon to Treasurer William McMahon seeking continued Government funding for transport of milk to India, 16 January 1967 — 410

A10. Resolution moved by the Prime Minister of India in the Indian Parliament regarding West Pakistan's attack on East Bengal, 31 March 1971 — 414

A11. Report on 'Relief aid in Bangladesh—Nagori' enclosed in letter from Mr Allen, Deputy High Commissioner for Australia, Dacca to Moira Dynon, 19 February 1972 — 416

A1

Table Talk report of wedding of Lily Johnston and Percy Shelton, November 1919

St. Patrick's Cathedral was the scene of a pretty wedding on Thursday evening, October 16, the bride being Miss Lily Johnston, only daughter of Mr. and Mrs. W. B. Johnston, "Naumai," Studley-avenue, Kew, and the bridegroom Dr. Percy G. Shelton, third son of the late Mr. Henry Shelton, B.A., and Mrs. Shelton, "Wimmera", Sutherland-road, Armadale. The ceremony was performed by Rev. J. Manly, of Kew, and Rev. Father Collins, of Elsternwick. Miss Anderson presided at the organ for the choral service.

The bride, who was given away by her father, wore an exquisite bridal gown of ivory satin charmeuse, gracefully draped, with tulle and silver bodice delicately hand-embroidered. The train of tulle was powdered with silver and was lined with flesh pink georgette over satin. A lovely veil of rare old Limerick lace was worn over a chaplet of orange blossom, and she carried a shower bouquet of white orchids, with a touch of pink introduced.

As she left the Cathedral a horseshoe of flowers was slipped on her arm. The bridegroom's gift was a pearl necklace.

There were four bridesmaids—Miss Margery Kelly and Miss Beryl Kelly (cousins of bride), Miss Eileen Shelton (sister of bridegroom), and Miss Rhoda Inell. They wore pretty pale pink frocks, daintily embroidered with silver beads, the same embroidered design being introduced on the drape skirts. Their large black tulle hats were trimmed with jet and long streamers, and they carried lovely bouquets of La France roses and forget-me-nots. The bridegroom's gifts were gold bangles and opal rings.

Mr. James Shelton (brother of bridegroom) was best man, and the groomsmen were Dr. Len Johnston (brother of bride), Dr. Brendon O'Sullivan, and Mr. Maurice Cussen.

Wedding breakfast was served at the Grand Hotel. The bride's mother received in a beautiful gown of black crepe meteor, with a tunic draped to one side of georgette. The corsage of metallic lace was partly veiled with the georgette and finished at the waist with a large tissue rose.

About 120 guests were entertained, only relatives and old family friends being invited.

Numerous costly and beautiful presents, including many cheques, were received by Dr. and Mrs. Shelton, who are spending their honeymoon in Sydney and the Blue Mountains. The bride travelled in a cream tricotine coat and skirt, smartly trimmed with silk braid, with a dainty front of georgette, prettily beaded in saxe blue and finished with lace. It was worn with a set of white fox furs and large picture hat.

On their return Dr. and Mrs. Percy Shelton will reside at "Illawarra", Glenhuntly-road, Elsternwick.[348]

A2

Flight Officer Moira Shelton's war service account

Flight Officer Shelton's Account

February 1943

Whilst on duty at No. 1 W.A.A.A.F. Depot I received instructions from No 1 Training Group to report to R.A.A.F. Headquarters, Directorate of Armament Arm. 6 Section (Chemical Warfare Section). Here I was interviewed by Wing Commander R.J.W. Le Fevre R.A.F. who, recently evacuated from Singapore, where he had been Chemical Advisor to the Air Officer Commanding, was temporarily filling Armament 6 appointment as Chemical Officer. Wing Commander Le Fevre told me that the R.A.A.F. was in need of officers with scientific training, as a Chemical Warfare Organisation was being set up. The work concerned both the offensive and defensive aspects of Chemical Warfare mainly on the armament and equipment sides. Wing Commander Le Fevre wanted an assistant urgently—someone with a University degree in Science including Chemistry and Biochemistry and someone who was readily available for duty. As I was in Melbourne at the time and possessed the necessary qualifications I was asked if I would be interested in the appointment. I was willing to accept it.

9th March 1943

I was posted to R.A.A.F. Headquarters, Directorate of Armament, Armament 6 section to fill Armament 6B establishment. On arrival at the Directorate I was interviewed by the Director of Armament, Group Captain Lightfoot who welcomed me to the section and wished me luck in my new appointment. He pointed out that I was the only female officer employed on Armament and

Chemical Warfare duties in the Service. The appointment was for a male, but as no one possessing the required qualifications could be obtained at short notice, the Service had decided to appoint a girl. However because of my sex I was not to expect privileges and must be prepared to "rough it" from time to time—a warning that I was to recall on numerous occasions during the next two and a half years. He informed me that for the first few months, I should accompany Wing Commander Le Fevre on inspection tours, interservice trials or any other trips that might be advantageous to my training as a Chemical Officer. I should also be required to undergo two courses of training at the Armament School—the Chemical Warfare portions of the Armament Officers' Course and that of the Aerodrome Defence Officers' Course.

That night I proceeded to Sydney to join Wing Commander Le Fevre who was supervising the unloading of a ship whose cargo contained bulk drums of liquid mustard gas (500 lb up to 880 lb) and miscellaneous offensive chemical warfare munitions.

To digress for a moment—just a few weeks previously the first shipment of Chemical Warfare munitions had come to Australia. This ship, the Idomeneus, had been redirected from Singapore and arrived in Sydney before the R.A.A.F. was equipped to take delivery. Unfortunately the consignment was in poor condition, many of the weapons having leaked. Consequently all the wharf labourers employed on the unloading developed burns of varying degrees and had to be hospitalised. One such case was fatal though only indirectly as a result of the burns. Service personnel were then called upon to carry out the unloading and over 80 of those who volunteered for the job from Bradfield Park were burnt. This puzzled the technical scientists who had tested the air in the ship's hold for gas and all the tests indicated that no gas was present. Senior technical officers from No. 1 T.M.O. R.A.A.F. Headquarters and Bradfield Park, including Wing Commander Le Févre were burnt and admitted to hospital suffering from temporary blindness and skin lesions. It was not until many months later that the real cause of the casualties was known—an experimental team working in the tropics discovered that mustard gas will under hot,

APPENDIX A2

humid conditions, particularly when the body is exercising, produce casualties when present even in minute concentrations—too minute to be detected by any of the then known chemical tests.

This unloading which I was to attend was the second shipment to arrive in Australia. 20 R.A.A.F. armourers were given a short course of training by Flight Lieutenant A.H. Trewin and formed the nucleus of the mustering which later became known as Armourer Chemical Warfare. These armourers working in special clothing unloaded the ship with only a few minor burns. The special clothing presented a comical appearance—it consisted of female vests and bloomers which had been treated with chemicals to afford protection against gas vapour and which were as a result brilliant pink in colour and sticky to touch. Over these were worn oilskin green fabric D jackets and trousers. Two pairs of gloves (cotton and rubber), chemically treated socks and hoods, rubber boots and a respirator completed the ensemble. Women's underclothing was particularly suitable for protective purposes as gas vapour acts most rapidly on those parts of the body which perspire freely—in the groins and armpits. Even so some of the tougher of the armourers objected strongly to wearing such apparel.

As part of my training I was told to don protective clothing and duly joined a working party. When thus dressed it was impossible to distinguish me from any one of the armourers. We worked in three shifts, twenty minutes unloading, thirty minutes rest and five minutes climbing in and out of the hold. The work was exhausting it being impossible to remain working longer than twenty minutes in the protective clothing. The unloading of the ship, took 11 days by which time we had all lost a considerable amount of weight.

A rather amusing incident occurred—one of the members of the ship's crew (all of whom incidentally kept a very safe distance during the unloading) saw me come out of the hold and perceived a woman when I removed my respirator. Apparently there was a superstition to be overcome and it took a lot of reassurance by Wing Commander Le Fevre before the Captain of the ship was convinced that I was indeed a member of a working party. He apologised at the end of the job for the misunderstanding and as a gesture of his appreciation, at the completion of the job, included me in the party, which he gave in his cabin for all the officers who had been connected with the unloading. On completion of this job, Wing Commander Le Fevre was advised from R.A.A.F. Headquarters that he was to proceed to Grafton to attend an Army trial.

(The Interservice Liaison in Chemical Warfare has always been very close and very complete. Many of the problems particularly on the defensive side were common to all Services and many investigations were done by the Munitions Supply Laboratories. Most of the stocks of defensive chemical warfare equipment were manufactured in Australia under the control of munitions. Whenever one of the Services or Munitions held a trial, representatives of the other organisations attended. The interservice body which controlled Chemical Warfare organisation and development for the South West Pacific Area was known as the Chemical Defence Board. This Board consisted of Army, Navy, Air Force, Civilian, and American Army (Chemical Warfare Service) personnel and was directly responsible to Defence Committee and War Cabinet. (Note Air Vice Marshal Hurley D.G.M.S., Group Captain Lightfoot, Director of Armament, and the Chemical Warfare Staff officer were R.A.A.F. representatives.)

On 9th April, I accompanied Wing Commander Le Fevre and Flight Lieutenant Trewin to Coffs Harbour by air (Loadstar) and thence by road to the Army improvised camp at Grafton. We were quartered in the town as I was the only female attending or participating in the trial. The trial lasted 12 days during which time I learned a little about the field assessment of chemical warfare weapons. It was here that I first witnessed the use of human volunteers (Army) for such purposes. Work was being done with mustard (vesicant) and B.B.C. (tear) gases and volunteers wearing varying degrees of protective clothing were exposed to field concentrations of the gases and the casualty producing power thus determined. These trials of course were always supervised by Medical as well as Chemical Warfare Specialists.

On completion of the trial we returned to Sydney by air (Hudson) for discussions at No. 5 M.G. regarding the storage and maintenance of Chemical Warfare munitions which were being stored at No. 1 Central Reserve near Lithgow and at various sub depots throughout the Blue Mountains. We then proceeded on an inspection tour of these depots accompanied by staff officers from No. 5 M.G. We stayed a couple of nights at No. 1 Central Reserve, where I, being the only female on the station, was accommodated in a small sitting room off the Officers Mess Ante Room. I was treated royally having a blazing fire, a wireless and a pile of overseas magazines in my room and was delighted on getting into bed to discover that a hot water bottle had been placed in it.

On completion of the inspection we returned to Sydney and thence to Melbourne. Within a few days I was posted to the Armament School at Hamilton to undergo two courses—a 3 weeks Chemical Warfare course for Aerodrome Defence Officers and a 12 days Chemical Warfare course for Armament Officers. The Commanding Officer of the Gas School was an Army Major who had been evacuated from Rabaul and who was on loan to the R.A.A.F.. He at first was sceptical that a girl should be posted to these courses but after the first few days appeared to become accustomed to the idea. In both of these courses I obtained the highest aggregate marks—93% in the first and 99% in the second—this latter being the highest marks on record in the school up to that date.

Early in June I returned to Air Force Headquarters, Directorate of Armament, Armament 6 Section to take up Chemical Warfare Staff work. My principal duties then were as follows—

a. To assist Wing Commander Le Fevre as required in both offensive and defensive preparations for Chemical Warfare.

b. In conjunction with the directorate of training, to arrange for the training (for personal protection only) of WAAAF personnel.

c. In conjunction with Munitions Supply Laboratories to devise methods for the sampling and analysis of mustard gas chargings in R.A.A.F. Chemical Warfare munitions.

At the end of June, 21 W.A.A.F. from all musterings were selected to undergo training to be Anti Gas Instructors W.A.A.F.. The qualifications required were similar to those required by the D.I. mustering but in addition required an elementary knowledge of chemistry. The girls were posted to the Armament School gas detachment then operating at Shepparton where I proceeded to supervise their training (period 3 weeks). Within a few days it was obvious that seven of the girls were unsuitable for the new mustering and so the course proceeded with a strength of 14. Of these 9 passed, were promoted to Corporal and then attached for 10 days to an Army Respirator Repair unit for further practical experience. They were then posted to units to carry out instructional duties and to assist the Aerodrome Defence Officer in Station Defence. It is interesting here to note that Corporal Gibbins and Corporal Gillies were required for instructional duties at No. 2 I.T.S. and No. 6 I.T.S. at Bradfield Park due to the shortage of R.A.A.F. anti gas instructors and Aerodrome Defence instructors at that time. According to the Aerodrome Defence Officer (Squadron Leader W. Turner) the girls proved themselves very capable both in training and controlling the class.

On completion of the course I returned to R.A.A.F. Headquarters for general staff duties which at this time consisted mainly of drawing up "Gas Defence Instructions" (RAAF Publication No. 295) and giving technical advice to D D E 2 and D T concerning gas defence equipment and gas defence training requirements of the R.A.A.F..

The R.A.A.F. at this time carried out smoke trials at Point Cook and at Dromana (here in liaison with RAN) and I attended these trials with Wing Commander Le Fevre. In August I accompanied W/Cdr Le Fevre and Flight Lieutenant Trewin on an inspection tour of gas defence equipment and training covering R.A.A.F.

units in North Eastern Area Headquarters. (I was not permitted[349] to accompany them to New Guinea or North Western Area and so returned to Brisbane to inspect R.A.A.F. units in the Brisbane area (these units included Toowoomba, Maryborough, Bundaberg, Amberley and several Radar units as well as units located in the vicinity of Brisbane. Some of the Station Defence Officers were surprised that a girl should perform these inspections but in every case I received their co-operation. As preparations for 'Gas Cleansing Centres' consisted in the main of minor adjustments to Ablution Blocks I experienced some embarrassing moments when carrying out inspections of these blocks. Because of my sex the blocks had to be put out of bounds while I carried out the inspections. Returning to R.A.A.F. Headquarters on 1st September, I was informed that as soon as my report on these inspections was completed, I was to proceed to North Eastern Area Headquarters. At that time considerable quantities of offensive gas stocks were being found in all Japanese forward areas (mainly Lewisite, Mustard and Prussic acid gases).[350] North Eastern Area Headquarters had requested that a W.A.A.A.F. Officer trained in gas proceed to North Eastern Area to assist the Area Defence Officer and to arrange and supervise the training of W.A.A.A.F. personnel in elementary gas defence for personal protection and the organisation of Decontamination Centres and Gas Cleansing Centres for W.A.A.A.F personnel. On 7th September, I proceeded to Townsville by air for these duties. Two weeks later Corporal Watt and Corporal Kimber arrived in Townsville to assist me. All W.A.A.A.F.were to receive the twelve hour course of training in the use of their equipment, procedure and first aid in the event of gas attack. The co-operation of the units was magnificent and by the end of November 800 W.A.A.A.F. in Townsville had received this training. I then returned to RAAF Headquarters leaving the two instructors W.A.A.A.F. to assist the Area Defence Officer in the organisation of general gas alarms for training purposes, the repair of gas defence equipment and the training of W.A.A.A.F. in units outside Townsville and any others in the area who had not been covered in the general scheme of training.

On my return I was sent immediately to the Chemical Warfare Detachment of the Armament School at Shepparton Victoria, to supervise the training of No. 2 Course of Gas Instructors, W.A.A.A.F.. Nine girls were put on course, but only five passed and were remustered.

A few days prior to the completion of the course, I was recalled for a day to R.A.A.F. Headquarters as Wing Commander Le Fevre was returning to United Kingdom on urgent compassionate grounds and Flight Lieutenant Trewin was to take over as head of Armament 6 Section. On my return on the completion of the course there was a new distribution of duties—An Aerodrome Defence Officer (ex. No. 6 Squadron) who had been given a special course at the Armament School and at the Munitions Supply Laboratories (Flying Officer P.A. Trompf) was now filling Armament 6A appointment and responsible for the Gas Defensive Preparations of the R.A.A.F. as regards training and equipment. Flight Lieutenant Trewin was now head of the section. I became his assistant and deputised for him at meetings of the Chemical Defence Board and Experimental and Research Committee in his absence. I remained at R.A.A.F. Headquarters until April 1944. About this time a great deal of interest was being taken in experimental work. A series of trials that had been conducted by an interservice team of medical and physiological personnel (British, Australian and American) had revealed that vesicant gases and in particular mustard gas were more effective and produced drastic results when employed in the tropics. This was due mainly to the skin being more receptive when moist and hot and also to the fact that the gas vaporised readily and produced casualties even when present in concentrations too low to be detected by any methods then known. Not only did protection for the head and lungs have to be provided for all personnel but some type of clothing practical for use in the tropics and yet capable of affording protection against mustard gas vapour had to be designed and then provisioned for. In addition it became obvious that Chemical Warfare munitions in particular those charged with mustard gas would be infinitely more effective when employed in tropical areas than in temperate zones. And so it was necessary to perform trials to determine the tactical value of munitions then held and provisioned by the Air Force and Army. In addition, existing defensive equipment had to be tested and if necessary new protection designed. To carry out this work an interservice unit, at first called No. 1 Australian Field Trials Company, and later known as the Australian Field Experimental Station, was formed. This unit (about 400 strength), consisted of English, Australian and American civilian and service scientists and highly specialised technical and medical personnel; there were also representatives from New Zealand and South Africa. R.A.A.F. and Army provided the other rank and non-commissioned personnel namely laboratory technicians, armament and general administrative personnel.

To carry out flying and purely R.A.A.F. aspects of the work, a special unit equipped with 4 Beaufort and 2 Vultee Vengeance aircraft and later known as R.A.A.F. Chemical Research Unit was formed. This unit was located at Bowen, North Queensland, though for many trials it was called upon to operate from Melbourne to Hollandia. For the first twelve months most of the work was carried out in the Innisfail, Cairns areas and on a group of islands off Cardwell, namely the Brook Islands. The programme of work for the A.F.E.S. (Australian Field Experimental Station) was drawn up in Washington by the Project Co-ordination Staff which consisted of Allied representatives (civilian and service) whose duty it was to estimate the amount of work required on both British and American equipment and then to distribute the work to the chemical research establishments. These were situated at Porton (England) Suffield (Canada) and Edgewood (Maryland, USA) — these carried out work under temperate conditions as required for the European theatre whilst the tropical stations were at Canniphore (India), Florida (USA), and Proserpine (Australia). The work was distributed according to the target types and facilities available at the particular units. Most of the work done in Australia was in jungle, densely vegetated islands and landing beaches such as would be encountered in the S.W.P.A. The programme of work was passed from the Project Co-ordination Staff simultaneously to the Chemical Board (London) and the Chemical Defence Board (Melbourne) and thence through the Experimental and Research Sub-Committee of the Board to the Australian Field Experimental Station. The reports of the work were published by the Chemical Defence Board and circulated to all field experimental stations.

To this unit I was sent as R.A.A.F. Headquarters Directorate of Armament Liaison Officer and after September (1943) filled the establishment at the Station as Air Force Experimental Officer. My duties in addition to armament experimental duties (charging bombs with mustard gas, supervising armourers and assisting in all trials with R.A.A.F. munitions) were to act as liaison officer with R.A.A.F. Headquarters and North Eastern Area Headquarters.

Conditions in the early days of the unit were difficult. Much of the technical equipment had not arrived from overseas and Australian manufacture, and the "teething troubles" which were encountered by the very nature of various services staffing the unit were enormous. For the first 15 months the unit was billeted in a group of houses on the edge of civilisation on the Johnston River about two miles out of Innisfail. This was really a delightful spot although the large programme of work gave us little time to appreciate the surroundings.

Our toxic stores were de-centralised about the area and trials were conducted over large areas extending to Mission Beach, Mourilyan Harbour and Cairns. In those days we would usually have to depart the unit at 5.30 a.m. and drive for about two hours to reach isolated parts of the jungle which provided the target areas. The aircraft bombed usually early in the morning and trials would last for anything up to 14 days when the air would be continually sampled and human volunteers used to assess the vapour gas dangers. Working in two layer impregnated clothing (woollen and cotton clothing specially treated with chemicals to afford protection) and respirator, boots, and hood, gaiters and two pairs of gloves for hours on end was indeed very trying in the heat and humidity of the tropics.

However the work was indeed interesting and the leadership displayed by Colonel Gorrill (the Commanding Officer) was an inspiration to all who participated in the trials. We conducted the field aspects of the trials during the day and in the evenings would plan trials and carry out the necessary chemical analyses. (In some of these trials AWAS and AAMWS personnel assisted the field chemical sampling teams, and in some I was the only female participating). All the typing of the unit was done by AWAS. All the work done and the very existence of the unit itself was classed as secret and confidential.

Some trials were carried out on the Brook Islands. For these a detachment from the unit would move to the extreme easterly point of Hinchinbrook Island (4 American Landing barges providing the necessary transport facilities) where an improvised camp would be made. From there we could travel to South Brook Island by barge, a distance of about 8 miles, where most of the work was done. The third series of island trials was employing Air Force munitions and was carried out in April 1944. Flight Lieutenant Turner Walker who was then Air Force Experimental Officer and I participated in these trials which took place shortly after my arrival at the unit. The detachment which proceeded to the island consisted of about 60 personnel and included 6 other girls—laboratory assistants, typists and cooks.

The barges were run up onto the river bank in front of the camp and loaded on 17th April. At dawn the following day the main party consisting of the Officer in Charge of the trial (Major Skipper, U.S. Army), technical scientific personnel (Messrs. Purkis and Pasquill ex Porton England), Dr. Ennor (Munitions), R.A.A.F. experimental officer (Flight Officer Shelton) and a team of medical, specialist Chemical Warfare, armament, meteorological and general labouring personnel departed. We sailed down the Johnston River to its mouth and thence due east for a distance of 20 miles. On this day the seas were extremely rough and as the barges were heavily loaded with technical equipment and most of the party seasick we put into Mouribyan Harbour for the night. The next day we proceeded arriving at Hinchinbrook Island in the late afternoon. The scenery during the trip was unbelievably beautiful—the seas were very blue and the coral and numerous tiny islands that abound in these parts very picturesque. We made our camp on the extreme point of Hinchinbrook Island where we had the benefit of two beaches. On one we set up tents to house the chemical and medical equipment, the other was used for barracks purposes. It was during this series of trials that I really learned to rough it. We had been unable to transport any beds and so at night slept on a ground sheet under the inevitable mosquito net. At all times the mosquitoes were very bad and it was necessary to continually apply mosquito repellent to our clothes and any exposed parts of the skin. (The repellent used was provided by Australian Army and U.S. Army). The island has an abundance of lizard, reptile and other fauna life—however we soon became accustomed to the visits the animals made to our sleeping quarters at night. Incidentally, there were six girls in the party and we had a certain section of the beach roped off for our use. The beach in front of this we used for washing clothes using, of course, sea water soap. Rations during the trial consisted of American and Australian dehydrated and tinned food.

We worked hard—we would rise at 4am, don our protective clothing, have breakfast, and depart at 4-45am for Brook Island. A considerable amount of chemical equipment would have to be set up before the aircraft bombed at 7am and this could not be done until very exact meteorological conditions prevailing were worked out. Fortunately the meteorologists were nearly always able to forecast accurately the winds and air movements for the day and it was only occasionally that a trial would be postponed or spoilt by changes in weather conditions.

R.T. communication was maintained with the mainland at all times and during a trial with the aircraft. During bombing the barges would stand off shore and once bombs were down the barges would run up onto the beach discharging the technical personnel who would sample the air continually over a period of days, inspect the bombs, etc. etc. These specialist personnel would be wearing full protective clothing. During this series of trials, human volunteers were not employed but goats were used to help assess the liquid and vapour gas dangers. Visitors from Melbourne, London and Washington both civilian and Service attended the large scale trials. These included at various times Major General Goldney, Colonel Paget, Mr. Kingon and Mr. Davidson Pratt from England, General Baunskill, Colonel Prentiss, Colonel Copthorne and Colonel Morgan (U.S.) in addition to senior officers from the R.A.F., South Africa and New Zealand Army and Army Medical Services.

It was during this series of trials that I had the unique experience of being marooned on a coral tropical island. A small party consisting of the Officer in Charge of the trial, two Army technical officers and I were doing some special work on one of the Brook Islands. At 6pm the party boarded the barge to return to Hinchinbrook and when the barge crew tried to start the barge they discovered the barge was stuck on a coral reef. We had to wait until the tide went out and then became full, before we could depart. This occurred at 2am the next morning. The experience was certainly not a pleasant one. There were no swaying palms, no soft music, no hula hula girls, but in their place millions of mosquitoes and coral that had a horrible smell once the tide ran out. In addition we were hungry having only one half bar of chocolate between us all.

The evenings on Hinchinbrook after the day's work certainly were very lovely. The usual routine was to build a large fire on the beach (to keep down mosquitoes rather than provide warmth) and have supper parties of toasted apples and oysters of which there were plenty on the rocks. One of the boys played the accordion and a general sing-song would usually develop. However as we had to make an early start, the camp curfew was at 9 p.m.

This series of trials lasted 22 days. On their completion we returned to Innisfail from where we carried out more jungle trials. During some of these we used human volunteers from Army and R.A.F.. These volunteers certainly were wonderful—they would volunteer to allow themselves to be used with varying degrees of protection to assess gas dangers and then for various treatments of gas burns. They were never allowed to be burnt so badly that their health would be impaired permanently though many of them sustained severe burns which were indeed painful. Trials continued until the middle of May (1944) when the bulk of the unit came to the University of Melbourne laboratories to carry out necessary laboratory medical, biochemical and chemical experimental work. This work was always done in the winter months as the temperature and humidity in the tropics were too low to be of value for tropical assessment trials.

I returned then to R.A.A.F. Headquarters to assist general staff work. Squadron Leader Trewin departed in early June on a visit to Washington and London for conferences on Tropical Chemical Warfare and Flight Lieutenant Trompf and I were left to carry on Armament 6 Section. At the end of August Squadron Leader Trewin returned. On 3rd September I departed for Bowen where I was to be Officer in Charge of a trial on Tropical Storage of R.A.F. bombs which were to be charged with different types of gases.

Working with me on this trial was a team of twenty eight specialist armourers. We charged several hundred bombs by direct pouring of the gas, designed and then fitted manometers to certain weapons to measure pressure developments and in the early stages recorded hourly any pressure that developed. The trial was a particularly tricky and precarious one—several of us sustaining burns despite our protective equipment—but at no time did I have any trouble whatsoever regarding discipline. Before the trial commenced I was uneasy being the only girl and then the officer in charge of the trial employed on the job. I made it a point not to ask the armourers to do any difficult or technical job that I did not first show them how to do it or work with them; during the anxious hours when the bombs were developing pressure I was constantly in the area remaining on the job at one time for a period of 49 hours. This I felt was necessary as I was the only Scientist working on the trial. My efforts were more than repaid by the co-operation I received.[351] Once the first difficult days were over and the necessary routine observations and inspections planned and decided upon, I left Bowen to proceed to Cairns and then Innisfail, the Headquarters of the Australian Field Experimental Station. On 12th November, I flew to Cairns in one of the Beauforts from R.A.A.F. Chemical Research Unit. This unit was located at Bowen but had detachments at Cairns and Innisfail. For all trials done in the Innisfail areas, the aircraft operated from Cairns. My next job was to set up storage areas for toxic munitions at Cairns for use during the new season of trials. This season I was the only R.A.A.F. Chemical Warfare Officer at the Australian Field Experimental Station. During the previous season, I was quartered in the W.R.A.N. officers barracks whilst on duty in Cairns, an arrangement which continued for convenience during the 1944–1945 season.

On November 14th, I returned to Innisfail. The Unit had acquired the services of 10 English civilian Scientists in addition to the technical personnel employed during the previous seasons.

Trials continued in the jungle around Innisfail until 17th January, 1945. One trial worthy of note was that of the assessment of an American tank charged with 30 gallons of thickened mustard gas. On 3rd January 4 Beaufort aircraft each carrying two tanks (one on each wing) took off from Cairns to release the gas on the Mission Beach target area. Unfortunately the tanks did not function properly and only portion of the contents were discharged over the target. And so, 4 Beauforts carrying partially emptied tanks proceeded (over the sea) to Bowen and of course heavily contaminated the drome as they landed. This necessitated the closing of Bowen drome for 48 hours. The aircraft themselves were contaminated but the splendid way in which all personnel on the unit co-operated to effect decontamination resulted in the aircraft being ready to depart Bowen the next day for Cairns to attempt the trial again. (Only the main runway was clear, the rest of the drome still being contaminated.) During take off from Cairns (5th Jan.) an electrical failure resulted—one of the tanks being released on the runway just as the aircraft became airborne. 30 gallons of thickened mustard gas were thrown on the main Cairns runway. This meant closing the drome for 24 hours whilst decontamination was carried out. Fortunately there were no major casualties. The trial was successfully done 10th January.

On 17th January, the Australian Field Experimental Station moved from Innisfail to Proserpine leaving only a small detachment to carry out the remaining minor trials in the Innisfail area. A really lovely camp had been built about 14 miles out of Proserpine for the unit with excellent field and laboratory facilities for trials. This became the new Headquarters of the unit and remained so until its termination on 15th November, 1945. The buildings and living quarters were excellent—quite a change after Innisfail, although the scenery compared to the latter was unimpressive. Facilities for recreation for personnel were not good although after a few months it became possible to arrange trips to Day Dream Island and other picturesque islands in the Whit Sunday Passage on Sundays.[352]

Completely isolated as the unit was in the Proserpine area with ample room for large scale field trials in comparatively close proximity to the camp and situated only 60 miles from Bowen (the Headquarters of R.A.A.F. Chemical Research Unit), working conditions were considerably easier than they had been at Innisfail. Some of the special equipment available at the unit was the best available in the world. This equipment included a large stainless steel gas chamber of 1500 cubic feet capacity and fitted with devices to maintain accurate conditions with regard to gas concentration, humidity and temperature. It was in this chamber that extensive work of physiological interest under the supervision of Mr. Legge (M.Sc. Melb.) and Dr. Robert Thompson (D.Sc. Oxford) using R.A.A.F. personnel as volunteers was carried out.

A trial worthy of mention was that carried out on 13th July, 1945. A Beaufort aircraft was sprayed with mustard gas to a density of 30 gms. per square metre. The object of the trial, which was a request from London, was to determine whether or not it would be safe to fly an aircraft covered with gas, how much protection the crew would require and the degree of decontamination necessary. Among the aircrew volunteers we called for a pilot and wireless operator for the job. Two technical personnel to operate the sampling apparatus, volunteers from Australian Field Experimental Station would fill the Navigator and Rear Gunner positions. Flight Lieutenant Barker and Warrant Officer Wells were the aircrew volunteers while Captain Andrews (Aust. Army) and I took the other positions. Preliminary trials were done to determine the safety of flying and landing in protective clothing and a respirator. In the trial proper the crew entered the heavily contaminated aircraft and flew over the sea for two hours though they were aware of the corrosive properties of mustard gas on perspex and aircraft fabric. Chemical sampling of the air inside the aircraft was carried out continuously. Owing to the exhaustion caused by flying in full protective clothing and a respirator it was necessary for the crew to be dosed with glucose and receive injections of hyoscine prior to take off. On landing it was discovered that the lining of the brakes had been corroded so we landed with no brakes; the pilot fortunately was able to avert a crash.

With the cessation of hostilities the future of the station was in doubt. However, it was decided that the present programme of work was to be finished and the station was placed on a care and maintenance basis awaiting a decision as to its peace time use. And so on November 15th, the unit commenced to close down.

I returned to R.A.A.F. Headquarters where I assisted in staff work concerning disposal of Chemical Warfare Munitions prior to being posted to No. 1 P.D. with effect from 23rd December, for discharge.

Comments and Suggestions Re the Use of Women for Chemical Warfare

Defensive

The efficiency with which W.A.A.A.F. anti gas instructors performed their duties both instructional and assisting the Aerodrome Defence Officers, illustrated that women were suited to this type of work. Maintenance and repair of respirators, anti-gas capes and suits, re-doping fabric D materials and routine chemical testing of impregnated clothing to watch for deterioration is work for which girls appeared to have a natural aptitude.

Armament

The protective clothing plus a respirator that must be worn continually during offensive work with Chemical Warfare munitions is very exhausting and trying. It took a long time to train men to work for long periods in protective clothing and though I trained to do likewise the work is indeed exhausting and in my opinion not suitable for women. In addition mustard gas burns are very painful and quite often scar. During my service I was burnt several times on the skin, eyes, throat, and lungs and though the only permanent damage is a scar on the skin the experiences certainly were unpleasant and painful.

Experimental

With regard to field trials the same remarks apply as for armament duties. However, for laboratory work connected with trials AWAS and AAMWS were successfully employed at Australian Field Experimental Station. This type of work is very interesting and here again girls showed a natural aptitude for attention to detail and the precision required.

Return September. Winding up camp November. Return R.A.A.F. Headquarters. General work. Released from Service 7th February, 1946.[353]

A3

Petition to Her Majesty under Section 59 of the *Australian Constitution* seeking disallowance or amendment of *Matrimonial Causes Act 1959*

Your majesty:

We, the undersigned petitioners in the Commonwealth of Australia, desire to express our devotion and loyalty to Your Majesty.

We wish to invite the attention of Your Majesty to a grave matter concerning the Matrimonial Causes Act, 1959, of the Commonwealth of Australia, with particular reference to Section 28 (m), assented to on 16th December, 1959.

Irrespective of the merit or demerit of the principle of Divorce itself, and without setting down herein Constitutional objections, it is our firm and sincere belief that the ground for Divorce as provided in Section 28 (m) is a clear denial of elementary justice and of basic human rights of an innocent spouse, who may be divorced in the interest and for the convenience of a guilty partner.

British people have inherited a deep respect for the majesty and justice of the law.

Centuries of British experience have led people of British tradition to the conviction that the law is just.

Section 28 (m) destroys this conviction. For the law to assist the wrongdoer against an innocent partner in this most personal and fundamental institution of family life is a vital and serious departure from principle.

The implementation of this Section could have a grievous influence destructive of the trust relationship of husband and wife in the family sphere.

In particular the legitimate rights of an innocent spouse are not protected in the case where such innocent spouse's unwillingness to accept a divorce is based on sincere religious conviction.

This is confirmed by the Attorney-General (Hansard 18 & 19, November, 1959, page 2858). Explaining the effect of Section 28 (m) referring to the case of an innocent spouse not wishing to be a party to divorce, the Attorney-General said: "He may say 'I have some religious or sentimental reason for not wanting to be divorced'. In speaking on this matter last night my proposition was that the interests of the community in ensuring that the other party to the marriage did not form an illicit union and was able to form a sound union would overbear these sentimental or religious scruples on the part of the respondent".

Concessions to human frailty, such as appear in this Section, endanger the true welfare of millions of children yet unborn by striking a fresh blow at the integrity of family life.

Although the law cannot make people moral we claim the right to expect that its aim should be to uphold accepted moral principles and not to condone immorality by clothing it in a garb of respectability.

Not only are we grievously shocked at this attitude towards a spouse innocent of any matrimonial wrongdoing, but it appears to us that Section 28 (m) is neither in the interests of the children of the marriage, the youth of the nation, nor of the community.

In addition, the thoughtful and expressed views of the leaders of the Anglican and Catholic Churches throughout Australia on this issue were obviously rejected.

We recall the words of the centuries old prayer said on the delivery of the sword to Your Majesty on the day of Coronation:

"With this sword do justice, stop the growth of iniquity, protect the Holy Church of God, help and defend widows and orphans, restore the things that are gone to decay, maintain the things that are restored, punish and reform what is amiss and confirm what is in good order, that, doing these things, you may be glorious in all virtue and so faithfully serve Our Lord Jesus Christ in this life and you may reign for ever with Him in the Life which is to come."

With respect we humbly pray Your Majesty to exercise Your Personal Prerogative and/or Your Power of Disallowance mentioned in Section 59 of the Commonwealth of Australia Act (63 & 64 Vic Chapter 12) in order to disallow this Act in its present form or alternatively delete Section 28 (m) in its present form.

We remain Your Majesty's humble and obedient servants.[354]

A4

Special Report on Australian-Japanese Children in Japan, July 1960

Special Report on Australian-Japanese Children in Japan

(Prepared by Mrs. John F. Dynon on behalf of the Australian-Asian Association of Victoria. July, 1960.)

Summary

1. A number of children were abandoned in Japan by their Australian fathers. Some of these children are legitimate.

2. The total number of mixed-blood children abandoned by their Australian fathers is at least 104.

3. Of these, a few have been adopted by families in Japan and in U.S.A. Of the remainder, approximately one half of the children are being cared for in orphanages and homes in Japan. These charitable institutions are in need of funds and warm clothing.

4. 52 of the children are living in dire poverty in the Kure area and are in great need of material assistance.

Background

The period of the Occupation of Japan by the British Commonwealth Occupation Force (including A.I.F.) was from early in 1946 until 28th March, 1952, when the Peace Treaty (Japanese) became effective. Under the Treaty "all Troops were to leave within 90 days." An agreement with the Japanese Government allowed troops to remain after this because of the Korean War. In February 1956, Sir Philip McBride, Australian Minister for Defence, announced that the "Australian Forces left in Japan would be progressively withdrawn." The last Australian troops left Japan later that year.

APPENDIX A4

Fraternisation

In the first years of the Occupation, Australian troops were under orders not to fraternise with the Japanese, and marriages between Australian servicemen and Japanese women were not recognized by the Army authorities.

Herald 5/3/1949 "Troops on the Duntroon (which returned to Sydney yesterday from Japan) told a reporter that they were bitter about the non-fraternisation policy."

Herald 5/3/1949 "Many Australian soldiers in Japan are marrying Japanese girls in defiance of the Army's non-fraternisation ban according to members of B.C.O.F., who returned to Sydney in the Duntroon yesterday. Among 427 on board were about 20 married to Japanese girls and anxious to return to them. Also aboard was an ex-serviceman who stowed away in a ship from Sydney nearly 18 months ago, and had resumed married life with his Japanese bride. Keith Morrison, 23, said there were others in the contingent anxious to be discharged and to apply for permission to return to Japan as civilians to marry Japanese girls. He said the next troopship from Japan would carry an even greater number of Australians who had married Japanese girls. Ken Gibbons, 25, of Thistlewaite St., South Melbourne, and Pat Stapleton, 28, of Ebly St., Bondi Junction, both said they had married Japanese girls according to Shinto rites. Keith Morrison said he had married a Japanese girl nearly three years ago."

Sun 14/6/1949 "No legal marriages have taken place between Japanese women and members of B.C.O. Forces" said Lt/Col. A.D. Gillespie last night. He has been with B.C.O.F. Public Relations for over 3 years and is the last New Zealander to leave Headquarters in Japan. He said, "A marriage ceremony, whether Shinto or Buddhist, in which a serviceman is involved cannot be performed without prior notification to the Occupation authorities. Moreover, every union must be registered with the local Japanese town or village authorities, otherwise it is not legal."

Official Army statements issued about that time indicate that Japanese registrars were forbidden by the Occupation authorities to conduct these marriages for occupation men. If the Army authorities heard that a Shinto rites marriage was going to take place, provosts would be sent to break up the ceremony.

Despite the ban on fraternisation by the Occupation authorities, a number of Australian members of the B.C.O.F. admitted on their return from Japan that they had married Japanese girls by Shinto rites. Some of these marriages were registered with local Japanese authorities. Mr. Denis Warner said in the Herald on 23/1/1960:

> "Many Australians married Japanese girls under rites which were legally binding under Japanese law, but which the Australian Army would not accept. Some of the children were born in what the Japanese women had every reason to believe was legal wedlock. Only when the troops were shipped off home and denied the right to take their "wives" with them, did the Japanese girls discover the deception."

Prior to September 1949, it was difficult for an Australian to obtain a visa to return to his "wife" in Japan.

Legal Effect of Army Ban

We are not aware that the international validity of any of these marriages has been tested in a Japanese or in an Australian Court of Law. The effect of the Army ban on the international validity of the marriage has not yet been determined by the Courts, so far as we know.

Representations have been made to the Federal Attorney General regarding the effect of the Army ban on such marriages. In February 1960, Sir Garfield Barwick replied as follows:

> "So far as the questions involve matters of law, I do not feel that it would be proper for me, as Attorney General, to attempt to provide answers, nor do I think that I can furnish you with a reply of a general nature which would serve any useful purpose."

There is so far no Australian Federal Act relating to Marriage. It may be of interest to note that Cheshire's "Private International Law" states:

"A marriage solemnised in Japan according to the local forms between an Englishman and a Japanese Woman was recognised as valid in England, upon proof that by the law of Japan marriage is the union of one man and one woman to the exclusion of all others."

The British Nationality Act states: —

"1. The following persons shall be deemed to be natural-born British subjects, namely... (b) (IV) his father was at the time of that person's birth in the service of the Crown."

The Commonwealth of Australia Nationality and Citizenship Act, which came into operation on 26th January, 1949, states: —

"11. (1) Subject to this section, a person born outside Australia after the commencement of this Act shall be an Australian citizen by descent if (a) at the time of the birth, (1) his father was an Australian Citizen and (b) the birth was registered at an Australian consulate within one year after its occurrence or, in special circumstances, within such extended period as the Minister allows."

According to both British and Australian law and according to Japanese law, a child born out of wedlock assumes the nationality of his mother, except in certain special circumstances where the mother is living abroad at the time of the birth.

Law of Japan regarding Marriage

The law of Japan requires no specific form of marriage ceremony. Legally, the only necessary procedure is registration of the marriage in the Family Register, which is held in the registry office according to the Census Registration Law, in the town in which the family lives. Therefore, although a couple have been married by Shinto or other rites and live together, they are not regarded as being legally wed until they have complied with the necessary registration.

Court precedents, however, show that informal, de facto marriages, which are socially considered binding, are given protection as close as possible to that of formal marriages.

Precedents have also established the judicial conception of informal marriages and the Courts have ruled that desertion by one of the parties renders such spouse responsible for compensation to the deserted.

In cases of the various Government Social Welfare Services, wives and widows of an "Informal Marriage" hold the same status as those of a formal marriage.

Change in Policy of Australian Government

Prior to 1952, the policy of the Australian Immigration Department did not permit Asian wives to join their husbands in Australia, nor were they eligible for admission to Australian citizenship by naturalization.

With regard to the question of bringing Japanese wives to Australia, in 1952 the new policy of the Australian Government permitted non-Europeans married to Australians and other approved non-Europeans to take out citizenship rights subject to certain conditions being fulfilled. Permission was given by the Federal Cabinet on the recommendation of the then Minister for Immigration, the Hon. H.E. Holt, on 27th March, 1952, in the case of Mrs. Gordon Parker. Each case was to be considered on its merits.

In 1955, The Commonwealth of Australia Nationality and Citizenship Act was amended to include: —

> "Part 3, Division 3, 15(4)(1). The Minister may, upon application in the approved form grant a certificate of naturalization as an Australian citizen to an alien who satisfies him: (a) that she is the wife or widow...of an Australian citizen".

After March 1952, applications by servicemen in Japan for permission to marry had to be received by the Australian Commander in Chief in Japan and by the British Consul. The proposed marriage had to be proved likely to last and the serviceman had to guarantee job prospects and accommodation for himself and his wife on their return to Australia.

Information available to our Sub-Committee shows that although a number of servicemen did marry and succeed in bringing their wives and children to Australia they had to overcome many difficulties and much discouragement. The serviceman having obtained Army permission to marry, it appeared to be necessary for him and his Japanese fiancee to undergo three forms of marriage, namely (1) Church, (2) Before Japanese Registrar, (3) Before British Consul.

Among the "war-brides" now living in Australia, some came to Australia with their husbands while others came alone and joined their husbands in Australia. Some Japanese women came to Australia as temporary visitors with the understanding that they may be permitted to stay permanently if the proposed marriage was solemnized within the specified time.

Deserted "Wives" and Children in Japan

Information available to our Sub-Committee shows that a number of Australian servicemen married Japanese girls before Japanese Registrars and/or by Shinto rites and/or by Christian rites or entered into Japanese Informal Marriages or formed illicit unions with Japanese girls. Later, for varying reasons, these abandoned their Japanese wives and/or their children in Japan.

We have not been able to ascertain the exact number of children who were left in Japan by their Australian fathers. On 23/10/1956 an Official of the Japanese Welfare Ministry denied statements that there were more than 1000 children of Japanese mothers and Australian servicemen in Japan. The Official said that the Ministry knew of only 104.

Many of these children are living in hovels and shanties and in conditions of poverty, want and hunger and in the words of a Tokyo Official of Japan's Welfare Ministry (16/11/1959) are "existing at a minimum living standard." He explained that while the Japanese Government helped to finance some orphanages and offered help to mothers caring for their children, it was feared that in a few years some children might turn to crime to try to improve their poor living conditions.

Some of the abandoned children have been adopted by Japanese families and some by non-Japanese couples living temporarily in Japan, some have been adopted by couples in U.S.A. and some are living with their mothers and step-fathers. The material needs of these children would seem to be satisfactory.

Some of the children abandoned by their fathers are living with their mothers and some have been placed in orphanages run by Church and charitable organizations. The National Catholic Council of Japan has arranged for the adoption of a number of mixed-blood children and some are being cared for in its orphanages and homes. Some of the school age boys have been gathered together in a Boys' Town run by the Catholic Church at Yokohama. In this way it is hoped that a good education will be given to them, and later that it will not be too difficult for them to find suitable employment in a big commercial and harbour city like Yokohama.

The International Social Service, Japan Branch, has arranged for the adoption into America of eight Japanese-Australian children. The Australian Council of the World Council of Churches raised a large proportion of the money needed to cover legal and other adoption expenses.

In addition, the I.S.S. financed by the Augustana Lutheran Mission in Japan, the Australian Council of the World Council of Churches, with supplementation by the I.S.S. and by logistic support from the Municipal Government of Kure conducted a survey in 1958 and since July, 1959, has assigned a Trained Social Worker to the Kure area to assist the mixed-blood children in that area. In the course of the project, considerable help, both material and "counselling" was mobilized for the children and their mothers. The programme was carried out in complete co-operation with the Department of Social Welfare of Kure City.

The survey has shown that there are 88 mixed-blood children living in Kure of whom 52, whose ages vary from 6 to 13 years, are children of Australian paternity. These children are living in extreme poverty and all are in need of material help for their maintenance and for their education and vocational training. These

52 children are living with their mothers or grand-parents or friends and it is the opinion of the I.S.S. that it is in the best interests of these children that they remain where they are. There are no longer any Japanese-Australian children whose interests would best be served by adoption outside Japan now. Social workers claim that separation of the child from the mother in cases where the child has been long enough with its mother to have formed a close emotional tie is known to have serious damaging effects. Many instances of later maladjustment, delinquency, and even actual mental breakdown have been traced to this kind of separation. Most of the children now living in Kure, Japan, have been a long time with their mothers or close relatives and social workers feel that poverty, even "dire poverty", does not constitute in itself a sufficiently grave reason for removing these children from their mothers.

The I.S.S., the National Catholic Council of Japan and the World Council of Churches, agree that the Australian-Japanese children and all mixed blood children need very special understanding, protection and help. In Japan, there is an urgent need for money. Any funds that can be made available will be used for food and clothing and for the enabling of the children to remain longer at school (up to 15 years as required by Japanese law) and to receive vocational training so as to equip them to compete later in the highly competitive Japanese employment market.

In December, 1959, Tsutomu Hiromoto, an official of the Kure City Social Welfare Office said of the 52 children of Australian paternity living in Kure: "I am afraid that the only hope of giving these children a happy future is aid from Australia. The problem is beyond our powers."

The International Social Service of Japan, 1959 Report of Kure Project states:

> "In November, 1957, a representative of the Australian Embassy in Tokyo approached I.S.S. for information about Japanese children of Australian paternity, with a view to obtaining assistance of some kind from the Australian

Government. Such information as was available was given to him, with a proposed plan of operation for practical assistance to the children. Information was also sent to I.S.S. Australian Branch; reply was received in March 1958, from the I.S.S, director in Australia reporting on the negative results of her discussion of the question with the Secretary of the Department of External Affairs in Canberra."

The members of our Sub-Committee believe that there is a moral responsibility for Australia to do what it can to help the Australian-Japanese children, who through no fault of their own were abandoned by their Australian fathers and are living in conditions of great hardship and extreme poverty. We believe that through the Australian-Asian Association of Victoria launching an Appeal for funds and for warm clothing for these children, we may be able to help alleviate the suffering of the children.

We must not ignore the plight of these children—rather let us give an example of charity. We contend that our Christian, Democratic civilisation here is a precious heritage in the Pacific area of the world. To help these children is a golden opportunity for us to demonstrate the practice of our convictions.

July, 1960[355]

A5

Joint Statement concerning Proposed Policy of the Commonwealth Government of Australia to Conscript a Minority of Aliens Resident in Australia for Military Service including Service Overseas by James M Galbally & Moira Dynon, 15 August 1966

Joint Statement concerning Proposed Policy of the Commonwealth Government of Australia to Conscript a Minority of Aliens Resident in Australia for Military Service including Service Overseas.

1. We call upon the Commonwealth Government of Australia to reconsider its announced decision to impose compulsory military service, including overseas service, on certain categories of aliens resident in Australia.

2. In view of the fact that there is a clear conflict of opinion between the Government of Italy and the Government of Australia as to the validity in International Law of such a proposal, we urge the Government not to implement this decision in any way unless and until the matter is adjudicated upon by the appropriate International Court of Justice.

3. We point out that there are many undesirable and unjust features of this proposal and of the concept of selective compulsory service, involving service overseas, of alien residents.

    - It is inequitable in that conscription is imposed by the Government on a minority of aliens whilst the Government is unwilling to inflict similar burdens on the majority of Australian people.

- It is <u>unjust</u> in that the minority being conscripted, through being denied the right to vote, has no prior say in the formulation of the policy.
- We note that there is <u>discrimination</u> against a minority of aliens, who are to be conscripted, whilst the vast majority of Australians remain unaffected.
- Further, we note that the proposed policy discriminates between aliens themselves, in that, of those who are required to register at the same time, only those who are "Balloted in" will be forced to the decision – "Serve or leave the country". This discriminatory and oppressive policy against a minority of aliens is in effect "Serve or accept expulsion".
- Furthermore, to the minority who accept expulsion, the result will either divide the family or lead to family emigration. Bearing in mind the strength of the family bond amongst Italians, we deplore this enforced choice to be imposed on a minority of the Italian families.

4. We remind the Government that Italian migrants have made an important contribution to the development of Australia in the post-war years—in primary and secondary industries, and in industrial development including the Snowy River Scheme.

5. The members of our Association work to facilitate the integration of the Italian migrants into the Australian community. We are vitally concerned with all matters affecting the welfare of the Italian community. We consider the proposed discriminatory policy directed against minorities of aliens must inevitably lead to misunderstanding and resentment.

James M. Galbally, President of Italo-Australian Welfare Association

Moira L. Dynon, President of Italo-Australian Welfare Association, Women's Division[356]

A6

Statement on Abortion prepared by Moira Dynon and released by National Executive Committee Australian Council of Catholic Women, 30 April 1968

We the Australian Council of Catholic Women, Hold these Truths about Abortion:

1. Directly intentional killing of an innocent human being is wrong. Each human foetus from the moment of conception must be considered a distinct, innocent, human being. To remove this from the womb before viability is to deprive it of the life that it already has, and so to kill it. This is seriously wrong. It differs from other forms of murder only in that the victim is smaller, more helpless and more innocent.

2. Abortion is wrong because it is the direct taking of innocent human life. Some may ask—if the life that is taken is really a human life, if the foetus is definitely a human being. We, and indeed the majority of mankind, take the view that the beginnings of life are indeed human and should not be deprived of the right to exist. To avoid the accusation of killing the innocent the abortionist would have to prove that the living foetus was not a human person. If he is uncertain he cannot act with a good conscience. If a man sees a form that may be a man or could be a kangaroo it is morally wrong to shoot. If a man is driving along in the evening and sees something lying across the road which looks like a sack but might be a man, he is not justified in

running over it. He has done wrong in taking such a grave risk without certain knowledge in such a matter of life and death. The onus of proof is on the abortionist and in this case he is unable to prove that he is not destroying an innocent human baby.

3. We answer the mistaken view that Catholics prefer the life of the child over that of the mother by replying with Pope Pius XII:

"Never and in no case has the Church taught that the life of the child must be preferred to that of the mother. It is erroneous to put the question with this alternative; either the life of the child or that of the mother. No, neither the life of the mother nor that of the child can be subjected to an act of direct suppression…On purpose we have always used the expression 'direct attempt on the life of an innocent person', 'direct killing'. Because if, for example, the saving of the life of the future mother, independently of her pregnant state, should urgently require a surgical act or other therapeutic treatment which would have as an accessory consequence, in no way desired nor intended but inevitable, the death of the foetus, such an act could no longer be called a direct attempt on an innocent life."

4. Also we quote Pope Paul VI:

"Innocent human life, in whatever condition it is found, is to be secure from the very first moment of its existence from any direct deliberate attack. This is a fundamental right of the human person, which is of general value in the Christian concept of life; and hence as valid for the still hidden life within the womb of the mother as for the life of the already born and developing outside of her…Whatever foundation there may be for the distinction between these varying phases of the development of the life that is born, or still unborn, in profane and ecclesiastical law, and as regards certain civil and penal consequences, all these cases involve a grave and unlawful attack upon the inviolability of human life".

5. The Declaration of the Rights of the Child made by a unanimous vote of the United Nations' General Assembly on the 20th November 1959, stated that "The child, by reason of his physical and mental immaturity, needs special safeguards and care including appropriate legal protection, before as well as after birth". It went on to call "upon parents upon men and women as individuals and upon voluntary organisations, local authorities and national governments to recognise these rights and strive for their observance by legislative and other measures." This Declaration was accepted by 78 nations—and Australia was one of them.

6. We deplore the movement to legalise abortion. We hold that abortion is the violation of a basic human right and we want our laws to defend basic human rights. We are not trying to impose Catholic morality on those who are not Catholics, but are defending the basic human right to life. God has said: "Thou shalt not kill" and it is our clear conviction that the whole of society benefits by defending the life of the innocent. Once we allow the right to life to be undermined, we make life in any society a very insecure thing and place the power over innocent human life in the hands of those in political power, thereby departing from democracy to despotic dictatorship. We do not claim that anyone who has an opinion differing from ours is in bad faith but we would not be contributing to the good of our society if we were silent when the life of an innocent human being was at stake. Legalising abortion would be an admission that our Australian society is so morally confused that its laws permit the killing of the innocent. Such a basic human right—the right to life itself—is inviolable. Society cannot benefit by undermining the right to life. If abortions were legalised,

then could follow the destruction of deformed live babies, the mentally sick and old helpless people suffering from incurable diseases.

7. Legalising abortion on the pretext of thereby lessening "backyard" abortions is like legalising murder in order to lessen the number of hidden murders.

8. If abortion is legalised the increased number of abortions will mean that a number of women in Australia will die, and even more will suffer ill health, merely as a result of abortion of normal pregnancies.

9. The vocation of a doctor is to preserve and not to destroy human life as is evidenced by the Hippocratic tradition.

10. If women were dying in pregnancy and childbirth because they had been denied therapeutic abortion in the early months, this would be apparent in a survey of the causes of maternal deaths. In fact this is not so. In practically none could the cause of death be foreseen in the early weeks as the deaths are due to unforeseen complications or accidents later in pregnancy or childbirth.

11. There is no evidence known to us that the number of "backyard" abortions has decreased in countries which have legalised abortion.

12. Society has an obligation to find a solution to the problems facing some women who see abortion as a solution to their social and economic problems.

13. Especially in a nation like ours, desperately short of population, there is urgent need to extend the assistance to parents already granted in a limited form, providing pre-natal care, maternity allowances, child endowment and child welfare provisions.

14. Perhaps abortion is the most cowardly of all crimes for it is often an attempt to gain either greater affluence, or a false reputation for chastity at the expense of a life too weak to defend itself.

15. For all these reasons, we the Catholic Women of Australia, are opposed to legalising abortion, and we call upon all people of good will to protect the unborn child.

Released by National Executive Committee, Australian Council of Catholic Women.

Affiliated Organisations of Australian Council of Catholic Women are:

1. Catholic Women's Social Guild of Victoria and Wagga Wagga.

2. Catholic Women's League, New South Wales.

3. Catholic Daughters of Australia, Queensland.

4. Catholic Women's League, South Australia.

5. Catholic Women's League, Western Australia.

6. Catholic Women's League, Tasmania.

7. Catholic Women's League, Canberra-Goulburn.

8. Catholic Women's League, Darwin, Northern Territory.

30th April 1968.[357]

A7

Letter to Moira Dynon from M.W.B. Smithies (for the Secretary) Department of External Affairs, 7 June 1965

Dear Mrs. Dynon,

When we talked on the telephone earlier this week I suggested you may like to come to Canberra in the near future so that we could discuss some of the problems that have arisen in the administration of the Government grant for freight on voluntary food aid given to India. This is to confirm that invitation, and to ask you to let me know which day in the week ending Friday 18th June would be suitable to you. We could cover the points for discussion in a couple of hours and so there would be no difficulty in your making the return trip Melbourne-Canberra in the one day.

You will recall that our main concern was to minimise some of the less desirable side-effects of the granting of Government assistance. Among these may be listed—

    a.   the possibility that if further publicity is given to the Government grant, more shipping companies may withdraw concessions previously given to donors of charitable consignments (in addition, that is, to the two companies that have already done so in respect of several consignments that have come to the attention of our Procurement Directorate in Melbourne). This would be regrettable in any case and even more so if the concession were withdrawn from donations that did not qualify for Government assistance—especially if, in the longer run, it were to result in less rather than more voluntary aid reaching India;

b. the difficulty the small staff of the Procurement Directorate is experiencing in dealing with prospective donors of consignments which, while as small as a few tins of milk, are addressed to specific recipients and would, if accepted by the Directorate, require individual attention and as much administrative work as consignments of several tons;

c. the Department's duty, in dealing with public money, to assure itself that the grant cannot be exploited by commercial interests and cannot lead to a charge of "favouritism" to members of any particular faith.

In the latter connection your own suggestion that Government assistance be confined in the future to consignments put at the disposal of the Indian Government or its instrumentalities is one that we welcome and would like to discuss with you in more detail. I might add that since I spoke to you we have had confirmation of the desirability of taking a course of action along these lines from our High Commission in New Delhi, following discussions that the High Commission has had recently with the Indian Government on the question of entry of goods for distribution to the poor and needy irrespective of race colour or creed; among other things the question arose of gifts allegedly designed to attract people to particular religious beliefs.

It seems fairly clear to us in Canberra that we shall have to take some action that is compatible with the spirit in which the gifts are offered in Australia, but at the same time does not arouse any sensitivities during the process of their distribution in India. Your offer to co-operate with us in looking at these problems is therefore especially welcome at this time, and we are hoping that you will feel free to accept some kind of co-ordinating role in respect of the smaller consignments offered in Melbourne.

Yours sincerely,

M.W.B. Smithies (for the Secretary)[358]

A8

Memorandum to Prime Minister Harold Holt regarding Australian Food Assistance to India, February 1966

Memorandum to the Prime Minister, The Rt. Hon. H.E. Holt, M.P. regarding Australian Food Assistance to India.

The Milk For India Committee wishes to bring the following points to your attention, regarding India's need for food assistance now and in the immediate future and Australia's capacity to assist.

The committee believes the Australian Government has shown some awareness of the Indian food crisis, indicated by—

a. The $8 million gift of wheat, processed milk, pesticides and machinery announced by the Minister for External Affairs, Hon. Paul Hasluck, M.P. on 18th February, 1966.

b. Co-operation with citizen efforts, particularly by the allocations of funds to cover freight costs and insurance of citizen's gift consignments of processed milk sent to the Government of India for the needy.

c. Assistance provided under Colombo Plan.

d. Participation in the Asian Bank, the World Bank and other monetary arrangements.

We wish to point out that India's need for assistance is still great and is likely to continue in the immediate future. May we refer to the Statements by the Secretary General of the United Nations, U. Thant, President Johnson and His Holiness Pope Paul, as well as to speeches by the Prime Minister of India, Mrs. Indira Gandhi, and the Indian Minister for Food and Agriculture, Mr. C. Subramaniam.

The Committee believes there is an overwhelming case for particularly generous assistance to India, not only on humanitarian grounds but also in the interests of long term trading and of political stability in India itself.

India is a country of about 470 million people, most of whom are badly undernourished. She is the largest nation in the world attempting to find national unity and stability by democratic process, and is our largest friendly neighbour in this area of the world.

It is important for the future democracy in Asia that India's political experiment should succeed. Nothing is more likely to ensure its failure than a continuation of serious food shortages. The recent serious riots are disturbing. According to current Indian Parliamentary reports, it appears that extremist groups are endeavouring to make capital out of the food shortage situation.

Food For India Committee believes that Australia can help in the following ways:—

    a. By supplies of wheat (including Rycena), and processed milk and egg powder. In this regard we believe that Sir John Crawford, former Secretary of the Department of Trade has made a valuable suggestion. In a message to a public meeting in the Melbourne Town Hall on February 23rd, 1966 (called by the Food For India Committee) Sir John stated that non-exporting nations as well as traditional exporters should contribute to the cost of acquiring wheat on the needed scale. "Indeed it is high time that Europe, North America and Australia reached agreement with India on a supply programme designed to complement but not to replace her own programme for expanding production." We urge the Australian Government to initiate a conference between nations of these areas to decide on a supply programme.

b. Another way of helping India would be to accept full or part payment in rupees for food and other supplies. Some of these rupees could be used to finance Australian long-term development projects in India and to finance the "Grow More Food" projects (as is done with supplies of grain by the U.S. under PL 480.)

In addition to helping India, such a scheme would help the development of Australian special skills, for example, the further development of the Rycena industry. This scheme could help stabilise the flour industry in Australia and could also lead to more markets for flour in the form of Rycena. This could also be financed by trade arrangements for increased purchases of Indian goods.

The Committee believes that there is enormous potential for the Australian Diary Industry in providing long-term assistance to India. We would suggest an arrangement between the Australian Government, the Dairy Produce Board and the Dairying Industry for the supply of fixed quantities of processed milk on similar repayment terms, for a minimum fixed period of, say, ten years. We are informed that such an arrangement would be welcome by the dairying industry and greatly assist its development. At present the dairying industry receives Government subsidies of approximately $26 million annually. This scheme would help in the expansion of overseas markets and help to keep down the subsidy.

We believe the Australian Government should give further encouragement to realistic citizen projects in the following ways:

a. Tax deductions on donations for Indian relief.
b. Continuation of freight cost payments for all consignments of processed milk sent for distribution to the needy by the Government of India.

In this regard we would like to point out the valuable assistance given by State Governments in Australia, particularly those in the States of Victoria, Tasmania and South Australia, which provide free rail freight for citizens' contributions of processed milk for India.

Another practical method of assistance would be for the Australian Government to encourage Australian investment in India by the promotion of the Government's own scheme for Australian companies to insure their capital investments in less developed countries with the Government. This is a highly commendable scheme and if applied with emphasis on Indian food production plans (for example, fertiliser production, milk schemes, etc.) could be very valuable.

We recognise the difficulty in foreign investment in India. However, we believe that it is in Australia's <u>long-term</u> interests for the Government to make investment less hazardous.

Indirect assistance to India can be given in the following ways: —

a. Australian Tariff Preference Proposal Australian people should be made more fully aware of the Government's action with regard to this proposal. In addition, the Government should examine the possibility of the extension of the number of items and the extension of the quotas which have been fixed. Australian representatives to continue to press for the adoption of this commendable and constructive Australian proposal in General Agreement on Tariffs and Trade.

b. Expansion of Schemes whereby Australians with specialised skills and training (especially in the field of agriculture) spend fixed periods in India in research and field work.

c. Extension of existing educational schemes in the Commonwealth Scientific and Industrial Research Organization, Australian Universities and other fields under which Indian specialists work in Australia for fixed periods for study and field work.[359]

A9

Letter from Moira Dynon to Treasurer William McMahon seeking continued Government funding for transport of milk to India, 16 January 1967

Dear Mr. McMahon,

I am writing to you because I am deeply concerned at the delay in the decision concerning the continuation of the original policy providing for the allocation of funds to meet freight and insurance costs to ship to the Government of India the processed milk contributed by private donors through my 19 Milk For India Committees.

As you are aware, it was the then Prime Minister, Sir Robert Menzies, who conveyed to me on 29th December 1964 the Government's decision to provide funds for shipping costs of the processed milk to India. At the beginning of the financial year in July 1965, I was advised without any application being made by my Campaign that a similar allocation of funds was being provided for similar purposes.

In more recent months, as you are aware because of the increase in contributions it has been necessary for me to make further applications to cover the further necessary freight and insurance costs involved. The Shipping Company, Royal Inter-Ocean Lines, has been providing generous concession rates for our consignments.

Prior to July 1966, any departmental expenses involved by the Department of Supply regarding transport, storage, and some crating, were not debited against the allocation.

APPENDIX A9

On 14th July I was delighted to receive your telegram advising that the Government had decided to provide an additional $5000 to cover freight and insurance costs involved in shipping the processed milk to India. This allocation in fact enabled us to send the Government of India all the processed milk then held in the various States (115 tons, our No. 8 Consignment.) At a later date a further quantity of milk was held but we were unable to send more than 7 tons (our Number 9 Consignment) because I was informed by Mr. Connor of External Affairs Department in Melbourne that there was sufficient money to send only this small quantity because expenses of the Department of Supply had been debited against the allocation of $5000 provided by you to cover freight and insurance costs.

Such debiting departed from the practice which had been followed consequent on the decisions by the then Prime Minister, Sir Robert Menzies on 29th December 1964. Such departure meant, in fact, that not nearly as much processed milk could be shipped to the Government of India from this allocation as our Campaign had anticipated if the established practice had been followed.

I was informed that the freight costs for our Number 10 Consignment to the Indian Government (60 tons) shipped per S.S. Straat Colombo, which sailed from Melbourne on 2nd December, was met from 'a balance of Colombo Plan funds'. This is the first advice I had received concerning freight and insurance costs for any of our consignments being met from Colombo Plan funds.

Further application was made to the Prime Minister on 4th December 1966 for freight costs and insurance and I have been advised that the Government "still has this matter under consideration." A substantial quantity of processed milk is currently held in various depots.

The January ship, S.S. Lombok, is now in Melbourne Port and no decision from the Government is yet to hand. Now it is a practical impossibility for the processed milk currently held to be shipped on this ship to Bombay. To me it seems inhuman that the despatch of powdered milk, urgently needed for the Indian Government's relief programmes for children, pregnant mothers and the sick and infirm, and donated in the spirit of friendship by thousands of Australian people, should be delayed.

I do not blame you or the Prime Minister. Both of you have so frequently expressed friendship and understanding for the people of India by words and action.

It seems to me that there are signs of resistance located in the ranks of External Affairs Department endeavouring to manoeuvre our Campaign into a 'hand to mouth' system in the shipment of this precious item of help and friendship. You may be interested to know that a responsible person, a member of one of my State Committees, considered that he had been reliably informed that External Affairs Department was most sympathetic to our efforts but that the Federal Treasury would 'fight every inch of the way'. I told my Committee that I could not believe this allegation. It is because of this allegation that I am writing to you to give you some background to the Campaign and its Milk For India programme.

Further, I have every reason to believe that our voluntary efforts are promoting friendship and goodwill and providing help for needy people during a most critical stage of India's development.

I have received numerous communications from Australian Government representatives in India telling of the goodwill that our efforts are creating and forwarding distribution particulars. Recently our Australian High Commissioner in New Delhi, Sir Arthur Tange, wrote to me:

> "It is most pleasing to hear of the continuing efforts of the Campaign…I know from personal contacts that members of the High Commission have with officials of the Food and Rehabilitation Ministries that there is a continuing appreciation here of the generosity of private Australian donors in gifting processed milk to India."

Our Campaign including Milk for India programme, is a purely voluntary initiative (there is no paid staff whatsoever) and is supported by all sections of the community including the State Governments of Victoria, Tasmania and South Australia, which provide free rail freight and other services. Milk For India now has been approved by the N.S.W. Department of Education as the official appeal in all N.S.W. public schools during 1967.

There have been press reports in Australia and elsewhere that claims have been made that the United States Government has pressured Australia into giving help to India. We believe that the voluntary Milk for India Campaign refutes such propaganda.

I am doing all in my power to have the processed milk shipped to India at the minimum cost. Representatives of Royal Interocean Shipping Company have indicated to me that the Company is prepared to continue to provide generous concession rates on our large shipments to the Government of India. R.W. Miller and Co. Pty. Ltd. very generously agreed to my request to carry 10 tons of powdered milk free of charge on the tanker R.W. Miller which sailed from Geelong, Victoria, yesterday (15th January). A gang of waterside workers voluntarily donated their time and labour to load the 10 tons at Geelong—which was a gracious gesture of support and concern.[360]

I hope and trust that you will continue to support our humanitarian gesture of friendship to the people of India. Should you require further information, please do not hesitate to ask me.[361]

A10

Resolution moved by the Prime Minister of India in the Indian Parliament regarding West Pakistan's attack on East Bengal, 31 March 1971

The tragedy which has overtaken our valiant neighbours in East Bengal so soon after their rejoicing over their electoral victory has united us in grief for their suffering, concern for the wanton destruction of their beautiful land and anxiety for their future. I wish to move a resolution which has been discussed with the leaders of the Opposition and, I am glad to say, approved unanimously.

Text of Resolution

This House expresses its deep anguish and grave concern at the recent developments in East Bengal. A massive attack by armed forces, despatched from West Pakistan has been unleashed against the entire people of East Bengal with a view to suppressing their urges and aspirations.

Instead of respecting the will of the people so unmistakably expressed through the election in Pakistan in December 1970, the Government of Pakistan has chosen to flout the mandate of the people.

The Government of Pakistan has not only refused to transfer power to legally elected representatives but has arbitrarily prevented the National Assembly from assuming its rightful and sovereign role. The people of East Bengal are being sought to be suppressed by the naked use of force, by bayonets, machine guns, tanks, artillery and aircraft.

APPENDIX A10

The Government and people of India have always desired and worked for peaceful, normal and fraternal relations with Pakistan. However, situated as India is and bound as the people of the subcontinent are by centuries old ties of history, culture and tradition, this House cannot remain indifferent to the macabre tragedy being enacted so close to our border. Throughout the length and breadth of our land, our people have condemned, in unmistakable terms, the atrocities now being perpetuated on an unprecedented scale upon an unarmed and innocent people.

This House expresses its profound sympathy for and solidarity with the people of East Bengal in their struggle for a democratic way of life.

Bearing in mind the permanent interests which India has in peace, and committed as we are to uphold and defend human rights, this House demands immediate cessation of the use of force and the massacre of defenceless people. This House calls upon all peoples and Governments of the world to take urgent and constructive steps to prevail upon the Government of Pakistan to put an end immediately to the systematic decimation of people which amounts to genocide.

This House records its profound conviction that the historic upsurge of the 75 million people of East Bengal will triumph. The House wishes to assure them that their struggle and sacrifices will receive the whole hearted sympathy and support of the people of India.[362]

A11

Report on 'Relief aid in Bangladesh—Nagori' enclosed in letter from Mr Allen, Deputy High Commissioner for Australia, Dacca to Moira Dynon, 19 February 1972

Relief Aid in Bangladesh – Nagori

Some 15 miles north west of Dacca, the village of Boira used to have a population of some 200 Hindus. After the pogrom initiated by the Pakistan Army on 25th March, many Hindus from Dacca and other centres fled to Boira, hoping that its isolation in the deep countryside would afford them some protection. Their hopes were belied. During April-May the Pakistan Army began fanning out from the cities into the villages. By that time Hindus had become one of the main targets.

During the third week of May, Boira was attacked and several hundred Hindus killed, not only the original inhabitants of the village, but also many refugees from elsewhere. Those who escaped the Army's bullets fled to Nagori, some six miles to the east, where a Roman Catholic mission, founded by Portuguese missionaries as far back as 1665, had a 17-acre property, including a boys high school, a girls high school, a dispensary, etc.

From then on Nagori became a haven of shelter for refugees fleeing from villages all around within a radius of 50 miles. From that day until the end of the year, Father Gaedeet and his team of American missionaries have been feeding, <u>every day</u>, refugees whose numbers varied, according to the location and degree of Pakistan Army pressure, between <u>5,500 and 14,000</u>. Supplies from Dacca being short and communications between Dacca and Nagori being difficult, the dimensions of the problem can be imagined. The schools and buildings and verandahs of the mission, indeed the entire Mission Compound, for months were crowded with destitute refugees, who needed not only food, but also clothes and other basic necessities.

Much the same story applied to a group of Hindu villages 80 miles south of Dacca, near Jhalakati, where a Protestant Mission is doing the same kind of work.

The $6,000 provided by the Melbourne Committee amounted to Rs. 31,000. Of this sum, in round figures, Rs. 17,000 were spent on food and clothing for Nagori, while Rs. 14,000 were spent on the Jhalakati area. Every dollar was spent in meeting real human needs.

Father Gaedeet writes: "I hope you will convey my thanks to all those people in Australia who made your gift possible. As for yourself you know I am grateful. God will bless you all since He is the One who said, 'When I was hungry you gave me to eat. When I was naked, you clothed me'".[363]

Appendix B

About the author John F Dynon—aspects of his life and family history by Michele Trowbridge and Jacinta Efthim

B1	John Dynon and Son	420
B2	Statue in St Francis Church in memory of Abigail	426
B3	James Dynon and his 1881 travel diary	430
B4	Alderman James Dynon	440
B5	John Francis Dynon and his siblings	445
B6	*Rerum Novarum*	453
B7	Carraig na bhFear	456
B8	The mystery of the marriage record	465

B1

John Dynon and Son

In 1856, John F Dynon's paternal grandparents, John and Abigail Dinan, left Ireland with their baby son James, bound for Australia. They travelled on the *Sir WF Williams*, which departed from Liverpool on 10 September 1856 and arrived in Hobart on 2 December 1856.

The *Hobarton Mercury* reported the arrival:

> The Clipper Ship, Sir W F Williams, 869 tons, arrived in port last evening, after an excellent run of 81 days: she is a new ship, and iron built: she spoke no vessels since leaving the Equator. She brings 335 emigrants under the care of Dr. Hardy formerly surgeon of the ill-fated Schomberg, two children under 7 years of age and 2 infants died during the passage, the following is the account of the emigrants: Married men 38, Married women, 49, Single men, 65, Single women, 74, Boys, from 7 to 14 years 26; Boys from 1 to 7 years, 23; Boys under 1 year, 3. Girls from 7 to 14 years, 25; Girls from 1 to 7 years, 25; Girls under 1 year, 11. They have arrived in good health, and the vessel presented a remarkable appearance of comfort and cleanliness, being admirably adapted for the purposes of a passenger traffic. We cannot refrain from expressing our obligation to Captain Rees for his courtesy in supplying us with the latest English News.
>
> The Sir W. F. Williams. — This magnificent ship, one of the Messrs. Baines's Black Ball liners, has excited the greatest admiration of nautical men; and even those whose eyes are unaccustomed to see ships of her size, as she lay in the river, have expressed their delight at her beautiful

appearance on the water.[364]

The 'Descriptive list of immigrants' included:

> John Dynan, 23[365], 'Dark complexion brown hair & whiskers tallish—rather slight figure'; Education: 'None'; whose 'trade, calling or qualification as stated by the immigrant' was 'Farm Labourer'.
>
> Abigail Dynan, 19, 'Reddish hair, fair complexion; Rather low in stature'; described herself as 'Farm Servant'.
>
> James Dynan, 11 months.

The family name in Ireland was Dinan but the immigrant list recorded the name as Dynan. Possibly when John and Abigail stated their name to the English officials at Liverpool, 'i' in an Irish voice may have sounded like 'y'. In any event, 'Dynan' did not last for long. According to family stories, when John and Abigail started their business, the signwriter spelt the name on the shop 'Dynon' and Abigail had said: 'Let it be. It will be more expense to change it.' From then on, the family name was Dynon.

John and Abigail settled in Melbourne. The family home was 405 William Street with views over the Flagstaff Gardens.

On their voyage to Australia, John and Abigail had brought with them chinaware to establish a business. Unfortunately, all of it broke whilst being unloaded. They arranged for another consignment to be shipped but this was badly packed and most was damaged in transit. John was then for giving up the idea of starting a china importing enterprise but Abigail was determined. At her insistence, a further consignment was ordered that arrived intact and the business started.[366] That was 1857, the year after they arrived in Melbourne.

That they had the means to purchase three shipments of crockery suggests that they did not arrive in Australia penniless. According to the shipping records, the cost of passage was £16 for each of John and Abigail and £4 for James—£36 in total. This was a substantial sum in 1856, particularly at a time when Ireland was still suffering from the effects of the potato famine. The 'person on whose application sent out' on the shipping record was Ellen Sheehan, who was most likely related to Abigail, whose maiden name was Sheehan. If Ellen Sheehan paid the £36 for the cost of passage, possibly Ellen also provided funds for John and Abigail to start the business.

Abigail may have stated her occupation on the shipping record as 'farm servant' but there is no doubt that she had the nous and, it seems, the knowledge to make a success of the crockery business. The 1841 Census of County Cork listed several Sheehans in Cork city who were in business as 'china & glass dealer' and 'glass china & earthenware dealer'. If any of these were related, then Abigail's family had knowledge of running such a business and undoubtedly would have offered advice. Family anecdotes confirm that Abigail was the brains behind the business. Moira Peters, our Dynon family history guru, said there was no question about this. Although Abigail had 12 children, the demands of a large family did not prevent her from taking an active part in the business.

Success did not take long. The young colony was growing quickly and there was a demand for household crockery. Operating in Lonsdale Street, Melbourne, the boast of the firm was that it could furnish any home, be it mansion or cottage, from ceiling to cellar 'at prices not to be equalled'. Melbourne newspapers reported regular deliveries of crates of imported earthenware and glassware to Hobsons Bay and, occasionally, Port Phillip Heads for John Dynon. The frequency and quantity of the imported goods increased steadily through the last four decades of the 1800s.

The business also operated very successfully in Sydney. This was run by Basil, the youngest son of John and Abigail. There was further expansion in the mid-1890s when the business opened in Perth. Basil's older brother, Dan, looked after this.

Newspaper articles at the time shed some light on the business:

John Dynon and Son

The proverbial bull in a china shop would have a rare time in the warehouse of Messrs John Dynon and Son. Many houses do business in similar lines, but Messrs Dynon, confining themselves solely to their original trade, stand in a deservedly high position as the glass and china merchants of Sydney.

One might as well try and catch the wind with a net as to describe their varied stock, but prominently there are fine examples of modern Worcester decorations, comparing favourably with the old and never-beaten designs. Examples, too, of Limoges, Sevres, Wedgwood, Crown Derby, Bohemian glass, &c, form a display of an excellence rarely seen. Especially suitable to the season for presents are tete-a-tete tea sets and others varying from such as would gladden the heart of a little maid from school to those of the rarest value. Then in dinner and dessert services the choice is equally large in all designs and values including plates on which "One could eat peas with the king or cherries with the beggar." The Hampden and other toilet sets are well known, but for Christmas gifts the most suitable probably of the varied stock are the art pots and umbrella stands.

The exhibit in Messrs. Dynon's window, in George-street, is alone well worth a visit, and the interior display is perhaps unrivalled in the colonies.[367]

John Dynon and Sons – A Flourishing Business

The Western Australian business of John Dynon and Sons has since its inauguration, seven years ago, kept apace with the development of the State, and is now one of the most important and largest in Western Australia. The headquarters of the firm are in Melbourne, where operations have been carried on for forty-five years, and at the present time Dynon and Sons rank amongst the largest importers of glass, china, and earthenware in Victoria.

The branch business in Sydney has developed into an important concern. The firm holds large contracts with the Tasmanian, N.S.W. and Victorian Governments, and these alone generate a considerable annual turnover. The handsome premises at 238 Murray-street, form a prominent feature of that busy thoroughfare. On entering the building the fine capacious showroom with its artistic and instructive display of ware at once attracts attention. Here may be seen almost every conceivable design in crockery ware, glassware, etc. Great care has evidently been taken in the selection of the stock, and the tastes and requirements of all sections of the community have been catered for. The old china ware is especially interesting, and an instructive time awaits any connoisseur who may visit the emporium. Innumerable designs in breakfast, dinner and tea-sets are to be seen. These goods have been selected with an eye to artistic effect, as well as utility, and the Royal art ware on show is of extreme beauty; its delicacy of design and construction make one marvel at the comparative smallness of the cost. Storekeepers and confectioners goods are to be found in profusion, and some very novel ideas have been introduced. The fancy ware is, of course, the main attraction of the showroom, and this is alone well worth seeing.

The stock is rich with all the latest designs and patterns from the leading American, English and continental manufacturers, and some of these are marked at prices which seem ridiculously small, when the extreme labor involved in their manufacture is taken into consideration. There has just been landed a beautiful shipment of flower epergnes, and these include many varieties hitherto unknown in Western Australia.

Over the showroom the whole floor is devoted to the toilet ware department. This is a very important part of the business and a very large turnover is done in connection with it. The different varieties of toilet ware are very numerous. The choice of articles is a very wide one. Here again the utmost care has been taken to cater for all classes. It is the boast of the firm that they can furnish any home, be it mansion or cottage, from ceiling to cellar.

At the rear of the main building and extending backwards about 200 feet are the bulk stores. Here one is immediately struck by the systematic packing and arrangement. The firm only employs those who are skilled in the handling of their goods, and as a result the breakages—usually so heavy in this class of business—are reduced to a minimum. The bulk stock is a very heavy and valuable one, and to enumerate the principal lines would occupy too great a space.

An excellent idea of the favourite beverage of the Western Australian public is to be found in the glass department, where the "long beer" glass occupies an overwhelming space in proportion to the other varieties. One cannot help admiring the systematic handling and packing of the goods. Not one foot of space seems to have been wasted and the stock held in the stores is enormous.

The operations in the packing department entail very careful supervision, and these are under the care of an experienced packer. Almost every day shipments of goods are arriving, and at the time of visiting the establishment there were no less than 60 crates of crockery awaiting unpacking. Mr. Dynon, the head of the firm, resides in England, where he conducts the purchase of all goods. Every article is imported direct by the firm, where operations are exclusively wholesale, and extends throughout the whole of the Commonwealth.[368]

B2

Statue in St Francis Church in memory of Abigail

Abigail and John Dynon had 12 children. **James**, the eldest, was born in Cork, Ireland, in 1855. Next was **Timothy**, who was born in Melbourne in 1858 but died the following year, aged one. Then **Annie** was born in about 1860. Annie married Michael Mornane and they had six children: Michael, Josephine, Frank, Rusty, May and Nancy. The next child was **Mary**, who was born around 1861. She did not marry and was a nun in the Loreto Order for a short time. Then came **Lena**, who married Patrick McGinnis. They had 12 children: Ita, Joseph, Nina, Patrick, Ina, Frank, Hilary, Rosa, Ignatius, Abigail, Agnes and Carmel. In 1866, **John Edward (Jack)** was born. He spent a few of his school years at Stonyhurst in England. He was unmarried and died in 1909, aged 43. **Abigail** was born in 1867. She married Patrick McMahon Glynn KC MHR and they had eight children: John, Joan, Elly, Dympna, Patrick, Alice, Mary and Gerard. Next was **Daniel**, who was born in 1869. He also spent a few years at Stonyhurst. He married Elizabeth Mitchel Robinson and had four children: John, Joe, Mary and Abbie. **Margaret Agnes** was born in 1870 but died when she was just nine months old. **Joseph** was born in 1874 and was married in Perth. **Francis** (Frank) was born in 1875 and educated at St. Ignatius' College, Riverview, in Sydney; while in Hobart on a business trip for John Dynon and Son, he died after a short illness, aged 23. **Aloysius Basil (Basil)** was born in 1878. He married Mary Ellen Hobbs and they had five children: Nell, Basil, John, Frank and Jeffrey. Another child, a son, was stillborn in 1879.

Abigail died on 24 October 1905, aged 70.

A noble and fervent Catholic in the person of Mrs. Abigail

Dynon, wife of Mr. John Dynon, a popular and respected merchant of Melbourne, was called to her eternal reward on the 24th ult. Mrs. Dynon and her husband arrived in Melbourne from Cork over fifty years ago, and resided ever since in that city, where they built up the well-known business of John Dynon and Sons, Lonsdale-street.

Mrs. Dynon always took the deepest interest in Church matters in Melbourne, and was particularly attached to St. Francis' Church, in that city, where she was a constant and most edifying worshipper. She was a most liberal benefactor of all Catholic charities, a lady of the most lovable and gentle qualities, and one whom to know was to esteem and revere. Her friendship was cherished by hundreds, and her words of comfort and consolation to those in distress or affliction have cheered and lightened many a heart. But she did not stop at words—her purse was always open to the needy, and the amount she spent in charity will never be made known. The number of poor people who called on her weekly for their pension was very large—she was never known to turn a deaf ear to the call of the poor, and now that she is gone, she will be sadly missed by them.

Mrs. Dynon had been in failing health for some time, and her death was not unexpected. During her illness she was attended by the Rev. Father Quilter, the priest in charge of St. Francis' Church, who was most assiduous in his attention, and she died fortified by the rites of the Church, the faith of which she loved and cherished as a priceless gift.[369]

In St Francis Church, Lonsdale Street, Melbourne, above the altar in the 'Ladye' Chapel, there is a life-size Carrara marble statue of the Blessed Virgin and Child. The plaque on the wall reads: 'This marble statue was erected by Mr John Dynon in memory of his late beloved wife Abigail Dynon R.I.P.' The statue was:

> the work of Sig. Palla, a leading Italian sculptor. The attitude of the Blessed Virgin, with her right hand extended, the divine expression of the features, the fine

lineaments of the modelling, combine to inspire devotion and tenderness in the heart of the devout client of Mary. With the left hand she supports the Divine Infant, whose tenderness, depicted in His divine face and extended little hand, invite all to come and ask favours through the intercession of His Immaculate Mother.[370]

The statue was unveiled on 8 December 1907, the Feast of the Immaculate Conception.

Large congregations attended St. Francis Church last Sunday, morning and evening. At 11 o'clock, the Very Rev. Dean Phelan, assisted by Very Rev. W. Quilter blessed and unveiled the beautiful Carrara marble statue, Our Lady Help of Christians, which has been placed over the altar in the Lady Chapel. It is the gift of Mr. John Dynon, and has elicited unstinted praise.

...Fr. Quilter...desired to thank Mr. John Dynon for his magnificent generosity in providing the marble statue of Our Lady of Help in memory of his dear wife, who, like her husband, had been most generous to the Church and to the poor of the parish. The gift was a worthy tribute to a noble, generous, and faithful wife, who had brought up her family in the fear and love of God. He (Fr. Quilter) hoped that when the people knelt before that beautiful statue they would offer a prayer for the repose of the soul of Mrs. Dynon.[371]

John Dynon died on 10 December 1912 and news of his death was reported widely:

We much regret to learn of the death of Mr. John Dynon, which occurred on last Tuesday, at his residence "Grenagh", William-street. The deceased was a well-known figure in the mercantile world, having been in business in Lonsdale-street for many years as the leading crockery importer of Melbourne. In conjunction with his sons he also opened establishments in Sydney and Perth.

Mr. Dynon had been a widower for the last seven years. Four daughters and three sons survive him. Amongst his children are Mr. James Dynon, who was an alderman of Melbourne City Council for nearly twenty years and resigned last November owing to ill health; Mrs. Glynn, wife of Mr. P. Mc M Glynn, M.P., and Mrs. Mornane, wife of Mr. M. Mornane, Solicitor.

The deceased's Melbourne business is being carried on by Mr. Jas. Dynon and his brother Mr. Daniel Dynon, while Mr. Basil Dynon, another son, is in charge of the Sydney business.

Mr. Dynon died at the advanced age of 87, after an illness of some months, borne with exemplary fortitude and patience.[372]

John Dynon's Victorian assets included five parcels of real estate in Wright's Lane, Melbourne. These five warehouses were purpose-built for John Dynon & Son. They were designed by William Pitt, the celebrated architect who designed the Princess Theatre. Wright's Lane was subsequently renamed Hardware Lane. Four of the warehouses remain (63-73 Hardware Lane) and have Heritage listing. At the top of one, 'Dynons Buildings AD 1889' is visible.

B3

James Dynon and his 1881 travel diary

James Dynon, the first child of John and Abigail, was 11 months old when he came to Australia.

In 1872, he travelled overseas with his mother.[373] At this time Abigail had seven children—James, who was 16 years old, Annie, Mary, Lena, Jack, Abigail and three-year-old Daniel. We can speculate that Abigail took James to the United Kingdom to meet his grandparents and to show him aspects of the business.

James journeyed to Europe again in 1881 when he was 25 years old. He recorded many experiences in his travel diary. A few entries are reproduced here:[374]

Particulars of my journey to England and the Continent leaving Melbourne February 2 1881

Left Melbourne on Wednesday the 2nd of February 1881 for Southampton calling at Adelaide, Albany, Galle, Aden, through Suez Canal, to Malta and Gibraltar en route.

Galle We arrived at Galle on Tuesday morning 6.30 am twelve days from Albany…The harbour at Galle is very poor and there is always a very heavy swell which makes it very inconvenient for small boats. We went ashore in a catamaran.

Cairo Bought a hat (fell off the bus style) of beautiful quality price 15/- a few engravings of interesting sights in Cairo, and then started for the Pyramids. We commenced to cross the Nile Bridge at 10 minutes to 10 (400 yards long) on the centre we had to stop till the Khedive who was coming from his Palace passed us. He was in an open carriage & Pair of horses & was dressed in very grand style, his embroidered shirt being covered with decorations, he saluted us at the moment of passing by gracefully lifting his hand first to his mouth & then the two forefingers to his forehead smiling at the same time, we lifted our hats.

The drive to the Pyramids is a beautiful one. The road is lined with Acacia trees & we passed several Grand Palaces. We arrived at the Pyramids at 11 o'clock and after walking around them (we each accompanied by three Arabs two walking in front holding candle in one hand & you with the other & the 3rd Arab walking behind to give you lift should you require it) we explored the Tomb of Cheops. The largest Pyramid is called Cheops, he was buried there. The Pyramid was built from the Centre viz a large room was built 24 feet wide 30 feet long and 40 feet high, this room was built with blocks of Red Granite some 15 feet long 5 feet wide 5 feet deep & after this was finished they commenced to build the Pyramid over it, leaving an intricate passage from the room to the Desert. The height of the Pyramid 470 feet. We entered & after a laborious walk of 10 minutes entered Cheops Tomb. The sarcophagus was in the Centre of the room but the mummy was not there it having previously been removed to the British Museum in London. After a stay of 10 minutes we came out & I felt very much relieved to find myself outside.

At half past eight we went to the Grand Opera to see Madame Favart. The Khedive & his suite & the ladies of the Harem were present. The Khedive was in an open Box, but the Ladies had a muslin veil in front of their Box. They could see everyone, but could not be seen.

Naples, Sunday 20th March This Hotel is beautifully situated on the embankment fronting the Bay, with Mount Vesuvius to the left, during the day there is a continual stream of smoke coming from the crater, & at dark the scene is very grand. The mouth of the crater presented a fiery appearance. It was half past five as we entered the Chiaia road on our way home. We were greatly impressed with the sight of carriages and Pairs driving to and fro, the scene was very grand and if you would like to see it, fancy posting yourself at the Post Office corner on Melbourne Cup day & seeing 10 times the number of carriages pass in excess of those you see on Cup Day, and all in the space of 20 minutes, we must have passed over 2000 Grand Carriages & Pairs in this drive. The sight was a grand one & I shall never forget it.

Tuesday. Today at eight o'clock we left Naples (a party of 7) for the Crater of Mount Vesuvius. We had a carriage of three horses, one in the shafts & one each side, the centre horse had a spur projecting from each side of the collar, to prevent the other horses from leaning over towards him thus making each do his own pulling. The horses were driven with a bit common to Naples but never to Melbourne viz no bar in the mouth, but two pieces of steel against the nostrils and attached to a curb chain under the jaw, when the horse bolts the curb tightens and forces the steel pins into the nostril. The streets were very slippery, we passed several fallen horses the road being paved with lava from Mount Vesuvius (Lava just like our Bluestone but a harder material). When the Mount is in a state of eruption or emitting streams of lava (as at present) the lava descends into the valleys beneath & when cooled, it is quarried for roads & building purposes.

We arrived at the Café – Restaurant at half past one (3000 feet above the sea). After lunch ascended Vesuvius by the wire railway, the ascent was at an angle of 63 degrees. We arrived at our destination in 8 minutes and were met by guides (3 to each of us) these took us to within 30 yards of the mouth of the crater and as the Sulphurous smell was very strong, the rocks under our feet very warm & the whole place enveloped in smoke I thought we were far enough & gave orders to retreat. We did so & arrived at the café in 15 minutes time. The drive up was very cold & when we were within 500 yards distance from the Café we were in the Clouds, after leaving the Café & during our journey up by rail, we could distinguish objects at a distance of 20 yards, no further, above before behind and all round us were dark clouds, & atmosphere very cold. When we got back to the Café our overcoats were saturated with the damp. We left the Café at a quarter to three in the afternoon & arrived at our hotel at five thus coming down almost twice as fast as we went up.

We passed several Macaroni manufacturers & if the lovers of this delicacy had seen the makers (as we did) engaged in the manufacture, I don't think they would think the dish such a delicacy.

There was an earthquake at Ischia a few miles from here last week, over 100 people killed, another slight shock was felt a few days ago. Earthquakes are thought nothing of in this part of the world. The traveller is greatly troubled here by beggars, pimps, walking stick vendors, flower girls, etc.

Ireland. Tuesday – May 9th 1881. We drove to the Phoenix Park, the grandest Park in the world, we were fortunate, as on our arrival we had a grand sight of the Review of the Troops about 5000 Infantry & 1000 Cavalry being engaged in the manoeuvres, we enjoyed this for upwards of an hour & unconsciously having advanced beyond the boundaries in our eagerness to see what was going on, we were surprised at the Cavalry who were going away from us, suddenly turning & galloping down towards us, we ran for our lives & did not feel safe till we reached the car.

This is the finest month to see Ireland. The trees just beginning to blossom & the farmers ploughing, & everything presents a smiling appearance.

Caught the train leaving Bray at half past five & arrived at Kingsbridge at 10 past six. Drove to our Hotel & had dinner then went to the Gaiety Theatre, Carl Rosa's company playing "Carmen". This being a first night the place was crowded, all the notables of Dublin being present, we had great difficulty to get a seat but the Queen's image was not refused. We arrived at 7.30. Theatre was full & as the orchestra was not playing, the crowd (Pit) was singing choruses, when presently someone in the Gallery sang (amidst terrible silence) "You'll remember me" & was rapturously encored. I never heard Annie Beaumont singing it as well as my gallery friend, being encored, he sang the last verse again & was again applauded. Then another sang "Over the Garden Wall" with a chorus all Pit & Gallery joining in, & being encored sang Bland Holt's "Fie for shame Mary Jane I'll tell your Ma", this was again demanded, but the Orchestra tuning up was the signal for silence, after the Carmen Overture the curtain was raised. The play was not as well mounted as in Melbourne & you could not compare the Soloists (with the exception of the Lady who played Michaela) to Rose Hersees crowd. After the first two acts I left & returned home & after answering a few letters went to roost.

Friday May 12th Returning to my Hotel I hired a Jarvey & drove to Garryowen, & saw the ruins of St. John Castle & old walls of Limerick then on by the Scarriff & Broadford road to "Clonlara", called on James Mornane at Mount Catherine & had a chat for about an hour, then on through Clonlara, over the Canal Bridge along Donass Road, to St. Brigids Well famed for wonderful cures, & on to the Shannon Rapids a lovely view, here I was initiated into the knack of casting the flies but could not catch a salmon. J Mornane gave me a sod of Turf for his brother in Melbourne & I also got one for ourselves at Castle Connaught & hope to be able to take them to Melbourne.

Left Limerick at half past ten next morning, prior to leaving I witnessed a very sorrowful scene viz Emigrants leaving for America. All their friends & relatives came to see them off. Mothers to see the last perhaps of their sons & daughters. I was very glad when we left the station. At every station on the line friends assembled to bid good bye & we were always pleased to hear the loving words addressed to their friends on parting: "God speed you" "Good Bye Pat" "Don't get sunburnt" etc.

Killarney May 18th Gap of Dunloe We left the Hotel at ten o'clock & drove through Lord Kenmare's property till we got on the Caluciveen & Valentia Road. We were shown the House Where Daniel O Connells nephew Sir Maurice O'Connell now lives & met His (Sir Maurices) brother at the entrance to the grounds. On our way we were followed by troops of women offering us Goats milk, Potheen or Mountain Dew as others called it.

Passing the house of Kate Kearney her granddaughter came out & gave us a drink for which we paid 6d each, further up the mountain we met an "echo man" (a man who makes his living in summer time by firing off cannon to enable the visitors to hear the echo) who fired his cannon & charged 6d, several others of the same class wanted to repeat the dose, but I couldn't see it.

We passed the "McGillicuddy reeks" & the "Eagles Nest". On the top of the Gap the view is very fine, a mist coming on, I complained to one of my lady friends, who were trying to induce me to take a drink of milk that the weather was very treacherous "Spose it only perspiration from the mountains" & another said—"Its O'Donohues blessing". These girls followed our party for five miles, they were barefooted & very scantily dressed, but were strong and healthy & are very good girls, one of our party an American offered 1/- for a kiss but that luxury the young lady said could not be bought for money.

Wednesday June 1ˢᵗ Derby Day Drag & four horses. A beautiful day, we left the White Horse Cellars, Piccadilly at 9.30 & after a nice drive arrived at Epsom at 12. The journey out was enjoyable. The In Cup is nothing as regards a crowd, but then from a racing point of view the In C is superior to the Derby. We were all Australians on our Drag & I Service of Melbourne was on a drag with another crowd of Australians. I think that there were over 500 Drags at the Epsom Derby. It seems an awful lot but people here don't value money like the majority of the Australians. We left Epsom at 5.30 & arrived in London after a glorious day at 9, had a Langham Dinner & finished up at the Pavilion.

Thursday Owing to the kindness of Mr. Craig the member for North Staffordshire I go today for the House of Commons. I went & had the pleasure of hearing Gladstone, The Marquis of Hartingdon, Sir Stafford Northcote & other notable persons in the Land Bill Debate.

Saturday I left London by the 10 a.m. train from Victoria Station for Paris via Dover and Calais, crossed the Channel in the Steamer Petrel passing the celebrated Double Boat (built to prevent passengers from getting sea sick) "Calais Douanes" and landed in Calais after a smooth passage. Left Calais at 2.30 and arrived at Paris at 8 o'clock & drove to the "Hotel De La Tamese" in the Rue D'Algei opposite the Tuilleries Garden. After Dinner strolled along The Boulevard D'Italian and Madeline, and The Place De L'Opera as far as the Grand Opera House.

The streets are wide & well lighted. The Place De L'Opera is lighted with The Electric Light & presents a very grand appearance. The shops are all 4 stories high & are of a uniform appearance. The Kiosks on the Footpaths for selling Newspapers would take well in Melbourne, besides they are used for advertising purposes. My bedroom is very fine. Furniture of Black & Gold with Maroon velvet seating, 3 large Mirrors, Black marble Wash Stand & every convenience in Tip Top style.

Sunday Went to the Madeline Chapel and then as the Grand Prix was going to be run the same afternoon I drove to the Bois De Boulogne Racecourse. The drive was very pleasant, starting from The Hotel we passed The Tuilleries, then through the Place De La Concorde, along Les Champs Des Elysees to the Course. From the Hotel to the Course is about 5 miles & all along the road are lovely plantations of choice trees and playing Fountains. At the Place De La Concorde there are two very large fountains and in front of The Mabille there are 6 Fountains.

The Bois De Boulogne course presented a very fine appearance. The 5 Grand Stands (capable of holding twice as many as our Melbourne stand) was crowded with the Beauty of Paris, dressed in style & oh what dresses. I thought the Melbourne Ladies dressed well but they don't come near the Parisian Ladies in Dress. One Lady was dressed in Pale Blue Silk (low neck) & instead of a sleeve wore a very elaborate silk threaded Glove. The Body was covered with Diamond Sprays & she had a Diamond Spray in her Gainsborough Hat. The Gainsborough and The Mother Hubbard are all the Fashion here. Marshall McMahon, The Rothchilds & all the nobility & men of note in Paris were present. I backed Foxhall for The Grand Prix for a few sous and won, thus having my days pleasure free of expense.

Monday We visited an agent for houses in the north of France his glass was very high, but I bought a few China Candlesticks Fancy shapes also some Butterfly Handle Cups & Saucers. He showed me a new invention viz a Portable Gas Forge, a very useful article. The Gas is made by the air passing through a valve of mineral oil attached to The Flange, & the latter is worked like a sewing machine by the feet. As it was close on five o'clock I drove home & after a good drive went to the Grand Opera House, to hear Gounod's latest production "Le Tribunal De Zamora". The House was crowded (it being the last night of this piece) & all the Boxes presented a grand appearance. The main or principal row of Boxes hold about 4 persons comfortably with the exception of 4 Corner Boxes, the Ladies sit forward & the gents behind, almost every Lady in this row wore diamonds. In Mrs. Mackey's Box there were 3 Ladies covered with diamonds. One had her hair knotted & the knots held with diamond Brooches, diamond earrings, lovely necklace & Brooch, Bracelets, Rings, & a large cluster of Diamonds, which showed to perfection on her black silk dress. Another wore all pearls about as large as Pigeons Eggs. I was astonished & never seen such a show of jewellery in my life as in this 'Diamond House'. All the Parquette seats (where I was) are covered with red velvet. After the second act I strolled out & had a cigar then came in to see the Ballet in the 3rd Act, about 150 performers assisted & it was very fine almost as good as San Carlo.

Thursday Drove by the 'Magasin Du Louvre' the most complete shop in France, and a place where everything merchantable is sold. The Building covers 3 acres & this morning there were over 100 carriages waiting outside the building whilst their occupants were shopping.

Called on Carlier, maker of Glass Shades, Clichy, La Garerue, Paris, drove through the St. Martin & St. Denis Arches erected by Louis XIV & had lunch at the Cafe Maise Boulevard St. Denis. After lunch called on the Baccart People in Rue Paradis Roissoniere & was shown through their grand showrooms. I never looked at a more magnificent collection of Glass. The Showroom is as large as our Back Store & is full of samples of Cut & Engraved Glass, Vases etc. They have Vases of £250 & £200 & down to 6d each. The manager showed me Two Cut Glass Tables standing about 40 inches high, price £100 each. Called on Landier & Handaille glass makers (in the same quarter) & bought a few lines. Then drove to the Rue St. Roch. The chapel of St. Roch celebrated for the splendid choir, is in this Street-corner Rue St. Honore & St. Rochs.

Returned home had dinner & drove to the Hippodrome, a very large building (150 yards long 100 wide oval shape illuminated with electric lights. The performance commenced with the Pony Race, 14 starters, one of the Ponies fell & the Rider was carried off the course insensible. The next items were a Chariot Race, a Ladies Race, Gymnastic Performances (very clever) Trick Horses seven in number (very clever) an interval & then a grand spectacular drama of Les Radjah very good, the best of the kind I have seen. There were over 100 horses & 250 ladies & gentlemen engaged in this mimic battle & rescue. The Ladies rode like the Gents & rode very well. There were also three cannons in the siege & these were discharged about a dozen times; you fancied yourself in a battle.

Leaving the Hippodrome a doctor who was of our party asked a French Gentleman who was with his wife where the Mabille was, the man turned pale & said he did not know, & next asked a Gendarme & he directed us. The Mabille, (alias Le Jardin Mabille and The Gay Mabile) was beautifully illuminated with coloured lamps & was crowded with people. There is one Band Stand in the centre & all around is boarded. The Garden is situated about 10 minutes walk from The Tuilieres in Les Champs Elysees, & being near Paris is always crowded.

Mirrors are placed in nooks & are surrounded with trees giving them a very pleasing appearance—cafes in any number. The first dance was a Polka, very nice music, then a waltz nice music & beautiful dancing. Next the celebrated Can Can. The Can Can is a set of Qiadrilles—usually danced by four parties—two ladies & two gents, the first and second figures are like the English quadrille, but the third fourth & fifth are something extraordinary. The ladies kicking off the onlookers top hats with the greatest of ease. I would not advise any of my friends to go there as the place once seen would not be revisited & is not even worth the first visit.

B4

Alderman James Dynon

On 10 January 1883, James married Alice O'Callaghan at St Patrick's Cathedral, Ballarat. The celebrant was the Right Reverend Monsignor Moore, the uncle of the bride. James and Alice resided at 'Grenagh', 26 Queens Road, Melbourne on the corner of Leopold Street, overlooking Albert Park.

James Dynon was first elected to the Melbourne City Council in May 1894. It was reported in 1897:

> The retiring councillor for Bourke Ward on this occasion is Mr. James Dynon, J.P., one of the most genial-hearted and popular men in the council. A proof of this is the fact that he has never yet been called on to contest his right to the seat, and this election has proved no exception, the day of nomination passing by without any other candidate's name being lodged. This makes his third term of office, and speaks well for his untiring energy and courtesy in his public duties.[375]

A marble plaque at the entrance of the Melbourne Town Hall names Alderman James Dynon J.P as one of the members of the Melbourne City Council at the time when the town hall was built, 1908–1910.

James frequently travelled abroad for business and, on one occasion in 1910, following a visit to China, his comments were reported in the *Brisbane Telegraph*:

> **Unrest in China. Possibility of Eruption. Australian Visitor's Impressions.**
>
> There is in China at the present time, says Ald. J. Dynon, of the Melbourne City Council, who is returning from a

visit to the orient by the J.M.S. Kumano Maru, a great deal of unrest, which may break out into open hostilities at any time. Indeed, the only factor wanting to bring about a recurrence of the Boxer rising of 1900, states Mr. Dynon, and the statement is corroborated by other passengers on the steamer, is some bold and capable leader to organise the discontented factions, amongst whom there is no cohesion. Side by side with this dangerous undercurrent, Mr. Dynon adds, there are marked indications that the ancient Empire is on the verge of a great forward movement, such as that upon which Japan embarked some 40 years ago.

China, Mr. Dynon is of opinion, never will make a fighting country, the yellow peril, as applied to the inoffensive celestial, is only a bogey, so far as invasion of neighbouring countries is concerned. But the Chinaman is a born trader, and when the occasion arises, he can fight more effectively with a boycott than many a nation can with force of arms.[376]

Alice died in 1905 and on 22 April 1908 James married Margaret Carruthers at St Mary's Star of the Sea Church, West Melbourne. Margaret's father was Hugh Carruthers, a farmer, and her mother was Mary Clancy. They came from Donald in rural Victoria. They were among the original selectors in the district.

RP Falla published an account of how the original selectors in the Shire of Donald became landowners:

> The Grant Land Act of 1869—so named after the Minister, James McPherson Grant—imposed strict conditions in an attempt to ensure that only bona-fide selectors were recommended. Each applicant, after selecting not more than 320 acres, was required to appear before a Local Land Board for assessment. When a "License to Occupy" was approved, the selector was required to live on the allotment, to fence it, and within the first three years to cultivate at least one acre in ten. He was required to pay an annual rental of two shillings per acre, which, after three years entitled him to a lease, and at the end of a ten year period,

or full payment of £1 an acre, to the issue of a Crown Grant.

Records show that many families toiled under harsh and primitive conditions in an effort to pay their rents so that they could some day own their allotments. Many failed to reach their objective, as inexperience, seasonal conditions and other hardships, which included the rabbit menace, proved to be too great. Records also show that other selectors overcame the difficulties, and became the pioneer families of the Donald district.

...Hugh Carruthers pegged allotment 110 (320 acres) on June 25, 1874 and received a licence to occupy on November 1, 1874. He received the Crown Grant (title) in 1900. ... Mary Clancy was recommended for allotment 98 (103 acres) on December 16, 1874, and received her licence to occupy on February 1, 1875. The Crown Grant was issued in her name in 1904.[377]

Mary Carruthers (nee Clancy) died at the age of 29, when Margaret was just two years old. It was reported in the *Donald Express*:

We regret to announce the death of Mrs. Carruthers, daughter of Mr. Clancy, a well-known resident of Jeffcott. The deceased had only a brief illness, which terminated fatally on Monday last. The funeral took place yesterday and was one of the largest that has taken place in the district for a considerable time.[378]

On 28 March 1909, Margaret and James had their first child, a daughter, Abigail. Fourteen months later, on 30 May 1910, their son, James, was born. In 1911, they had another son, Cyril, who survived for just three days.

During 1912, James and Margaret travelled to the United Kingdom and Europe. Postcards to three-year-old Abbie and two-year-old Jimmy reveal another side of James, who was in his early fifties when he became a father for the first time:

APPENDIX B4

My Dear little Abb. I hope you & Jimmy are well & good & give no trouble. My thoughts are always with you. Your father. (Naples 17 January 1912)

Dear little Abbie. How are you. We have been looking for a little gift for your birthday & hope to get it sent on next mail. Look after Jimmy & be a good little girl. Your fond father (Venice 4 February 1912)

My Dear Little Abbe. Mother joins in sending you our love. I hope you look after Jimmy & are a good little girl. I will send you a little dress and one for Jimmy, all Red. How will you like that. With fondest love to you & dear little Jimmy from father xxxxxxxxxxxx (Paris 3 March 1912)

My Dear Little Abb. I hope you will like this card. Keep all Mother & daddy sends you & see Jimmy keeps his also. love from daddy & mummy. Teach Jimmy to say his prayers. (Paris 5 March 1912)

My Dear Little Abbe. Mummy & daddy got your letters & kisses also Dear Jimmy. I bought this card & hope you will like it. We hope you are looking after Jimmy and are a good little girl. Daddy xxxxxxxxxxxxxxxxxxxxxx (Paris 14 March 1912)

My Dear Little Daughter. I miss you & your little brother very much. I hope you are taking care of him & that you are a good little girl. Daddy loves you Abbie xxxxxxx (London 25 March 1912)

My Dear Jimmy. I hope this will find you & dear Abbie in good health & taking care of each other—be good & I will bring you & Abbie some toys Daddy & Mummy (Edinburgh 27 April 1912)

My Dear little Abbie. Your proud father loves & hopes you are well. Will send you some nice toys. I think of you morning noon & night. (Ceylon)

In November 1912, James resigned from the Melbourne City Council due to ill health.[379] On 22 October 1913, James and Margaret welcomed their youngest son, John Francis—a brother for Abbie and Jimmy. The following year, on 1 November 1914, James Dynon died from pneumonia, aged 59.

The business of John Dynon and Son did not survive for long. By 1916, only Dan was involved in the firm. On 5 September 1926, it was reported that the Perth staff of John Dynon and Co. 'were absorbed by Boans Ltd. The latter firm has bought out the entire stock and fittings of Dynon's, who have been in the glass and china business in Perth for 30 years'.[380]

B5

John Francis Dynon and his siblings

John was about 10 years old when he commenced school at Studley Hall[381]. James was then at Xavier College Kew and Abbie was at Sacré Coeur, Glen Iris. Abbie loved her days at Sacré Coeur. She was Head of the School in 1927 and also in 1928 when she was awarded the First Medallion—a prestigious award that was not awarded every year. Abbie donated various gifts to the Sacré Coeur chapel, including a stained-glass window depicting Jesus blessing the children.

James was Captain of Xavier in 1928. Father Paul Keenan, SJ recalled that James was 'a notable influence in the School. In sport he was a sturdy defender on one of Father O'Keefe's 1st XVIII and proved a talented cricketer'.

In 1929, the family travelled overseas. Margaret Dynon was well prepared, armed with a letter of introduction from the Australian Prime Minister, Stanley Bruce.[382]

John, who was 15 years old at the time, kept an account of this trip in his travel diary. A few excerpts are reproduced:

> **Rome** We have at last reached Rome, and in it we hope to see many treasures of the ancient world. Tonight Saint Peters is a glorious sight. At the entrance to the big square stand two fountains, spraying their waters up towards the red glow of the evening sky. Darkness falls and this magnificent basilica fades from sight to appear again just as glorious, the next morning, with the early sunrise. The Forum was the meeting place of the tribes around Rome. This is the place where Generals triumphed, Cicero spoke, Caesar ruled and Horace dictated. It was the heart of a mighty empire, until its fall, when hordes of invaders

buried its magnificence in ruins. The Vatican Library was founded in 1477 by Nicholas V, and there are many famous and historic manuscripts contained in its cases. Autographic letters by Anne Boleyn, Luther, Thomas Aquinas, Raphael, Tasso, Petrarch and Michelangelo are kept here. There is also Dante's Divine Comedy, dedicated to Boccaccio. An Augustan Virgil of the 2nd or 3rd century, and a Vatican Virgil of the 4th century are kept, together with ancient Gospels and Papal coins. The Holy Stair, in a small building, stands in front of the north east corner of the Lateran Palace. It is said that the twenty-eight marble steps, now covered over by wood, were brought by St. Helena, from Pontius Pilate's house in Jerusalem. One goes up these stairs on their knees, and there are small glass rounds, under which are the traces of the blood of Jesus.

Frascati After driving through Genzano, we drove around part of Lake Nemi. This is the lake that Mussolini is drying up to find the long lost galleys. But we now have the results of the enterprise, to hand.

Rome It was some time before twelve o'clock, on Thursday the 21st March, that we entered the rooms in which we were to have an audience with the Pope. We were taken through several rooms, until we came to the second room. At twelve thirty, there was a stir in the room, on our right, and the Pope had begun. Soon, he came into our room and all went down on their knees. As he passed by the kneeling figures, they each kissed his ring. And then, after this was done, he stood back and gave his blessing. Very briskly, he was out into the next room, and we all stood up. The day before I left Rome, I was summoned to the office of Mussolini to collect an autographed photograph of himself, which I had written and asked him for. I was truly delighted, as I had not expected him to give me one. Hoorah!

London The day after we arrived, Jim and myself went to Australia House, and got there just in time to see the Prince of Wales. On the 27th April, we attempted to get into Wembley, to see the soccer final between Portsmouth and the Bolton Wanderers, but we found that all the tickets had been sold some months before. However, we went along to Stanford Bridge and saw Chelsea defeat Reading by 3 goals to 2. On Sunday, we walked into Hyde Park and listened to the orators for a few hours. One of the men speaking for the Catholic Guild was a convert and was extremely interesting. On May 4th, Jim and myself went to Wembley and saw the Rugby final between Wigam and Dewsbury. The first named won easily. On the 30th May, Jim and myself went to Brooklands and the racing was very good. Some of the drivers included Kaye Don who won one of his races by a brilliant finish and a man named Cobb, who was also successful. While in London, Jim and myself saw some of the cricket played at Lords. I went to the first morning of the England v South Africa test and saw Sutcliffe and Hendren put up a good partnership with Morkel bowling for the South Africans. I spent many interesting afternoons at Wimbledon and it was only on the first two days that I was able to get a seat.

Ireland In the evening, we walked down the main street of Dublin across the 'Liffey river'. We saw the monument erected to Daniel O'Connell who brought about Emancipation by uniting the Irish. There is also the tall Nelson monument, the Parnell monument and several other statues of different statesmen of Ireland. We visited the Pro Cathedral, which is too small to be made a Cathedral. The Christ Church Cathedral, which could seat 3,000 people never has more than 300 for the Protestant services. The Catholics hope that they may soon be able to obtain their own cathedral back again. In the afternoon, at 3 p.m., the Government were holding a special meeting to pass a few bills. Cosgrave and de Valera were there.

Cork In the evening, we went to see Al Jolson in "The Singing Fool". Talkies have just been introduced into Cork. I saw, in the morning, the St Finbar cathedral. There was a monastery here in the 7th century, founded by that Saint, built on the site of a pagan temple, Blarney Castle. In the 15th century, Cormac MacCarthy built the castle. The attraction of this castle is the Blarney stone, for if you kiss it, you are endowed with the gift of eloquence. To kiss the stone, you lie on your back with two men holding your feet down. You then lean back and downwards in order to kiss the stone. There are two iron bars fastened to the wall, and you cling to these. There is rather a long drop if the men let go of your feet.[383] We now drove on to Glengarriff. From here to Killarney is a lovely drive. Before coming to Glengarriff, we passed through Macroom and past the Inchigeelagh Lake. The scenery in Southern Ireland is beautiful. It often makes the English scenery appear artificial.

From the Arc de Triomphe From the top of the arch, we obtained a magnificent view of Paris. First of all, you are attracted by the twelve avenues that all meet at the foot of the Arch. At the head of each of these, there are built twelve similar houses. Now we look along one of the best of the avenues—Avenue de le Grande Armee, so called because Napoleon led his large army out of Paris by this road, when going to invade Russia. It is six miles long and you can look right along it, until it seems to run off the hill. To the left now, is the Avenue de Michael Foch, recently having been known as L'avenue du Bois de Boulogne. Just behind this avenue, you could not miss seeing Le Bois de Boulogne, the largest of the parks in Paris, having an area of 2250 acres. Behind the wood rises a small mountain on which the Germans had a fortress in 1871. Now we turn further to the left passing L'Avenue Victor Hugo, and look along L'Avenue Kleber. On the left we saw La Trocadero and the Eiffel Tower rising high above the rest of the city. Now as we keep moving around to the left we see the Hotel Des Invalides, with the Pantheon, and Jardin du Luxembourg further behind. Looking now along the

Avenue Des Champs Elysees, we see many buildings. Le Palais du Louvre in the foreground, with Notre Dame and the river Seine on the right. Further to the left is the Madeleine and L'Opera. Looking over L'Avenue Hoche, we see the Clock tower of the church of the Sacre Coeur rising 360 ft above the famous hill of Montmartre, which is itself 330 ft above the Seine. I may have made many important omissions in describing the view from the Arc de Triomphe, but as I am just beginning to learn something of Paris, I cannot describe the view very fully, as yet.

In June 1929, Abbie was presented at Buckingham Palace. She was one of about 300 Australians presented at Court and this was reported in several Australian newspapers. After the trip, Abbie remained in Italy to attend a finishing school. From the mid-1930s, Abbie decided to make England her home. She did not marry but was romantically involved for a time with an officer from the French Foreign Legion who was a member of the French nobility. She settled in Dover and lived there until her death on 6 May 2001, aged 92.

During their world trip, John and James attended Mass every day. Even when they were on a ship, they would go ashore to find a Mass. James was 19 years old and he knew then that he wanted to be a priest. On his return to Australia, James entered the Jesuit Novitiate in Sydney. He studied arts as an external student from the University of Melbourne and philosophy at Loyola College, Watsonia. James was ordained as a Jesuit priest on 8 January 1944 at St Mary's Basilica in Sydney. To John, he was 'Jim' but Moira said that, as he was a priest, it was more respectful to call him 'Father'. So to his nephews and nieces and to Moira, he was 'Father James'.

Following his ordination, Father James spent some years teaching at Xavier College. In 1952 he was appointed socius to the Jesuit Provincial in Hawthorn, Austin Kelly. 'This was a wise choice for he was judicious, discreet, and totally reliable and committed. He remained eleven years in this office.'[384] During the 1960s, he worked as director of the Australian Jesuit Mission in India and later as Parish Priest at St Mary's, North Sydney. In the early 1970s, his health declined and he moved to Perth where it was warmer. There he spent many happy years as college chaplain at St Thomas More College at the University of Western Australia.

After the family's world trip, John returned to school at the beginning of 1930. He was a gifted all-rounder:

> **Dynon is Versatile** That graceful, well-modelled athlete John Dynon, fresher of Newman, has a remarkable record of versatility.
>
> At Xavier College he was captain of the cricketers, the footballers, the athletes, and the school. For three years he played centre half-back; and as a batsman he many times reached the seventies. Three times he has recorded even time for the 100 yards—when he defeated B. Maher in a trial, in inter-club sports at Olympic Park, and at the freshers' sports some time ago. Ten seconds equals the University record, but his time was not allowed because of a slight assisting breeze.
>
> In 1931 he distinguished himself at the public school sports by winning the 100 yards and long jump, he was second in the 220 and third in the hurdles. In the same season he was third in the Victorian long jump championship. Dynon is always fit, for if he is not playing cricket or football he is engaged in athletics. Last season he played cricket and football with Old Xavierians.
>
> One who has played in his company told me that Dynon has the gift of leadership and just cannot help being popular.[385]

In 1932, his final year at Xavier, John kept a diary with photos, letters and telegrams glued to many of the pages. Here he kept the autographed photo of Mussolini, under which he had written: 'The wonder leader of the age who saved Italy from revolution and disaster.'[386]

APPENDIX B5

On the first page of John's diary, he had two photos; both were of his brother. Most of the letters and telegrams glued to the diary were messages of congratulations on his appointment as School Captain or following a victory or great effort in football, cricket or athletics. Even more welcome may have been the words of encouragement from his brother after a loss:

> My dear John, Have you ever said to yourself as the final bell rang out its melancholy note, what a "funny" game this is? One moment on the crest of the wave and the next bowled off our feet. My eye! But it's grand to see the team getting up again and having another go. And if you get nothing from the footy season except that right spirit, you've got a treasure. Hold on to it and pray for your philosophising brother. Jim

...or before an important event:

> My dear Johnny, This is to wish you every blessing in your efforts on Friday. Don't be discouraged if a little disappointment comes along but go simply ahead for your school remembering that the cross comes first then the crown. Above all, trust in our Lord and you will be able to get over a lot of your nervousness by having everything in His Loving Hands. He will give you what is best and be grateful, John, in failure or success. A little prayer that I like very much might appeal to you too. "Dear Lord, beware of me, take care of me, Lest I may, this very day, betray Thee". Pray for me John, and I will be praying for you on Friday that you may be true to our Lord and your school, love from Jim.

Over the years, Father James was a regular visitor to 7 Haverbrack Avenue. He and John were close. He was very supportive of Moira's works and he took great interest in the lives of his nephews and nieces. He was particularly keen on cricket and he enjoyed the family cricket matches on the front lawn. On one memorable occasion, his nephew James had hit the cricket ball through the lounge-room window. There was an almighty crash and glass went everywhere. Fortunately, it missed the Venetian vase, which was still standing on the ledge with shattered glass all around it. As Moira arrived on the scene, Father James was quick to tell her that it wasn't James' fault. It had been a bad delivery and James had played a splendid cricket shot!

Father James officiated at John and Moira's wedding in 1950 and he was also the celebrant at the marriages of his nieces—Michele to Tony Trowbridge and Jacinta to John Efthim—and of his nephew James to Vicki Anderson.

In October 1976, Father James travelled from Perth after receiving John's phone call and he was there to comfort Moira with spiritual counsel and blessings in the hours before she died. He concelebrated her Requiem Mass with nine other priests at St Joseph's, Malvern.

John's fatal heart attack on 8 July 1984 was sudden and unexpected. Father James flew from Perth to be with the family. The Requiem Mass was at St Ignatius', Richmond, which was John's parish after he moved to 7 The Righi in 1979. The priests entered in procession and crowded around the altar. There was no more room but still they kept coming. Thirty priests including Father James concelebrated that Mass.

Father James died on 24 September 1991 in Perth, aged 81. 'Dynon was a man of faith, a loyal Jesuit, a faithful friend, a wise counsellor and much loved by all who knew him'.[387]

B6

Rerum Novarum

In 1891, Pope Leo XIII wrote an encyclical letter, *Rerum Novarum*, 'On the condition of the working classes'. This made a deep impression on John F Dynon when he read it. It was also dear to the heart of Father James:

"The Workers' Charter"

60th Anniversary of Encyclical "Rerum Novarum" By Rev. James Dynon, S.J.

SIXTY years ago, Pope Leo XIII looked out on the world and saw human society in the throes of revolutionary change, disorganized and in confusion. He saw wealth increasing rapidly, but unjustly distributed; a few men owned land and capital, but the masses were a propertyless proletariat. He saw false economic principles and political philosophies swaying the thinkers of the day, telling governments not to intervene—*laissez-faire*—thus preventing the workers from gaining a fair share from their toil and even preventing them from uniting to better their conditions. In brief, he saw rich men, through greed and false doctrine, perverting the divine purpose of national economies—the satisfying of the needs of all—and laying "upon the masses of the poor a yoke little better than slavery itself."

Doctrinal Thunderbolt

On May 15, 1891, Pope Leo, as the Supreme Pontiff and Vicar of Christ, spoke to the world in the best-known and most widely influential social encyclical ever issued from the Vatican, entitled *Rerum Novarum*, generally called in English *The Condition of the Working Classes*. At the time, the document came as a thunderbolt and was regarded by many as little short of revolutionary, even though today most of its principles have become familiar and commonplace to us.

Rerum Novarum presented a summary of modern Catholic social thought that had developed since the birth of the new industrialism, together with the wisdom of past centuries of the Faith and the authoritative teaching of the Scriptures. In addition, it had a vigour of expression, a concentration of thought, a sweep of vision, which implied more than mere genius. Finally, it uttered solemn warnings, which have since been tragically fulfilled, because its words have not been fully heeded. Leo XIII stood apart as the champion of the exploited workers of the world, the pleader for the oppressed and disinherited and the vindicator of the rights that were ignored by those who possessed wealth and power. Hence, he was given the title of *The Pope of the Workingman*...[388]

In April 1951 while on his honeymoon, John took time out to attend a conference at Oxford University organised by the International Federation of Catholic Employers 'to pay homage to Pope Leo XIII on the occasion of the sixtieth anniversary of the Encyclical "Rerum Novarum"'.[389] The Catholic employers were working towards the social justice that was urged by Pope Pius XI in his 1931 encyclical, *Quadragesimo Anno*, 'On the Reconstruction of the Social Order'. John was actively involved in various Catholic Action groups—both Australian and international—which promoted the message of these two encyclicals. John described this work:

> The call of Our Holy Father is a clear appeal to Catholic Employers to strive to overcome class struggle through an organic co-ordination of employer and employee. In this regard proper human relationships in Industrial and Business sphere is a vital necessity.[390]

In the year before he married, John spent over 12 months in the United Kingdom, Europe, Canada and the United States, where he, in his own words, 'carried out human relations studies'. During this period, John wrote many letters to Moira. These letters reveal his dedication and enthusiasm for this work.

He wrote to Moira in considerable detail about the conferences and meetings he attended, the factories and mines he visited, also his thoughts on the law in Belgium regarding workers' representatives on Work Councils. He wrote of his meetings with Catholic Employers' Associations in England, France, Belgium and Holland and meetings with Christian Trade Unions. He was enthusiastic about the book he was reading, *Partnership for All* by John Lewis, and about the London business he was to visit where all of the employees were partners. His letters were filled with details about the woollen weaving mill in Marlborough, Ireland, the meat works in Roscrea, the aluminium factory at Namagh, and the bakery dispute where men had been sacked for joining a union. He wrote about the conference on the resettlement problems of disabled miners and he gave her a detailed description of the two mines he inspected in Wales: one was so damp they were continually pumping water out and the other was so dusty they needed to infuse water. He wrote about the public meeting he attended involving UK Labour MP Ness Edwards, the Parliamentary Secretary of the Ministry of Labour and the questions he later asked Edwards regarding Labour's policy of nationalising industry. He also wrote about the Wedgwood factory and the clever girl who hand-painted the line around the cup. And there were pages of commentary on the impending 1950 UK general election.

Moira was not deterred. On the day John returned to Melbourne after 12 months abroad, Moira was waiting at the bus stop to welcome him. Moira told the story that, as she waited for the bus to arrive, she had a lovely conversation with a priest who was also at the bus stop waiting for someone. It turned out that they were waiting for the same person. The priest was Father James.

B7

Carraig na bhFear

Jacinta's search for the Dinan family home in Ireland

John F Dynon's father, James Dinan, was born in Cork, Ireland on 4 December 1855 and baptised on 9 December 1855. These facts are verified by the records of Cork Cathedral. Beyond this, John knew little of his family's Irish origins. His father died a week after John's first birthday and both of his paternal grandparents had died before he was born. Although James was survived by seven siblings, it seems no one in the extended family in Australia could shed any light on the location of the Dinan family home in Ireland.

In 1983, Michele visited Cork and met a Tim Dinan, presumably a relation, with whom John had been corresponding. Then in his seventies, Tim told Michele that the Dinans and the Sheehans had adjoining farms in Cork. This was a vital clue.

We searched for more clues in James' travel diary. During his visit to Cork in 1881, James had written: 'Drove to Whitechurch Burying Ground to see the grave of my Grandfather & Grandmother & then on to Carrignavar…' He wrote nothing more in his diary about Carrignavar—the purpose of his visit, what he did there, whom he saw or spoke to. But the mere mention of Carrignavar immediately after seeing the grave of his grandparents suggested the possibility of a family connection. This was worth exploring.

My husband John and I travelled to Ireland in October 2014, hoping to find some more clues. Wasting no time after arriving in Dublin, our first stop was the office of the National Archives of Ireland. We knew that James had seen the grave of his grandparents in the Whitechurch Cemetery in 1881. If we could find the burial records, this would reveal names, relationships, dates of birth and

APPENDIX B7

death. This would be a good start. Unfortunately, we left empty-handed. They had no burial records. If such records existed, we were told, they would be in the local parish.

In anticipation, I telephoned the parish priest of St Patrick's Church, Whitechurch, only to be disappointed again, as he had no records of persons buried in the Whitechurch Cemetery. By way of consolation perhaps, he said that it was a public cemetery and we were welcome to visit and look around.

In our hire car, we journeyed south to Cork and spent a few days exploring the city. The highlight was Cork Cathedral, also known as the Cathedral of St Mary and St Anne. I knew that James Dinan had been baptised in this Cathedral. The baptismal font was easy to find. It was prominently positioned, of solid marble and beautifully sculptured. It was clearly very old and I allowed myself to believe that this was the very font where my grandfather had been baptised.

Next stop was Cobh and specifically the Cobh Heritage Centre. There we met with Christy, a researcher who knew how to access the limited historical records. Christy pointed out that, during the 1800s, the land in Ireland was owned by mostly absentee English landlords and the Irish people occupied the land merely as tenants. He consulted *Griffith's Valuation*. Published between 1847 and 1864, this consisted of a printed valuation book for each barony or poor law union in the country. It recorded the names of occupiers of land and buildings and the names of persons from whom these were leased and the rent. There were even maps. The Parish of Carrignavar was formerly known as Dunbullogue. An electronic search of *Griffith's Valuation* for places within Dunbullogue where Dinans and Sheehans had adjoining land revealed a concentration of Dinans and Sheehans in Glashaboy South. The records showed that in 1843 a Timothy Dinan leased a sizable land holding in Glashaboy South and sub-leased parts to various persons, including several Sheehans. This was a very promising lead.

It was a 15-minute drive to Carrignavar from Cork city. We parked and had a look at the lovely church in Carrignavar, the Church of the Immaculate Conception. The best decision I made that day was to knock on the door of the parish priest, Father Michael Regan. He was very welcoming. We introduced ourselves and explained that we were from Australia, visiting Ireland for the first time. I told him that my grandfather was born and baptised in Cork in December 1855 before coming to Australia as a baby, that I had great-great-grandparents buried in Whitechurch Cemetery and that my grandfather had visited Carrignavar in 1881, so it was possible that the family homes of my great-grandparents, John Dinan and Abigail Sheehan were located in Carrignavar. I told him that the Dinans and the Sheehans had adjoining farms in the 1850s.

Father Michael said that Dinans and Sheehans still lived in the parish. He told us that he had been in this parish for only three years but one of his parishioners, Maurice Spillane, had lived his whole life in Carrignavar and was familiar with the history of the local families. He telephoned Maurice who, fortunately for us, was at home and even more fortunately, was happy to come over to the presbytery and talk to us.

Maurice told us that there were several Dinans living here but there was only one place in Carrignavar where Dinans and Sheehans had adjoining properties. This was very exciting news. But there were some questions. Why would a family who lived in Carrignavar use the cemetery in Whitechurch, which was the neighbouring parish? Maurice said this was not uncommon and that he also had deceased relatives buried in the Whitechurch Cemetery. Also, I had wondered why my great-grandparents (and also my grandparents) named their family homes in Melbourne 'Grenagh'. I asked Maurice if this word meant anything to him. He told us that Grenagh was a village just up the road! A shiver went through me when he said this. I sensed that this could well be the place. I thought of Michele. We'd been working closely on our family history. How she would have loved to be here. Maurice offered to drive us around. I think he was as excited as we were.

Maurice told us that the Gaelic name of the town was Carraig na bhFear, meaning Rock of the Men. He said that the 'American' spelling, 'Carrignavar' had no meaning. It was just a word. As we left the church, Maurice pointed to a tree and monument. This monument was erected to honour 12 local poets from the 18th century. It encompasses the triangular grassed park and is called 'Faiche na bhFili' (the Poets Park). Opened in 1962 by the Irish President, Eamon De Valera, this was a wonderful occasion for the town.

Maurice drove down the narrow roads that are so typical of Ireland. Along the way, he showed us a derelict footbridge over the Glashaboy River and the shell of what had been the Glashaboy school that Maurice had attended as a young boy. He stopped the car and reminisced. All the children in the area walked to school. He told us of four families, including the Dinans who walked from one direction and the Spillanes who walked from the opposite direction. On reaching this intersection, they would place a pebble on the stone fence before turning into the road leading to the school. As the children of each family reached this intersection and saw the pebbles, they could tell who was already at school. But how could you know who had left any particular pebble? He said they all knew.

Further up the road, Maurice stopped outside a house and told us that this was the home of Christy and Mary Dinan. He said that in the past, Sheehans had lived next door. This was a modern house with a pretty garden. First impressions gave nothing away of its history. Maurice didn't know if Christy and Mary were at home but he said they wouldn't mind if we drove down the driveway, so we did. What we saw at the end of the driveway was like going back in time. I stepped out of the car and took it all in. There was an old two-story house—uninhabited and in a state of disrepair but rock-solid; also outbuildings and a stable. Maurice said that this would have been the family home of Dinans many years ago. We drove back to the house at the front where Christy and Mary lived. They were at home and warmly welcomed us. Christy confirmed that Dinans had lived on this land for many generations but he had no records going back earlier than 1900.

It was almost surreal. I was thinking, this might actually be the place. I might be standing on the very ground where my great-grandfather, John Dinan, spent his childhood and that my great-grandmother, Abigail Sheehan, may have lived next door.

But knowing that there were and still are many Dinans and Sheehans in this part of Ireland, I had to wonder whether it was possible to be 100 per cent sure that this was the place of the original home of *our* John Dinan. Certainly, the words in my grandfather's diary—that his grandparents were buried in the Whitechurch burying ground together with his visit to Carrignavar—pointed to the family home being in this area.

Later, as we enjoyed afternoon tea and the generous hospitality of Maurice and his lovely wife Carmel at their home, Maurice showed us a map of the area and he pointed out precisely where the Sheehan home had been. At the time, Maurice was confident that this was the place. By email several weeks later, he was more circumspect:

> I was careful to point out on our little tour that it was not possible to say for definite that we saw the correct ancestral home or that in meeting with Christy and Mary Dinan, that we were definitely meeting with the closest relatives of your late Grandfather, but we were in very close proximity to where your [great] Grandfather grew up. We were in the correct part of the correct Townland. We were at the old farmstead of the most likely descendants of your Grandfather's people and we were in the presence of the most likely descendants.

It may not be a 100 per cent certainty but a 'most likely' was so much better than a 'don't know'.

It was lovely to have my husband John with me. In 1978, while on our honeymoon, I was with John when he saw for the first time the birthplace in Greece of his parents and grandparents. That was an exciting time. It was wonderful that he was with me as I was discovering all this information about my own family.

Maurice drove us to Whitechurch Cemetery and he knew where to find the Dinan graves. Unfortunately, we couldn't find any Dinan graves with dates going back to the mid-1800s. It didn't help that the inscriptions on many of the very old graves were indecipherable. Certainly, this was the 'Whitechurch burying ground' that James visited in 1881. Of course, if the grave James saw was of his maternal grandparents, it would be a Sheehan grave, not a Dinan grave. In all the excitement of the day, we hadn't thought to look for Sheehan graves. With the benefit of subsequent research, it now seems more likely that the grave James saw in 1881 was of his maternal grandparents. James and his mother, Abigail, had travelled to the United Kingdom in 1872 when James was 16, leaving six younger siblings at home. The timing of that trip was possibly due to the ill health of one or both of Abigail's parents. And on James' return nine years later, he visited their graves.

We noticed many rocks on the ground in the cemetery. Maurice said that the rocks would have marked the spot where people had buried family members who died during the potato famine of the late 1840s. They would not have been able to afford a headstone. I asked Maurice how the area had suffered during the famine. He said that Carraig na bhFear had been very fortunate to have a landlord who was more humane than most of the other English landlords. As a result, Carraig na bhFear was spared many of the worst effects seen in other parts of Ireland. Maurice said that the McCarthys were the landlord family in this area, sometimes spelled McCartie, sometimes known as the McCarthy More (the Great McCarthy) or the McCarthy Spaineach (Spanish McCarthy).

Maurice drove the short distance to Grenagh. We were not looking for anything specific. We just wanted to see the place that so impressed John and Abigail who gave this name to their homes in Melbourne. John and Abigail were married, we believe, in February 1854, their son James was born in December 1855 and they left Ireland to come to Australia in September 1856. It is possible that their first home after they married was in Grenagh, not far from their parents' homes in Carrignavar. This is pure speculation as there is no record or story to support this. Certainly, Grenagh must have been the source of some very happy memories for John and

Abigail. There were at least four separate Dynon properties in Melbourne called 'Grenagh'. Newspapers reported that John Dynon died on 14 December 1912 'at his residence 'Grenagh', 408 William Street'; that James' first wife, Alice, died on 17 February 1905 'at her residence, 'Grenagh', Queen's Road, South Melbourne'; that James died on 1 November 1914 'at his residence, 'Grenagh', Royal Parade, Parkville'. Also, James' widow, Margaret, moved the family home to 'Grenagh', Urquhart Street, Woodend.

Endeavouring to gain more clues, we looked at James' 1881 diary. He mentions Carrignavar only once. Some of the writing is hard to decipher. His longhand scrawl appears to be:

> Went to St Peter & Pauls Chapel in Careys Lane to 11 o'clock Mass (a very pretty chapel.) Drove to Whitechurch Burying Ground to see the grave of my Grandfather & Grandmother & then on to Carrignavar & lovel passing Kihoh on the way.

Maurice also looked at these diary entries. He had a different view:

> The word after Carrignavar is, in my opinion, House. I am not sure of his route to Whitechurch and Carrignavar and the return journey to Cork. My interpretation of the end of the sentence 'then on to Carrignavar...passing...on the...' is 'then on to Carrignavar House passing Kilard on the way'. I have difficulty with this because there is no place between Carrignavar and Whitechurch with a name remotely like what is written, but, there is a place called Killard between Cork and Blarney and it is possible that he would have travelled through Killard on his outward journey or on his return from Whitechurch. Killard might have been spelled with one l instead of the present spelling with 2 ls. I have taken a look at the Ordnance Survey map and identified some of the locations mentioned in the Diary and you will note from the attached scan that there could be a connection with all of them if doing a short tour of the area.

If Maurice is right, the diary entry was '& then on to Carrignavar House', suggesting that James visited the family home. James' footprints were clearly all over this area.

Several days after we left Cork, Maurice sent me an email: 'Among my souvenirs, I came across the attached "Extracts from an Old Census".' He had attached a scanned 10-page article. This was an absolute gem of a find. In 1906, the author of the article, Tollamh o Donnchanha (Torna), went to the Public Records Office in Dublin to consult a 1766 Census that had been ordered by the Irish Parliament to ascertain the number of Protestants and Catholics in the country. Torna was interested specifically in the Parish of Dunbullogue (now known as Carrignavar). He wrote: 'At the time, my main interest was in the Dunbullogue area and so I made a verbatim copy of that portion of the census.' Torna said that the census was conducted on a parish basis. 'Fortunately, the gentleman who compiled the census of St Peter's and its "appanage", Dunbullogue, the Rev. Samuel Meade, set about his task in a conscientious manner, and so has given us a highly interesting and valuable document of contemporary local history.'[391]

What makes this article all the more valuable is that the original census no longer exists. It was destroyed during the bombing of the Public Records Office in 1922. Maurice pointed to page 72, which listed the occupants of 'Glasseboy'. The household of 'Jno. Deanane' had six Catholics and the household of 'Danl. Sheehane' had 10 Catholics. Maurice commented:

> It's interesting also that where the inhabitants of Glashaboy are listed that the Dinan name is followed immediately by the Sheehan name. It's also interesting that this census was taken almost 100 years before your grandfather was born and that both Dinan and Sheehan families lived in Glashaboy.

So in 1766, there were Dinans (Deanane) and Sheehans (Sheehane) living in Glashaboy in the Parish of Dunbullogue. As Maurice pointed out, the names were not listed alphabetically, and so it is significant that the Deananes and the Sheehanes were listed together, indicating that they were most likely neighbours as far back as the mid-1700s. Maurice also pointed out:

Note the top of page 76 refers to Tim Deanane (Dynan) (Dinan). The address Dallainin is a more precise part of the Townland of Glashaboy and is exactly where we met with Christy and Mary Dinan.

Knowing now that the original census was lost forever in the bombing of the Public Records Office, how fortunate were we that the census information relating to Dunbullogue was copied verbatim, and that it was published, and that we had met Maurice who had a copy of it!

With each new piece of information, a picture was emerging of a very long history of Dinans and Sheehans living in and around Carrignavar.

Nell Dynon, the daughter of Basil Dynon (the youngest of John and Abigail's children), recalled that her father used to say that the family originally came from France. Certainly, this is possible, but it may have been a few centuries earlier than they thought.

B8

The mystery of the marriage record

John F Dynon was unable to find a record of the marriage of his paternal grandparents. The Cork Cathedral, which had records of his father's birth and baptism, had no record of the marriage of his father's parents. Among John's papers was a handwritten note: 'I want certificate—write to P.P. at Whitechurch to ascertain if any record of marriage between John Dinan & Abigail Sheehan in 1855, 54, 53, 52, 51, 50.' He was on the right track.

Father Michael in Carrignavar thought that John and Abigail would most likely have married in their local parish. When Abigail had her baby in Cork, she would have been encouraged to have him baptised at the earliest opportunity. This would explain why James was baptised in Cork city.

Father Michael told us that the marriage records for the parishes of Carrignavar and Whitechurch were held in the Glanmire Parish. He telephoned Eileen in the Glanmire Parish Office seeking her assistance. We followed this up with an email:

> Dear Eileen
>
> Father Michael of the Church of the Immaculate Conception in the Parish of Carrignavar telephoned you yesterday on my behalf. I have been searching for the marriage certificate of my great grandparents John Dinan and Abigail Sheehan. They both resided in the parish of Carrignavar. Their baby son James was born on 4 Dec 1855 and he was baptised in the Cathedral of St Mary and St Anne in Cork on 9 Dec 1855.
>
> We presume that John and Abigail would have married between 1852 and 1855. The Cork Cathedral has no record

of the marriage but we now think that the marriage would have taken place in their local parish. I would be very grateful if you could search the records for the marriage certificate.

Eileen's response was not what we had hoped for:

After Fr Michael called to the office I went through our marriage register and unfortunately we have no record of marriage here of John Dinan and Abigail Sheehan.

Possibly we needed to search wider.

Thank you for your email Eileen. And thank you for taking the time to search for the marriage record. Can you please let me know the ambit of your search? Did it include Whitechurch as well as Carrignavar? What years did you search?…it's possible that they married as early as 1850. Thank you very much for your time and trouble. My family and I are very appreciative.

Eileen very kindly made a thorough search of the records:

Our records go back to 1803. There were three Abigail Sheehan's married here in the 1800's the dates are as follows:

27th January, 1838 Abigail Sheehan married Daniel Kelly.

21st November 1840 Abigail Sheehan married William Dorgan.

25th February 1854 Abigail Sheahan married John Sheahan, Clashabuy.

At that time there was very little information listed. Perhaps they were married in Cathedral of St Mary and St Anne as you state their son was baptised there.

This was actually very welcome news.

Dear Eileen,

Thank you so much for taking the time and trouble to check through your marriage records for me. I am extremely encouraged by your results. I believe that the entry for 25th February 1854 could well be the one. I think it is possible that when writing John Dinan they wrote Sheehan again by mistake. I assume that "Clashabuy" would mean from Glashaboy, which would pinpoint the home. What are the odds of 2 Abigail Sheehans from Glashaboy being married within a year or 2 of each other? What are the odds of a Sheehan marrying a Sheehan?

Eileen sent us a certificate of the marriage. It records both the bride and the groom having the same family name 'Sheahan'. The witness's family name was 'Sheehan'. The town was 'Clashabuy'.

That a bride and groom who are unrelated should have the same family name would, in any circumstances, be an extraordinary coincidence. For this to happen in a small rural town is simply inconceivable. With several apparent mistakes on the marriage record, the logical explanation is that the person who recorded the details in the marriage register was distracted or perhaps had started celebrating too early!

The family is satisfied that on 25 February 1854 Abigail Sheehan married John Dinan from Glashaboy. It is always possible that, down the track, a marriage record between John Dinan and Abigail Sheehan will turn up. But we don't expect this will happen. In any event, we are no longer looking, as everything points to this being the one.

Appendix C

Three autobiographical chapters by John F Dynon

C1	Memories of childhood	470
C2	Memories of pre-war Europe	474
C3	My three loves	479

C1

Memories of childhood

Now 70, grey or, rather, white-haired, with heart trouble and on a non-fat diet, and for all practical purposes having completed my biography of Moira, I commence to set down some material for an autobiography. It is not because it is in any real way unusual but because my family may like to know more than they do. Just how can I divide up my life for recording purposes? I suppose it is hard to divide it up into sections. Sometimes one makes one's own decisions; sometimes decisions seem to be made by others; sometimes things happen for no apparent rhyme or reason.

I was born on 22 October 1913 and my father died on 1 November 1914. Of course, I have no memory of him. I was one year old when he died. I never felt directly the aftermath of his death. I did not know what a father could have been to me.

My first memory is waking up and running downstairs, having been frightened by loud noises coming from the street. This was most likely during the World War I period and could have been the night that peace news came through. I remember playing in the grounds of our home, on the corner of Walker Street and Royal Parade, Parkville. I also remember riding on the horse tram to Melbourne Zoo. We lived in Royal Parade until 1919 or 1920 then moved to Goodall Street, Auburn for about two years. Jim had been attending school at St Patrick's whilst living at Royal Parade. After we moved, he went to Xavier College as a boarder early in 1920. Abbie had attended Loreto, South Melbourne whilst living at Royal Parade. Eventually, she went to Sacré Coeur, Glen Iris as a boarder. A Miss Batten used to come to the house as a teacher for me. My special memories of Goodall Street are of me hiding school books under the carpet before a governess came to give me special lessons on certain days of the week. Then there was the occasion when I cut my leg near the ankle whilst on a swing in the backyard. It was a deep cut made by a kerosene tin. It was a Saturday afternoon and a hot day. The doctor was nearly a mile away. He put several stitches in my leg. I don't know how she did it but my mother carried me in her arms all the way without stopping.

From Auburn, we moved to 'Scarborough' in Fitzroy Street, St Kilda. I went from there to Loreto, South Melbourne as a day boy. I was not particularly concerned with study and found it all quite a bore. It was probably because I was not responding well enough to the call of education that it was considered that it would be best for me to become a boarder at what was then called Studley Hall at Kew. Later Studley Hall was to become Burke Hall. This prep school of Xavier was then under the directorship of such identities as Father James O'Dwyer SJ and the scholastic RJ Tyndall SJ. Father Tyndall was in my opinion, after Father O'Dwyer, the most outstanding personality of the time. The matron was quite an identity—Miss McDougall. She looked after me very well; a lovable matron, she was a wonderful influence. I participated in all sports: cricket, football, athletics. Also, we played hockey on the asphalt playground down below the school building. We all played 'Charlie over the water' in the early evenings, and one of the school 'gangs' was the 'Ratty' gang led by Leo Confoy.

I loved sport but not work. I remember being strapped prolifically by Bill Tracy and Mr Charlton. Also Mr McArthur—God rest his soul, was a great character—a lay teacher whose strap was thin and of unusual length. He used to take a firm grip of it by winding it around his hand and then finish up by winding it around mine.

Whilst I was there, the chapel was behind the Study Hall; in fact, was part of it. The new chapel was built later. I remember being confirmed in the old chapel and being amazed at the lightness of the slap to the face, which I had been led to believe could be delivered with quite some severity by the officiating bishop—in this case, Dr Mannix. Dr Mannix presented the prizes for Aths on Sports Day. That was a big event.

When I commenced at Studley Hall, Mother moved to Urquhart Street, Woodend. During the school holidays there were good days at Woodend. I particularly remember Brother Jackson, the Flynns and Jim Edwards.

My first real loss was the death of my maternal grandfather, Hugh Carruthers, in 1932. He was a lovely grandfather. He was always kind to me and that was not just because he often brought me a gold sovereign at Christmas time. He used to holiday often at Mother's home in Woodend. He had been in hospital for some time. Grandpa was to be buried at Charlton in the country on the Saturday. My mother and my sister were to drive to Charlton for the funeral. I felt that it was my duty to my mother to accompany her on this journey. But a competition Public School cricket match was on Friday and Saturday at school. I was Captain of the School and Captain of the first XI. It was taken for granted that my duty lay with my team on the field, and it was my duty to perform with the team. I carried that through with a heavy heart. I do not know how much that incident affected my mother at the time. She never said. She never complained.

After my mother's death on 5 March 1958, I received a letter from Father Tyndall SJ:

> My dear John,
>
> I am indeed very sorry for you, Jim and Abbie. Father Stephenson had reason to write to me and included the sad news of your mother's death. Though really she has gone into eternal life and glory. Yet no one who has already tasted the bitterness of the loss of one's mother can exaggerate the deprivation.
>
> I have known her since Studley Hall 1922 and I always admired her. Beautiful, dignified, saintly, courageous and so kind.
>
> I regret that I was in Limerick the last time she visited Ireland and tried to find me in Dublin. God reward her gentle soul! I shall say Mass immediately for her happiness

and for your comfort and resignation. I would write to Abbie had I her London address.

With renewed sympathy and every good wish.

I remain, as always,
Yours very sincerely
Robert Tyndall S J[392]

My mother's death was the first time I attended at the graveside of a member of my family. That day I took stock of my life and rededicated myself to the cause of the family. My closest now were Moira and the children.

C2

Memories of pre-war Europe

In March 1936, after two years' residence at Newman College, University of Melbourne, I left on the *Orion* en route to Europe, Ireland and England, to commence my studies at Oxford in October.

I had been looking forward to a brief glimpse of Italy, but this time the ship did not make its scheduled call at Naples. Such a call was considered inadvisable in view of the strained relationship which had developed between the United Kingdom and Italy arising out of Benito Mussolini's continuing military adventure in Abyssinia.

As we passed through the straits of Messina, I recalled our family journey overseas in 1929. Then, as a boy of 15, whilst staying at the Hotel Savoia in Rome, I had written to Mussolini asking for an autographed photograph. This was at the time Italy had signed the Concordat with the Vatican, and this Church-State treaty and reconciliation made a deep impression on my mind. Within days, Italian officials arrived at the hotel and I was informed that Mussolini wished to see me. My brother accompanied me in a taxi to the official address at the appointed time. I must admit that I was rather apprehensive. Having presented myself for inspection, Mussolini autographed a postcard photograph and we left, somewhat relieved.

Much water has since flowed under the bridge.

During 1936, we attended the Salzburg Festival and travelled in Germany. The following year we motored to Vienna and Budapest and down to Lake Balaton. In 1938, the Nazi forces of Germany marched into Austria. Engelbert Dollfuss had been murdered in July 1934 by a Nazi group unsuccessfully seeking power. Kurt von Schuschnigg had become Chancellor on the death of Dollfuss.

Hitler's occupation of the demilitarised zone in the Rhineland in March 1936 had demonstrated to Schuschnigg the ineffectiveness of the Western powers. He negotiated a compromise with Germany in July 1936 but Hitler showed his hand when, at Berchtesgaden in February 1938, he dictated the terms of surrender to Schuschnigg. In an attempt to halt the inevitable, Schuschnigg called a plebiscite for Sunday, 13 March 1938 so that the Austrian people could decide whether or not to become part of Germany. Hitler's answer was swift and final. With his troops, he entered Austria on 12 March, thus outflanking the southern Czecho-Slovakian frontier. In fact, Dr von Schuschnigg had broadcast his last speech on Friday, 11 March 1938:

> Austrian men and Austrian women. This day has placed us in a tragic and decisive situation. I have to give my Austrian fellow countrymen the details of the events of the day... President Miklas asks me to tell the people of Austria that we have yielded to force, since we are not prepared in this terrible situation to shed blood, and we decided to order the troops to offer no serious— to offer no resistance...So I will take leave of the Austrian people with the German word of farewell, uttered from the depths of my heart, 'God protect Austria'.

Whilst I was holidaying at Biarritz in March 1939, the German army moved into Bohemia and Moravia and it was obvious that the independent nation of Czecho-Slovakia, created after World War I, was being erased from the map of Europe. The issue involving the German minority in Czecho-Slovakia had been simmering for some years. Prime Minister Neville Chamberlain's flying visit to the German Führer at Berchtesgaden on 15 September 1938, their discussions at Godesburg on 22 September, and the four powers conference (Hitler, Chamberlain, Mussolini and Daladier) at Munich on 29 September were all to be fruitless in avoiding the inevitable. Mr Chamberlain was to remain convinced that, for good or ill, his endeavours had delayed German action for almost six months.

I vividly recall speeding north through France to Dunkirk and crossing by boat to England. I was down to my last francs, and an English family also returning to England from the continent kindly came to my aid and loaned me some money so that I could pay my fare.

This period, 1936–39, had witnessed the 'civil war' in Spain, Leon Blum's Socialist interlude in France, the Japanese onslaught on China, Mussolini's incursion into Abyssinia and the Nazi crusade. In 1939, Dr Franz Borkenau wrote:

> There is no use denying that the German ideal of a Fascist world revolution is a challenge to our whole western civilization. If the challenge succeeds, it will not be due to overwhelming force of arms, but to the weakness of the moral, religious, and political impulses of the opposing side.[393]

During these years, I had as base my mother's London apartment in Grosvenor Square, and Christ Church, Oxford, affectionately referred to as 'The House'.

Following the end of the final term at Christ Church in 1939, with a third class in the Honour School of Jurisprudence, I left England and returned to Melbourne, travelling first to Paris and thence to Toulon, where I joined the *Otranto*. Some seven weeks later, I was at the Hotel Australia in Sydney on the day Neville Chamberlain announced the declaration of war on Germany and heard the rather famous pronouncement by RG Menzies, Prime Minister of Australia, that Australia was 'automatically' at war. On Friday, 1 September 1939, German forces had invaded Poland. On Sunday, 3 September, Great Britain found herself at war with Nazi Germany. Mr Neville Chamberlain, the Prime Minister of Great Britain, in a broadcast, *Talk to the German People*, on September 4, demonstrated the inevitability of war:

> Your country and mine are now at war…You may ask why Great Britain is concerned. We are concerned because we gave our word of honour to defend Poland against aggression. Why did we feel it necessary to pledge ourselves to defend

this Eastern Power when our interests lie in the West? The answer is—that nobody in this country any longer places any trust in your Leader's word. He gave his word that he would respect the Locarno Treaty; he broke it. He gave his word that he neither wished nor intended to annex Austria; he broke it. He declared that he would not incorporate the Czechs in the Reich; he did so. He gave his word at Munich that he had no further territorial demands in Europe; he broke it. He gave his word that he wanted no Polish provinces; he broke it. He has sworn to you for years, that he was the mortal enemy of Bolshevism; he is now its ally.

The German-Polish Agreement of 26 January 1934, expressed to be valid for 10 years, provided that, should any disputes arise between them, in no circumstances would either party proceed to the application of force for the purpose of resolving such disputes. Hitler claimed in April 1939 that this agreement was incompatible with the Anglo-Polish promises of mutual assistance and therefore was no longer binding. This was shortly after the German occupation of Prague. Poland's independence was threatened by Germany and thereafter England assured Poland 'in the event of any action which clearly threatened Polish independence, and which the Polish Government accordingly considered it vital to resist with their national forces, His Majesty's Government would feel themselves bound at once to lend the Polish Government all support in their power. They have given the Polish Government an assurance to this effect'.[394]

On Monday 4 September, the British liner *Athenia* was sunk. Just prior to the outbreak of war on 28 August my mother and sister cabled to advise that they were in Dublin awaiting shipping to Australia. My mother wrote to me from Dublin:

> Well my darling what are you going to do. It can be truly said we are all in the hands of God & he will direct everything. I pray for you constantly & put my petitions in Our Lady's hands. I intend going back when I can get a boat. The boat leaves Cobh near Cork for New York. The American Embassy stipulate that a through ticket to

Australia is necessary before they issue the visa—so at the moment I am waiting for a berth—it may be next week or next month. Anyhow there is nothing to do but wait...I hope to be able to help here in some way while I am waiting for my boat.

...It would be wonderful if even now some peace plan could be arranged. Be happy & pray. I suppose the Air force will be your decision.

My love,
Mother[395]

In due course, my mother did cross the Atlantic in an English ship and arrived home safely after much delay and danger.

Abbie stayed in Dublin to finish a nursing course necessary for war work. She then returned to England and was soon to work with the Voluntary Aid Detachment and later the Auxiliary Territorial Service in the United Kingdom.

During 1940, I had applied to join the RAAF but was rejected on account of my eyesight. I joined an AASC Officers' Training course and was eventually commissioned and posted to various places in Australia, including Alice Springs and Atherton.

In February 1946, the Army finally released me to the Reserve so that I could return to complete my studies at the University of Melbourne. I completed my final year Law whilst resident that year at Newman College, and, following Articles with Doyle and Kerr was admitted to practise as a barrister and solicitor by special leave of the Full Court of the Supreme Court of Victoria on 11 February 1948, upon the motion of Mr McInerney and Mr Ellis.

The following day, I left for London on the *Orion* to return to Gray's Inn to finish my Lord Justice Holker (Bacon) Scholarship on constitutional law and criminal law. I was 'called' to the Degree of Utter Barrister by the Honourable Society of Gray's Inn on 17 November 1948.

C3

My three loves

On 21 July 1939, I departed Toulon on board the *Otranto* for Australia. As I was a university student, the shipping company had offered a return trip for the price of a single ticket during the long vacation. I jumped at the chance. In the normal course of events, I was going to return to England on the same ship after it had completed a cruise in the Pacific. I was to return to sit for the Final Bar Examination in London.

After the outbreak of the war, I contacted Professor Bailey at the University of Melbourne and the examiners in London and arrangements were made for me to sit the examination in Melbourne late in 1940, with the papers being sent out from London. On this occasion, I was not successful.

Marie-Anne, by air mail and telegram, was entreating me to return to Paris and marry her there, come what may. For good or ill, I had looked at the family situation, the practicability of working and sitting for the examination in London, the war situation, and my personal position with regard to war service and marriage. There were a lot of complications. I felt that I should not risk a marriage which I considered, at the time, to be premature. I doubted whether Marie-Anne, with her intellectual capacity, would really have found contentment and fulfilment in Australia.

On my return to Melbourne and before the war broke out for Australia, I had lunch with my first love, Julie, at Menzies, and told her of my second love and that I was returning to England to complete my Bar examination. At that very moment, unknown to me, my future third love was studying science at the University of Melbourne and near the end of her first year.

When, in December 1982, I looked back through some of Marie-Anne's many letters to me (which I had kept), I realised what a wonderful relationship we had established in the years 1937–39. I recalled that, despite the fact that war clouds were on the European horizon, I still believed that I would be returning to England to complete the examination in London and consider the whole future. Hitler had indeed been expanding Germany's frontiers steadily but the final onslaught could have been delayed a year or two. But that was not to be. I felt myself caught in a vice in Australia with shipping held up, pressed by conflicting loves and loyalties and drowning in near-despair.

In 1950, when I became engaged to Moira, I told her of my friendship with Marie-Anne. In fact, Marie-Anne was one of the first people I told of the engagement. Marie-Anne wrote wishing us well and enclosing a fresh flower for luck. Indeed, on our honeymoon, whilst in Paris, Moira and I called on Marie-Anne and her mother.

Marie-Anne had married early during the war. She had a persistent suitor. They had one child, a boy, who had the good looks of Marie-Anne, and, I guess, the enthusiasm and depth. We had corresponded during 1939–1940 but when I went into the Army in 1940, the correspondence ceased. There had been problems regarding mail and censorship and I also felt powerless to do anything.

A few months following the invasion of Europe, Marie-Anne posted me a card dated Paris 22.9.44 (postmarked Melbourne 13 March 1945):

Dear John,

I am sending you at the same time this card to Melbourne and another to your brother hoping one will arrive at the destination. I have a lot of things to tell you about me but I am anxious to have news from you. Four years...

Meilleurs souvenirs
Marie-Anne

In 1944–45, we contacted one another by telegrams and letters and I think it was then that she first told me of her marriage. In 1948, I met Marie-Anne again in Paris and we parted in friendship, still wondering what might have been if the war had come one year or even three months later. It prompts reflection on the efficacy of 'free will' in a world where one's destiny often seems to lie in the hands of fate—as on a roulette table. Marie-Anne was pro-Republican in Spanish Civil War conflict, a devotee of Proust, and believed in sincerity and idealism rather than accepting the materialism of the age, which disgusted her.

Excerpts of translated letters from Marie-Anne to John:[396]

Monday 27th August Received your letter from Colombo, surprising that I have too the feeling that you are quite near me. Please tell me as soon as possible what you have decided to do…I wish you bon voyage. Believe me, no matter what happens, I will not forget you.

Sunday …My sister and my brother in law are as nice and kind to me as one can be. I don't know how I will be ever able to express my gratitude but my soul my spirit my mind are continually hurt and I only wish you took me as soon as possible away from here… I won't fear any more as long as I have faith in you and you faith in God. You are for me the greatest proof of the existence of God.

Thursday I read a beautiful book yesterday, which enchanted me 'Portraits sans modèles' ['portraits without models'] by Suarès. The portrait of Ignace Loyola is splendid. If you feel courageous enough to read one of the passages, I encourage you to do so. Suarès notes this saying of Loyola's 'What use is the empire of the world if I don't have my soul' and compares it to the materialism of our epoch. There is also a conversation between Loyola and Calvin which highlights the difference between the characteristics exhibited by the Protestantism and those exhibited by Catholicism. Predestination is to my mind a horrible thing in every possible case.

I went this afternoon to see the collection of the couture house, Lucile Paray. Dresses are such lovely things. I am walking every day in the woods or at Bagatelles and doing lots of German. I went to a Picasso exhibition, which is causing a stir at the moment and led to some contention between Jacques and me because I liked it a lot.

Wednesday 12th October Les Pelouses I do not know whether to be happy to have you safe in Australia, or to cry from your absence. While asking you to return quickly, I worry about that long voyage on unsafe seas. There my love, this is the last chance that we have to be reunited and happy despite everything, <u>do not let it get away.</u>

Now if you can't come to France I can come to Australia. I can perhaps work too. I know that it can be almost hellish for me to live in Melbourne the half of my life is my mother and the intellectual activity of Paris. The other half is you. Maybe I can find a way to satisfy a little the first half even in Melbourne, but I will never be able to satisfy the second half if I don't marry you.

Monday 16th October …As long as you think that the danger is too big on the seas, don't come back. I will be so frightfully anxious as long as the travel will last. I wish you could come back by aeroplane, it seems safer. We are listening to the news. Now I am going to sleep hoping that my sleep will last up till the day you reach Toulon. Goodnight my love, God bless you and protect you. Marie-Anne

Friday 20th October I have just come back from the hairdresser, who by his joyfulness and his stupidly chatty personality, made me laugh a lot. While my hair dried I flicked through an American fashion magazine, the first that I have had the courage to open since the war. Nearly everything was from Paris. Something adorable in its fragility and beauty, especially in Paris where it is within reach of almost everyone.

Jacques reopened his shop, with very little hope. He comes here on weekends. Mom, Vera and I are very occupied by François who is very cute and unbearable. Children really have a death wish. If we stop watching them for just a second, we turn back to them on the brink of taking out one of their eyes or falling on their heads.

I wait for you even more impatiently each day. Come back to me quickly. The Mediterranean seems calm at the moment and we should make the most of it. During the whole voyage send me your news often. I went into a little church the other day, perched on the top of a cliff, which is used only by fishermen, it is the church of sailors. I asked the holy virgin to protect you for as long as you will be at sea. I put you in her care up until Toulon, after that I will take control.

Jacques wants us all to return to Paris in 3 weeks, if there are no bombings. Come back, I am dying from waiting for you here. If you accept the proposition which I made to you …I hope that your mother won't find too many inconveniences with it. You said to me that I would certainly not like Australia. Do you like it?

Paris. Thursday 4th November It is now 2 weeks, my dear, that I have not written a single word to you. The responsibility falls on François who has been a little ill, and on a hindered return to Paris. We needed two cars to move everything we had moved out bit by bit, because we have completely relocated to Paris. In case of bombing, Jack, Vera and François will return immediately to Étretat and maybe Mum and me, but for the moment we are comfortable here…This morning I went to the Conservatorium concert, the programme: Franck's Redemption; Mozart's Sonata in D major; Beethoven's Seventh Symphony. The sonata charmed me completely, I was next to a big guy, with a round nose and a friendly face, a great audience member, he got enthusiastic about all that he heard and was going to hear, and during the intermissions was trying to give his wife an idea of the seventh symphony with cries of "Pam Pa Pam", he was shouting more than singing and it greatly amused me.

Have you received any of my letters since the 6th of November, the date of your last letter, complaining that you hadn't received anything from me? I hope that your mother arrives safe and sound in Melbourne. Attached is a photo of me which you may already have? Yesterday I went to the cinema with Mum, an American burlesque film, a very funny story about a leopard. Every evening we are terribly anxious because the houses are under surveillance by agents who whistle as soon as they notice the tiniest crack of light, since we never know for sure who the whistles are aimed at, and despite the effort we make with the curtains, we feel guilty.

Paris 16th November 1939 Three weeks of your silence is sad and long. I have received only one letter, and it was two months old. It made me happy anyway. Next week I am beginning to learn how to drive. I hope that my learning will take place without too many squashed dogs.

Saturday 9th December I received on Thursday morning your two letters from the 14th and 18th of November, they petrified me with sadness, and since I have done nothing but move from one room to another like a robot, without even the strength to cry. I have not slept either and my thoughts have been turning more and more quickly like mad ones. Luckily I have reacted rather quickly and this morning I woke up more happy and with a calm spirit. I have been able to have a more healthy judgment of the situation and I told myself that after all this situation isn't hopeless, and we are both cowards. You because you are a little too scared to "throw yourself into the water without knowing how to swim". Me because I don't have the courage to wait for you. My love, happiness is something which is won painfully and we will have it only by working. I shall try to wait for you as long as possible.

Thursday 31st December Let this year bring you the rarest joys and the most precious happiness. I hope that we will have the upper hand on this bitch life. We have to be tenacious and not let go…My last two letters were very hard my dear, but…I think that we both need to be shaken, it was too stupid to abandon our love at the first real difficulty…Happy new year to all and ruin to those criminals Hitler and Stalin!!

30th December 1950 Very dear John, I was very touched by your last two letters and to be undoubtedly one of the first to be told your big news! I wish to both of you every happiness possible and that harmony reigns in your home and in your hearts, nothing bad will be able to reach you then. Do not forget to come and see me when you pass through Paris. I would be delighted to meet Moira, your future wife. In France it is the lily of the valley and the violet which are lucky. I am sending a sprig in a letter which I am sending in the same post. I will be with you in spirit on the 2nd of December.

Very affectionately to both of you.
Marie-Anne.

Appendix D

Just Mum and Dad—the 'Dynon children' share some reflections and memories of their parents and life at home by Michele Trowbridge, Jacinta Efthim, James Dynon and David Dynon

Jacinta

When I first read Dad's manuscript, I was overwhelmed by the magnitude of their good works. At home, they were just Mum and Dad. As I write, the calendar shows October 2013. It is 37 years since Mum died. Despite the years, childhood memories remain strong.

One of my most enduring memories is of Mum doing the ironing in the dining room, listening to records on the stereo—always classical music. She enjoyed Tchaikovsky, Beethoven and Rachmaninoff but most of all she loved Puccini's operas—*Madame Butterfly*, *La Bohème* and *Tosca*. I can still hear her humming softly as she listened to her favourite arias.

It was always work before play. When we were young, there was a rule of no television on school nights, which later became no television before homework (although if Mum was out when we came home from school, we watched *Superman*). Our parents took our education very seriously. It was instilled in all of us that after school came university. It didn't matter what we studied but it was important to go to university and get a degree. We needed to be able to support ourselves. 'You must be able to stand on your own two feet', Mum would say. Another favourite saying of hers was: 'If it's worth doing, it's worth doing well.'

During school holidays, each of us had a list of jobs to do every day, but after we finished, our time was our own. We could ride our bikes anywhere, as long as we were home by dinnertime. We always had dinner together as a family. However hectic her daily schedule, Mum made a point of being home in time to cook dinner. If she thought she might be running late, she would tell us in the morning before we went to school and sometimes asked me to put on the potatoes if she was not home by 5 o'clock. Dinners were well planned and potatoes took the longest to cook.

After dinner, Mum usually went into her study to either sew on her sewing machine or work on a letter or a talk. She rarely watched TV, which was in Dad's study. Dad was happy for us to watch TV while he worked. He sometimes watched TV with us, then he'd make a pot of tea and join Mum in her study and they talked. They were in tune with each other. They never argued or raised their voices at each other—not ever.

We loved our big backyard at 7 Haverbrack Avenue. We were encouraged to play outside in the fresh air. Mum did not object to us getting dirty in the garden. We were allowed to play in the rain as long as we didn't get cold. When we came inside, we changed into dry clothes. We played football and cricket. We climbed trees, we built cubbies from wooden greengrocer's boxes and even slept in them occasionally, although the novelty of sleeping in uncomfortable cubbies wore off pretty quickly.

Dad took us to the football and cricket at the MCG until we were about 12 years old, when we could go by ourselves, as long as we caught trams—which had conductors. In summer, Dad often took us to the beach—Sandringham, Mt Martha, Dromana and, after we discovered surf beaches, Point Leo. He often bought fish and chips for dinner, which we ate in the car on the way home.

Gar was our maternal grandmother. For much of our childhood, Gar lived nearby, in an upstairs apartment in Malvern Road. Her best friend from schooldays, Rhoda Foote, lived in the downstairs apartment. Gar often made surprise visits to 7 Haverbrack Avenue. She let herself in and, when she was halfway down the hallway heading towards the kitchen, she would call out: 'Oo whoo. Can I come in?' This always amused us because she was already in.

Our brother John developed mild asthma when he was about six years old. Before long, the four of us (not David who was just a baby) started exercise classes in the city once a week after school. A taxi picked us up from Loreto and drove us to 601 Elizabeth Street where we changed into shorts and T-shirts and did exercises for an hour, then a taxi took us home. Looking back on this, it was apparent that Mum did not want to single John out for exercises, so we all went.

I remember an incident one day with a babysitter. Some of our babysitters were regulars but this particular afternoon we had a new babysitter, who told us to play outside. This wasn't a problem as we loved playing outside, but we made it a bit of a game to go inside. The babysitter started locking the doors and we found windows to get in. I thought it was fun and was enjoying it. But my brother John became annoyed and ended up breaking the glass in the back door so that he could go inside. I was worried that he would get into trouble but when Mum and Dad came home, they praised John for doing this and said the babysitter had no right to lock us out. Bravo John!

Mum enjoyed sewing and she made most of our party dresses. The Singer sewing machine table was a permanent feature in the centre of her study. Michele reminded me recently that we would stand on the kitchen table when Mum measured the hems for our dresses. I never acquired Mum's sewing skills. In my Year 8 sewing class at school, one of the projects was to make a skirt with a waistband, a zip, darts and a hem. This was quite a challenge for me and on the Saturday afternoon, two days before the skirt was due to be handed in, I showed my skirt to Mum and asked her what she thought. Mum said if I cooked dinner, she would make a new skirt. I cooked tuna mornay and rice for the family while Mum made the new skirt, which I proudly presented to the teacher on the following Monday. She looked at it closely and asked: 'Did you sew this?' I said that Mum had helped me and she told me that I failed and that maybe my mother could help me do detention!

In the garden, Dad grew tomatoes and looked after the rhubarb. Mum looked after the flowers. She put on barrier cream and gardening gloves and pottered around—weeding and planting. When there were water restrictions, Mum had us filling brown beer bottles with water and inverting them at the base of the azaleas and hydrangeas for slow-release watering.

We had lots of fruit trees including an apricot tree and about six plum trees. Every summer, Mum cooked stewed apricots, which were delicious, and we ate these while they were still warm. We couldn't wait until they had cooled down. We also had stewed plums, which were lovely at first but we got a bit tired of stewed plums so Mum made plum jam, which lasted for months.

During our childhood, bottled milk was delivered to the front door every day. We left out six empty pint-sized glass bottles and the milkman would replace them with full bottles. Sometimes, we had more milk than we needed and Mum would make custard or junket as after-dinner desserts. And of course we all remember Mum's delicious cream sponge cakes. Sometimes she made a big batch for a school fete or fundraiser. It wasn't until some years later that I realised you could make a cake without White Wings!

I remember the time when I was about 10 years old and my brother James and I had been climbing on a wobbly fence, although we had been told not to. As punishment, Dad had us write out the Ten Commandments 10 times. We sat at the kitchen table and it took us all afternoon and a lot of paper. During a school lesson a year or so later, the teacher asked if anyone knew the Ten Commandments. Generally, I wasn't one to speak up much in class but on this occasion, I put up my hand, stood up and confidently recited them all: 'I am the Lord thy God etc...' Everyone was amazed. I recall the teacher asking me how I knew them. I was too embarrassed to say the real reason and mumbled something like 'I just know'. I was relieved at the time that I wasn't pressed to elaborate. Thinking about this now, I wish that I had been brave enough to share with the class the full story of how I came to learn the Ten Commandments.

I remember standing with Dad in the grounds of St Francis Church just inside the Lonsdale Street entrance when he was collecting signatures for the Petition. I was seven years old. People walked up to him and shook his hand and talked and then they signed the Petition. I also recall many years later standing on the steps of Parliament House with Dad, Michele and David protesting against the death penalty before Ronald Ryan was hanged.

Our parents had strong religious faith but Mum sometimes surprised me with comments that seemed unusual for a Catholic. I recall the controversy that followed the Papal Encyclical of Pope Paul VI, *Humanae Vitae*, which prohibited artificial birth control. It was around this time that I remember Mum saying that the Pope was infallible only on matters of faith.

We were encouraged to be independent and to look after ourselves. We all did household chores. As Mum's work took her away from home occasionally, we all just pitched in and life went on. Among her papers, Mum had kept a letter that I had written to her in 1969, when she was in India:

> Dear Mum,
>
> How's life? I hope the seminars went quite all right. We all said prayers for you. Yesterday, as you know, was John's birthday and we cooked pavlova—it was not soft in the centre (like yours) but everyone loved it and it was soon finished. We (John & I) started to cook it at about 10.15 the night before, because we were going to the beach the following day. We didn't get to bed until about 3.00 because it took nearly four hours to cook. As it happened we did not go to the beach yesterday because the weather was not hot enough. In the afternoon we went into Campion Press to get our school books. Gar came over about five minutes before we left. For my birthday she gave me a yellow pair of cotton, nylon and polyester (all in one) shorty pyjamas. The boys each received a sports shirt.
>
> About the pavlova. As we were taking off the brown paper (which had stuck) a lot of it crumbled but the cream soon covered that. On the top we had about 60 strawberries.

APPENDIX D

Yesterday also meant David's return to school which proved to be quite satisfactory. As you probably have experienced, cleaning up David's mess is a full time job.

Wilsons came this morning at 8.00 which pulled me, unexpectedly, out of bed. After the man had loaded about 1/3 of the milk on to his truck, a telephone call came to him which said that there was some stoppage at the wharf. After much conversation had finished, the remainder of the milk was packed on to the truck. The load finally got away at about 12. Apparently the wharfies have gone on a strike which will end at 10.00 tomorrow. The "Vishva Prabha" will leave on Monday.

What is the weather like? I hope it is to your satisfaction. Melbourne's weather, if you have not already heard, is absolutely tremendous. Several times the temperature has neared the century. The other day I bought a pair of slacks. They are lime green with a navy blue stripe going down it. They match perfectly with the green Kashmir silk shirt.

The Advocate's article about you and your work was very good. Don't you think? As school is so near I am quite busy. I seem to be running out of space so I had better stop writing.

With love Jacinta

I remember the time when Michele and I joined Mum on a trip to Sydney. We were enjoying a relaxing afternoon on the beach at Manly. It was 17 December 1967. Mum had her transistor radio with her and switched it on to hear the news. There was a report of a search for a missing person off the beach at Portsea. The person wasn't named but I remember Mum saying that she thought it was Harold Holt.

As an adult reflecting on the time when the Australian Government decided it would no longer pay the shipping costs to send the milk to India, knowing the pressure that Mum and Dad would have been under, one might expect that this would have been a difficult time for the family. In fact, family life went on as usual. Mum and Dad calmly discussed and dealt with each issue as it arose. They knew that what they were doing was worthwhile and they took everything in their stride, dealing with each setback as it came along.

In the summer after Mum died, Dad took us on a road trip to Perth. We stayed at St Thomas More College where Father James was the chaplain. We played tennis for hours each day, we went to the fabulous beaches, including Cottesloe and Scarborough. We also took the boat to Rottnest Island, hired pushbikes and rode around the island. Dad joined in everything. Thinking back, it wasn't until he had his first heart attack in 1982 that he slowed down.

As I edit this chapter, today is 23 October 2016. It is 40 years since the day Mum died and I reflect. We knew she was unwell but we didn't know that her illness was terminal. For me, the shock came when I saw Dr Morrison in the corridor at Cabrini Hospital in early September 1976. I told him that Mum had said she was much better and that she wanted a vertical griller for her birthday. He said very plainly she wasn't getting better and most likely wouldn't live more than another two months. I don't recall anything else of the conversation. I remember telling Dad that night as we were doing the dishes after dinner. I think I expected him to disagree with Dr Morrison but he didn't say anything. Maybe he didn't want to believe it. I didn't mention it again. I didn't say anything to Michele or John or James about this. David wasn't there. He was boarding at Xavier at the time. None of us children had seen anyone die before and you don't expect your mum to die. We never talked about this possibility. I think we all just expected that she would get better.

Two weeks before she died, Mum came home from hospital. She was very weak but she liked being home. On the Thursday before she died, I came home from work at lunchtime to find Aunty June doing the ironing. Something was obviously wrong. She said Mum had gone back to hospital. James and I drove to Cabrini and saw

Mum in bed surrounded by nurses who were attaching drips. Gar was there as were some of the McCanns. At that point, we realised the inevitable. A priest from St Joseph's gave her the Last Rites. Dad telephoned Father James and Sister Ruth Winship. David came home.

During the last two days, someone was with Mum all the time. At one point on the Friday, Mum sat up in bed and asked for a cup of tea and a cigarette and I wondered if this was a miracle. I also remember my brother John and I were with Mum during Friday night when John was talking to the doctor and nurses about giving Mum stronger pain relief. Then, early Saturday morning, as it started to get light outside, Father James arrived. He went over and talked to Mum. He knew the right words to comfort her. After being up all night, John and I went home to have a sleep. When I awoke, I didn't know what time it was. I looked out of my bedroom window at the trees outside. It was bright and sunny but very quickly it started to get dark. It was eerie. It was mid-afternoon but it became as dark as night. This was a total eclipse of the sun. It was dark for about three minutes and then it was sunny again. I went back to Cabrini and as I reached the corridor leading to Mum's room, I saw Michele and Dad and Father James walking towards me. Shelly said, 'It's over. She's at peace'.

James

I was born in February 1955 whilst the family lived in Elizabeth Street, Malvern and my family moved to Haverbrack Avenue, Malvern later that year. I spent all my childhood living in our home at Haverbrack Avenue. I was the fourth-born child of my parents, and David was subsequently born in 1960. I was a twin but sadly my twin brother was stillborn.

I have very fond memories of my childhood at Haverbrack Avenue. When I reflect back on my childhood, I recall that family, school and sport were central parts of my life. Mum and Dad and my siblings each contributed to my childhood in his or her own way.

Dad worked as a solicitor and was very often engaged in working at home in his study, where the TV was located. I'm unsure how we fitted in watching the various shows and sports on TV whilst Dad was busily working in the same room. Dad was able to watch me play football and cricket on many occasions over the years.

Mum was always very busy in her numerous voluntary organisations which occupied a great deal of her time. I vividly recall that the Milk for India Campaign impacted on our life at home with donated tins of powdered milk stored in all sorts of available locations at home, with my role helping to pack tins into cartons before trucks arrived at various times to transport the milk cartons to various locations destined for India.

Although Mum's involvement with her numerous voluntary organisations and raising her five children kept her very busy, she had some involvement with my school. When I was at Kostka, Mum was a member of the Ladies' Committee of which she was President for a year. In my final year at Xavier, she helped out with the preparation and serving of afternoon teas in conjunction with the mothers of the boys who were in the First XI cricket team.

Despite the busy nature of the lives of my parents, they were always there for me and encouraged me very much in pursuing my schooling and sporting interests. I loved sport and was very fortunate to have a large front lawn and area for a cricket pitch in the rear at home on which a great deal of football and cricket was played during my childhood.

Overall, I had a very happy childhood and was much loved.

David

A recollection of Mum was that I went on a trip to Canberra with her for her work and had to take a week off school to do so. Just before we left Melbourne, Mum turned to me and said, 'We are going to Sydney for another week after Canberra but don't tell Dad'. I didn't say a word to anyone. I was going to enjoy the holiday and two weeks off school in Grade 6. Was Mum training me in diplomacy skills?

Another recollection of Mum, when in her final months, was that she was watching Abba on a colour TV in hospital and turned to me and said, 'David, girls are good'. Abba has since become one of my favourite bands and I still often watch them on DVD. Maybe Mum was also encouraging me with my music as I was playing in my first rock and roll band at the time.

Another memory I have as a child was that Dad occasionally drove all the children to the drive-in cinema. He was a firm believer that each car entering should be paying the same price, whether there be one or several patrons in the car. The logic was that one car space required one speaker attached to the window; nothing extra was required for more than one person. Unfortunately, the drive-in charged by the head. So Dad, sticking up for his principles of what was right and fair, although technically in breach of the law, put some of us in the boot of the car as we went through the entrance. This was just another example of standing up for what is just and at the same time training his children to do the same.

One more point which I find rather curious was that in Dad's den (meaning his office with the family TV and his library), he had two large pamphlets close together on the mantelpiece. On the front of one of these was a picture of the US White House containing the US Constitution and next to it was a pamphlet with the Kremlin on the front cover. What were we children expected to think of these? Maybe just another lesson in not to believe in too much propaganda. Dad led by example. He didn't always give a wordy explanation about what he did or why.

When I was young, Dad took me to the footy every Grand Final day, arriving in the first quarter of the under 19s. That is at about 9.30 a.m. The seniors did not start until about 2.10 p.m. Dad must have thought that I wasn't going to last the distance but he took me early anyway. I really treasure those football games and Dad's kindness in devoting his whole day just to me.

Another memory I have of Mum's kindness was when Collingwood lost the 1970 Grand Final to Carlton after being 44 points up at half time. I was rather upset. I barrack for Collingwood as did Dad, and I was in tears all night. Mum made me one pint of junket just for me and, I tell you what, it did the trick!

Michele

When we were growing up, we used to play sometimes in what we called Pap's House. Mr Papworth, who did repair jobs around the house, built this structure. There were two good-sized rooms and a roof, of course, but no doors. There was also an outside laundry and toilet. My recollection is that the Malvern Council wouldn't let the building be completed as it was too close to the back fence. As children, we enjoyed playing in there. It was fun also on rainy days. Later, Mum used the shed as a place to store tins of milk in readiness for packing and shipping to India.

In the 1950s and early 1960s, Mum had a dressmaker who lived locally. Miss Whitaker made some exquisite gowns and cocktail dresses for her. Mum learned dressmaking at Caulfield Tech and over the years she made beautiful clothes for the whole family.

Mum admired Tagore's writings and poetry. She quoted his prayer to me: 'Give me the strength to surrender my strength to Thy Will with love.'

During my final year at school, I was preparing for a debate and I asked Mum if she had any ideas. She told me: 'The greatest challenge facing Australia today is to reconcile our history with our geography.' I used this as my opening words.

On some weekends, Dad took us for a drive, often to Sandringham or Frankston or Woodend. Sometimes, when we passed a park with swings, we'd ask Dad to stop and he usually did. He often stopped for ice-creams.

We called Mum's mother 'Gar' because, when I was little, that was my first attempt at Grandma. From then on, to the Dynons she was always Gar.

Dad didn't believe me when I told him that President Kennedy had been assassinated. Jacinta and I had been watching *The Bugs Bunny Show* on TV on Saturday morning and we saw the news flash. I raced in to tell Mum and Dad. They were in bed. I woke Dad and told him.

APPENDIX D

In February 1969, when Mum was in India, I wrote her a letter that she brought home and kept:

Dear Mummy,

I have taken this opportunity to write to you as it is early in the morning and the sounds of silence make it relatively easy to collect thoughts. Since you left (just over a week ago) the usual daily procedure is a trip to the beach. Occasionally this is varied to outings of primary import such as the purchasing of school books, the getting of school clothes and picking up of school shoes etc. As well on Wednesday night we went to the Drive-In and saw "The High Commissioner" and a supporting feature "The fast lady" (which is a car). To my amazement the second and latter was the better.

Today David and John are going to get their hair cut—an essential evil. Then, after David has prepared all his clothes for school which resumes tomorrow we plan to go to the beach.

I hope you're enjoying your stay over there. As I know, the conference begins tomorrow so remember that our prayers and thoughts are with you, however, there is no need for you to worry. Just get up and give it to them.

I have also supposed that you are living to a strict timetable and this I know helps to make one alert and prepared. Enclosed is a clipping from "the Advocate" January 30th 1969. I thought that the last few paragraphs were most subtle but directly to the point.

Wishing you all the best and all are hoping to hear from you (after the conference perhaps)

With love Michele

PS. Michele Jacinta John James David and Dad send their best wishes and love.

Mum had a scar on the inside of her left forearm—about the size of a 20-cent coin. She said that it was from a mustard gas burn during the war. She didn't talk much about this work. It was top secret, 'hush hush'. But she did tell us that they had wanted a man in the role but, as no men were available with the right scientific qualifications, she was chosen; that she had attained the top score in a test, beating all the men and achieving a mark that was higher than anyone had achieved before; that she was thrown out of a jeep and hurt her back; and that she pulled the pin on a hand grenade during a training exercise and was lucky to escape injury.

The evening meal was the time of day when the whole family came together. Mum prepared dinner and the seven of us shared the day's events. Sometimes conversation turned to topical issues or maybe a major world happening.

Christmas 1975—I am very clear about the year because James was just a few weeks old. Mum said she had presents on her bed for James, me and Tony. Very near the gifts I saw beautiful white rosary beads. I said to Mum: 'What lovely rosary beads. Are these for me?' Mum said something like: 'Oh, I hadn't intended to give them to you. They were given to me by a kind lady but yes, it's right that you have them.' I also remember seeing rosary beads under Mum's pillow at home during the time when Mum was very unwell.

I was present at Mum's death at Cabrini. Dad and Father James were on either side of her and I was next to Dad. Mum's breathing changed and then was silent. Father James had a mirror in his coat pocket which he put under her nose and we realised that she had gone. I noticed that, at the time of her death, there was a total eclipse of the sun. A short time after she died, daylight returned.

Acknowledgements

We don't take our blessings for granted. Michele and Jacinta are very grateful to the many people who have helped and encouraged us. We want to single out a few for special thanks:

Christopher Darling for so generously proofreading numerous drafts and for his eagle-eyed attention to detail. Coincidentally, it was Christopher's mother, Honor Darling, who co-authored a book on the WAAAF, which included a chapter on Moira—Darling, H. & Stevenson, C., *The WAAAF Book*, Hale & Iremonger, 1984.

Kathleen Powrie for her truly inspirational advice and guidance, and especially for keeping us focused.

Dr Val Noone who worked with Moira in the St Albans Milk for India appeal and with John in the anti-conscription movement of the late 1960s—for sharing his memories of Moira and John, for his expert and invaluable analysis of the manuscript and especially for his enthusiasm for our project in ensuring that Moira and John were better known.

Felicity Taylor, Susan Pierotti, Merril Darling, Gabby Mahony, Sue Hardy, Karen Tait and the members of the **Lyceum Club Writers' Circle** for their valuable editing suggestions.

Babette Francis, a friend of Moira's and a supporter of Moira and John's many causes, for reading the draft manuscript and for her welcome feedback, recollections and written tribute.

Paul F Ormonde for meeting with Michele and Jacinta and sharing his recollections of Moira and the Milk for India days. Paul was a journalist during the 1960s and 1970s and was Hon. Publicity Officer for Aid for India for a few years.

Werribee Secondary College for honouring our mother by naming one of the eight college houses 'Moira Dynon' with the very apt house value of Resilience. In 2008, the students at the college nominated various Victorians or Australians who had lived worthily ('Live Worthily' being the college's motto). Moira Dynon was selected as one of the house names and sits well alongside the names of other worthy Australians.

The Assistant Principal of Werribee Secondary College **Kevin O'Neil** and the **Dynon House** leaders at the college in July 2015 who so warmly welcomed Michele, Jacinta and David with a wonderful guided tour and who showed us that our mother's life continues to be an inspiration for the students of the college.

Elizabeth Lusby for sharing with us the wonderful stories that her late father, Pat Hogan, had recorded about the friendship and wartime experiences of Moira's brother, Alan Shelton and the RAAF crew NR179; and for keeping alive the memory of their heroic sacrifice.

The late **Moira Peters** for so enthusiastically sharing with us her knowledge of the Dynon family history and stories about our shared great-grandparents. One of the highlights of our research was the time we spent with Moira, over many enjoyable lunches at her home, chatting about family history.

Giles Robinson with his exceptional knowledge of languages, who so generously gave his time and skills to translate Marie-Anne's letters and opened a window on an early chapter in John's life.

Maurice Spillane with his extensive knowledge of the history of families in Carraig na bhFear, Cork, for his valuable assistance in our search for the Dinan family home in Ireland.

Sonya Clark who has been invaluable from the outset and so cheerfully and expertly converted into a workable format over a thousand pages of draft manuscript and notes that John had typed with his manual typewriter or had handwritten.

Michelle Pirovich for her wonderful typesetting and design work and for her above and beyond assistance in bringing this book to life.

Our uncle **David Shelton,** Moira's brother, now in his nineties, for his stories of Moira and their brother Alan; and especially our aunt **June McCann,** Moira's sister, who, in her mid-nineties, read every page of the draft manuscript and gave us her warm and unqualified support.

And most of all, our family—our brothers James and David, who join us in this tribute to our parents, our wonderful children who inspire us and who have encouraged and assisted us in so many ways and to Jacinta's husband, John, for his enduring love and support and for his welcome distractions including horseracing adventures.

Moira on the lawn at 230 Glenhuntly Road Elsternwick. c. 1942

Moira c. 1922

Family group at Glenhuntly Road. Lily Shelton sits between David and Valda. Sitting in front are (L to R) June, Alan and Moira. 1934

WAAAF Flight Officer
Moira Shelton. c. 1942

Moira (centre) charging LC 65 lb
bombs with mustard gas during
tropical storage trial, Bowen.
25 October 1944

Crew climbing into Beaufort aircraft, sprayed with mustard gas for trial. (L to R) W/O WC Wells (pilot); Flt/Lt Ronald Barker (W/T op) and Scientists for the trial, Flt/Off Moira Shelton and Captain Andrews (Australian Army), Bowen. 13 July 1945

Crew NR179 466 Squadron RAAF. (Top L to R) Greg Dixon, RAAF Wireless operator; Bill Bullen, RAAF Rear Gunner; Roger Laing, RAAF Mid Upper Gunner; Wally Welsh, RAF Flight Engineer. (Bottom L to R) Roger Johnson, RAAF Bomb Aimer; Alan Shelton, RAAF Pilot; Patrick Hogan, RAAF Navigator. Photo taken at Driffield. January 1945

Moira c. 1947

ARGUS, MON, SEPT 16/46

The Life of Melbourne

A Topping Topper

"WHERE DID you get that hat?" Moire Shelton had this question fired at her from left and right at Helen Webster's cocktail party on Saturday night—from girl friends lost in admiration and from boys who for a second—only a second, mind you—glanced higher than the attractive face beneath THE HAT.

A real top hat it was, but it was not the shape so much as the material which made it exciting—tropical red flowers and gold lame on black slipper satin.

Moira told me she bought the material in Sydney and had it made up in Melbourne, so, for once, two rival states share the honours.

Moira and that hat.

Just married. John and Moira in Xavier College chapel. 2 December 1950

John and Moira on the chapel steps.

Moira's parents, Percy and Lily Shelton. 2 December 1950

Moira and John in London during their honeymoon. 1951

John and Moira enjoying honeymoon travels. 1951

Michele, aged 5, with Mrs Chen Tai Chu and Mr Chen Tai Chu, Chinese Minister Plenipotentiary. AAUN Malvern Branch schoolchildren's rally, Metro Theatre Malvern. 29 March 1957

Michele, aged 9, preparing for the Dance of the Cherry Blossom at a Japanese evening at St Andrews Hall, Gardiner. 1960

Moira Dynon, Secretary, Australian-Asian Association, meeting the Prime Minister of Malaya, Tunku Abdul Rahman at Malaya Hall. 1959

John and Moira enjoying an Easter celebration with Dr Vittorio Strigari, Consul-General of Italy. 1964

James, John, Jacinta and Moira stacking milk in the shed known as Pap's House, at the back of 7 Haverbrack Avenue. c. 1966

Moira and children, (L to R) James, Michele, John, David and Jacinta with tins of milk inside the entrance of the Dynon home. December 1964

John and Moira with His Excellency Mr DN Chatterjee, High Commissioner for India. c. 1966

His Excellency Mr DN Chatterjee speaking to a group of schoolchildren at Metro Theatre Malvern, alongside Moira, John F Dynon and the Mayor of Malvern, Cr TH King. 27 September 1966

Moira and John welcome Mrs Vijaya Lakshmi Pandit, former President of the United Nations. 7 Haverbrack Avenue. May 1966

Mrs Pandit visiting Moira, her family and officials of the Campaign. Included in the gathering are Mrs Pat Mutimer, Chairman, Mentone Milk for India (standing, next to Moira), Mrs J D'Arcy, prominent Milk for India worker (standing next to Mrs Mutimer) and Fr F O'Hanlon, Mentone Parish Priest (centre back). May 1966

(L to R) Mr RE Arthur, Assistant Traffic Manager, Victorian Railways; The Most Rev Bishop J Cullinane DD; Mr LS Reid MLA; Mr Newman Rosenthal, Head, Audio-Visual Aids Department, University of Melbourne; Moira Dynon; His Excellency Mr AM Thomas, High Commissioner for India; Mr Rohan Rivett, journalist, editor and author; Dr SN Ray, Head of the Indian Studies Department, University of Melbourne at the launching of the 1969 Milk for India Appeal. Hotel Australia. 1969

(L to R) Mr G Raj, Deputy High Commissioner for India; John F Dynon; Mr Lindsay Thompson MLA, Minister of Education; Moira Dynon and Dr Jim Cairns MHR at the launching of the 1970 Milk for India Appeal. 1 June 1970

John, aged 13, with His Excellency Mr A M Thomas, High Commissioner for India. August 1967

Moira meeting children being cared for at the Red Cross Welfare Centre at Najaf Garh, 35 miles from New Delhi. c. 1969

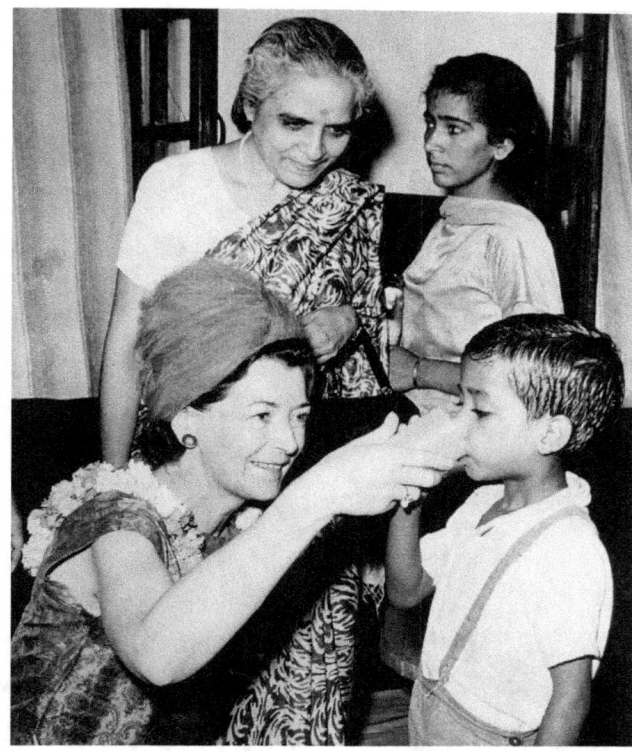

'It is a deeply moving experience to give a cup of milk from Australia to a child in need.'

Moira at Kasturba Niketan, New Delhi. 1967

Moira distributing milk at a nursery school in Madras. 1969

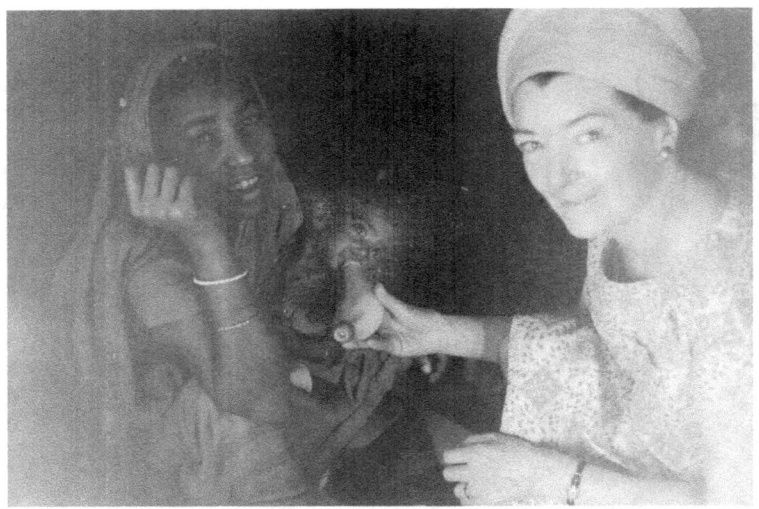

Moira feeding milk to a baby at the home of Brother Andrew MC in Calcutta. 28 January 1969. Photo taken by Dr Val Noone.

Opening of Guild of Service / UNESCO Seminar on Human Rights. (L to R) Mrs Mary Clubwala Jadhav, Director of the Seminar and Chairman, Guild of Service; Sardarni Ujjal Singh, wife of His Excellency the Governor; Hon P Govinda Menon MP, Union Minister for Law and Social Welfare; His Excellency Sadar Ujjal Singh, Governor of Madras State; Hon Dr T Satvavanimuthu MP, Minister for Health and Social Welfare, Madras State Government; Mrs Moira Dynon, National President Aid India Campaign (Australia); Hon Mr A Manickavelu Naicker MLC Chairman, Madras Legislative Council; Dastoor ND Minocheher Homji, Bombay (Parsee High Priest). Rajah Hall Madras. February 1969

Moira c. 1965

L.D.M.

Missionaries of Charity,
54A, Lower Circular Road,
Calcutta-16.

24th August, 1970.

Mrs. J. F. Dynon,
National President,
Aid India Campaign,
7, Haverbrack Avenue,
Malvern,
Victoria,
Australia.

Dear Mrs. Dynon,

    On behalf of the Missionaries of Charity and our Poor, especially the leprosy patients, I take this opportunity of thanking you for sending us 33 bags of wheat ex s.s. VISHVA KALYAN under B/L No:4 of 6.6.70 which reached us in good condition on 6.8.70.

    You will be very happy to hear that these 33 bags of wheat reached us just in the nick of time to help us tide over a crisis. As you know our leprosy patients receive each week very strong medicine, which requires them to take plenty of nourishment to complement it, otherwise they may become very weak and even face death. Divine Providence came to our rescue and helped us clear this consignment to give each of them sufficient ration for the week. Thanks to your generosity and the trouble taken. God reward you a hundredfold for your kindness for the Poor of India.

    Assuring you of our prayers and in return requesting yours,

God bless you
M Teresa mc

Letter to Moira from Mother Teresa M.C.

ALAN BIBLE, NEV., CHAIRMAN
WAYNE MORSE, OREG.   WINSTON L. PROUTY, VT.
THOMAS J. MCINTYRE, N.H.   PETER H. DOMINICK, COLO.
ROBERT F. KENNEDY, N.Y.
JOSEPH D. TYDINGS, MD.

CHESTER H. SMITH, STAFF DIRECTOR

United States Senate

COMMITTEE ON
THE DISTRICT OF COLUMBIA

February 9, 1967

Mrs. J. F. Dynon
National Chairman
Aid for India Campaign
7 Haverbrack Avenue
Malvern, S.E.4
Victoria, Australia

Dear Mrs. Dynon:

    Thank you very much for your fine letter and the clippings from <u>The Age</u>. I just recently received the copy you sent and I apologize for not answering sooner. I am always pleased to receive your thoughtful views and suggestions.

    You are probably aware that the day after you mailed your original letter the United States agreed to ship 900,000 tons of food grains to India during February and March.

    Last week the President authorized an emergency shipment of 2 million tons. He also asked Congress to approve of 3 million additional tons to be shipped in the near future, with the condition that appropriate amounts also be given by the other developed countries of the world.

    As you know, I share your sincere concern for the people and democracy of India. I was very pleased to see our government take these much-needed steps.

    Thank you again for writing. I hope I will be hearing from you again concerning matters of mutual concern.

Sincerely,

Robert F. Kennedy

Robert F. Kennedy

Letter to Moira from US Senator Robert F. Kennedy.

PRIME MINISTER
India.

No.688-PMO/68 New Delhi,
July 27, 1968.

Dear Mrs. Dynon,

You have helped us in the past. Now I learn of your latest gift of milk powder. I appreciate your genuine humanitarian concern and thank you on behalf of the many to whom you have brought succour.

It was a pleasure meeting you again in Australia. I have pleasant memories of my visit.

With good wishes,

Yours sincerely,

(Indira Gandhi)

Mrs. J. F. Dynon,
National President,
'Aid for India Campaign',
7 Haverbrack Avenue,
Malvern, S.E.4
(Victoria)

Letter to Moira from Prime Minister of India, Mrs Indira Gandhi.

Moira with baby James
at 7 Haverbrack Avenue.
1955

Brothers Fr James
Dynon SJ and John
F Dynon with brothers
John and James.
c. 1963

Michele, Jacinta, John and James at Loreto Convent Toorak. c. 1959

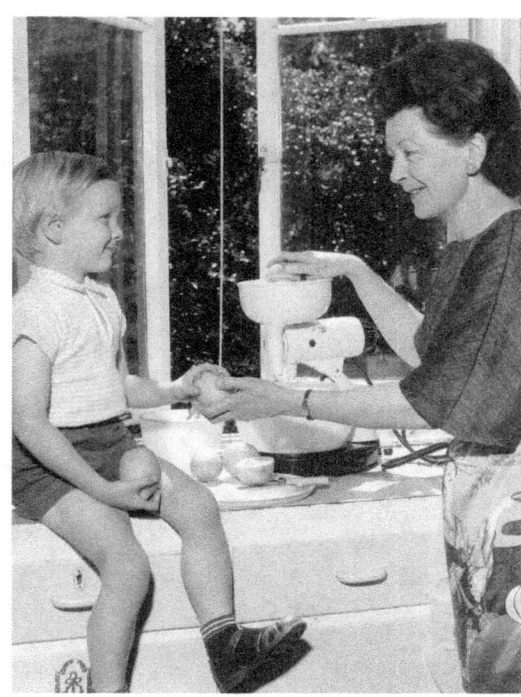

Left: Moira with David in the kitchen.

Below: Family cricket match on the front lawn at 7 Haverbrack Avenue.

Michele and Jacinta at Manly Beach, Sydney. 17 December 1967. Photo taken by Moira.

Moira at Jacinta's law graduation, Monash University. 9 April 1976

John F Dynon in his study. c. 1980

Index of names

A
Abo, Satoyo 163
Ackeroyd, Mrs 42
Adachi, Fumiko 163
Adams, Judge Arthur 309
Adams, Julie 309, 479
Ajgaonkar, Nama 277, 528
Alan, Eric 203
Albryts, Dr and Mrs 86
Andrew, Professor R 530
Allen, James L 328, 329, 338, 416-17, 531, 534
Alley, Steve 143, 154
Aloysius, Sister Mary 514, 105
Aluffi, Count 68
Alva, Violet 301, 302, 311
Anderson, Senator Kenneth 252
Andrew, Rev Brother MC (Ian Travers-Ball) 276, 277, 303, 304, 355, 528, 532
Andrews, Captain 383
Anthony, Doug 331
Arnott, L J 207, 208, 209, 522
Arvio, Duc 88

B
Bailey, Professor 479
Balakrishnan, P 534
Bankowski, Mrs 203
Barber, A 290
Barker, Flight Lieutenant 382
Baron, Rev Father 48
Barry, Mother Gonzaga IBVM 9, 94, 95, 102, 511, 513, 514
Barwick, Sir Garfield 126, 129, 131-34, 136-37, 139-41, 148, 149, 386, 390
Baunskill, General 379
Bayart, Phillipe 77
Beazley, Kim (Snr) 134-35
Beermann, Dr 245
Bergin, Mr 292
Bernard, Rev Mother PBVM 24, 25, 64
Bhoot, Captain 304
Bilek, Mr 515
Billings, Dr John and Dr Evelyn 180
Bird, Mrs Andrew 61
Blacklow, Mr 268
Blogg, Sylvia 142, 143, 517
Bloomfield, Sir John 114, 145
Body, Dr 65
Bolte, Sir Henry 143, 144, 198, 322, 336, 517
Bowen, Nigel 334, 531
Bowles, Chester 234
Boyle, Colonel Henry and Mrs Boyle 67, 70, 86
Bray, Gertrude 177, 200, 519
Brooks, Sir Dallas and Lady Brooks 96, 104, 514
Bruce, Stanley 445, 535
Bruno, Dr G 170
Buchan, Councillor John 127

Buck, W W 519
Bullen, Bill 40, 47, 51, 52
Bunting, Sir John 270, 273, 527
Burnet, Sir Frank Macfarlane 27, 28, 511
Burns, Councillor F 519
Buxton, Douglas 63
Buxton, Richard R 63, 152, 315, 519, 530
Byatt, Rev Frank 159, 519, 521

C

Cairns, Dr James F 163, 164, 242, 288, 293, 318, 319, 519, 521, 530
Calanchini, Betty 61
Callow, Mr 68
Calwell, Arthur 169, 208, 522, 524
Campbell, Mrs Hugh 519
Carr, Surgeon Rear Admiral 30
Carruthers, Hugh 441, 442, 472
Carruthers, Mary (Clancy) 441, 442
Carse, Rev Maurice SSS 237
Chain, Professor 68
Challis, Dr John 267, 268, 271, 272, 526, 527
Chatterjee, DwarkaNath 108, 236, 246, 266-69, 271, 525, 527
Chatterjee, Mr and Mrs (Sheila) 304
Chen, Tai Chu, Dr 107
Cherian, Dr and Mrs PV 311
Chessels, Arthur and Carmel 85
Chettiar, Mrs AMM Murugappa 316
Chipp, Don 532
Chisholm, Professor Alan R 107
Chittiak, R 279-80, 528
Churchill, Sir Winston 36, 512
Clark, E 226, 524

Clarke, Monsignor LM 219, 222-25, 524
Clarke, Rev Father L 519
Clunies Ross, Lady Janet 519
Clunies Ross, Sir Ian 57
Coates, Sir Albert 152
Coleman, Kevin 59, 513
Colombiere, Rev Mother IBVM 94, 100-1, 514
Connor, Mr 411
Copley, Mrs H 519
Copthorne, Colonel 379
Costigan, Rev Michael 526
Coulthard, Mrs JL 519
Coumbos, Nicolas D 515
Courtnay, Mr 520
Coutts, Mrs J Grant 530
Cowen, Sir Zelman 108, 515
Cox, EH 136, 172, 291, 517, 520
Crawford, Sir John 407, 523
Crosbie, John 63
Crosbie, Margaret 60
Crowther, George 112
Cullinane, Bishop John 321
Cummins, Mr 80
Curtain, Sister Katherine PBVM 24-25, 511

D

Dalton, Rev Father Bill SJ 88
Daly, Dame Mary 519
De Brass, Mr and Mrs 290-91
del Castillo, Captain E 515
Dell'Acquin, Cardinal 100
De Souza, Dr L 263
Denning, Mr Justice 148, 518
Dhar, Mr 264
Dias, Mr and Mrs 312-13, 315
Dimmick, S 152
Dinan, Christy and Mary 459-60, 464

Dixon, Greg 40, 43, 47, 50-51, 84
Dobson, Mary and Roy 94, 309
Dobson, Nancy 295-6, 529
Dobson, Mrs W 530
Downer, Sir Alexander 154, 159-63, 170-71, 175, 282-83, 293, 519-20
Dunlop, Dr Sir Edward E 152, 159, 328, 353, 519, 521, 530, 532
Dunne, Mother Pauline IBVM 94
Dunstan, Keith 159, 518
Dwyer, Hiliary 96, 309
Dynon, Abigail (Sheehan, Dinan, Dynan) (JFD's grandmother) 420-22, 426-27, 428, 430, 458, 460-61, 465-67, 535
Dynon, Abigail (Abbie) (JFD's sister) 82, 442-45, 449, 470, 472-73 477-78
Dynon, Alderman James (JFD's father) 12, 60, 63, 420, 421, 426, 429, 430-39, 440-43, 456-57, 461-62, 470, 535
Dynon, Alice (O'Callaghan) 440, 441, 462
Dynon, Basil 422, 426, 429, 464
Dynon, Cyril 442
Dynon, Daniel 422, 426, 429, 430, 444
Dynon, David Francis (Moira & JFD's son) 93, 168, 296, 299, 310, 486, 494-95, 497
Dynon, Dr John Damian (Moira & JFD's son) 93, 97, 169, 296, 301, 303, 305, 308, 310, 488
Dynon, Francis (Frank) 426
Dynon, James Newman (Moira & JFD's son) 93, 96, 303, 452, 493-94
Dynon, John (Dinan; Dynan) (JFD's grandfather) 420-30, 458, 460-62, 464-67, 534-35
Dynon, John Edward 426, 430
Dynon, Joseph 426
Dynon, Margaret (Carruthers) (JFD's mother) 18, 60, 62-63, 65, 86, 95-97, 417-72, 441-42, 444-45, 462, 471, 477-78, 513, 535-36
Dynon, Mary 426, 430
Dynon, Nell 426, 464
Dynon, Rev Father James SJ (JFD's brother) 17, 19, 63, 82, 97, 294, 298, 304, 361, 442-47, 449-55, 470, 474, 492-93, 498, 533, 536
Dynon, Timothy 426
Dynon, Vicki (Anderson) 452

E

Edwards, Jim 472
Efthim, Moira Jacinta (Dynon) 93, 97, 107, 294, 296, 301, 303, 305, 310, 315, 452, 456-64, 486-93, 496-7, 512, 522, 529
Efthim, John 452, 456, 460
Elizabeth (Queen mother) 44
Elizabeth, HRH Princess (later Queen Elizabeth II) 44
Ellis, Mr 478
England, Mary 101
Ennor, Dr 377

F

Fader, Julian 515
Falla, RP 441, 535
Ferguson, Alex J 164, 199, 323, 519
Ferguson, Noel 164, 519
Fernandez, Mr and Mrs 307
Fitzgerald, Senator J 165
Fontana family 169-171, 283, 289, 294, 520
Foote, Rhoda (Inell) 365, 487
Forster, Dr HC 57

INDEX OF NAMES

Fox, EMC 521
Francis, Babette 359, 533
Francis, Charles QC 289-90, 529
Frost, Mrs G 521
Fujii, Kazuko 163

G

Gaedeet, Rev Father 416-17
Gaffney, Joan 60, 82
Gair, Senator 524
Galbally, James M 173, 397, 398, 520, 534
Gallagher, Rev Father 70
Gandhi, Mrs Indira 12, 233, 236, 239, 248, 256, 262, 274, 275, 292, 308, 312, 319, 323, 330, 338, 344, 406, 414-5, 527, 530, 532, 534
Gault, Professor Edward 521
George VI, His Majesty 44
Gera, Mr 312
Gibbins, Corporal 372
Gibbons, William C 269, 527
Gill, JS 249, 526
Gillies, Corporal 372
Girvan, Rev H 519
Glynn. Abigail (Dynon) 176, 426, 429-30, 534
Glynn, Dympna 65
Glynn, Patrick McMahon 426, 429, 534
Goldney, Major General 379
Gomez, Archbishop 311
Gorrill Mrs Muriel 36
Gorrill, Lieut Colonel FS (Freddie) 36, 377
Gorton, John G 273, 292, 318, 530
Gracias, Cardinal Valerian 260
Grant, Bruce 530
Grant, Dr KB 279, 528
Groves, Flt/Sgt Ken 44

H

Hagelthorn, Florence 196-200, 522
Hall, Graham R and Mrs Hall 107, 515
Hall, Mrs GWT 519
Harmel, Leon 76
Harmel, Monsieur 76
Harper, Professor Norman 530
Harriman, Averell 213-14, 226, 523
Harris, Mr 307
Hasluck, Sir Paul 216-17, 241-44, 253-54, 406, 523-5
Hay, HS 515
Haydon, Dr 180
Hayes, B 327
Hayward-Butt, Commander 515
Hill, Dr Robin 82
Hogan, Patrick 39-52, 356, 512, 532
Holt, Harold 114-24, 131, 131-34, 145, 172, 214-16, 240-41, 243-46, 254, 262, 267-68, 270-74, 392, 406, 491, 516-17, 523-27, 534
Holt, Dame Zara 104-5, 119, 297, 305
Howard, Mr G and Mrs Mary 283-84, 294, 298-99, 528
Humblet, John 78
Hurley Air Vice Marshal 370
Hurley, Dr JG 521
Hymavathy, Mrs T 278, 528

I

Imajo, Mr 166
Infantino, Luigi 168
Ito, Yone 158, 165-167

J

Jackson, Brother 472
Jacobucci, M 169, 170, 520

Jadhav, Mrs Mary Clubwala 312, 315-16, 526, 529
Jeewa, Mr and Mrs 298-99, 301
Johnson, President Lyndon 213, 226-29, 234-35, 270, 292, 406, 524
Johnson, Roger 38, 40, 43, 47, 48, 50-51, 84
Johnston, Alan 24
Johnston, Charlotte Howard (Burd) 24
Johnston, Dr Len 24, 366
Johnston, Eliza (Brophy) 24
Johnston, George Keane 23
Johnston, Margaret Ellen (McCarthy) (Moira's grandmother) 24, 59, 364
Johnston, Mary (Peppard) 24
Johnston, Maurice 24
Johnston, Nancy (Rutherford-Smith) 24
Johnston, William Bowen (Moira's grandfather) 24, 364
Joshi, Dr Martand S 354, 532
Joske, Percy 125-127, 130-32, 140, 143
Jovy, Dr M 107

K

Kaines, AB 519
Kamil, Dato Nik A 108
Kay, Douglas 29, 511
Keans, Bernadette 277-78, 528
Keating, Frank G 344-45, 530, 532
Keenan, Rev Father Paul SJ 445
Kelly, Mr and Mrs Paul 82
Kelly, Rev Father Austin SJ 449
Kelly, Vincent 168
Kennedy, US President John F 178, 270, 496

Kennedy, US Senator Robert F 12, 229-37, 269-70, 524-25, 527
Kent, BA 266, 526
Khan, R Axel 252
Kimber, Corporal 373
King, Councillor John 103
Kingon, Mr 379
Knox, Archbishop (later Cardinal) James Robert 225, 303, 311, 331-32, 531

L

Laing, Roger 40, 50, 52
Lal, Muni 107
Lancaster, IG 527
Langenbacher, Alice 358, 533
Lawrence, Mrs 70, 82
Lawson, Dr Don 93, 353
Lazerian, Sister PBVM 24, 25, 511
Le Févre, RJW 31, 33-35, 367-372, 374, 512
Legge, John 382
Leo XIII, Pope 13, 453-54
Leung, KY 515
Lewis, Mary (O'Collins) 62, 65
Lightfoot, Group Captain 367, 370
Lowe, Sir Charles 151, 153, 518
Lunn, Arnold 86, 88
Lusby, Elizabeth (Hogan) 512
Lyons, Mother Ursula IBVM 94

M

MacArthur II, Douglas 230-32, 524
Macgillicuddy, Ellie 65, 534
Madain, Mr 264
Magdalen Rev Mother IBVM 94
Malcolmson, RD 519
Maluste, Mr and Mrs 305, 308

INDEX OF NAMES

Manly, Joan 365, 514
Mannix, Archbishop Daniel 39, 471, 512
Margaret, HRH Princess 44
Marie-Anne 479-85, 536
Marron, Richard 63
Martin, Bill 26
Martin, David 26
Martin, Geoff 26
Martin, Judge William (Bill) 25-26, 59
Martin, Margaret 26
Martin, Paul 26
Martin, Valda (Moira's sister) 24-25, 58-59, 61, 63, 75
Massand, BK 188-89, 521
Mathias, Rev 519
Matthews, AG 57, 513
McArthur, Mr 471
McBride, Miss 176
McCann, Dr Charles 26, 59, 80, 511
McCann, Elizabeth 26
McCann, Genevieve 26
McCann, Joan 26
McCann, Judy 26
McCann, June (Moira's sister) 24, 26, 37-38, 58, 59, 61, 78, 79-81, 511-12
McCann, Margaret 26, 310
McCann, Patricia 26
McCarthy family (Ireland) 461
McDonald, Nancy 69, 103, 514
McDougall, Miss 471
McEwen, Sir John 273, 524
McGinnis, Patrick 426
McGinnis, Lena (Dynon) 426
McGuire, Paul 99, 100, 104, 514
McGullicuddy, Ellie 65, 534
McInerney, Sir Murray 223-25, 352-53, 478, 524, 532

McKay, Andrew 247
McMahon, William 172, 216-17, 238-39, 252, 273, 293, 331-33, 334, 337, 410, 523-25, 531, 534
McManus, Senator Frank 155-56
Mehta, Mr and Mrs AS (Calcutta) 303-5
Mehta, RS (Bombay) 307
Menzies, Sir Robert Gordon 125, 132, 136-37, 149-50, 153, 159, 164, 172, 188, 191-93, 205, 208-9, 210-14, 239, 254, 292, 322-23, 327-28, 410-11, 476, 516-18, 521-23, 530
Moline, Archbishop Robert 147-8, 517
Molomby, John 309
Molomby, Leah 309
Molony, Bill and Mona 70
Molony, Rev Father John 70
Mooney, RH 289
Moore, Right Rev Monsignor 440
Moorees, Gwen 82
Moraes, Frank 190-91, 309, 522
Moran, Bishop 177, 222
Morgan, Colonel 379
Moriau, Robert 515
Mornane, John 63
Mornane, Michael 426, 429
Mornane, Annie (Dynon) 426, 430, 429
Morrison, Dr George C 492, 514
Morton, Lord (of Henryton) 138
Moss, Joe 49
Moulik, J 246
Murphy, Elsie (Shelton) 23
Murphy, Father Jeremiah SJ 63
Murphy, Maude 61, 63
Mussolini, Benito 12, 446, 450, 474
Muthachen, Mr and Mrs 304

Muthiah, Mr and Mrs 314
Mutimer, Pat 204, 530

N

Nagarajan, Dr 307
Nagarajan, Usha 307
Naidu, Mrs J 530
Nanjappa, Mr and Mrs V 315
Nehru, Jawaharlal 179, 190, 523
Newman, Eileen (Shelton) 23, 67, 365
Newton, Robert 43
Nomoto, Mr and Mrs M 163, 515
Noone, Dr Val 203, 206, 522

O

O'Collins, Maeve 62
O'Collins, Dympna 513
O'Collins, Glynn 97
O'Collins, Joan 62
O'Connell, GJ 520
O'Dwyer, Rev Father James SJ 471
Okuhara, Y 519
Oldham, Trevor and Kathleen 106, 514
O'Mahoney, Rev Father M 63
Opperman, Hubert 164, 172, 282, 519-20
Ottonello, Dr Luciano 74

P

Paget, Colonel 379
Paltridge, Senator 165
Pandit, Mrs Vijaya Lakshmi (Nehru) 215, 523
Parslow, HE 289, 290
Pasquill, Mr 377
Pathak, Captain and Mrs 304
Pearce, Lord Justice 138
Peters, Moira 66, 422, 535

Phillips, Rev H Palmer 514
Pisetti, Professor 73
Pius XII, Pope 67, 86, 88, 100, 400
Pollack, Cr Julius 530
Powicke, Professor FM 18, 511
Pratt, Davidson 379
Prentiss, Colonel 379
Preston, Rev Arthur 530
Pringle, JN Douglas 300, 303, 529
Probyn, Miss I 519
Purkis, Mr 377

R

Rahman, Sheikh Mujibur 334, 336, 338
Ranger, Rev Father Peter 280, 528
Ray, Professor S 521
Regan, Father Michael 458, 465
Reid, Len S 166, 328, 339, 519, 521, 530
Reid, Sir George 355, 532
Ridley, Stanley 515
Rivett, Rohan 347-8, 523, 530, 532
Robinson, Giles 536
Rodeck, Mrs Ernest 60
Rodgers, JA 166, 519
Rosenblum, Alec A 109, 110-13, 114, 120-22, 124, 515-16
Rosenthal, Adelaide 310, 313
Rosenthal, Newman 310, 313, 519, 521, 523, 530
Ryan, Mr JP and Mrs Leonore 203, 530
Ryan, Susan 23

S

Sadiq, Hon G 263-65, 526
Salisbury, Sir Edward 82

INDEX OF NAMES

Sambell, Rt Rev G T 519
Sangtani, Mr and Mrs Atur 311
Sapru, Shri SN 300-3, 338, 531
Sathaye, SN 307
Scott, David 521, 523
Selby, Mr Justice 137, 138
Sen, Mr and Mrs SK 306, 310, 313
Shann, KCO 526
Shannon, Sqdn Leader Dave 40
Shar, Sarla 302, 306
Shastri, Lal Bahudur 12, 190-91, 194, 199, 323, 521-22
Sheehan, Ellen 422
Shelton, Alan P W (Moira's brother) 24, 26, 37-54, 83-4, 356, 512
Shelton, Carol 26, 356
Shelton, David (Moira's brother) 24, 26, 38, 52, 59, 63, 65
Shelton, Dr James 23, 366
Shelton, Dr Grantley 23
Shelton, Dr Percy (Moira's father) 23- 26, 27, 29, 37, 59-60, 63, 97, 98, 365-66, 511-512, 514
Shelton, Harry 23
Shelton, Henry 23, 27, 365
Shelton, Jill 26, 356
Shelton, Katrina 26, 356
Shelton, Lily (Johnston) (Moira's mother) 18-19, 23-24, 29, 36, 59-60, 63, 365-66, 511
Shelton, Mark 26, 355-56, 532
Shelton, Valery (Mornement) 26
Simonds, His Grace Archbishop J D 219, 222-25
Sinha, Dr NH 530
Skipper, Major 377
Smith, Bernadette 357-58, 532
Smith, KJ 286, 289, 293, 528-29
Smith, Pat 97

Smithies, MWB 194, 207, 404-05, 522, 534
Snedden, B (later Sir Billy) 282, 285-88, 528-29
Spillane, Maurice 458-64
Stivala, Captain GF 515
Stoneham, Hon C 521
Strigari, Dr Vittorio 169, 175
Subramaniam, Hon C 193, 232-33, 406
Suhr, Mrs N 530

T

Tagore, Rabindranath 180, 496
Tange, Sir Arthur H 195, 412
Temby, Harold 514
Teresa, Rev Mother MC 12, 262, 276, 303, 319, 320, 527-28, 530
Thiagaraj, D Henry 354, 526, 532
Thomas, AM 302, 304, 312, 330-31, 531
Thompson, Lindsay HS 145, 321
Thompson, Major Robert 382
Thompson, N, SM 289, 291, 292
Thomson, Peter 519
Tobin, Wilf 48
Trewin, Squadron Leader AH 369, 370, 372, 374, 380
Trompf, Flying Officer PA 374, 380
Trowbridge, Michele Mary (Dynon) 93, 96, 301, 310, 350, 452, 456, 458, 496-98
Trowbridge, Tony 452
Turner, Squadron Leader W 372
Tyagi, Dr Mahavir 194, 280, 522, 528
Tyndall, Father Robert J SJ 536, 471, 472, 473

V

Vaccari, Dr V 73-74
van Straaten, Captain FGA 515
Veitch, HA 282, 284-85, 287-89
Verma, R 357, 532
Vinayakam, Mr and Mrs 313
Vincent, Senator 156-57, 518
Vokes, Miss 84

W

Walker, Turner 377
Ward, Mary IBVM 98, 514
Warner, Denis 151, 186, 187, 357, 390, 518, 519, 521, 530, 532
Watt, Corporal 373
Wearne, Norman 530
Webb, Rex 203
Webster, Gwen 94, 96
Wedgwood, Senator Ivy 139, 142
Wells, Warrant Officer 382
Welsh, Wally 41, 45, 47, 50-51
Whitaker, Miss 496
White, Dr Glynn 96
White, HD 523
Whitlam, E Gough 149, 187, 240, 251, 252, 526
Wickham, Benjamin and Tabetha 24
Williams, Frank 309
Williams JR 527
Wilson, Jenny 106, 514
Winship, Sister Ruth (Mother Assumpta) IBVM 19, 94, 101, 102, 493, 511, 514
Wood, Rev Dr AH 519
Wright, Davern 180
Wright, Senator Reginald 135-36, 138

Y

Yamanishi, Makiko 163
Yarnold, Rt Rev SE 519

Z

Zietek, Mrs GG 515
Zutshi, Mr 264

References

1. Mother Gonzaga Barry IBVM (Institute of the Blessed Virgin Mary).

Chapter 1 'Those whom the gods love, die young.'

2. Professor FM Powicke, Regius Professor of Modern History at University of Oxford, delivering the Riddell Memorial Lecture on 'History, Freedom and Religion' before the University of Durham at King's College Newcastle on Tyne. November 1937.
3. Sister Ruth Winship IBVM was a friend of Moira's. As school girls, they had been contemporaries at Loreto Convent, Toorak and both studied science at the University of Melbourne.

Chapter 2 Moira Lenore Shelton—the early years

4. 'Weddings. Dr. Percy Shelton to Miss Lily Johnston', *Table Talk* (Melbourne, Vic.: 1885-1939) Thursday 6 November p. 10. See Appendix A, A1 for full report.
5. Notes taken by John F Dynon during his meeting with Sister Katherine Curtain, Presentation Convent, Elsternwick, 10 June 1982.
6. Notes taken by John F Dynon during his meeting with Sister Lazerian, Presentation Convent, Elsternwick, 10 June 1982.
7. McCann, C & J, *Our Story*, self-published, December 2010, pp. 8, 10.
8. ibid, p. 10.
9. Later, Sir Frank Macfarlane Burnet, a highly decorated Australian scientist. Knighted in 1951, he was awarded the Nobel Prize for physiology or medicine for 'discovery of acquired immunological tolerance' in 1960 and was the first recipient of Australian of the Year Award (1960).
10. 'Influenza Virus Tests on Medical Students', *The Herald* (Melbourne, Vic.), 6 September 1940, p. 5.
11. Excerpts from letters from Douglas S Kay to John F Dynon, 27 April 1983 and 26 May 1983.

Chapter 3 Moira's war service and the mustard gas trials

12 It was not until 31 August 1942 that the War Cabinet decided that women's auxiliaries were to be 'enlisted' under the Defence Act.

13 Royal Australian Air Force Certificate of Service and Discharge for Moira Lenore Shelton.

14 'New W.A.A.A.F. Officers; Many from Ranks', *The Age* (Melbourne, Vic.), 9 October 1942, p. 3.

15 Flight Officer Moira Shelton's war service account. This was written by Moira after she had been released from service. A copy of this account was among Moira's personal papers. See Appendix A, A2 for full account.

16 'Woman's Hazardous Job in Chemical Warfare Unit', *The Argus* (Melb, Vic.), 28 August 1946, p. 9.

17 Open letter from RJW Le Févre, Professor of Chemistry, University of Sydney, 26 November 1946.

18 'Churchill Wanted to Gas the Germans', *The National Times*, 16–22 May 1982, quoting Paxman, J. and Harris, R., 1982, *A Higher Form of Killing: The Secret History of Chemical and Biological Warfare*, Chatto and Windus.

Chapter 4 Moira's brother, RAAF Flying Officer Alan Shelton

19 Letter to Moira from her sister, June Shelton, 11 March 1945.

20 Letter to Dr P Shelton from Catholic Archbishop of Melbourne, Dr D Mannix, 15 March 1945.

21 Auxiliary Territorial Service

22 The editors compiled this account from notes taken by John F Dynon during his meeting with Pat Hogan on 12 October 1980; supplemented by Statement of PJ Hogan, 5 June 1945: 'Re – Loss of Halifax Aircraft NR.179 on the night of 3rd March 1945'; and copy of personal record of Pat Hogan dated 2 November 1980 and other records provided by Pat Hogan's daughter, Elizabeth Lusby, to Jacinta Efthim on 11 September 2017.

23 Batchelder, A, 'His Life was Selfless and Unsullied', *Aerogram*, June 2016. The Friends of the RAAF Museum Inc.

REFERENCES

Chapter 5 Moira's post-war social activities and her newsworthy hats

24 Matthews, AG and Shelton, ML, 'A Streptomycin Sensitivity Test', *The Medical Journal of Australia*, 27 September 1947, p. 387.

25 'Demobilised', *The Argus* (Melbourne, Vic.), The Life of Melbourne, 12 August 1946, p. 6.

26 "A Topping Topper', *The Argus* (Melbourne, Vic.), The Life of Melbourne, 16 September 1946, p. 6.

27 'Government House Party for Royal Navy', *The Sun* (Melbourne, Vic.), 15 July 1947.

28 'Oaks Day 1947', *The Argus* (Melbourne, Vic.), 7 November 1947, p. 10.

29 'Small Crowd at Flemington Races', *The Argus* (Melbourne, Vic.), The Life of Melbourne, 1 December 1947, p. 7.

30 This engagement did not proceed. Moira decided that Kevin was not the one for her. Coincidentally, Kevin Coleman married Dympna O'Collins, the second cousin of John F Dynon.

31 'Interesting engagement', *The Argus* (Melbourne, Vic.), The Life of Melbourne, 5 August 1948, p. 7.

32 'Caulfield Cup eve cabaret ball', *The Advocate*, (Melbourne, Vic.), 28 October 1948, p. 16.

33 'Party at Club for Friends', *The Argus* (Melbourne, Vic.), 26 January 1950, p. 8.

34 'Engaged Today', *The Herald* (Melbourne, Vic.), 21 August 1950, p. 13.

35 'Cherry Red', *The Age* (Melbourne, Vic.), 16 November 1950, p. 7.

36 'Pre-Wedding', *The Age* (Melbourne, Vic.), 20 November 1950, p. 5.

37 'Household Hints Tea', *The Age* (Melbourne, Vic.), 22 November 1950, p. 5.

38 'Gift Tea', *The Herald* (Melbourne, Vic.), 6 November 1950, p. 13.

39 'Pre-wedding', *The Age* (Melbourne, Vic.), 25 November 1950, p. 5.

Chapter 6 Wedding and honeymoon

40 'Bride in Blue at College Chapel', *The Herald* (Melbourne, Vic.), Woman's World, 2 December 1950.

Chapter 7 The Spirit of Loreto Federation

41 Excerpt from letter from Mother Gonzaga Barry IBVM in *Eucalyptus Blossoms*, Loretto magazine, 8 December 1897. Ballarat.

42 Letter from Moira to Mrs Margaret Dynon, 2 March 1955.

43 'Dr P.G. Shelton', *The Age* (Melbourne, Vic.), 31 October 1955.
44 http://www.loreto.org.au/about-us/our-spirituality/pray-with-mary-ward/;http://www.congregatiojesu.org/en/maryward_her_story.asp; https: //ibvm.us/About/Mary-Ward; http://www.marywarddocumentary.com/life.htm [Accessed 4 January 2020].
45 Letter to Moira from Mr Paul McGuire, Australian Legation Rome, 29 November 1955.
46 Letter to Moira from Mother Colombiere IBVM, Provincial Superior of the Institute in Australia, 17 December 1955.
47 Excerpt from letter to Moira from Mother Assumpta IBVM, 1 October 1965.
48 Letter written by Mother Gonzaga Barry IBVM in *Eucalyptus Blossoms*, Loretto magazine, 7 March 1887. Ballarat.

Chapter 8 Australian Association for the United Nations Malvern Branch

49 Reverend H Palmer Phillips, President of the Victorian Division of AAUN.
50 23 October 1951 was the eve of United Nations Day. United Nations Day is celebrated on 24 October each year. The UN was officially created on 24 October 1945 when the UN Charter was signed by representatives of 50 countries.
51 AAUN Malvern Branch Office Bearers for 1952 were: President, the Mayor of Malvern; Vice Presidents, Dr George Morrison, The Hon. Trevor Oldham, MLA, Mr H Temby and Mr John F Dynon; Hon. Secretary, Mrs Moira Dynon; Assistant Hon. Secretary, Miss Nancy McDonald and Hon. Treasurer, Miss Joan Manly.
52 Excerpt from Programme for United Nations 7th Birthday Eve celebrations, AAUN Malvern Branch, Malvern Town Hall, 23 October 1952.
53 23 October 1952 at Malvern Town Hall.
54 General Sir Dallas Brooks was also patron of the Victorian Division of AAUN.
55 Letter from Sister Mary Aloysius, Holy Eucharist School, Chadstone to John F Dynon, 17 November 1953.
56 Letter from Jenny Wilson, President of the United Nations Club, St Catherine's School, Toorak to John F Dynon, dated 2 April.

REFERENCES

57 Schools represented at fourth Malvern AAUN schoolchildren's rally at Metro Malvern on 28 March 1958 were De La Salle College, Caulfield Technical School, Christian Brothers College, Malvern Central School, St Kevin's College, Malvern Girls School, St Catherine's, Loreto Convent, Lauriston Girls School, Kildara College, St Joseph's Girls School, Holy Eucharist School, Korowa and St Mary's School.

58 The Official Party at fourth Malvern AAUN schoolchildren's rally at Metro Malvern, 28 March 1958 comprised: **America**: Mr Graham R Hall, Consul-General and Mrs Hall; **Austria**: Mrs GG Zietek (Le Gerant de Consulat) and Mr LW Zietek; **Canada**: Mr HS Hay; **Czechoslovak Republic**: Mr Bilek; **The Republic of China**: Mr KY Leung, Consul and Mrs Leung; **Dominican Republic**: Mr Stanley Ridley, Consul and Mrs Ridley; **France**: M. Robert Moriau, Vice-Consul and Madame Moriau; **Greece**: Mr Nicolas D Coumbos, Consul; **Japan**: Mr M Nomoto, Consul and Mrs Nomoto; **Malta**: Captain GFL Stivala, High Commissioner and Mrs Stivala; **Netherlands**; Captain FGH van Straaten, Naval Attache and Mrs van Straaten; **Phillipines**: Captain E del Castillo, Armed Services Attaché and Mrs del Castillo; **Thailand**: Mr Julian Fader, Consular Secretary and **United Kingdom**: Commander Hayward-Butt, Staff Service Liaison and Mrs Hayward-Butt.

59 UN General Assembly Resolution 1353 (XIV) of 1959, New York.

60 Later, Sir Zelman Cowen, who became the 19th Governor-General of Australia.

Chapter 9 President and Secretary of Stonnington Branch of the Liberal Party

61 'Forming a new party', *The Age* (Melbourne, Vic.), Letters to the Editor. 6 November 1953.

62 'State Election in Malvern', *The Age* (Melbourne, Vic.), Letters to the Editor. 14 November 1953.

63 'Federal Elections – 10th December, 1955. The Campaign in Higgins'. Report by Alec A Rosenblum, Chairman, Higgins Electorate Committee, 20 February 1956. (Copy report was among the papers of John F Dynon).

64 'Federal Elections 22nd November 1958; The Campaign in Higgins'; Report by Alec A Rosenblum, Chairman, Higgins Electorate Committee, 9 January 1959. (Copy report was among the papers of John F Dynon).

65 Resolution passed by special meeting of members of Stonnington Branch LCP, 20 April 1959 (included in letter to members of Stonnington Branch LCP, 4 May 1959).

66 Excerpt from letter from Treasurer, Harold Holt to Moira, Hon. Sec. of Stonnington Branch LCP, 24 April 1959. ©Commonwealth of Australia

67 'Branch wants to sack Mr Holt', *Daily Mirror* (Sydney, NSW), 27 April 1959. Quoted in Confidential Information from John F Dynon to members of Committee of Stonnington Branch LCP, 20 May 1959.

68 *Daily Mirror* (Sydney, NSW), Letters to the Editor; Quoted in Confidential Information from John F Dynon to members of Committee of Stonnington Branch LCP, 20 May 1959.

69 'Mr Holt has influenza', *The Age* (Melbourne, Vic.), 18 May 1959, p. 3.

70 Letter from Alec A Rosenblum to John F Dynon, 30 April 1959, quoted in Confidential Information from John F Dynon to members of Committee of Stonnington Branch LCP, 20 May 1959.

71 Confidential Information from John F Dynon to members of Committee of Stonnington Branch LCP, 20 May 1959.

72 Letter from Moira, Hon. Sec. Stonnington Branch to Mr McConnell, General Secretary LCP, 2 May 1959.

Chapter 10 Section 28 (m)

73 Printed Joint Policy Speech of Prime Minister The Rt. Hon. RG Menzies, delivered in the Canterbury Memorial Hall on 29 October 1958, p. 18; and supplementary statements published conjointly with the broadcast speech, p. 29.

74 Section 51, (xxi, Marriage); (xxii, Divorce and matrimonial causes) of the *Australian Constitution*.

75 'Liberal Party has no mandate for Divorce Bill. Branch President Threatens to Resign', *The Advocate* (Melbourne, Vic.), 26 November 1959.

76 Australia, House of Representatives 18 November 1959, *Debates*, vol. 47, p. 2858.

77 Australia, House of Representatives 17 November 1959, *Debates*, vol. 47, pp. 2756–2760.

78 Australia, House of Representatives 17 November 1959, *Debates*, vol. 47, p. 2773.

79 Australia, House of Representatives 18 November 1959, *Debates*, vol. 47, p. 2860.

REFERENCES

80 Australia, House of Representatives 18 August 1959, *Debates*, vol. 34, p. 291.

81 Australia, House of Representatives 18 August 1959, *Debates*, vol. 34, p. 288.

82 Australia, Senate 27 November 1959, *Debates*, vol. 48, p. 1971.

83 Australia, House of Representatives 17 November 1959, *Debates*, vol. 47, p. 2773.

84 Cox, EH, 'Safeguards Plan for Divorce', *The Herald* (Melbourne, Vic.), 19 November 1959, p. 7.

85 Excerpt from letter to John F Dynon from Prime Minister The Rt. Hon. RG Menzies, 17 April 1962. ©Commonwealth of Australia

86 'Divorce curb "dead letter"' *The Herald* (Melbourne, Vic.), 8 September 1967, p. 5.

87 Australia, Senate 24 November 1959, *Debates*, vol. 48, p. 1783.

88 Letter from John F Dynon to all members of Stonnington Branch LCP, 22 December 1959.

89 Excerpt from letter from Moira to Mrs E Haynes, Secretary of the Women's Sections of the LCP, December 1959.

90 Letter to John and Moira Dynon from Mrs Sylvia Blogg, East Malvern, c. January 1960.

91 Letter from The Hon. Henry E Bolte (later Sir Henry Bolte) Premier of Victoria to Mr J Dynon, 11 January 1960.

Chapter 11 The petition to Her Majesty

92 'LCP Branch: No OK yet for Holt', *The Herald*, (Melbourne, Vic.), 29 March 1960, p. 1.

93 Section 59 of the *Australian Constitution*.

94 Petition to Her Majesty under Section 59 of the *Australian Constitution* seeking disallowance or amendment of *Matrimonial Causes Act 1959*. See Appendix A, A3 for full text of petition.

95 Letter to John S [sic] Dynon, from ML Tyrrell, Official Secretary to the Governor-General, Government House Canberra, 16 December 1960.

96 Letter to John F Dynon from Anglican Archbishop of Perth, Robert Moline, 5 January 1961. Published by permission of the Anglican Diocese of Perth, Western Australia, Archives.

97 Printed notes among John F Dynon's papers: 'Precis of Address by The Hon. Mr Justice Denning. In 1947, at Kings College London, The Hon. Mr Justice Denning delivered a lecture on 'The Divorce Laws'.

98 Australia, House of Representatives 22 March 1961, *Debates*, vol. 12, p. 489.

99 ibid.

100 Reproduced verbatim from John F Dynon's manuscript.

Chapter 12 Australian-Japanese children in Kure

101 Denis Warner was a distinguished Melbourne journalist, war correspondent and historian. He was later awarded an OBE and CMG.

102 Special Report on Australian-Japanese Children in Japan (Prepared by Mrs. John F. Dynon on behalf of the Australian-Asian Association of Victoria. July, 1960.) See Appendix A, A4 for full report.

103 Spoken by Sir Charles Lowe in January 1960. Reported in Moira's AAAV Progress Report No. 3 Australian-Japanese children, December 1962.

104 Australia, House of Representatives 8 September 1960, *Debates*, vol 36, p. 1052 (Prime Minister The Rt. Hon. RG Menzies responding to question on notice by Mr E Ward to the Acting Treasurer).

105 Australia, House of Representatives 29 March 1960, *Debates*, vol. 13, p. 701.

106 ibid. p. 646.

107 Australia, House of Representatives 1 October 1959, *Debates*, vol. 40, p. 1636.

108 Resolution moved at LCP Victorian State Conference, 1958, as recorded by John F Dynon.

109 Australia, Senate 28 September 1961, *Debates*, vol. 39, pp. 728–729.

110 ibid. p. 732.

111 Excerpt from letter from Moira to Senator Vincent, 10 October 1961.

112 Moira's Progress Report No. 2 Australian-Japanese children, 2 October 1962.

113 Keith Dunstan was quoted in Moira's 1964 address, 'The Australian-Japanese children'. www.moiradynon.com.au

114 Moira's AAAV Progress Report No. 3 Australian-Japanese children, December 1962.

REFERENCES

115 Excerpt from Press statement by Minister for Immigration, AR Downer, 1 December 1962. ©Commonwealth of Australia

116 'Statement on waifs criticised', *The Herald* (Melbourne, Vic.), 3 December 1962.

117 Australia, House of Representatives 4 December 1962, *Debates*, vol. 49, p. 2839.

118 ibid.

119 Afternoon tea hosted by Moira at her home, Monday, 29 April 1963.

120 The AJ Ferguson Memorial Appeal for Australian-Japanese Children in Japan. The Appeal Director was Mr JA Rodgers, and the committee members were: President: LS Reid, MLA, Vice-Presidents: Dr Jim Cairns, MHR, Rev Father L Clarke, Lady Clunies Ross, Dame Mary Daly, Dr EE Dunlop, RD Malcolmson, Rev Mathias, Rt Rev GT Sambell, Denis Warner, Rev Dr AH Wood, Rev SE Yarnold. Committee: Mrs Gertrude Bray, WW Buck, Cr F Burns, RR Buxton, Rev Frank Byatt, Mrs Hugh Campbell, Mrs HH Copley, Mrs Moira Dynon, NA Ferguson, Rev H Girvan, Mrs GWT Hall, Miss I Probyn, Newman Rosenthal, Peter Thomson, Hon. Treasurer: AB Kaines FCA, Secretary: Mrs JL Coulthard.

121 Address by Moira: 'The Australian-Japanese children', 1964. www.moiradynon.com.au

122 Australia, House of Representatives 12 May 1964, *Debates*, vol. 20, p. 1797.

123 Excerpt from letter to Moira from Minister for Immigration, Hubert Opperman MHR, 22 September 1964. ©Commonwealth of Australia

124 Australia, Senate 21 October 1964, *Debates*, vol. 43, p. 1146.

125 ibid.

126 Mrs JF Dynon, Messrs LS Reid, NA Ferguson, WW Buck and Reverend F Byatt were appointed, by an executive meeting of Australian-Asian Association of Victoria on 29 March 1965, trustees to administer the fund for the AJ Ferguson Memorial Appeal for Australian-Japanese Children in Japan.

127 Letter from Mayor of the City of Kure Japan, Y Okuhara, to NA Ferguson, Trustee of the Fund The AJ. Ferguson Memorial Appeal, 11 June 1969.

Chapter 13 Italian welfare

128 Special benefit concert at the Palais Theatre, St Kilda, Thursday, 7 September 1961.

129 Italo-Australian Welfare Association fundraising party, 3 December 1961.

130 Letter to Moira from Vice-Consul of Italy in Australia, M Jacobucci, 14 December 1962.

131 Australia, House of Representatives 27 November 1962, *Debates*, vol. 48, pp. 2556–2557, in answer to a question by Mr Courtnay MHR.

132 Press conference held on 30 January 1963.

133 The English translation of the medical reports certified to by the Consul-General of Italy in Australia.

134 Excerpt from letter to John F Dynon from AR Downer, Minister for Immigration, 14 June 1963. ©Commonwealth of Australia

135 'The Fontanas are together again. Tears, laughter at the airport', *The Herald* (Melbourne, Vic.), 3 August 1963.

136 Australia, House of Representatives 14 October 1965, *Debates*, vol. 41, p. 1813, Mr Opperman, Minister for Immigration.

137 Australia, House of Representatives 11 November 1964, *Debates*, vol. 46, pp. 2784–2785.

138 *The Australian*, 1 April 1966.

139 Cox, EH, *The Herald* (Melbourne, Vic.), 31 March 1966, p. 1.

140 Joint Statement concerning Proposed Policy of the Commonwealth Government of Australia to Conscript a Minority of Aliens Resident in Australia for Military Service including Service Overseas by James M Galbally and Moira Dynon, 15 August 1966. See Appendix A, A5 for full statement.

Chapter 14 Catholic Women's League

141 In 1970, the Catholic Women's Social Guild of Victoria and Wagga Wagga was renamed the Catholic Women's League (CWL).

142 The Australian Women's Register 2000-2015 http://www.women australia.info/biogs/AWE0765b.htm [Accessed 4 January 2020].

143 Victoria, Legislative Council 29 April 1964, *Debates*, pp. 4079, 4089, 4094 and 4132. (The Hon. GJ O' Connell MLC).

144 Excerpt from talk written by Moira in 1965, 'Friendship in the World'. www.moiradynon.com.au

145 ibid

146 *Statement on Abortion* prepared by Moira Dynon and released by National Executive Committee Australian Council of Catholic Women, 30 April 1968. See Appendix A, A6 for full statement.

147 Address by Moira, 'Be of Good Courage' at Corowa, NSW, Friday 6 March 1970. www.moiradynon.com.au

Chapter 15 Milk for India

148 Drieberg, T, 'Hunger Racks India. Children faint in School from lack of food', *The Herald* (Melbourne, Vic.), 9 November 1964, p. 5.

149 Editorial, 'World can Aid India', *The Herald* (Melbourne, Vic.), 10 November 1964, p. 4.

150 Excerpt from letter from Denis Warner to John F Dynon, 12 July 1977.

151 The speakers at this meeting were Mr Len S Reid, MLA; Mr Clive Stoneham, MLA, Leader of the State Opposition; Dr JF Cairns, MHR; Mr EMC Fox, MHR; Rev F Byatt, Secretary, Victorian State Committee for Inter-Church Aid; Professor S Ray, Head, Indian Studies Department, University of Melbourne; Mr Newman Rosenthal, Head, Audio-Visual Aids Department, University of Melbourne; Mr David Scott, Director, Community Aid Abroad; Dr EE Dunlop, Chairman, Australian-Asian Association of Victoria; Dr JG Hurley, President, Jesuit Indian Mission Committee; Mrs G Frost, President, National Council of Women of Victoria, and Executive Committee Member, Freedom from Hunger Campaign; Professor Edward Gault, Royal Australasian College of Surgeons.

152 Letter from Moira to Prime Minister The Rt. Hon. RG Menzies, 24 November 1964.

153 Excerpt from letter from Moira to BK Massand, High Commissioner for India in Canberra, 26 November 1964.

154 Excerpt from letter to Moira from BK Massand, High Commissioner for India in Canberra, 4 December 1964.

155 'A family with 2600 presents for India', *The Sun* (Melbourne, Vic.), 18 December 1964.

156 Telegram from Moira to The Prime Minister of India, 24 December 1964.

157 Telegram to Dynon Chairman Aid for India Special meeting from Joint Secretary to the Prime Minister India Foreign (date indecipherable; 'Ack 8-1-65').

158 Moraes, F, *Nehru – Sunlight and Shadow*, Jaico Publishing House, Bombay, 1964.

159 Telegram to Moira from Prime Minister The Rt. Hon. RG Menzies, 30 December 1964. ©Commonwealth of Australia

160 Excerpt from telegram from Moira to Prime Minister The Rt. Hon. RG Menzies, 30 December 1964.

161 Excerpt from letter to Moira from Prime Minister The Rt. Hon. RG Menzies, 29 December 1964. ©Commonwealth of Australia

162 Excerpt from letter from Moira to Prime Minister The Rt. Hon. RG Menzies, 20 January 1965.

163 Telegram to Moira from Joint Secretary to the Prime Minister Foreign, July 1965.

164 Excerpt from letter to Moira from Mahavir Tyagi, Indian Minister for Rehabilitation, 3 September 1965.

165 Florence Mary Hagelthorn (1905–1994) was a Catholic poet, writer and journalist.

166 Hazlethorn, FM, 'Friendship in the World', *The Advocate* (Melbourne, Vic), 26 August 1965.

Chapter 16 Feeling sorry won't help—milk will

167 Dr Val Noone, 'NOTES on Val Noone's Milk for India file, 15 May 2019 for Jacinta Efthim'.

168 Moira's address at PSA (Pleasant Sunday Afternoon) Adelaide, 17 April 1966.

Chapter 17 Reconsidering the policy of Prime Minister Menzies

169 Dr Val Noone, Notes on draft Moira Dynon biography, 24 May 2019.

170 Excerpt from letter to Moira from MWB Smithies, for the Secretary, Department of External Affairs, 7 June 1965. ©Commonwealth of Australia. See Appendix A, A7 for full letter.

171 Excerpt from letter to Moira from LJ Arnott, Assistant Secretary, Department of External Affairs, 13 July 1965. ©Commonwealth of Australia

172 Excerpt from letter from Moira to Arthur Calwell, Leader of the Federal Opposition, 15 July 1965.

173 Excerpt from letter from Moira to the Secretary, Department of External Affairs, marked 'attention: Mr LJ Arnott', 19 July 1965.

REFERENCES

174 ibid

175 Excerpt from letter to Moira from HD White, Acting Assistant Secretary, Department of External Affairs, 3 November 1965. ©Commonwealth of Australia

176 Telegram from Moira to Prime Minister The Rt. Hon. RG Menzies, 2 December 1965.

177 Telegram from Moira to Prime Minister The Rt. Hon. RG Menzies, 10 December 1965.

178 Telegram to Moira from Prime Minister The Rt. Hon. RG Menzies, 15 January 1966. ©Commonwealth of Australia

179 Excerpt from telegram from Moira to Prime Minister The Rt. Hon. RG Menzies, 15 January 1966.

180 Telegram from Moira to Averell Harriman, US President's Envoy to Australia, 9 January 1966.

181 Telegram to Moira from Averell Harriman, 11 January 1966.

182 Excerpt from letter to Moira from DO Hay, First Assistant Secretary, Department of External Affairs, Canberra, 18 February 1966. ©Commonwealth of Australia

183 Food for India meetings at Melbourne Town Hall on Wednesday, 23 February 1966. Speakers included Sir John Crawford, Mr Newman Rosenthal, Mr Rohan Rivett and Mr David Scott.

184 Memorandum to the Prime Minister The Rt. Hon. HE Holt, regarding Australian Food Assistance to India, February 1966. See Appendix A, A8 for full memorandum.

185 Letter to Moira from Prime Minister The Rt. Hon. HE Holt, 7 March 1966. ©Commonwealth of Australia

186 Mrs Pandit was a distinguished Indian diplomat who, in 1953, was the first female President of the United Nations General Assembly. Her late brother, Jawaharlal Nehru, was the first Prime Minister of India.

187 'Feels so much left undone', *The Herald* (Melbourne, Vic.), 20 May 1966, p. 2.

188 Telegram from Moira to Prime Minister The Rt. Hon. HE Holt, c/- The Prime Minister of the United Kingdom, 10 Downing Street, London, 8 July 1966.

189 Excerpt from telegram from Moira to Paul Hasluck, Minister for External Affairs, 8 July 1966 (and similar telegram from Moira to Federal Treasurer, William McMahon, 8 July 1966).

190 Excerpt from telegram to Moira from Treasurer William McMahon, 14 July 1966. ©Commonwealth of Australia

191 Excerpt from letter to Moira from Paul Hasluck, Minister for External Affairs, 13 July 1966. ©Commonwealth of Australia

Chapter 18 A Pleasant Sunday Afternoon

192 This letter is not reproduced. Copyright resides elsewhere.

193 John and Moira later learned that this Catholic man was Arthur Calwell.

194 Letter from John F Dynon to Right Reverend Monsignor LM Clarke, Vicar General, St Patrick's Cathedral Melbourne, 18 June 1966.

195 Letter from Moira to Right Reverend Monsignor LM Clarke, Vicar General, St Patrick's Cathedral Melbourne, 18 June 1966.

196 Excerpt from letter from John F Dynon to His Honour Mr Justice McInerney, Supreme Court of Victoria, 19 June 1966.

Chapter 19 Politicians, politics and resilience

197 Letter from Moira to President LB Johnson, US President, 15 October 1966. This letter was enclosed in a letter from Moira to Mr E Clark, US Ambassador, Canberra, 15 October 1966.

198 Telegrams from Moira to Prime Minister The Rt. Hon. HE Holt; Leader of the Opposition, AA Calwell; Leader of the Country Party, J McEwen; and Leader of the Democratic Labor Party, Senator Gair, 24 November 1966.

199 Telegram from Moira to US Senator Robert F Kennedy, Washington, USA, 22 November 1966.

200 Letter to Moira from US Senator Robert F Kennedy, 15 December 1966.

201 Excerpt from copy letter to US Senator Robert F Kennedy from Douglas MacArthur II, Assistant Secretary for Congressional Relations, Department of State, Washington, 12 December 1966. (This copy letter was enclosed in letter to Moira from US Senator Robert F Kennedy, 15 December 1966).

202 Letter from Moira to US Senator Robert F Kennedy, 22 December 1966.

203 Telegram from Moira to US Senator Robert F Kennedy, 23 January 1967.

204 Letter to Moira from US Senator Robert F Kennedy, 9 February 1967.

REFERENCES

205 Excerpt from letter from Moira to Treasurer William McMahon, 16 January 1967. See Appendix A, A9 for full letter.

206 Excerpt from telegram from Moira to Treasurer, William McMahon, 22 February 1967.

207 Excerpt from letter to Moira from Treasurer, William McMahon, 14 March 1967. ©Commonwealth of Australia

208 Excerpt from letter from Moira to Prime Minister The Rt. Hon. HE Holt, 10 March 1967.

209 Australia, House of Representatives 14 March 1967, *Debates*, vol. 11, p. 598.

210 ibid.

211 ibid. pp. 598–599.

212 Australia, House of Representatives 16 March 1967, *Debates*, vol. 11, p. 825.

213 Excerpt from letter from Moira to Prime Minister The Rt. Hon. HE Holt, 18 March 1967.

214 Excerpt from letter to Moira from Paul Hasluck, Minister for External Affairs, 17 March 1967. ©Commonwealth of Australia

215 Telegram from Moira to Prime Minister The Rt. Hon. HE Holt, 21 March 1967.

216 Telegram to Moira from Prime Minister The Rt. Hon. HE Holt, 22 March 1967. ©Commonwealth of Australia

217 Excerpt from telegram from Moira to Prime Minister The Rt. Hon. HE Holt, 28 March 1967.

218 Excerpt from letter to Moira from Prime Minister The Rt. Hon. HE Holt, 2 May 1967. ©Commonwealth of Australia

219 Excerpt from letter from Moira to Prime Minister The Rt. Hon. HE Holt, 8 January 1967.

220 Excerpt from letter to Moira from Prime Minister The Rt. Hon. HE Holt, 26 January 1967. ©Commonwealth of Australia

221 Letter to Moira from DN Chatterjee, High Commissioner for India in Australia, 14 March 1967.

222 'In Black and White', *The Herald* (Melbourne, Vic.), 13 April 1967.

223 'India gets our milk', *The Herald* (Melbourne, Vic.), Letter from Moira to the editor, 15 April 1967.

224 Letter from Acting High Commissioner for India JS Gill to the editor, *The Herald* (Melbourne, Vic.), 6 July 1967. (A copy was sent by JS Gill to Moira).

225 Excerpt from letter from Moira to Mr KCO Shann, CBE First Assistant Secretary, Dept. of External Affairs, 15 May 1967.

Chapter 20 Offer from Shipping Corporation of India

226 Excerpt from letter from Moira to EG Whitlam, Leader of the Opposition, 29 May 1967.

227 Excerpt from letter from Moira to Prime Minister The Rt. Hon. HE Holt, 9 August 1967.

Chapter 21 Eight weeks in India

228 Costigan, Rev. ME, 'With Mrs Dynon in India, Organiser of milk powder campaign Interviewed after eight-week tour', *The Advocate* (Melbourne, Vic.), 2 November 1967.

229 Moira's address for Radio Australia, 8 November 1967.

230 Excerpt from letter from Moira to Mary Clubwala Jadhav (Hon Director of the Bombay seminar), 27 November 1967.

231 Costigan, Rev. ME, *The Advocate* op cit..

232 Excerpt from letter from Moira to D Henry Thiagaraj, Information Officer, Government of Madras, 11 December 1967.

233 Moira's address for Radio Australia op cit..

234 Excerpt from letter from Moira to Prime Minister The Rt. Hon. HE Holt, 6 November 1967.

235 Letter from Moira to GM Sadiq, Chief Minister, Government of Jammu and Kashmir, Srinagar, 28 November 1967.

Chapter 22 The ABC 'Noises Off' Affair

236 Excerpt from letter to Moira from BA Kent, A/Supervisor of Education, ABC Melbourne, 1 May 1967. Reproduced by permission of the Australian Broadcasting Corporation – Library Sales © ABC

237 Excerpt from letter to Moira from Dr John Challis, ABC, 17 July 1967. Reproduced by permission of the Australian Broadcasting Corporation – Library Sales © ABC

238 Programme number 7 was one of the 10 radio programmes in the ABC series for secondary schools –*7 FREEDOM FROM WANT* – to examine the aid work in Asian countries by voluntary aid organizations in

REFERENCES

Australia'. Reproduced by permission of the Australian Broadcasting Corporation – Library Sales © ABC

239 Telegram from Moira to Prime Minister The Rt. Hon. HE Holt, 20 July 1967.

240 Excerpt from letter from Moira to Dr Challis, ABC, 7 August 1967.

241 Letter to Moira from John Challis, ABC, 10 August 1967. Reproduced by permission of the Australian Broadcasting Corporation – Library Sales © ABC

242 Extract from the transcript of an interview between the Indian High Commissioner, Dr Chatterjee and Dr J Challis, recorded in the office of the High Commissioner, 13 March 1967. Reproduced by permission of the Australian Broadcasting Corporation – Library Sales © ABC

243 Letter to Moira from US Senator Robert F Kennedy, 24 July 1967.

244 Excerpt from copy report of William C Gibbons Director, Congressional Liaison, Department of State, Agency for International Development Washington, DC to Robert F Kennedy, United States Senate, 14 July 1967 (enclosed in letter to Moira from Senator Robert F Kennedy, 24 July 1967).

245 Letter to Moira from Prime Minister The Rt. Hon. HE Holt, 26 September 1967. ©Commonwealth of Australia

246 Letter from EJ Bunting, Secretary Prime Minister's Department (63/2918) to JR Williams, Acting General Secretary NSW Teachers' Federation, 24 October 1967. ©Commonwealth of Australia (Copy forwarded to Moira by JR Williams).

247 Letter from Moira to IG Lancaster, General Secretary, NSW Teachers' Federation, 6 November 1967.

248 Excerpt from letter from Moira to Prime Minister The Rt. Hon. HE Holt, 3 November 1967.

249 Excerpt from letter to Moira from EJ Bunting, Secretary, Prime Minister's Department, 16 January 1968. ©Commonwealth of Australia

250 Address by Moira, 'India and The Revolution of Rising Expectations' at PSA Sunday, 21 January 1968. www.moiradynon.com.au

Chapter 23 Making a difference

251 Letter to Moira from Mrs Indira Gandhi Prime Minister of India, 27 July 1968.

252 Mother Teresa MC was the founder of the Missionaries of Charity; now Saint Teresa of Calcutta.

253 Letter to Moira from Mother Teresa MC, 1 January 1970.

254 The Rector of Xavier College referred to Brother Andrew: 'a former student of the College who was known to us as a boy as Ian Travers-Ball. Many of you will have heard of his working out of his Christian commitment for the help of the dying and starving in Calcutta and more recently of his endeavours for the refugees of the current political crisis in Pakistan. Time does not allow me to give a full picture of what this man is or does, but I will be happy to go on record as saying—even if Xavier had produced no-one else in the course of its history that such heroic Christianity would have made the enterprise worthwhile.' (*Xavier College 94th Annual Report* 1971).

255 Letter to Moira from Brother Andrew MC, 25 November 1970.

256 Letter to Moira from Miss Nama Ajgaonkar, Superintendent, Dadar School for the Blind, Bombay, 22 January 1970.

257 Letter to Moira from Bernadette Keans, St Columba's Hospital, Hazaribagh, 1 October 1967.

258 Excerpt from letter to Moira from Mrs TG Hymavathy, Stree Seva Mandir, Women's Tutorial Institute, Madras, 9 July 1969.

259 Letter to Moira from Dr KB Grant, Poona Medical Foundation, Poona, 22 December 1970.

260 Letter to Moira from R Chittiak, social worker and Hon. Liaison Officer, Rangaraya Medical College, Gollaprolu East Godavari District Andhra Pradesh, 26 November 1969.

261 Excerpt from letter to Moira from Indian Minister for Rehabilitation, Mahavir Tyagi, 24 October 1965.

262 Excerpt from copy letter from Father Peter Ranger, Maria Busti parish, Pedong, to the local bishop, 9 October 1968.

Chapter 24 The Prosecution

263 Excerpt from letter to Moira from Mary Howard, India, 17 January 1966.

264 Excerpt from letter from John F Dynon to Mr Snedden, Minister for Immigration, 22 August 1968.

265 Letter to John F Dynon from B Boothby, Private Secretary to the Minister for Immigration, 30 August 1968. ©Commonwealth of Australia.

266 Letter to John F Dynon from KJ Smith, Commonwealth Director of Migration for Victoria, 3 October 1968. ©Commonwealth of Australia.

REFERENCES

267 Excerpt from letter from John F Dynon to Mr Snedden, Minister for Immigration, 9 October 1968.

268 Letter from John F Dynon to Mr Snedden, Minister for Immigration, 26 October 1968.

269 Letter to John F Dynon from 'Webster for Commonwealth Director of Migration', 25 October 1968. ©Commonwealth of Australia

270 Quoted in letter from John F Dynon to Dr Ferrari de Carpi, Consul-General of Italy, 29 November 1968.

271 Charles Francis was appointed a Queen's Counsel in 1969.

272 John F Dynon's notes from the Magistrates' Court hearing, 2 May 1969.

273 'Solicitor freed on charges', *The Age* (Melbourne, Vic.), 3 May 1969.

274 Mr KJ Smith had been present at the Royale Ballroom function in 1967 when John F Dynon was awarded an honour by the Italian government in recognition of his work in reuniting Italian families in Australia.

Chapter 25 India revisited—Letters between Moira and John

275 Letter to Moira from Nancy Dobson, Hon. Sec. Australian-Asian Association of Victoria, 22 January 1969.

276 Letter to Moira from John F Dynon, 27 January 1969.

277 Sydney Morning Herald.

278 The Prosecution.

279 Letter from Moira to John F Dynon, 26 January 1969.

280 JN Douglas Pringle was editor of the *Sydney Morning Herald*.

281 Letter to Moira from John F Dynon, 28 January 1969.

282 Letter to Moira from John F Dynon, 29 January 1969.

283 Letter from Moira to John F Dynon, 31 January 1969.

284 Letter from Moira to John F Dynon, 2 February 1969.

285 Postcard from Moira to John D Dynon, 2 February 1969.

286 Letter to Moira from John F Dynon, 31 January 1969.

287 Letter from Moira to Jacinta Dynon, 7 February 1969.

288 Letter from Moira to John F Dynon, 9 February 1969.

289 Letter from Moira to John F Dynon, 14 February 1969.

290 Letter from Moira to Mary Clubwala Jadhav, Chairman Guild of Service, 7 March 1969.

Chapter 26 Surplus Australian wheat for India

291 Hooper, K, 'A bumper crop but nobody wants it', *The Age* (Melbourne, Vic.), Thursday 22 January 1970.

292 Letter from Moira to Prime Minister The Rt. Hon. John G Gorton, 13 January 1970.

293 *The Herald* (Melbourne, Vic.), early edition, 14 January 1970.

294 Matthews, V, '$3.5M. wheat gift', *The Herald* (Melbourne, Vic.) late edition, 14 January 1970.

295 'Govt. fails on aid – Cairns', *The Herald* (Melbourne, Vic.), 15 January 1970.

296 Press statement issued by Moira, 15 January 1970.

297 Letter to Moira from Mother Teresa MC, 24 August 1970.

Chapter 27 Twenty-five million pints of milk

298 Press release by Michael Rosel on launch of 1970 Milk for India Appeal on 1 June 1970.

299 At the launch of the 1969 Milk for India Appeal.

300 Moira's address at launch of 1970 Milk for India Victorian Appeal.

Chapter 28 Disasters in East Pakistan

301 Australia, House of Representatives 10 October 1972, *Debates*, vol. 41, p. 2310. (Len Reid MHR).

302 Letter to Moira from Sir Robert Menzies, 19 November 1970.

303 Committee for East Pakistan Disaster Relief: Chairman Moira Dynon; Vice Chairman, Dr NH Sinha; Secretary, Mrs Leonore Ryan; Treasurer, Mr Frank Keating; Publicity Officer, Mrs W Dobson. Committee: Professor R Andrew, Mr RR Buxton, Mrs J Grant Coutts (Victorian State President, Country Women's Association), Sir Edward Dunlop, Mr JF Dynon, Mr Bruce Grant, Professor Norman Harper, Mrs Pat Mutimer, Mrs J Naidu, Mayor of Malvern (Cr Julius Pollack), Mr Rohan Rivett, Mr Newman Rosenthal, Mr JP Ryan, Mrs N Suhr, Mr and Mrs Denis Warner and Mr Norman Wearne (representing Reverend Arthur Preston.)

304 'Milk for India rallies help for Pakistan', *Progress Press*, (Chadstone, Vic.), 2 December 1970.

305 Resolution moved by the Prime Minister of India in the Indian Parliament regarding West Pakistan's attack on East Bengal, 31 March 1971, See Appendix A, A10 for text of resolution.

REFERENCES

306 Included among the many donations was a most generous and practical gift of 1,155 cases of high-protein baby foods from HJ Heinz Company for use in camps and centres for refugees and displaced persons, conducted by the Indian Government.

307 Excerpt from letter from Moira to AM Thomas, High Commissioner for India in Canberra, 10 May 1971.

308 Excerpt from letter to Moira from AM Thomas, High Commissioner for India in Canberra, 14 May 1971.

309 Excerpt from letter from Moira to The Archbishop of Melbourne, Dr J Knox DD, 20 May 1971.

310 Excerpt from letter to Moira from Prime Minister The Rt. Hon. William McMahon, 16 August 1971. ©Commonwealth of Australia.

311 '"Pakistani babe weighed only two pounds" – Moira Dynon', *The Advocate* (Melbourne, Vic.), 23 September 1971.

312 Telegram from Moira to Nigel Bowen, c/- Australian Delegation, United Nations Headquarters, New York, 23 September 1971.

313 Telegram from Moira to Prime Minister The Rt. Hon. William McMahon, 14 October 1971.

314 'Comments by Moira Dynon' made at public meeting at Melbourne Town Hall, Friday 22 October 1971.

315 Address by Moira, 'The Bangla Desh Issue', Wesley Church Sunday Forum, 28 November 1971. www.moiradynon.com.au

316 Telegram from Moira to Prime Minister The Rt. Hon. William McMahon, 3 November 1971.

317 Excerpt from letter to Moira from Prime Minister The Rt. Hon. William McMahon, 3 December 1971. ©Commonwealth of Australia.

318 Excerpt from letter to Moira from Shri SN Sapru, Hon Secretary Indian Red Cross Society, Delhi, 29 November 1971.

319 Excerpt from letter to Moira from Mr Allen, Deputy High Commissioner for Australia, Dacca, 19 February 1972, enclosing Report on 'Relief Aid in Bangladesh – Nagori'. See Appendix A, A11 for full report.

320 Australia, House of Representatives 10 October 1972, *Debates*, vol. 41, p. 2320.

Chapter 29 Winding down the Campaign

321 Address by Moira, 'India Today', Bairnsdale, Victoria, 25 February 1971. www.moiradynon.com.au

322 Letter to Moira from Mrs Indira Gandhi, Prime Minister of India, 29 April 1971.

323 Moira's typed notes, 'The late Mr. Frank Keating', Aid for India Committee Special Meeting, 2 April 1971.

324 John F Dynon identified this person as Mr D Chipp MHR, Minister for Customs and Excise.

325 Moira's typed notes, 'Future of The Campaign', Aid for India Committee Special Meeting, 2 April 1971.

326 Letter to Moira from Rohan Rivett, 17 April 1971.

327 Minutes of Meeting of Aid India Campaign held on 22 June 1972.

Chapter 30 Into Eternity

328 Tielhard de Chardin, P., *The Phenomenon of Man*, 1955.

329 Tielhard de Chardin, P., *The Spirit of the Earth*, 1931.

330 Letter from Murray McInerney (later Sir Murray) to John F Dynon, 25 October 1976.

331 Excerpt from letter from Sir Edward Dunlop to John F Dynon, 26 October 1976.

332 Excerpt from letter from Dr Martand S Joshi, President, Australia India Society of Victoria to John F Dynon, 28 October 1976.

333 Excerpt from letter from D Henry Thiagaraj, Deputy Director of Tourism, Government of Madras, to John F Dynon, 11 December 1976.

334 Excerpt from letter from Sir George Reid, retired former Attorney-General of Victoria, to John F Dynon, 18 November 1976.

335 Letter from Brother Andrew MC to John F Dynon, 3 November 1976.

336 Letter from Mark Shelton (aged 12) to John F Dynon, 24 October 1976.

337 Card from Pat Hogan to John F Dynon, c.1976.

338 Excerpt from letter from R Verma, Acting High Commissioner for India, Canberra, to John F Dynon, 28 October 1976.

339 Excerpt from letter from Denis Warner to John F Dynon, 12 July 1977.

340 Excerpt from letter from Bernadette Smith to John F Dynon, 8 December 1976.

REFERENCES

341 Excerpt from letter from Alice Langenbacher to John F Dynon, 26 October 1976.

342 Francis, B, 'A Bird's Eye View', *The Toorak Times*, 10 November 1976.

343 Newsletter, Australian-Asian Association of Victoria, 1977.

344 St Joseph's Record, Malvern, November 1976.

345 Excerpt from the Reading at the Memento for the Dead following a special Loreto Federation Mass at Loreto Convent, Claremont, Western Australia, 23 October 1977.

346 Excerpt from letter to John F Dynon from Rev Fr James Dynon, SJ, 14 October 1977.

347 *The Blue Book 1971–72: Leaders of the English-Speaking World*, 1971 Entrants Edition. St James Press Limited, London & Chicago.

Appendix A Reports, documents and letters

348 *Table Talk* (Melbourne, Vic.) 6 November 1919, p. 10.

349 Pursuant to a War Cabinet ruling regarding service women.

350 The extent of the threat that gas could be used against us was laid bare in *the National Times* 1–7 November 1981, pp. 3–4: 'By 1945 Japan had a huge stockpile of germs, vectors and delivery equipment unmatched by any other nation.'

351 One gift which Moira kept until the end of her life was the soft leather folder inscribed, under Royal Australian Air Force insignia: 'To Miss Shelton, In appreciation of your efforts on behalf of the boys while at Bowen & wishing you the Compliments of the Season. From the 19 RC and 1 CR boys.'

352 Moira told her family about these Sunday trips. If personnel from the unit wanted to attend Sunday Mass, they would miss the boat to the islands. Moira saw the priest and arranged for the Mass time to be changed so that they could attend Mass and also catch the boat.

353 Flight Officer Moira Shelton's war service account. This was written by Moira after she had been released from service. A copy of this memoir was among Moira's personal papers.

354 Petition to Her Majesty under Section 59 of the *Australian Constitution* seeking disallowance or amendment of *Matrimonial Causes Act 1959*.

355 Special Report on Australian-Japanese Children in Japan (Prepared by Mrs. John F. Dynon on behalf of the Australian-Asian Association of Victoria. July, 1960).

356 Joint Statement concerning Proposed Policy of the Commonwealth Government of Australia to Conscript a Minority of Aliens Resident in Australia for Military Service including Service Overseas by James M Galbally and Moira Dynon, 15 August 1966.

357 Statement on Abortion prepared by Moira Dynon and released by National Executive Committee Australian Council of Catholic Women, 30 April 1968.

358 Letter to Moira from MWB Smithies, for the Secretary, Department of External Affairs, 7 June 1965. ©Commonwealth of Australia.

359 Memorandum to Prime Minister The Rt. Hon. HE Holt, regarding Australian food assistance to India, February 1966.

360 Letter to Moira from P Balakrishnan, Attache, Indian High Commission Canberra, 23 January 1967 requesting the full names and addresses of the wharf labourers who loaded the milk free of charge—so that he could write personal letters of thanks to each of them for giving their time and services so generously.

361 Letter from Moira to Treasurer William McMahon, 16 January 1967.

362 Resolution moved by the Prime Minister of India in the Parliament in New Delhi on 31 March 1971; *Bangla Desh Documents*, Printed at The B.N.K. Press Private Limited Madras -26, 1971. 'This collection of documents is intended to provide to the world a primary source of information on developments pertaining to the crisis that overtook East Bengal in March 1971'.

363 Letter to Moira from Mr Allen, Deputy High Commissioner for Australia in Dacca, 19 February 1972.

Appendix B About the author John F Dynon—aspects of his life and family history

364 'Miscellaneous Shipping.' *The Hobarton Mercury* (Tasmania: 1854-1857), Wednesday 3 December 1856, p. 2.

365 John Dinan (Dynan; Dynon) was actually 31 years when he travelled to Australia. He was born in Cork, Ireland, on 28 June 1825.

366 As related in 1984 to John F Dynon by Ellie Macgillicuddy (granddaughter of John and Abigail Dynon; daughter of Abigail and Patrick McMahon Glynn).

367 John Dynon and Son', *Sydney Morning Herald*, (Sydney, NSW), 16 December 1896, p. 8.

REFERENCES

368 'John Dynon and Sons. A Flourishing business', *The Daily News*, (Perth, WA), 30 August 1902, p. 7.

369 'Mrs John Dynon', *Freeman's Journal* (Sydney, NSW), 11 November 1905, p. 19.

370 'St Francis' Church – Feast of The Immaculate Conception', *The Advocate* (Melbourne, Vic), 7 December 1907, p. 21.

371 'St Francis' Church – Feast of The Immaculate Conception – Statue "Help of Christians" unveiled', *The Advocate* (Melbourne, Vic), 14 December 1907. p. 20.

372 'Mr. John Dynon.', *The Advocate*, (Melbourne, Vic.), 14 December 1912, p.35.

373 Moira Peters related a story that Abigail had travelled to the UK with her son, James, when he was a teenager. A newspaper report supports this. *The Geelong Advertiser* (Geelong, Vic.), Thursday 19 September 1872 reported the 'Arrival of the Great Britain' in Melbourne, on 18 September 1872, having sailed from Liverpool on 26 July 1872: 'This noble ship arrived yesterday after a splendid passage of 53 days'; the saloon passengers included Mrs. Dynon and James Dynon'.

374 Excerpts from the 1881 diary are reproduced. Some of James' handwriting is indecipherable and some words may have been inadvertently misrepresented.

375 'Bourke Ward', *The North Melbourne Gazette*, (Vic.), Friday 5 November 1897, p. 3.

376 'Unrest in China. Possibility of Eruption. Australian Visitor's impressions', *The Telegraph*, (Brisbane, Qld.: 1872-1947), Monday 27 June 1020, p.2.

377 Falla, RP, *The Selectors in the Parish of Jeffcott*, 1992; Publication No. 25 of the History and Natural History Group of MLA, Donald.

378 *The Donald Express*, 12 November 1886. (Supplied by the Donald District Archive Centre).

379 'About People', *The Age* (Melbourne, Vic.), 11 November 1912.

380 'From Dynon's to Boans Ltd', *Sunday Times* (Perth, W.A.), 5 September 1926.

381 Later known as Burke Hall—Xavier Preparatory School.

382 Letter from Prime Minister of Australia, Stanley Bruce, introducing 'Mrs Margaret Dynon, a respected citizen of Melbourne who is proceeding on a visit to Great Britain and Europe', 20 December 1928.

383 John's 1932 diary includes a photo: 'Jim kissing the Blarney Stone'.

384 Rev. Strong, David SJ, 2017, *The Australian Dictionary of Jesuit Biography 1848–2015*, NSW Halstead Press.

385 'Dynon is Versatile', *The Argus*, (Melbourne, Vic.), 26 May 1934, p. 23.

386 By the late 1930s, John gave committed support to the war against Fascism.

387 Rev. Strong, David SJ, 2017. op cit..

388 Rev. Dynon, James SJ, 'The Workers' Charter', *The Advocate* (Melbourne, Vic.), 10 May 1951, p. 11.

389 Paper by John F Dynon, *Two Papal Encyclicals—Our Basic Documents*, c. 1952.

390 Letter from John F Dynon, Executive Officer of the League of St Thomas More to members, 5 November 1952.

391 Tollamh o Donnchanha, *'Extracts from an Old Census'*, 1906. Cork Historical and Archaeological Society, p. 69 ff.

Appendix C Three autobiographical chapters by John F Dynon

392 Letter to John F Dynon from Fr Robert Tyndall SJ, 16 March 1958.

393 Borkenau, F., *The New German Empire*, 1939. The Viking Press: New York, p. 166.

394 Statement by Prime Minister in the UK House of Commons, 31 March 1939.

395 Letter from Margaret Dynon to John F Dynon, c. September 1939.

396 Bundled together with John's typed pages titled 'An autobiography with one chapter perhaps entitled "My three loves"' was a packet of letters from Marie-Anne to John F Dynon during 1939 and 1940. Written mostly in French, they have been skillfully and sensitively translated into English by gifted linguist Giles Robinson.

"There will be much praise for Moira Dynon and her great work for pro-family values, and for the needy and vulnerable. But what I cherish in my memories of her is her personal kindness to me. When I had my last baby in 1974, Moira, despite her own frail health, visited me at Cabrini Hospital and spent time with me. I was deeply concerned about her loss of weight but she switched the focus of our conversation to the wellbeing of my new baby and me. This was typical of her unselfishness, her graciousness and care for others."

Babette Francis

www.ingramcontent.com/pod-product-compliance
Lightning Source LLC
Chambersburg PA
CBHW070728020526
44107CB00077B/2079